WHO
COMES
AFTER THE
SUBJECT?

E D I T E D   B Y

EDUARDO CADAVA
PETER CONNOR
JEAN-LUC NANCY

ROUTLEDGE
NEW YORK AND LONDON

Published in 1991 by

Routledge
An imprint of Routledge, Chapman and Hall, Inc.
29 West 35 Street
New York, NY 10001

Published in Great Britain by

Routledge
11 New Fetter Lane
London EC4P 4EE

Library of Congress Cataloging in Publication Data

Who comes after the subject? / [edited by] Eduardo Cadava.
     p.   cm.
    Essays translated from the French.
    ISBN 0-415-90359-9.   ISBN 0-415-90360-2 (pbk.)
    1. Subject (Philosophy) I. Cadava, Eduardo.
  BD223.W49 1991
126—dc20   90-20555

British Library Cataloguing in Publication Data

Who comes after the subject?
  1. Man. Consciousness—Philosophical perspectives
  I. Cadava, Eduardo II. Connor, Peter III. Nancy, Jean-
Luc
  126

  ISBN 0-415-90359-9
  ISBN 0-415-90360-2 pbk

Contents

Preface

The essays collected in this volume present the current research of nineteen contemporary French philosophers on one of the great motifs of modern philosophy: the critique or the deconstruction of subjectivity.

The project was initiated by Ermanno Bencivenga, joint editor (with Enrico M. Forni) of the international review of philosophy *Topoi*. Bencivenga wished to devote a special issue of *Topoi* to an important aspect of contemporary philosophical activity in France. The organization of the project was entrusted to Jean-Luc Nancy, who served as guest editor of the September 1988 issue of *Topoi*, in which a number of these essays first appeared, and who proposed to organize the issue around the question "Who Comes after the Subject?" The following year a French edition of this issue of *Topoi* was published as the final number of *Cahiers Confrontations* (no. 20, Winter 1989), under the direction of René Major. The French version included new contributions by Etienne Balibar and Mikkel Borch-Jacobsen, plus the entirety of Nancy's interview with Jacques Derrida, only partially published in *Topoi*. In the summer of 1989, we approached Nancy about the possibility of bringing out an American edition of these and other essays addressing this topic. The present collection therefore includes all texts from the earlier English and French versions, together with previously unpublished essays by Sylviane Agacinski and Luce Irigaray, and previously untranslated essays by Sarah Kofman and Emmanuel Levinas.

We have sought to bring to each of the translations a single notion of consistency, even while respecting as much as possible the individual contributions of each translator. We want to thank each of the translators for their patience and help with this work. We would also like to thank René Major, Michel Delorme, and the D. Reidel Publishing Company for their cooperation. Finally, we would like to express our gratitude to William P. Germano for his enthusiasm and support.

E.C. and P.C.

Introduction
Jean-Luc Nancy

Philosophy, today, world-wide: what might this mean? It would not mean a diversity of fields, schools, streams, or tendencies within philosophy. At least, it would not mean only this, or perhaps it would not mean this at all. This has been the traditional way of looking at such a topic. Nowadays, it would rather mean: different ways of thinking about philosophy itself. Different ways of understanding the word itself, and even ways of understanding that the thing it names is gone, or finished. Or different ways of inquiring about philosophy as something essentially linked to Western civilization, something with which other civilizations—or a general shifting of cultures, also within the Western area—now have to deal (and what does "to deal with" mean here? What between or beyond "praxis" and "theory" would this imply? Do we have a philosophical language for this task?).

It is very likely that no one "philosophy"—if something like this still exists, and is not merely something shelved in our libraries—is able to grasp this situation, nor to think it through. It is very likely that there is no "Weltanschauung" for it. "Weltanschauungen" belong to the epoch when the world had not become the world, world-wide. The becoming-world of the world does not mean what is usually called the "uniformization" of everything and everyone—even through technology, which one assumes to be essentially identical to itself. In many respects, world also differentiates itself, if it does not indeed shatter itself. The becoming-world of world means that "world" is no longer an object, nor an idea, but the place existence is given to and exposed to. This first happened in philosophy, and to philosophy, with the Kantian revolution and the "condition of possible experience": world as possibly of (or for) an existent being, possibility as world for such a being. Or: Being no longer to be thought of as an essence, but to be given, offered to a world as to its own possibility.

Such a program (if we can use this word) is not to be completed in a day. It does not take "a long time," but the totality of a history: our history. The history of philosophy since Kant (if not indeed since the remote condition of possibility of Kant himself at the beginning of the "Western" as such, of the Western "Weltanschauung") is the history of the various breaks out of which emerges, out of the "possible worlds" (the "Anschauungen"), as well as out of a simple necessity of the world (another kind of "Anschauung"), *the world as possibility*, or the world as chance for existence (opening/closing of possibility, unlimitation/disaster of possibility).

Each of these breaks is a break of philosophy, and not within philosophy. Therefore they are incommensurable with and incommunicable to one another. They represent a disarticulation of the common space and of the common discourse of "philosophy" (of what one assumes to have been such a commonplace). Their names (I mean their emblematic names up to the first half of this century) are well known: Marx, Nietzsche, Freud, Heidegger, Wittgenstein.

We are the second half of the century. A "we" without "we," a "we" without philosophical community (apart from the fake one of conferences, congresses, etc.). Many lines of rupture traverse *us*—which does not necessarily imply any "hostility," but which means this: philosophy separated from itself, outside of itself, crossing its own limits—which means, perhaps, discovering that it never did have proper limits, that it never was, in a sense, a "property."

One of the most visible lines of rupture runs between two ensembles (each of which is itself heterogeneous). These ensembles are most often designated, especially in Anglo-Saxon countries, in an ethnogeographic manner: "Anglo-Saxon philosophy," "continental philosophy," and, more particularly, "French philosophy" (a kind of partitioning, therefore, of the Western itself). These appellations are, of course, extremely fragile. There is "Anglo-Saxon" philosophy in Europe, as there is "continental" and "French" philosophy in the Anglo-Saxon world (to say nothing of the one and the other in the rest of the world, nor of this rest itself, of this immense "rest" as the space of unimaginable possibilities for these philosophies, beyond each of them . . .).

These names have no simple, absolute reference, nor pertinence, but their meaning is nonetheless not void. The ethnonational partitioning of "philosophy" (languages, cultures, institutions, etc.) would require a very long and complex analysis. This collection of essays proposes nothing of the kind. In this regard, it simply proposes, at once *under* the name and *on* the name "French," a kind of practical exercise.

These ensembles are also identified by "theoretical" names, the pertinence of which is no less problematic. One says "analytic philosophy," for example, which leads to a misconception about both the diversity of kinds of "analysis" with which it deals, and the variety of logical, linguistic, ethical, aesthetic, and political preoccupations within the "Anglo-Saxon" domain. One says, on the other hand, "post-structuralism"—which, in this case, is a baroque designation, because there has never been *one* structuralism, and because what it deals with did not come "after," nor as a "posterity." Moreover, what this word claims to cover is similarly of a very great diversity. But the more than insufficient nature of these denominations is itself a testimony to the line of rupture—whose traces are complex, sinuous, sometimes difficult to grasp, multiple, or effaced.

It must surely seem unfair to have restricted this collection to French thinkers: there is outside of France more than one thinking, more than one kind of work, that would answer to what "French" denotes here. But not only would the project have become excessive from a practical point of view, it would moreover have been no less unfair to have blurred the contours of a French specificity recognizable in certain characteristic traits—although neither systematic nor even simply convergent—over the last thirty years (let us say, very broadly, since the closure, on the one hand, of a certain type of French "rationalism" and/or "spiritualism"—in this respect, "French" thought today proceeds in part from a "German" rupture with a certain philosophical "France" (which is also a rupture within a certain "Germanity")—and on the other hand, since the close of the Sartrean enterprise).

However, one will find no unity here. The differences are extreme, and opposing views are not lacking. The invitation to participate in this issue left entirely open the potential range of philosophical approaches. With one exception, brought about by the choice of the theme (for which I am responsible and the reasons for which I will give later), I did not send my question ("Who comes after the subject?") to those who would find no validity in it, to those for whom it is on the contrary more important to denounce its presuppositions and to return, as though nothing had happened, to a style of thinking that we might simply call humanist, even where it tries to complicate the traditional way of thinking about the human subject. If I state that such a return stems in fact from the forgetting of philosophy, I am no doubt speaking only for myself. But it is no less true that I am also encouraged to say this by virtue of all the contemporary work witnessed in the authors brought together here. Those among them who challenge the terms of my question—and some do, as shall be seen—at least do not do so in the name of a return backward, something that has never had any meaning or sense, in philosophy or elsewhere.

The reader of these essays will no doubt perceive their diversity, and, should he or she perceive also something that is neither a unity nor a homogeneity but something that partakes of a certain "tonality," this will be a kind of "French accent" in many different philosophical tongues. I sent out my invitations keeping in mind at once the work of each contributor in regard to the question asked (I accept responsibility for its arbitrariness—but it is a reasoned arbitrariness, as we shall see in a moment)—and the distribution of current research in France.

One will recognize some of the principal axes at the source of this distribution: for example, the Husserlian, the Marxian, the Heideggerian, and the Nietzschean traditions. But one will not find anything like a "tradition" in the ordinary sense. Nobody here stands within a custom or a school. Each entertains a complex rapport to many of these traditions (and in such a way that it would be perfectly impossible, short of a lengthy study, to endeavor to present them one by one: it is incumbent on the texts to do this). Several have already been recognized as what I would risk calling the inventors of a thinking. All are concerned in one way or another with an unreserved questioning of "philosophy" and its "traditions," with a determined reevaluation of the "philosophical" as such and not with variations of "Weltanschauungen." All are the thinkers of an age in rupture. Which means also: they take responsibility for this age, because the questions they are discussing, and especially here, obviously engage all the ethical and political challenges of our time (as well as the debates *about* what "ethics" and "politics" mean today).

I asked the question: "Who comes after the subject?" to settle on one of the principle rupture lines. The critique or the deconstruction of subjectivity is to be considered one of the great motifs of contemporary philosophical work in France, taking off from, here again and perhaps especially, the teachings of Marx, Nietzsche, Freud, Husserl, Heidegger, Bataille, Wittgenstein, from the teachings of linguistics, the social sciences, and so forth. (But one should not forget the practical, ethical, and political experience of Europe since the 1930s: the fascisms, Stalinism, the war, the camps, decolonization, and the birth of new nations, the difficulty in orienting oneself between a "spiritual" identity that has been devastated and an "American" economism, between a loss of meaning and an accumulation of signs: so many instances for the investigation of the diverse figures of the "subject.") The question therefore bears upon the critique or deconstruction of interiority, of self-presence, of consciousness, of mastery, of the individual or collective property of an essence. Critique or deconstruction of the firmness of a *seat* (*hypokeimenon, substantia, subjectum*) and the certitude of an *authority* and a *value* (the individual, a people, the state, history, work). My question aimed in the first place to treat this motif as an event that had indeed emerged from our history—hence the "after"—and not as some capricious variation of fashionable thinking. But at the same time I wanted to suggest a whole range—no doubt vast—in which such a critique or deconstruction has not simply obliterated its object (as those who groan or applaud before a supposed "liquidation" of the subject would like to believe). That which obliterates is nihilism—itself an implicit form of the metaphysics of the subject (self-presence of that which knows itself as the dissolution of its own difference). There is nothing nihilistic in recognizing that the *subject*—the property of the *self*—is the thought that reabsorbs or exhausts all possibility of *being-in-the-world* (all possibility of *existence*, all existence as being delivered to the possible), *and* that this same thought, never simple, never closed upon itself without remainder, designates and delivers an entirely different thought: that of the *one* and that of the some *one*, of the singular existent that the subject announces, promises, and at the same time conceals.

Moreover, one will see in the texts that follow at least two very different uses of the word "subject." Sometimes it has the value of the metaphysical concept I have just recalled, sometimes (for example, for Granel or Rancière) it has the value of a singular *unum quid*, less present to *itself* than present *to* a history, an event, a community, an oeuvre, or another "subject."

Not only are we not relieved of thinking this some *one*—this some *one* that the subject has perhaps always pointed towards or looked for, and that brings us back to the same figures: the individual, a people, the state, history, production, style, man, woman, as well as "myself" and "ourselves" . . . —but it is precisely something like this thought that henceforth comes toward us and calls us forth. Such at least was the hypothesis I was following, thinking not to be too disloyal to a certain singularity of the era, common to all and particular to no one, circulating anonymously amidst our thoughts. This is what I tried to indicate with the verb "comes," and with the pronoun "who?": With which "one" have we henceforth to deal?

I reproduce here the passage from my letter of invitation (February 1986) that presents the question:

> *Who comes after the subject?* This question can be explained as follows: one of the major characteristics of contemporary thought is the putting into question of the instance of the "subject," according to the structure, the meaning, and the value subsumed under this term in modern thought, from Descartes to Hegel, if not to Husserl. The inaugurating decisions of contemporary thought—whether they took place under the sign of a break with metaphysics and its poorly pitched questions, under the sign of a "deconstruction" of this metaphysics, under that of a transference of the thinking of Being to the thinking of life, or of the Other, or of language, etc.—have all involved putting subjectivity on trial. A wide spread discourse of recent date proclaimed the subject's simple liquidation. Everything seems, however, to point to the necessity, not of a "return to the subject" (proclaimed by those who would like to think that nothing has happened, and that there is nothing new to be thought, except maybe variations or modifications of the subject), but on the contrary, of a move forward toward someone— *some one*—else in its place (this last expression is obviously a mere convenience: the "place" could not be the same). Who would it be? How would s/he present him/herself? Can we name her/him? Is the question "who" suitable? (My formulations seem to presuppose that none of the existing designations—for example, *Dasein* or "the individual"—would be suitable. But my intention of course is to leave open all possibilities.)
>
> In other words: If it is appropriate to assign something like a punctuality, a singularity, or a hereness (*haecceitas*) as the place of emission, reception, or transition (of affect, of action, of language, etc.), how would one designate its specificity? Or would the question need to be transformed—or is it in fact out of place to ask it?

At this point I have fulfilled—at least I hope I have—my role as editor, and I will let the texts speak. They are the "subjects" of this issue.

The role of editor, I must admit, has made me forget that I could and probably should, having asked the question, have written a response myself. It's too late to do this now, and perhaps this is not such a bad thing. In the interview with Derrida, I make some observations that will perhaps serve to clarify my position. But I will add a few words here to indicate the precise direction my answer might have taken.

The dominant definition of the philosophical (or "metaphysical") *subject* is to my way of thinking the one proposed by Hegel: "that which is capable of maintaining within itself its own contradiction." That the contradiction would be its *own* (one recognizes here the dialectical law), that alienation or extraneousness would be ownmost, and that subjectity (following Heidegger here, and distinguishing the subject-structure from anthropological subjectivity) consists in reappropriating this proper being-outside-of-itself: this is what the definition would mean. The logic of the *subjectum* is a grammar (cf. Nietzsche—but also Leibniz: *praedicatum inest subjecto*) of the subject that re-appropriates to itself, in advance and absolutely, the exteriority and the strangeness of its predicate. (A canonic Hegelian example, at least according to the way it is usually read: "The rational is actual.") This appropriation is made by the verb "to be." "To be" thus has the function here of an operator of appropriation: in fact it means "to have" or "produce" or "understand" or "support," etc. In a rather hasty manner, I could endeavor to say it is the technological interpretation of Being.

Still, for this to be the case, it would be necessary that the subject *be*, absolutely and without predicate. It is at this point that the institution of the subject of modern philosophy begins: *ego sum*. "To be" means then that which the Cartesian redundancy states: *ego sum, ego existo*. Being is the actuality of existence (or again, this "notion which belongs in an absolute way to all the individuals of nature"— Spinoza). Existence as actuality "is not a predicate but the simple position of the thing" (Kant); existence is the essence of the subject to the extent that it *is*, prior to any predication. (And this is why—again Spinoza—the essence of an infinite substance—or God—necessarily envelops existence.)

Descartes, Spinoza, Kant—one could continue: metaphysics itself indicates that what is posed here as the question of an "after" (in history) is just as much a question of the "before" (in the logic of being—but this would invite a different kind of retracing of history: that which comes to us has preceded us). Before the subject of a predication (let us say: before the *subject-of*) there is (*il y a*—this is Levinas's "word"—Heidegger's word is: *es gibt*, it is given, it gives) the Being of the subject, or the subject without "of," the subject-being, existence. Metaphysics, de-constructing itself (this is its logic *and* its history), indicates this "before" as "after": existence. Not the subject of existence but existence-subject: that to which one can no longer allot the grammar of the subject nor, therefore, to be clear, allot the word "subject."

But what existence? It is not an essence, it is the essence whose essence it is to exist, actually and in fact, in experience, "hic et nunc." It is the *existent* (and not the existence *of* the existent). With this in mind, the question asks "who?" Which means that the question of essence—"What, existence?"—calls forth a "who" in response. The question was therefore a response to the question of existence, of its "being" or its "meaning," nothing more and nothing less. (But whenever one responds to a question with another question, what one does is defy the first question from ever coming to be asked. . . .)

Every "what" that exists is a "who," if "who" means: *that* actual, existent "what," as it exists, a factual (even material) punctuation of Being, the *unum quid* (and it is not by chance that this is Descartes's formula for the quasi-third substance that is the union of soul and body, the reality of human existence, as evident as the reality of the *ego*).

"Before/after the subject": *who*. This is first of all an affirmation: the being is *who*. In a sense, it is Heidegger: Being is simply existing withdrawn from every essence of Being and from every being of essence. (But this still does not tell me if it is proper to determine this existent in the way Heidegger describes the *Dasein*— supposing that this description is sufficiently clear to us now. "After the subject": men, gods, living beings, and what else? I would not go further than this.)

But this is also a question: *who* is *who?* It is not "What is who?"—it is not a question of essence, but one of identity (as when one asks before a photograph of a group of people whose names you know but not the faces: "Who is who?"—is this one Kant, is that one Heidegger, and this other one beside him? . . .). That is to say, a question of presence: Who is *there?* Who is present there?

But what, presence? It is the presence of the existent: it is not an essence. Present is that which occupies a place. The place is *place*—site, situation, disposition—in the coming into space of a time, in a spacing that allows that something *come* into presence, in a unique time that engenders itself in this point in space, as its spacing. (Divine places, where presence withdraws, places of birth, where presence presents itself, common-places, where places are shared, places of love, where presence comes-and-goes, historic places, geography of presences, etc.).

There where there was nothing (and not even a "there"—as in the "there is no there there" of Gertrude Stein), something, some *one* comes ("one" because it "comes," not because of its substantial unity: the she, he, or it that comes can be one and unique in its coming but multiple and repeated "in itself." Presence *takes place*, that is to say it *comes into* presence. It is that which comes indefinitely to itself, never stops coming, arriving: the "subject" that is never the subject of itself. The "ipseity" of presence lies in the fact that it engenders itself *into* presence: presence to itself, in a sense, but where this "self" itself is only the *to* (the taking-place, the spacing) of presence. "I engender time" is the phrasing of Kant's first schema (schema: tracing, spacing). Strictly speaking it means: I engender "I," I engender myself as the "a priori form of internal meaning" that is time. The "internal" engenders itself as exteriority—in order to be the "internal" that it is, in order to exist. It *is* most intimately in this coming into presence. Presence *to*: To what? To whom? To the world, but the world is the shared taking-place of all places. Presence thus comes *to* presence, without being to *its*-self (this is why "to engender oneself" is a poor metaphor for "to exist," which is the metaphor for the carrying over of the self outside of the self before the self . . .). Presence to the world: and the so-called "technological" world should not be excluded from this, from the moment the technological interpretation of Being will have allowed some places to come about as the places of a presence *to* technology.

This presence-to that is not to-itself is not a "contradiction," and does not imply a dialectical power that "would retain it within itself." I can find no other name for this than the name of "freedom." Not freedom as the property of a subject ("the subject *is* free"), but freedom as the very experience of coming into presence, of being given up to, necessarily/freely given up to, the *to* (the *to* of the "toward," of the "for," of the "in view of," of the "in the direction of," of the "alongside," the *to* of abandoning to, of the offering to of "to one's core," of the "with regard to," of the "to the limit," and also of the "to the detriment of," "to the bitter end": freedom is wherever it is necessary *to make up one's mind to . . .*).

"I engender time" as the schema, the spacing of the place where *I* (who) takes place, where *I* comes into presence. (Who? I am coming—here I am). The "I" does not preexist this schematization. It does not come after it either; it "is" it, or it "exists" it, if one can (if "I" can) use the verb like this. If existence, as Heidegger insists, exists according to the *Jemeinigkeit*, the "in each case mine," it is not in the manner of an appropriation by "me," at each moment, of every taking-place. Freedom is not a quality, nor an operation of the existent: it is her/his/its coming into the presence of existence. If presence is presence to presence and not to self (nor of self), this is because it is, in each case, presence *in* common. The coming into presence is plural, "in each case ours" as much as "mine." This community without the essence of a community, without a common being, is the ontological condition of existence as presence-to. The plural coming is a singular coming—and this is not a prediction. But how could one say what it "is"? One (Who?) might try by saying: the plural liberates (or shares) the singular, the singular liberates (or shares) the plural, in a community *without subject*. This is what we have to think about. *Who* thinks, if not the community?

1

Another Experience of the Question, or Experiencing the Question Other-Wise

Sylviane Agacinski

What I hear in the question that has been put *to me by someone* is, first of all, an inquiry as to the responsibility for, and of, the question: Who is asking it? Who is being asked? In order for there to be a question "on the subject of" a *who*, should there perhaps first of all be someone who questions and someone who is questioned? Should perhaps someone *address himself* (or herself) to someone else? Following this hypothesis, one could emphasize the questioning agency (who is it?), while the gesture with which the question turns to someone, with which it *addresses itself*, would remain secondary. Another possibility, however, would be to stress, within the structure of the question, the very gesture of address. In this case *I* will not ask *myself* what agency is even capable of questioning, and especially of questioning *itself* (for it would no longer be a subject), but instead "I" would feel surprised that a question should get through (to me) at all. Is not the possibility of calling on, or of being called on, to answer—or more simply, of calling or being called—a more crucial matter than questions concerning *who* or *what*? The different philosophies of the subject (since it is clearly impossible to speak of *the* philosophy of the subject) always attribute to the subject the faculty of questioning *itself*, or asking *itself* questions, in such a way as to appropriate the alterity or obscurity that troubles it, either from "without" or from "within." In a sense, the status of the subject is inseparable from the status of the question, as well as of the origin of the question. The subject puts the question *to itself*. The claim of subjective consciousness consists in believing that, essentially, it can question itself and answer for itself.

For this reason, and to anticipate slightly, I would argue that if it is possible to speak in terms of a "someone" who can "come" after the subject, this "someone" would be one who would have another experience of the question. That is to say, it would have an experience of the question that would not be an experience of

Translated by Michael Syrotinski and Christine Laennec.

thought or of consciousness turning back on itself, but that would be a more radical experience of that which comes (to me) or happens (to me) or calls (me). How can the experience of the question be described?

The philosophical question is not generally thought to imply a process of address; the question is not addressed to me by another, it is not a foreign question from abroad, it is not conveyed by a call from another or an elsewhere. It cannot take me completely unawares or tear me away from myself (as one could say, for example, about being called by God, or about a cry of distress, or about a chance event). In its very necessity, the philosophical question is a product of my freedom: indeed, the question is posed as if it poses itself, it imposes itself on one's reflections, but it originates in the questioning thought that intends to answer *for* its own question. This questioning thought is free, in regard to the question it gives, or addresses, or sends to itself. It would thus exclude the process of address, in that this implies something that has come from afar. Questioning thought takes no responsibility for this coming—it takes no responsibility for, say, the question *of the other*, the question from the other. In this respect, philosophy's subject (meaning both *the subject* who questions philosophically, as well as the concept with which philosophy determines man in general) is a subject with a limited responsibility, if I may say so. It makes great demands on itself, it obliges itself to answer *for* its question, and this in turn obliges it to answer for itself. This is what Descartes sets out to do in the *Meditations*. But the thinker of questioning thought is also liable to remain deaf to the call of the other or to the question of the other, is liable to substitute "the other's question"—that is, the philosophical question that the philosopher puts to *himself* or *herself* about the other, about the question *of the other*, the question asked *by* another, that *comes* from the other, or rather from *several* others. Likewise, questioning thought runs the risk of substituting the "question of responsibility" for the "receptiveness" through which the timbre of another's voice could get through to it, has always already gotten through to it.

What I am challenging here is not simply the "logical egoism" about which Kant writes about in his *Anthropology* (§2): "The *logical egoist* considers it unnecessary to test his judgment by the understanding of others, as if he had no need at all for this touchstone (*criterium veritatis externus*)."[1] Indeed, it is not only a question of confirming our *own* judgment on the basis of this receptivity, and of testing its exactness. All the more so since rightfully (and as Kant stresses later on in the text I have just quoted from) in philosophy we do not have to "appeal to the judgment of others to corroborate our own."[2] For me, it is more a matter of knowing whether subjective consciousness's gesture of self-questioning, such as it functions in the *cogito* or such as it unfolds in Hegel's *Phenomenology* as the "experience of consciousness"—whether this gesture does not, from the outset, reject any possibility of address or of receptivity—that is, does not reject an openness to the "question" *of the other*, of another.[3] Which I would not a priori presume to be necessarily *the same* as me (another me, another subject, another "man," another consciousness, even another *Dasein*).

For what seems remarkable in the questioning of the philosophical subject is that the "experience of the question," as an experience that consciousness would carry out *on itself*, remains an "inner experience"—thought's relationship to itself. (This of course has nothing to do with the paradoxical sense that Georges Bataille gives to the "inner experience,"[4] and that we will have to come back to later. . . .) Heidegger, for example, writes about this experience of consciousness turning upon itself: "Knowledge in this experience retreats further and further behind itself."[5] One could likewise say that consciousness as a questioning agency endeavors to no longer have anything "behind" or "in front of" it. For philosophies of the subject, if one understands by "philosophies of the subject" thinking that posits consciousness as the foundation of all beings, the question can only come from consciousness itself. It is its own need. But in this case it would be impossible to speak of an "experience" of the question, since in an experience the alterity of a given always emerges (even if this given is elaborated by the subject), whereas consciousness "questions" even "before" it can be "questioned."

Moreover, the question can appear as something that takes the place of the gift or of a certain experience of the gift. In reading Descartes's address to the Deans of the Faculty of Theology, we could consider philosophical questioning, or the activity of the human mind "reflecting back on itself," as a substitute for the gift: it fills in for the lack of faith, which is "a gift of God."[6] One can, through reflection, show to those who have not received the gift of faith, that "everything that can be known about God can be made manifest by reasons drawn from a source none other than *in ourselves*, and which our *mind alone* is able to provide."[7] With philosophy, God becomes a *question*, the question the mind puts to itself and to which it can *alone* reply. Descartes announces that the object of his *Meditations* will be the *question* of God and that of the soul.

This, then, is the difference between the question that comes from the other and that presupposes an experience *[épreuve]* of the gift, and the question of the other, a question that comes from me and is about the other. However, this does not mean that the other is necessarily God. (A parenthetical remark: the philosophical tradition would lead us to think that the question is bound up with the essence of thought, but this essence only appears historically with Socratic *eironia*, with the questioning that Socrates directed at others. At that time, the question, in the course of a dialogue, presupposed a meeting with the other, and a partitioning of thinking: into several voices.)

If I referred earlier to God's call as an example of a call from the other, it is by no means intended as an invitation to look back nostalgically to men of faith, or as a call for a return to religious thought. Religious thinkers can make us aware of the finite nature of experience, but this existence is at the same time condemned or even sacrificed: finitude is only conceived of with a view to going beyond it. In particular, the religious bond, the common relationship of all mortals to the eternal (insofar as they all leave themselves in the hands of this great Other) always creates a kind of united community, a community of those who are likeminded—the community of the faithful—and always creates an exclusion *of* others, an *ex*communication. I think that the question *of the other* is only possible if the other is irreducibly plural, if it is *others*, and if they are not thought of in the perspective of an *us* (a collective subject). If religious thought has always interested me, particularly while I was reading Kierkegaard,[8] it is especially because of the resistance it offers to a kind of philosophical thinking that only ever yields to itself: to its own reason, its own law. . . . Job and Abraham are sublime in the humility and sacrifice of their intellect, whereas the moral subject only makes sacrifices to its own principles. In his *Religion Within the Limits of Reason Alone*, Kant manages, with the concept of a purely rational faith, to conflate the religious and the moral.[9] It may be, however, that neither divine law nor moral law leaves any room for a true experience of the other: that is, an experience of the bond by which I am already "tied" to the other, already dependent on it prior to any question of coexistence or autonomy. The "subject" only encounters the "problem" of the other and of coexistence because it has begun by detaching itself (from the world and from others), and by forgetting that it is, before anything else, in-the-world and with-others. Nothing is more remarkable than this operation by which thought withdraws into itself and dis-engages itself from existence.

This withdrawal has reached the limits of its possibilities with the transcendental subject or even with the Absolute Subject. "Afterward," for Kierkegaard or Heidegger, the difficulty will have been to "come back" to existence. It is true that Kierkegaard speaks of the living being as a "subjectivity," but it is never a matter of a consciousness that believes it can begin with itself, with its demands and questions, its freedom, or its autonomy. On the contrary, it is a question of an existent that undergoes the experience of its birth, of its derivation (the experience of its filiation) and of the originary lag of consciousness behind existence. Existence, it seems to me, names everything that I must experience (the body, matter, languages, others, responsibility, love . . .), the thing behind which my consciousness cannot go or situate itself in order to assure its return. Thus it is also grounds for a resistance to the subject's purely theoretical gaze.

However, the same cannot be said of "subjectivistic" thought, where the philosophical question of the other rightfully precedes the experience of the other. In this case one thinks of others on the basis of what consciousness discovers for itself (by itself and about itself). Subjectivist morality implies respect for the other (for the other subject) by grounding itself first of all in the freedom of the subject and the autocracy of practical reason (this autocracy is also attributed to the other). Thus it is on the basis of a rational being's subjective freedom that its relation to the other can be regulated, and not on the basis of its "empirical" encounter with others. The other can thus be my *equal* in terms of dignity and earn my respect because it is *my* equal. The subject essentially resolves the question of the other within itself, not *with* the other—for then it would have to *begin* with the experience of coexistence or community. Aristotle said that "the experience of the things of life" was "the point of departure and the object of the reasonings of political science" (which the *Ethics* encompass).[10] Indeed, it is crucial for political thought to know whether it begins with the questions consciousness puts to itself, or whether it begins instead with the experience of communication—which is also the experience of my inadequacy. Furthermore, we have to clarify which communication we are talking about.

If Habermas's theory of the *communicative act*, for example, asserts the irreducibility of communication, it does not, for all that, break with a theory of the subject, that is, of an individual or communal thinking that coincides with itself. Thus Habermas writes in his "Preliminary Observations" to the *Theory of Communicative Action* that the discourse of argumentation allows interlocutors to "overcome their merely subjective views" and to come together in a "mutuality of rationally motivated convictions."[11] However, this approach to communication still presumes "*initial* subjective conceptions*" (my emphasis), and thus presumes an original atomization of subjects that are still isolated or capable of being isolated (this would mean every subject for itself, unshared and undivided: this would mean individuals). One would, then, have to attribute these presumed initial "subjective conceptions" to subjects that would *not yet* have communicated, and, even, that would not yet have spoken; for if this subjectivity speaks, it is divided, different from itself, and its initial plenitude or adequacy is already shared. Moreover: Would the discourse of argumentation be the only one to allow for an "unconditional union" and "consensus"? It is remarkable, to say the least, that in the aftermath of various manifestations of fascism one can calmly claim to distinguish the "consensus bringing force of argumentative speech" from the "manipulation" of others. And it is difficult to see how the "yes" of acceptance uttered by actual interlocutors (however many of them there may be), and its "illocutionary success," could guarantee the "rationality" of arguments within a given discourse.[12] Communicational rationality thus maintains a certain subjectivism (or initial atomism), and, what is more, it cannot "go beyond" this subjectivism without recourse to the myth of a community of consensus—which is another form of subjectivity that is close to itself and that speaks with a single voice.

Aristotelian empiricism, in the final analysis, allows us to get closer to the kind of thinking that might begin with the experience of communication and the acknowledgment of the question of others, with the irreducible plurality of voices that such thought presupposes—with the impossibility of reducing coexistence to a self-sufficient or undifferentiated unity (of the individual or of the community). In this respect, the way in which Aristotle broaches the idea of justice, if one compares it to the Kantian doctrines of morality and Right, is a good illustration of the difference between a form of empiricism (which is what we have to rethink: the experience of the other as the point of departure) and a form of subjectivism (autonomy as the point of departure).

On the one hand, we are dealing with a reflection on questions of sharing, distribution, the complex mix of powers and obligations, etc. Exchanges, links, and others are already in place: it may entail carefully mediating these relationships, rather than creating or founding them in an absolute sense. On the other hand, the philosophical subject questions itself about the conditions of its freedom and of the compatibility of this freedom with that of other subjects which are just as abstract as it is. It endeavors to define, a priori, the conditions of the coexistence of free subjects. Whence this powerlessness of the metaphysics of morals to free itself from legalism in order to concern itself with the singularity of actual cases, and the difficulty of conceiving of jurisprudence other than as an application of the law.[13] Moreover, it is difficult to see what could prevent legislative reason from subordinating singularity to the universality of the law, since legislative reason has already decided *who* the other is—it has decided that it is another rational subject that must necessarily have a passion for autonomy—and since it can determine in advance what others can rightfully lay claim to. Even if legislative reason tells me what it is due, the law mediates a priori my relationship to the other. It is because the subject believes it can begin with itself, with its own unity and freedom, that it must also lay the foundations for any possible instances of sharing. The subject, this foundation, and the law are just so many figures of that which transcends the experience of communication and the experience of any form of "bond." If, on the contrary, the experience of coexistence entails an "encroachment" of existences and singularities on each other, then what articulates them, what binds, associates, or exposes them to each other, does not need to be founded, and, indeed, cannot be founded. (And "what binds them" should not here be conceived of as a bond between two sufficient beings who were originally separated. This bond could be "what tears them together," to borrow the expression Georges Bataille uses in talking about Tristan and Yseult's love.)[14]

Thinking that concerns itself with justice, if it begins with coexistence and the experience of division, could be founded not on the law that a reasonable subject is able to make (for itself), but, I would say, on complaints. The question would be one of knowing *who is complaining*, and where these complaints come from. Meting out justice would amount to finding acceptable compromises, to arbitrating, rectifying, settling, repairing (and not simply constraining or sanctioning).

Even then, if one wants to make room for questions from others, one would have to be careful not to prejudge *who* has "the right" to complain (even if, in the judicial domain, complaints are necessarily a determined procedure). Accounting for complaints must therefore precede the law. If the possibility of determining the law a priori (as an ethical or juridical imperative) precedes the complaint, then there will always be those who do not have the right to complain, because the law has not yet anticipated their case, because they were children, or women, or foreigners, or lunatics, or animals. As we know, the "Rights of Man" themselves cannot remain merely formal concepts: they must be applied to a humanity that is supposedly universal and in fact is always determined. After all, the actual evolution of the Law has never been determined on the basis of the philosophical question of duty or of right, but on the basis of actual complaints, revolts, and struggles. Philosophy has always intervened to rationalize the legitimacy of these complaints, revolts, and struggles after the fact.

Indeed, sometimes one form of legitimacy (political, for example) is tolerable, acceptable, and agreed upon, while at other times this is no longer the case. The very same reality becomes unjust—just think of the condition of women, whether from an economic, legal, or political perspective. . . . But can we state here that there is a rational foundation to legitimacy, without stemming or arresting the free play of political life in the wider sense of the term, without limiting it to an ideological program, whose principles the more enlightened among us would be familiar with, and whose implementation we would then be able to ensure? If a political philosophy were possible, if thinking alone could determine what it is that founds a community, it would destroy political experience and political life (or what we understand by democracy). And yet the experience of the question (coming) from the other *is* the experience of community: it takes place every time several singularities happen to be traversed by the same "event." Those who share are also divided among themselves. (I would like to speak more at length and more rigorously about sharing, but Jean-Luc Nancy, in response to the question for which I am answering in this essay, has done it better than anyone else in *La communauté désoeuvrée*,[15] in which he shows in particular how singular existences are constituted by sharing, exposed as they are to one another . . .)

It is also this theme of sharing and of en-gagement that could allow us to account for the experience of what we call "love," an experience that cannot be thought of in terms of a "bond" between two adequate subjects. If one of the features of the philosophical subject is to constitute itself as a consciousness which is originally free, it seems that it can only conceive of commitment as its own act, its decision, the act by which it agrees to enter into a contract, into a relationship, to associate itself with others, etc. If one accepts that subjective consciousness is that thought capable of resting upon itself, of always coming back to itself, of always appropriating what is outside it for itself (a thought that thereby reveals its passion for autonomy or adequacy), one can see how the subject is able to desire (the desire of the other as an object, or the desire for the desire of the other subject), but one can hardly, without laughing, imagine it loving, or worse yet, *"falling* in love." The English and the French expressions both say the same thing: a fall is involved, or rather, the experience of a weakness, through which existence would discover, or rediscover itself, in the mode of absence, the fact of its non-presence to itself. It is as if it found that, despite itself, it was entrusted to the other, under the keep of the other, pledged to the other. This experience is neither that of having a hold over another, nor that of the gift, at least not of the gift of the self, of a self keeping its pride, and free either to "give itself" or not to do so. Furthermore, at the same time as he (or she) would recognize his (or her) inadequacy, the person who loves also feels electively responsible for the other (even before any demands are made of him or her) and concerned about the other as only a finite, mortal, being can be concerned about another mortal.

But the love relationship, if it is thought of within the horizon of subjectivity, implies either a sublation (*Aufhebung*) of sexual difference in marriage and the family (Hegel),[16] or else demands that the lovers recover their "personality" through marriage. Let us consider the strange way in which Kant demonstrates the necessity of marriage: "If the man and woman want to enjoy one another reciprocally, they must necessarily marry. . . . Indeed, sexual enjoyment *[la jouissance]* is the natural use that one sex makes of the sexual organs of the other."[17] Kant continues: "This is therefore only possible under one condition: that is, that one person is acquired by the other *as a thing*. The first person acquires the other reciprocally in his or her turn; in effect he or she thus *reconquers his or herself* and reestablishes his or her personality" (my emphasis).[18] I admit that I am not able to understand very well exactly how the reciprocity of possession, the fact that the two spouses are things in each other's eyes according to a rigorous reciprocity guaranteed by a contract, can restore their personality. This would rather resemble a sort of mutual disrespect and a possible unleashing of a reciprocal and legal hold over one another. The experience of the commitment of those who are in love *[l'engagement amoureux]* could suggest something else: rather than a double mastery or hold over each other, it could be a shared weakness.

Now, either weakness is a sickness of the subject, a provisional crisis from which it can recover (alone), or else it is a structure of existence, one that certain experiences or certain "events"—birth, love, death, procreation . . .—bring to light. Weakness (and I should here refer to a certain number of texts that are literary, philosophical, or both, from Kierkegaard to Lacoue-Labarthe) is, in fact, the existent's experience that the *subjectum* hides itself and that the existent is not therefore its own subject, it does not rest upon itself, it is not its own foundation (if it were, it would have to duplicate itself, like the philosophical subject that redoubles itself into an empirical and a transcendental subject). "To be" weak also means not beginning with oneself, it means being *born*, experiencing the lag of consciousness behind carnal existence, knowing that a child is something that can happen to us and that death will necessarily surprise us. It is to *hold* (to remain, to remain "standing," to be, to be stable . . .) only to find supports or props "outside of the self ": the earth, the mother, but also any form of support one can think of, including all the prostheses usually classed as technical objects or instruments. (Only God is supposed to rest upon himself absolutely.) For example, to say that when one loves, one *holds* the other dear, is not a metaphor any more than what one calls *collapse*, which accompanies death or the loss of those whom one "holds" dear. It may seem paradoxical that weak beings could also support one another, but it is precisely because all are insufficient (all mortals, all living beings, all animals and vegetables) that they are like supports and supplements for one another. What is more, the fact of *finding oneself* by chance someone else's *support* (as for so many of Victor Hugo's heros; for example, the young Gwynplaine in *The Man Who Laughs*, who, in the depths of despair and deprivation, takes into his care another child[19]) gives a semblance of necessity to existence, or at least commits it to a certain resistance.

This inadequacy of sexual and mortal existences is already the inadequacy of bodies, which are less separate than it might seem and which are, before anything else, excrescences of other bodies. This in turn brings up the question of borders, of the borderlines of property, of limits, of what is inside and what is outside organic existence (that existence which *is repugnant* to consciousness; "to be repugnant to" meaning, in the fourteenth century, "to resist"). All mammals' infants graft themselves to, or "plug themselves into," the body of their mothers while they breastfeed, such that each one is momentarily the organ of the other (and the infant is no less necessary to the breast than the breast to the infant). This troubling connection (one that troubles the opposition of the self and the other in the same way that sexual relations also trouble it) cannot be described as a subject/object relationship, any more than it allows one to say who or what is active or passive. On the contrary, to relate to the body of the other as an object that can be used, that one can instrumentalize or think of as a means, is a way for subjective consciousness to reappropriate this outside, to prevent the other's flesh from infringing on its own, to prevent its "own" body from spilling over onto another's.

The concern with not allowing oneself to be overtaken by one's own body is a central concern of the philosophical subject: making the first move, getting ahead of the body, programming it oneself, being in command, and, in order to do that, *representing to oneself* if possible all the processes, foreseeing them, calculating them, setting them off or holding them in check . . . This is what constitutes the effort of consciousness, even that of the philosopher in his life, in his existence. There is something moving and comical, even pathetic (but here we all recognize ourselves) in the efforts Kant makes, in his everyday existence, not to let himself be bothered or surprised by his body (I refer here especially to the account given by his last secretary, Wasianski): a permanent vigilance, very strict rules for living—not to sweat, not to cough, not to sneeze, so to "breathe exclusively through the nose"—to digest well, to be comfortable in his clothes (whence the invention of a suitable suspenders-belt), etc.[20] So many examples of techniques capable of making this celibate philosophical machine function neatly (celibate or almost: his faithful and punctual servant was in a sense the indispensable supplement of this existence). One should ask, as a very serious question, why Kant tolerated neither coughing nor sneezing (and no doubt, in all likelihood any sort of spasm). Indeed, it seems clear that the autonomy of a subject that coughs is, if not gravely, at least distinctly weakened. A free subject must know how to prevent itself from coughing.

Here it would be necessary—and I will only touch upon this point—to pursue a reflection on the status of the organ and the status of technique in their relationship to consciousness. One could say, roughly speaking, that the subject's thoughts conceive of technique as a calculation and an implementation of means toward an end that consciousness represents. The representation of this end thus appears as the criterion of free action, that is to say, of human action. And because I earlier spoke of the mother and the child, I will quote what Spengler says about parental conduct in *Man and Technics*: "It is not true that the female animal 'cares' for her young. Care is a feeling that implies the projection of a mental vision into the future, concern for what is to be. . . . An animal can neither hate nor despair. Its parental activity is, like everything else above mentioned *[Spengler here refers to generic techniques specific to certain species of animals]* an obscure unconscious response to an impulse of the same order as that which underlies a great many forms of life."[21]

I do not wish to dwell on the question of despair, even though an animal, as we know, can allow itself to die: but it can no doubt be argued that the animal does not know that it is despairing (any more than it knows it is going to die), whereas man knows it. And this situation, for the very reason it is desperate, sometimes saves him from dying of it. What I want to emphasize here above all is the opposition between the *projection of a mental vision* and *the obscure unconscious response*, which distinguishes men from animals, and which allows Spengler, good humanist that he is, to say that the female does not care about her offspring. It is remarkable that Heidegger, who gives a completely different meaning to care, should nevertheless make it a structure specific to *human* existence, and absent from animal life.

As far as Spengler's theory is concerned, it implies or presupposes a clear opposition between instinctive animal technique and human technique (human technique being "technique," in the proper sense of the term), the latter implying the primacy and authority of consciousness. The implications of Marcel Mauss's approach to the body's techniques (in *Sociology and Anthropology*) are another matter altogether.[22] As Mauss describes them, in the course of a highly original argument, these traditional techniques of the body, examples of which he takes from human societies, call into question the primacy of consciousness and bring to light a technicity that precedes the traditional division between, on the one hand, the biological (a pure animality) and, on the other hand, the psychic, social, and technical "in the proper sense of the terms." Organs or gestures are one of a number of technical apparatuses. They are, one might say, natural prostheses, natural tools, just as parts of an animal's body can be (in the case of an animal that swims, flies, hunts, etc.). This would allow for a *rapprochement* of generic (animal) techniques and traditional (human) techniques. What is more, Mauss speaks of the body's techniques as "syntaxes of gestures that are traditionally effective," such as the techniques of sleeping, erotic techniques, walking, swimming, grooming, eating techniques, etc. (Thus we come back to the infant and its mother.) Now, these syntaxes of gesture are "physio-psycho-sociological constructs in which psychological phenomena are simple 'cogwheels,' " writes Mauss, who makes thought into a technical element, and not a consciousness that transcends and grounds the technical process.[23] In the case of these bodily techniques, and at least in this case, subjective consciousness is not the cause of the construct. This is why, for example, Mauss, as a swimmer who early on picked up this habit, continues to swim while swallowing and then spitting out the water again: "It's stupid, yet I still have this habit: I can't rid myself of my technique."[24] As for reflective thought, not only is it not the source or the cause of the gestural mechanism, but it is rather these mechanisms themselves, these techniques, that make it possible. "Nerves," resistance, seriousness, *presence of mind*, classically attributed to the control of subjective consciousness, would in fact be possible, for Mauss, only as a function of delaying mechanisms, of the inhibition of uncoordinated movements that stem from culture and from physical techniques, and that allow for a "resistance to the invasion of emotion."[25]

In any case, I would like to know what "mental vision" the mother, the true mother, the human mother, "projects" when she *worries* about her children. What does a mother think about, exactly? Does she, individually, set herself free from this "generic constraint" by which an animal is supposedly entirely dominated? Poets sometimes have another way of talking about it; for example, in *Ninety-Three*, Hugo writes: "Maternity is inexplicable; you cannot argue with it. What makes a mother sublime is that she is a type of animal."[26] Humanist thought can, moreover, accommodate itself to a discourse such as this; it suffices merely to reinscribe the difference between man and animal within humanity itself, so that the dividing line runs between man and woman. Because the question that has been put to us cannot avoid making reference to the deconstruction of metaphysics, that is to say, in its modern form, of the metaphysics of the subject, I would like to say a few words about this questioning, about this experience of the question, that are specific to *Dasein*. *Dasein* is certainly a new name for one who questions, and who is no longer a *subject*, for it is no longer this "fiction" of a consciousness without a world and without others. *Dasein* is not this consciousness that represents the world and others to itself, but rather the one that refers to the world and others in the mode of concern (*Besorge*), assistance or solicitude (*Fürsorge*). It is with-others *[avec-autrui]* and in view of others, even if this coexistence may actually change into indifference. The way in which we mutually *worry* about one another (*Fürsorge*) thus belongs to an existential and ontological determination. But *Dasein*, at the outset, insofar as it is originary and quotidian, is neither someone nor somebody: "not this one, not that one," but a neutral *They*, from which it will have to find itself, this *They* that had released it in advance from any decision and from all responsibility. "In *Dasein's* everydayness the agency through which most things come about is one of which we must say that 'it was no one.' "[27] *Dasein's* access to its own being is therefore contemporaneous with its access to responsibility.

What interests me here, as far as our question is concerned, is that the *who* is dissociable neither from responsibility nor from the question: for responsibility is conceived of from the perspective of a new experience of the question, which is also a new determination of freedom, insofar as the question is the decision that most properly belongs to spirit and its freedom (I refer here to Jacques Derrida's book, *Of Spirit*[28]). What I myself would like to emphasize, in Heidegger, is at the same time a questioning that breaks with the self-questioning of subjective consciousness, that is also a questioning that does not essentially bring into play a process of address *between* questioners. Questions are not events that happen between us or that pass from one to another through singular experiences (this is what interests me, and is what my thinking has been revolving around . . .). The "we" in Heidegger, is not a "*we* that each of us questions," for example. It is *we* who determine ourselves as those who experience the fundamental question, who experience the question of being. See for example what Heidegger says, in §2 of *Being and Time,* about "the formal structure of the question of being."[29] In examining the formal structure of any question, he writes that all questions are determined as a search that inquires about what is being asked: to ask is always in some way to address a question "to something." This "something," which first of all orients the question, however indeterminate it may be, is that *towards which* the question is directed. This *something* is not *someone*: I mean that the question may well be asked *about* a who, the question, "*Who?*" may well be asked, of course, but the "*who*" (who orients the question in this case) is not the who *to whom* or *to which* a question can be put in the sense of *being addressed.* The thing about which the questioner is inquiring, insofar as he is himself the questioner, no longer seems to come from someone who might ask him. In this sense, the questioning beings that "we" are, are less responsible for one another than we are for what, fundamentally, calls us: that is to say, Being. And nothing determines us essentially "before" this possibility of letting ourselves be called, that is to say, of answering, already by asking it, the question of being. As for myself, I will retain the following: that the experience of the question precedes the determination of the *who*. Who am I, who are you, could be articulated thus as: For what or whom, to what or whom, do you answer?

But is it possible to ask, for example, *Who are we?* Is it possible, in other words, to presuppose a common experience of the question? Can one say it is that which authorizes us to say "*We* who experience this"? In general, what authorizes the philosopher to say "*we*"? After all, Descartes does not say *we*, he says *I* in his *Meditations.* The event that he recounts is a certain experience of the philosophical question, a *singular* experience of thought. An experience of doubt and of certainty that is readable as a story. This seems to contradict what I was saying above: namely, that there cannot really be an experience of the question for a consciousness that begins with itself, or at least that draws from within itself its questions, that is its own resource, that locates itself as the foundation of all knowledge and claims to be the determination of man in general. One can nonetheless speak of experience in the case of the *Meditations* to the extent that the subject's certainty of self is not a beginning, but the consequence of an effort to overcome a singular experience: the experience of error and of doubt—"*I perceived* that I had taken a number of false opinions to be true. . . ."—"I *felt* that these senses deceived me"—"Yesterday's meditation filled my mind with so many doubts that today *it is no longer in my power* to forget about them"[30] (my emphasis). The certainty of the self is consequently an event that happens to "Descartes the doubter," as Heidegger will come to call him, that is to say, to someone who launches himself recklessly into a "sudden abolition of all the privileges of authority."[31] But as always, to abolish authority is also to set oneself up as an authority. In philosophy, Descartes in a sense started a Revolution and created an Empire.

Heidegger summarizes his story in the following way: "As the doubter, Descartes forced men into doubt in this way: he led them to think of themselves, of their 'I.' Thus the 'I,' human subjectivity, came to be declared the center of thought. It is here that the point of view of the 'I,' and the subjectivity of the modern age, had its source."[32] But this proclamation, and the "becoming-source" of the event of the *cogito* can only mask its sudden appearance, for the source cannot be its own resource, any more than it can go upstream from itself, just as the subjective consciousness cannot go behind itself. Whence the question, asked by Valéry and, also, to some extent by myself, that one might call the question of an underground of the subject, of a nonsubjective, unconscious, opaque support of the subject. For Valéry, this support of the cogito, which subjectivity as a philosophical concept in fact betrays, is a singularity, a *someone*—"he means to say that it is Descartes who is thinking, and not just anybody"[33] —it is the timbre of a voice, a style, the bid for power (*le coup de force*) of a "Self" that appeals to all of its *egotistical* strength. . . . Might there be *bids for power* in philosophy just as there are in politics (and is this not the expression that Heidegger uses in referring to Plato's gesture of determining being as *idea*)? In order to rediscover the event in philosophy, one must read it as one reads literature, admitting that someone exposed himself or herself and took a risk in writing it (in entering into this experience of writing); one must read it while asking to what or for what, to whom or for whom, is it answering (without perhaps knowing it); one must read it without succumbing to a kind of philosophical authority (the tone adopted by philosophers always has something authoritarian about it, and their style something "virile"), in such a way as to recover within it very singular experiences or events. One must perhaps also read it as the letter written to you by someone who would write you a letter.

After the subject, there would also be another experience of reading. But, above all, another experience of the question—or, if you like, of the other—that is to say, another experience of the question of the other.

Post-scriptum: After the subject, who signs? A "me" who would say, again with Valéry, "My fate is more me than myself. A person is only made up of answers to a number of impersonal incidents."

Notes

1. Kant, *Anthropology From a Pragmatic Point of View*, trans. Mary Gregor (The Hague: Martinus Nijhoff, 1974), §2, p. 10.

2. Ibid., p. 11.

3. See Hegel, *Phenomenology of Spirit*, trans. A. V. Miller (Oxford: Oxford University Press, 1977), Pt. A, pp. 58–103.

4. See Bataille, *Inner Experience*, trans. Leslie Anne Boldt (Albany: State University of New York, 1988).

5. Heidegger, *Hegel's Phenomenology of Spirit*, trans. Parvis Emad and Kenneth Maly (Bloomington: Indiana University Press, 1988), §2.

6. See Descartes's epistle to the Sorbonne written for the purpose of obtaining the approval of the Doctors for the publication of *Les Méditations*: "A messieurs les doyens et docteurs de la sacrée faculté de théologie de Paris," in *Oeuvres philosophiques*, ed. Ferdinand Alquié (Paris: Garnier, 1967), vol. 2, pp. 383–89. [TN: All translations of Descartes are our own.]

7. Ibid., p. 384.

8. See my *Aparté: Conceptions and Deaths of Søren Kierkegaard*, trans. Kevin Newmark (Tallahassee: Florida State University Press, 1988).

9. Kant, *Religion Within the Limits of Reason Alone*, trans. Theodore M. Greene and Hoyt H. Hudson (New York: Harper and Row, Publishers, 1960).

10. Aristotle, *Nichomachean Ethics*, trans. David Ross (Oxford: Oxford University Press, 1987), book I, §§2 and 3.

11. Jürgen Habermas, *Theory of Communicative Action*, trans. Thomas McCarthy (Boston: Beacon Press, 1984), vol. 1, p. 10.

12. Ibid.

13. I here refer to Kant's *Die Metaphysik der Sitten*, in *Werkausgabe*, 12 vols., ed. Wilhelm Weischedel (Frankfurt: Suhrkamp, 1956), vol. 8.

14. Bataille, *Inner Experience*, p. 22.

15. Nancy, *La communaute désoevrée* (Paris: Christian Bourgois Editeur, 1986). Soon to appear in English as *The Inoperative Community*, trans. Peter Connor (Minneapolis: University of Minnesota Press, 1990).

16. See Hegel, *Philosophy of Right*, trans. T. M. Knox (Oxford: Oxford University Press, 1975), §§158–69, pp. 110–16.

17. Kant, *Die Metaphysik der Sitten*, p. 483.

18. Ibid.

19. Hugo, *The Man Who Laughs*, 2 vols. (Boston: Little Brown and Co., 1888).

20. See Thomas De Quincey's summary of Wasianski's account in his "The Last Days of Kant," in *The Collected Writings of Thomas De Quincey*, ed. David Masson, 14 vols. (Edinburgh: Adam and Charles Black, 1890), vol. 4, p. 337. See also *Kant intime: I. E. Borowski, R. B. Jachmann, E. A. Wasianski*, ed. and trans. Jean Mistler (Paris: Grasset, 1985).

21. Spengler, *Man and Technics: A Contribution to a Philosophy of Life*, trans. Charles Francis Atkinson (New York: Alfred A. Knopf, 1932), p. 30. [TN: we have modified this translation slightly.]

22. See Mauss, "Les Techniques du Corps," in *Sociologie et anthropologie* (Paris: PUF, 1966), pp. 365–86.

23. Ibid., p. 371.

24. Ibid., p. 367.

25. Ibid., p. 385.

26. Hugo, *Ninety-Three*, (Boston: Colonial Press, Co., 1910), p. 274. [TN: translation modified slightly.]

27. Heidegger, *Being and Time*, trans. John Macquarrie and Edward Robinson (New York: Harper and Row, Publishers, 1962), §27, pp. 164–65.

28. See *Of Spirit: Heidegger and the Question*, trans. Geoffrey Bennington and Rachel Bowlby (Chicago: University of Chicago Press, 1989).

29. *Being and Time*, §2, p. 24.

30. Descartes, *Les Méditations*, in *Oeuvres philosophiques*, 2:404, 405, and 414.

31. Cf. Paul Valéry, "A View of Descartes," in *Masters and Friends*, trans. Martin Turnell (Princeton: Princeton University Press, 1968), p. 40. See also, in the same volume, "Sketch for a Portrait of Descartes," "Descartes," and "A Second View of Descartes."

32. See *What is a Thing?* trans. W. B. Barton Jr. and Vera Deutsch (South Bend, IN: Regnery, 1967), p. 99. [TN: Translation modified slightly.]

33. Valéry, "Descartes," in *Masters and Friends*, p. 31.

2

On a Finally Objectless Subject
Alain Badiou

What does our era enjoin us to do? Are we equal to the task? It seems to me too easy to claim that the imperative of the times is one of completion, and that, as modern Narratives linking subject, science and History are foreclosed, we must either explore the formless *dis-covered* this foreclosure bequeaths us or sustain— turning back towards the Greek origin of thinking—a pure *question*. I propose instead the following hypothesis: what is demanded of us is *an additional step* in the modern, and not a veering towards the limit, whether it be termed "post-modern" or whatever. We know, thanks in particular to mathematics, that making an additional step represents a singularly complex task as the local status of problems is often more difficult and muddled than their global status. The predication of an "end" is an enjambment that prohibits resolution when one is unaware of how to proceed on to the next step. Rather than ask "what is there beyond?" because of methodical distrust of the beyond, I will formulate the question as follows, on the basis of the hypothesis that modern thinking requires its continuation: what concept of the subject *succeeds* the one whose trajectory can be traced out from Descartes to Husserl, and which wore thin and fell into ruin between Nietzsche and Heidegger, as well as throughout the whole of what should be called "the age of the poets" (Hölderlin, Hopkins, Mallarmé, Rimbaud, Trakl, Pessoa, Mandelstam, Celan)?

Which amounts to asking: can we think an *objectless* subject? In the twofold sense in which, concerning such a subject, one can neither designate its correlate in presentation, nor suppose that it answers to any of thought's objectives. I would argue that the process of the destitution of the subject has, over the course of a complex history going back at least as far as Kant, been confused with the ineluctable process of the destitution of the object. From within the modern imperative— to which the predication of an "end" opposes but a dissipated torment—we must base what succeeds on the fact that the form of the object cannot in any way sustain

Translated by Bruce Fink

the enterprise of truth. This imperative thus raises the following question: Is it possible to de-objectify the space of the subject?

If it is possible: What is thus beyond the subject if not the very same subject dissociated or subtracted from reflexive jurisdiction, un-constituting, untied from all supports unrelated to the process of a truth—of which the subject would be but a finite fragment?

I call subject the local or finite status of a truth. A subject is what is *locally born out*.

The "subject" thus ceases to be the inaugural or conditioning point of legitimate statements. It is no longer—and here we see the cancellation of the object, as objective this time—that *for which* there is truth, nor even the desirous eclipse of its surrection. A truth always precedes it. Not that a truth exists "before" it, for a truth is forever suspended upon an indiscernible future. The subject is *woven* out of a truth, it is what exists of truth in limited fragments. A subject is that which a truth passes through, or this finite point through which, in its infinite being, truth itself passes. This transit excludes every interior moment.

This is what allows me to deny that it is necessary—"truth" henceforth being disjoined or dissociated from "knowledge"—to suppress the category "subject." While it is impossible in our era to identify "truth" with a status of cognitive statements, it cannot be inferred that we can thereby go beyond what modern thought (post-Galilean or post-Cartesian) has designated as its own locus using the term "subject." Granted: the meaning of the word "truth" may hang on the question of being; still it seems more apposite to make this meaning depend on the supplementation or exceeding-of-being that I term "event." Does it follow that the "subject" is obsolete? That would be to confuse the classical *function* of the subject (as transparent punctuality on the basis of which the true or its limit is established) and *being*, which props up this function (i.e., the finite that, since Galileo, must endure truth's infinite nature).

Let us dissociate this being from its hereditary function.

Axiomatic Provision

An irrevocable step forward has been made through the critique of earlier concepts of the subject, a critique thoroughly based on the notion that truth is not a qualification of knowledge nor an intuition of the intelligible.[1] One must come to conceive of truth as making a hole in knowledge. Lacan is paradigmatic on this point. The subject is thus convoked as a border-effect or a delimiting fragment of such a hole-piercing.

To conceptualize the subject outside of any object position makes no sense except from the point of view of a doctrine of truth that has been so completely recast as to go well beyond the critique of correspondence theories of truth, and to out-radicalize hermeneutics of unveiling. Such a doctrine cannot be laid out here in its ontological complexity. I will simply summarize it in four theses, fully aware though

I am that in philosophy summary is impracticable; one would better conceive of it as an axiomatic shortcut. The four theses that follow must thus be solidly founded as everything else depends upon them.

(a) A truth is always post-eventual.[2] Its process begins when a supernumerary name has been put into circulation—extracted from the very void that sutures every situation to being—by which it has been *decided* that an event has supplemented the situation.

(b) The process of a truth is fidelity (to the event), i.e., the evaluation, by means of a specific operator (that of fidelity), of the degree of connection between the terms of the situation and the supernumerary name of the event.

(c) The terms of the situation that are declared positively connected to the supernumerary name form an infinite part of the situation, which is suspended on a future, as this infinity only comes into being through a succession of finite evaluations, and is thus never presented.

(d) If this infinite part *will have avoided* (we have here the future anterior as truth's own temporal regime or register) coinciding with what knowledge determines as known, consistent, or discerned sets in the situation—if, thus, the part in question is indiscernible for knowledge, i.e., absolutely indistinguishable or generic—then we will say the post-eventual procedure produces a truth. A truth is therefore, in substance, a procedure of post-eventual fidelity that will have been generic. In this sense, a truth (indiscernible within knowledge), is the metonymy of the situation's very being—i.e., of the pure or unnamed multiple into which this being is resolved.

Let us call "subject" every finite state of a generic procedure.

Negative Delimitation of the Concept of the Subject

From the preceding definition, we can infer a whole series of negative consequences that make it clear that we are *proceeding* (through discontinuous continuity) forward from the classical concept of the subject.

(a) A subject is not a substance. If the word substance has a meaning, it designates a multiple that is counted as one in a situation. The intrinsic indiscernibility into which a generic procedure resolves excludes a subject's being substantial.

(b) Nor is a subject an empty point. The void, which is a proper name of being, is inhuman and a-subjective. It is an ontological concept. In addition, it is clear that a truth is realized as multiplicity and not as punctuality.

(c) A subject is in no sense the organizing of a meaning of experience. It is not a transcendental function. If the word "experience" means anything, it designates presentation as such. Now a generic procedure, hinged as it is on the event that a supernumerary name qualifies, in no way coincides with presentation. We should also differentiate meaning and truth. A generic procedure realizes the post-eventual truth of a situation, but this indiscernible multiple in which a truth consists yields up no meaning.

(d) A subject is not an invariant of presentation. The subject is *rare* in that the generic procedure runs diagonally to the situation. One could add that each subject is rigorously singular, being the generic procedure of a situation that is itself singular. The statement "There is subject" *[il y a du sujet]* is uncertain or haphazard: it is not transitive with respect to being.

(e) A subject is neither a result nor an origin. It is the *local* status of the procedure, a configuration that exceeds the situation.

Let us now examine the twists and turns of the subject.

Subjectivization: Intervention and the Faithful Connection Operator

The subject is at the core of a problem of twofold origin concerning fidelity procedures. We have the name of the event, which I say results from an *intervention*, as well as a faithful connection operator that regulates the procedure and institutes truth. To what extent does this operator depend upon the name? And doesn't the emergence of this operator constitute a second event? Let us take an example. In Christianity, the Church is that through which connections to and disconnections from the Christ-event, originally called the "death of God," are evaluated. As Pascal says, the Church is thus verily "truth's history," as it is the faithful connection operator sustaining "religious" generic procedures. But what is the link between the Church and Christ? or between the Church and the death of God? This point is continually under debate and (like the debate concerning the link between the Party and the Revolution) has given rise to all kinds of schisms and heresy. One suspects the faithful connection operator itself of being originally unfaithful to the event in which it takes pride.

I will call *subjectivization* the emergence of an operator that is consecutive to the interventional naming that decides the event.

Subjectivization takes the form of the Two. It is oriented towards the intervention in the vicinity of the eventual site. But is also oriented towards the situation by its coincidence with the rule of evaluation and proximity that grounds the generic procedure. Subjectivization is the interventional naming *from the point of view of the situation*, i.e., the rule governing the intrasituational effects of putting a supernumerary name into circulation.

Subjectivization, i.e., the singular configuration of a rule, subsumes the Two of which it consists in the absence of meaning of a proper name. St. Paul for the Church, Lenin for the Party, Cantor for ontology, Schoenberg for music, but also Simon or Claire, should they declare their love, are all designations—made by the "one" of a proper name—of the subjectivizing scission between the name of an event (the death of God, the revolution, infinite multiples, the destruction of the tonal system, or an encounter) and the setting into motion of a generic procedure (the Catholic Church, Bolshevism, set theory, serialism, or singular love). The proper name here designates that the subject, *qua* situated and local configuration, is neither the intervention nor the fidelity operator, but rather the advent of their Two, i.e., the incorporation of the event into the situation in the form of a generic procedure. The absolute singularity of this Two, dissociated as it is from its meaning, is *shown* by the un-signifying nature of the proper name. But this un-signifying nature also clearly recalls that what the interventional naming convoked was the void which is itself the proper name of being. Subjectivization is the proper name *in situ* of this general proper name. It is an instance of the void.

The commencement of a generic procedure grounds, as its horizon, the collecting of a truth. Subjectivization thus is that which makes a truth possible. It turns the event towards the situation's truth for which this event is an event. Thus the proper name bears the trace of both the event and the situation, being that by which one comes to be for the other, *qua* generic trajectory of a truth. "Lenin" is at once the October Revolution (the eventual component) and Leninism—true-multiplicity of revolutionary politics for half a century. Similarly, "Cantor" is at once the madness that requires the conceptualization of pure multiples and articulates and relates the infinite prodigality of being-as-being to its void, and the process of total reconstruction of mathematical discursivity (up until Bourbaki and even beyond). The fact is that the proper name contains both the interventional naming and the faithful connection rule.

Subjectivization—as the aporetic nexus of a name-too-many and an un-known operation—is what *traces in situ* the becoming multiple of the true, starting from the nonexistent point at which the event has convoked the void and interpolated itself between the void and itself.

Randomness, from Which Every Truth is Woven, is the Subject's Material

If we consider the local status of a generic procedure, we notice that it depends on simple encounters. The faithful connection operator prescribes if one or another term of the situation is linked or not to the supernumerary name of the event. It in no way prescribes, however, that we examine one term before, or rather than, another. Thus the procedure is regulated in terms of its effects, but entirely random in its trajectory. The only empirical evidence in this respect is that the trajectory begins just at the outskirts of the eventual site. Everything else is lawless. There is thus an essential randomness in the procedure's itinerary. This randomness *is not visible in its result*, which is a truth, for a truth is an ideal collecting of "all" the evaluations: it is a *complete* part of the situation. But the subject does not coincide with this result. Locally there are only illegal encounters, for nothing ordains—neither in the name of the event nor in the connection operator—that one term be evaluated at a certain moment and in a certain place. If one considers *the subject's material* to be the terms submitted to the fidelity operator, this material—as multiple—has no assignable relationship with the rule dividing the positive results (where connection is established) from the negative ones (where disconnection is established). Conceived of in its operation, the subject is qualifiable though singular: it breaks down into a name (of the event) and an operator (of fidelity). Conceived of in its multiple being, i.e., in the terms that figure in the actual evaluations, the subject is unqualifiable in that these terms are arbitrary with respect to its twofold qualification.

Of course, a finite series of evaluations of terms encountered by the fidelity procedure is a possible object of knowledge. But the *active element* of the evaluation—its evaluating—is not, as it is only accidental that the terms evaluated therein by the faithful connection operator turn out to be presented in the finite multiple of the evaluations. Knowledge can retroactively enumerate the components of this multiple, as they are finite in number. As knowledge cannot, at that very moment, anticipate any meaning whatsoever of their singular regrouping, it cannot coincide with the subject whose whole being is in the encounter with terms within a random trajectory. Knowledge never encounters anything.[3] It presupposes presentation, representing it in language by discernment and judgment. That which, on the contrary, constitutes the subject is the encounter with its material, though nothing in its form (the name of the event and the fidelity operator) orders this material. If the subject has no other being-in-situ than the multiple terms it encounters and evaluates, its essence—having to include the randomness of these encounters—is rather the trajectory that links them. Now this incalculable trajectory comes under no determination within knowledge.

There is, between the knowledge of finite regroupings, their principled discernibility, and the subject of the fidelity procedure, this indifferent-difference that distinguishes the result (finite multiples of the situation) from the partial trajectory of which this result is a local configuration. The subject is "between" the terms the procedure regroups, while knowledge is the retrospective totalization of these terms.

The subject is neatly separated from knowledge by randomness. It is randomness vanquished term by term, but this victory, subtracted from language, is accomplished only as truth.

Subject and Truth:
Indiscernibility and Nomination

I axiomatically stated that "a-truth"—infinitely gathering the terms positively evaluated by the fidelity procedure—is indiscernible in the language of the situation. It is a generic part of the situation.

As the subject is a *local* configuration of the procedure, it is clear that truth is equally indiscernible "for it." For truth is global. "For it" means exactly that a subject that effectuates a truth is nonetheless incommensurate to it, the subject being finite, truth being infinite. Moreover, the subject, being within the situation, can only know (i.e., encounter) terms or multiples presented (counted as one) in this situation. And finally, the subject can only *construct his idiom [langue]* out of combinations between the supernumerary name of the event and the language *[langage]* of the situation. It is in no way assured that this idiom will suffice to discern a truth, a truth being in any case indiscernible by the resources of the language of the situation alone. One must absolutely abandon every definition of the subject that would assume that it knows the truth or is adjusted to it. Being the local moment of the truth, the subject fails to sustain its global adjunction. Every truth transcends the subject precisely because its whole being consists in supporting the effectuation of that truth. The subject is neither consciousness nor unconsciousness of the true.

The singular relationship of a subject to the truth whose procedure it supports is the following: the subject believes that there is a truth, and this belief takes the form of knowledge. I term this educated belief *confidence*.

What does confidence mean? The fidelity operator locally discerns connections and disconnections of multiples of the situation with or from the name of the event. This discerning is an *approximative truth*, for the terms positively connected are yet to come—in a truth. This "yet to come" is the distinctive characteristic of the subject who judges. Belief here is the yet-to-come that goes by the *name* of truth.

Its legitimacy derives from the fact that the name of the event, having supplemented the situation with a paradoxical multiple, circulates in the evaluations as that on the basis of which the void—as latent and wandering being of the situation—has been convoked. A finite series of evaluations thus possesses, in a manner at once effective and fragmentary, the being-in-situ of the situation itself. This fragment materially pronounces the yet-to-come for, though it is locatable by knowledge, it is the fragment of an indiscernible trajectory. Belief consists merely in the fact that the encounters' randomness is not vainly gathered up by the faithful connection operator. Held out as a promise by the event alone, belief represents what is generic of the true as possessed in the local finitude of the stages of its trajectory. In this sense the subject is self-confidence, in that he does not coincide with the retroactive discernibility of these fragmentary results. A truth is posited as the infinite determination of an indiscernible of the situation, the latter being the intrasituational global result of the event.

That this belief may take the form of knowledge results from the fact that *every subject generates namings*. Empirically, this point is born out. What one can most explicitly connect with the proper names that designate a subjectivization is an arsenal of words that make up the deployed matrix of fidelity marks. Consider "faith," "charity," "sacrifice," and "salvation" (St. Paul), or "party," "revolution," and "politics" (Lenin), or "sets," "ordinal numbers," and "cardinal numbers" (Cantor), and everything that then articulates, ramifies, and stratifies these words. What is their particular function? Do they simply designate terms presented in the situation? In that case they would be redundant as concerns the established language of the situation. One can in fact distinguish ideological sects from truth's generic procedures on the basis of the fact that whereas the words used by such sects only replace—through meaningless shifts—those declared appropriate by the situation, the names used by a subject in supporting a generic truth's local configuration *generally have no referent in the situation*. They do not thus double over the established language. But what purpose do they then serve? They are words that clearly designate terms, but terms that "will have been" presented in a *new* situation, one that results from the adjunction of an (indiscernible) truth of the situation to that same situation.

Belief is sustained by the fact that with the resources of the situation—its multiples and its language—a subject generates names whose referents are in the future anterior. Such names will have been assigned referents or meanings when the situation will have come to be in which the indiscernible, which is only represented (or included), is finally presented, as a truth of the former situation.

On the situation's surface, a generic procedure draws attention to itself above all by the nominal *aura* that surrounds its finite configurations: the subject. He who is not involved in extending the procedure's finite trajectory—who was not assessed positively regarding his connection to the event—generally considers the names to be empty. He obviously *recognizes* them, as these names are fabricated on the basis of terms of the situation. The names with which a subject surrounds himself are not indiscernible. But the outside observer, noticing that the names are mostly lacking in referents in the situation as it is, considers that they make up an arbitrary and contentless language. Which explains why revolutionary politics are always thought to involve utopian (i.e., unrealistic) elements, scientific revolutions are greeted with skepticism or viewed as nonexperimentally confirmed abstractions, and lovers' babble is cast aside as infantile madness by prudent people. Now these observers are, in a certain sense, right. The names generated—or rather composed—by a subject are suspended, as concerns their meaning, upon the yet-to-come of a truth. Their local use is to sustain the belief that the terms positively polled designate or describe the approximation of a new situation in which the truth of the actual situation will have been presented. Every subject is thus locatable by the emergence of a language inside the situation, whose multiple-referents are, however, *conditioned* by an as yet uncompleted generic part.

Now a subject is separated from this generic part (of this truth) by an infinite series of random encounters. It is entirely impossible to anticipate or to represent a truth, as it comes to be only in the course of evaluations or connections that are incalculable, their succession being solely ruled by encounters with the terms of the situation. It follows that, from the subject's point of view, the referentiality of the names remains forever suspended upon the uncompletable condition of a truth. It is only possible to say that *if* such and such a term, when it will have been encountered, turns out to be positively connected to the name of the event, *then* such and such a name will be likely to have a certain referent, for the generic part that remains indiscernible in the situation will have such and such a configuration or partial property. A subject is that which uses names to make hypotheses about truth. But as it is itself a finite configuration of the generic procedure from which a truth results, one can equally maintain that a subject uses names to make hypotheses about itself, "itself" meaning the infinite of which it is the finite. An idiom *[la langue]* here is the fixed order in which a finitude attempts to postulate— within the condition of the finite effectuated by the finite—a referentiality yet-to-come. Finitude is the very being of truth in the combination of current finite evaluations and the future anterior of a generic infinity.

One can easily show that this is the status of names such as "communism," "transfinite," "serialism," or names/nouns used in a declaration of love. Let us note that these names can support the future anterior of a truth (be it religious, political, mathematical, musical, or existential) in that they combine local evaluations (predications, statements, works, addresses) and (re)appropriated or recast names, already available in the situation. They slightly *shift* the established meanings so as to leave the referent empty, the referent that will have been filled if the truth comes to be as a new situation (the reign of God, the emancipated society, absolute mathematics, a new musical order with a range comparable to that of the tonal order, a thoroughly amorous life, etc.).

A subject is that which fends off the generic indiscernibility of a truth—a truth it effectuates in discernible finitude by an act of naming that leaves its referent in the future anterior of a condition. A subject is thus, by the good graces of names/nouns, at once the *real* of the procedure (the assessor of the assessments) and *the hypothesis* of that which its unachieved result would introduce once again into presentation. A subject emptily names the universe yet-to-come that is obtained from the fact that an indiscernible truth supplements the situation. It is concurrently the finite real, the local stage of this supplementation. Naming is only empty insofar as it is pregnant with what its own possibility sketches out. A subject is the antonym[4] of an empty idiom *[langue]*.

Notes

1. For the "axiomatic" theses on truth, I refer the reader to my book *L'être et l'événement* (Paris: Seuil, 1988) of which this article is in many respects a fragment.

2. "Eventual" will always be used here in the sense of "having to do with an event."

3. One would have to follow this up, using the notion of a "return to knowledge," by the study of the dialectic truth/veridicality whose subject is the *forcing* point.

4. A term in discourse that designates itself.

3

Citizen Subject

Etienne Balibar

I

Both following Hegel and opposed to him, Heidegger proposes Descartes as the moment when the "sovereignty of the subject" is established (in philosophy), inaugurating the discourse of modernity. This supposes that man, or rather the *ego*, is determined and conceived of as subject (*subjectum*).

Doubtless, from one text to another, and sometimes even within the same "text" (I am primarily referring here to the *Nietzsche* of 1939–46), Heidegger nuances his formulation. At one moment he positively affirms that, in Descartes's *Meditations* (which he cites in Latin), the *ego* as consciousness (which he explicates as *cogito me cogitare*), is posited, founded as the *subjectum* (that which in Greek is called the *hypokeimenon*). This also has, as corollary, the effect of identifying, for all of modern philosophy, the *hypokeimenon* and the foundation of being with the being of the subject of thought, the other of the object. At another moment he is content to point out that this identification is implicit in Descartes, and that we must wait for Leibniz to see it made explicit ("called by its own name") and reflected as the identity of reality and representation, in its difference with the traditional conception of being.

Is this nuance decisive? The fact is that it would be difficult to find the slightest reference to the "subject" as *subjectum* in the *Meditations*, and that in general the thesis that would posit the *ego* or the "I think/I am" (or the "I am a thinking thing") as *subject*, either in the sense of *hypokeimenon* or in the sense of the future *Subjekt* (opposed to *Gegenständlichkeit*), does not appear anywhere in Descartes. By evoking an implicit definition, one that awaits its formulation, and thus a teleology of the history of philosophy (a lag of consciousness, or rather of language), Heidegger only makes his position more untenable, if only because Descartes's position is actually incompatible with this concept. This can easily be verified by examining

Translated by James B. Swenson, Jr.

both Descartes's use of the noun "subject," and the fundamental reasons why he does not name the thinking substance or "thinking thing" "subject."

The problem of substance, as is well known, appears fairly late in the course of the *Meditations*. It is posited neither in the presentation of the *cogito*, nor when Descartes draws its fundamental epistemological consequence (the soul knows itself "more evidently, distinctly, and clearly" than it knows the body), but in the third meditation when he attempts to establish and to think the causal link between the "thinking thing" that the soul knows itself to be and the God the idea of whom it finds immediately in itself as the idea of the infinite being. But even there *it is not a question of the subject*. The term will appear only incidentally, in its scholastic meaning, in the "Responses to the Objections," in the context of a discussion of the real difference between finite and infinite, and between thinking and extended substances, for which the *Principles* will later furnish a properly formulated definition. Along with these discussions we must consider the one concerning the union of body and soul, the "third substance" constitutive of individuality, the theory of which will be exposed in the "Sixth Meditation" and developed in the *Treatise on the Passions*.

From consideration of these different contexts it becomes clear that the essential concept for Descartes is that of *substance*, in the new signification that he gives to it. This signification is not limited to objectifying, each on its own side, the *res cogitans* and the *res extensa*: it allows the entire set of causal relations between (infinite) God and (finite) things, between ideas and bodies, between my soul and my (own) body, to be thought. It is thus primarily a relational concept. We should understand by this that the essential part of its theoretical function is accomplished by putting distinct "substances" into relation with one another, generally in the form of a unity of opposites. The name of substance (this is its principal, negative characteristic) cannot be attributed in a univocal fashion to both the infinite (God) and the finite (creatures); it thus allows their difference to be thought, and nevertheless permits their dependence to be understood (for only a substance can "cause" another substance: this is its second characteristic). Likewise, thought and extension are really distinct substances, having no attributes whatsoever in common, and nevertheless the very reality of this distinction implies a substantial (nonaccidental) union as the basis of our experience of our sensations. All these distinctions and oppositions finally find their coherence—if not the solution of the enigmas they hold—in a *nexus* that is both hierarchical and causal, entirely regulated by the principle of the *eminent causality*, in God, of the "formal" or "objective" relations between created substances (that is, respectively, those relations that consist of actions and passions, and those that consist of representations). It is only because all (finite) substances are eminently caused by God (have their eminent cause, or rather the eminence of their cause, in God) that they are also in a causal relation among themselves. But, inversely, eminent causality—another name for positive infinity—could not express anything intelligible for us except for the "objective" unity of formally distinct causalities.

Thus nothing is further from Descartes than a metaphysics of Substance conceived of as a univocal term. Rather, this concept has acquired a new equivocality in his work, without which it could not fill its structural function: to name in turn each of the poles of a topography in which *I* am situated simultaneously as cause and effect (or rather as a cause that is itself only an effect). It must be understood that the notion of the *subjectum/hypokeimenon* has an entirely evanescent status here. Descartes mentions it, in response to objections, only in order to make a scholastic defense of his *realist* thesis (every substance is the real subject of its own accidents). But it does not add any element of knowledge (and in particular not the idea of a "matter" distinct from the "form") to the concept of substance. It is for this reason that substance is practically indiscernible from its principle attribute (comprehensible: extension, thought; or incomprehensible: infinity, omnipotence).

There is no doubt whatsoever that it is essential to characterize, in Descartes, the "thinking thing" that I am (therefore!) as substance or as substantial, in a nexus of substances that are so many *instances* of the metaphysical apparatus. But it is not essential to attach this substance to the representation of a *subjectum,* and it is in any case impossible *to apply the name* of *subjectum* to the *ego cogito.* On the other hand, it is possible and necessary to ask in what sense the human individual, composed of a soul, a body, and their unity, is the "subject" (*subjectus*) of a *divine sovereignty.* The representation of sovereignty is in fact implied by the ideal of eminence, and, inversely, the reality of finite things could not be understood outside of a specific dependence "according to which all things are subject to God."[1] That which is valid from an ontological point of view is also valid from an epistemological point of view. From the thesis of the "creation of eternal truths" to the one proper to the *Meditations* according to which the intelligibility of the finite is implied by the idea of the infinite, a single conception of the subjection of understanding and of science is affirmed, not of course to an external or revealed dogma, but to an internal center of thought whose structure is that of a sovereign decision, an absent presence, or a source of intelligibility that as such is incomprehensible.

Thus the idea that causality and sovereignty can be converted into one another is conserved and even reinforced in Descartes. It could even be said that this idea is pushed to the limit—which is perhaps, for us in any case, the herald of a coming decomposition of this figure of thought. The obvious fact that an extreme intellectual tension results from it is recognized and constantly reexamined by Descartes himself. How can the absolute freedom of man—or rather of his will: but his will is the very essence of judgment—be conceived of as similar to God's without putting this subjection back into question? How can it be conceived of outside this subjection, for it is the *image* of another freedom, of another power? Descartes's thought, as we know, oscillates between two tendencies on this point. The first, mystical, consists in *identifying* freedom and subjection: to will freely, in the sense of a necessary freedom, enlightened by true knowledge, is to coincide with the act by which God conserves me in a relative perfection. The other tendency, pragmatic, consists in *displacing* the question, playing on the topography of substances, making my subjection to God into the origin of my mastery over and possession of nature, and more precisely of the absolute power that I can exercise over my passions. There are no fewer difficulties in either one of these theses. This is not the place to discuss them, but it is clear that, in either case, freedom can in fact only be thought as the freedom of the *subject*, of the subjected being, that is, as a contradiction in terms.

Descartes's "subject" is thus still (more than ever) the *subjectus*. But what is the *subjectus?* It is the other name of the *subditus*, according to an equivalence practiced by all of medieval political theology and systematically exploited by the theoreticians of absolute monarchy: the individual submitted to the *ditio*, to the sovereign authority of a prince, an authority expressed in his orders and itself legitimated by the Word of another Sovereign (the Lord God). "It is God who has established these laws in nature, just as a king establishes laws in his kingdom," Descartes will write to Mersenne (letter of 15 April 1630).[2] It is this very dependence that constitutes him. But Descartes's subject is not the *subjectum* that is widely supposed—even if, from the point of view of the object, the meaning has to be inverted—to be permanently present from Aristotle's metaphysics up to modern subjectivity.

How is it then that they have come to be confused?[3] Part of the answer obviously lies in the effect, which continues to this very day, of Kantian philosophy and its specific necessity. Heidegger, both before and after the "turn," is clearly situated in this dependence. We must return to the very letter of the *Critique of Pure Reason* if we are to discover the origin of the projection of a transcendental category of the "subject" upon the Cartesian text. This projection and the distortion it brings with it (simultaneously subtracting something from and adding something to the *cogito*), is in itself constitutive of the "invention" of the transcendental subject, which is inseparably a movement away from and an interpretation of Cartesianism. For the subject to appear as the originarily synthetic unity of the conditions of objectivity (of "experience"), first, the *cogito* must be reformulated not only as reflexivity, but as the thesis of the "I think" that "accompanies all my representations" (that is, as the thesis of self-consciousness, which Heidegger will state as: *cogito = cogito me cogitare*); then this self-consciousness must be distinguished from both the intuition of an intelligible being and from the intuition of the "empirical ego" in "internal sense"; and finally the "paralogism of the substantiality" of the soul must be dissolved. In other words one and the same historico-philosophical operation *discovers the subject in the substance* of the Cartesian cogito, and *denounces the substance in the subject* (as transcendental illusion), thus installing Descartes in the situation of a "transition" (both ahead of *and* behind the time of history, conceived of as the history of the advent of the subject), upon which the philosophies of the nineteenth and twentieth centuries will not cease to comment.

Paraphrasing Kant himself, we can say that these formulations of the *Critique of Pure Reason* form the "unique text" from which transcendental philosophies in particular draw "all their wisdom," for they ceaselessly reiterate the double rejection of substantiality and of phenomenality that forms the paradoxical being of the subject (being/nonbeing, in any case not a thing, not "categorizable," not "objecti-fiable").[4] And this is valid not only for the "epistemological" face of the subject, but for its *practical* face as well: in the last instance the transcendental subject that effectuates the nonsubstantial unity of the conditions of experience is *the same* as the one that, prescribing its acts to itself in the mode of the categorical imperative, inscribes freedom in nature (it is tempting to say that it *ex*scribes it: Heidegger is an excellent guide on this point), that is, the same as the one identified in a teleological perspective with the humanity of man.

<h1 style="text-align:center">II</h1>

What is the purpose of this gloss, which has been both lengthy and schematic? It is that it is well worth the trouble, in my view, to take seriously the question posed by Jean-Luc Nancy, or rather the form that Nancy was able to confer, by a radical simplification, to an otherwise rather diffuse interrogation of what is called the philosophical conjuncture, but on the condition of taking it quite literally—at the risk of getting all tangled up in it. Not everyone is capable of producing a truly sophistic question, that is, one able to confront philosophy, in the medium of a given language, with the aporia of its own "founding" reflection, with the circularity of its enunciation. It is thus with the necessity and impossibility of a "decision" on which the progress of its discourse depends. With this little phrase, "Who comes after the subject?" Nancy seems to have managed the trick, for the only possible "answer"—at the same level of generality and singularity—would designate the nonsubject, whatever it may be, as "what" succeeds the subject (and thus puts an end to it). The place to which it should come, however, is *already* determined as the place of a subject by the question "who," in other words as *the being (who is the) subject* and nothing else. And our "subject" (which is to say unavoidably ourselves, whoever we may be or believe ourselves to be, caught in the constraints of the statement) is left to ask indefinitely, "How could it be that this (not) come of me?" Let us rather examine what characterizes this form.

First of all, the question is posed *in the present tense*: a present that doubtless refers to what is "current," and behind which we could[5] reconstitute a whole series of presuppositions about the "epoch" in which we find ourselves: whether we represent it as the triumph of subjectivity or as its dissolution, as an epoch that is still progressing or as one that is coming to an end (and thus in a sense has already been left behind). Unless, precisely, these alternatives are among the preformulations whose apparent obviousness would be suspended by Nancy's question. But there is another way to interpret such a present tense: as an *indeterminate*, if not ahistorical present, with respect to which we would not (at least not immediately) have to situate ourselves by means of a characterization of "our epoch" and its meaning, but which would only require us to ask *what comes to pass* when it comes *after* the subject, at whatever time this "event" may take place or might have taken place. This is the point of view I have chosen, for reasons that will soon become clear.

Second, the question posed is "*Who* comes . . . ?" Here again, two understandings are possible. The first, which I sketched out a moment ago, is perhaps more natural to the contemporary philosopher. Beginning from a precomprehension of the subject such as it is constituted by transcendental philosophy (*das Subjekt*), and such as it has since been deconstructed or decentered by different philosophies "of suspicion," different "structural" analyses, this understanding opens upon the enigma into which the *personality* of the subject leads us: the fact that it always succeeds itself across different philosophical figures or different modes of (re)presentation—which is perhaps only the mirror repetition of the way in which it always precedes itself (question: Who comes *before* the subject?). But why not follow more fully the indications given by the language? If a question of identity is presupposed by Nancy's question, it is not of the form "*What is* the subject?" (or "What is the thing that we call the subject?"), but of the form "*Who* is the subject?," or even as an absolute precondition: "Who is subject?" The question is not about the *subjectum* but about the *subjectus*, he who is subjected. Not, or at least not immediately, the transcendental subject (with all its doubles: logical subject, grammatical subject, substantial subject), which is by definition a *neuter* (before becoming an *it*), but the subject as an individual or a person submitted to the exercise of a power, whose model is, first of all, political, and whose concept is juridical. Not the subject inasmuch as it is opposed to the predicate or to the object, but the one referred to by Bossuet's thesis: "*All men are born subjects* and the paternal authority that accustoms them to obeying accustoms them at the same time to having only one chief."[6]

The French (or Anglo-French) language here presents an advantage over German and even over Latin, one that is properly philosophical: it retains in the equivocal unity of a single noun the *subjectum* and the *subjectus*, the *Subjekt* and the *Untertan*. It is perhaps for lack of having paid attention to what such a continuity indicates that Heidegger proposed a fictive interpretation of the history of metaphysics in which the anteriority of the question of the *subjectus/Untertan* is "forgotten" and covered over by a retrospective projection of the question of the *Subjekt* as *subjectum*. This presentation, which marks the culmination of a long enterprise of interiorization of the history of philosophy, is today sufficiently widely accepted, even by philosophers who would not want to be called "Heideggerians" (and who often do not have the knowledge Heidegger had), for it to be useful to situate exactly the moment of forcing.

But if this is what the subject is *from the first* (both historically and logically), then the answer to Nancy's question is very simple, but so full of consequences that it might be asked whether it does not underlie every other interpretation, every reopening of the question of the subject, including the subject as transcendental subject. Here is this answer: *After the subject comes the citizen*. The citizen (defined by his rights and duties) is that "nonsubject" who comes after the subject, and whose constitution and recognition put an end (in principle) to the subjection of the subject.

This answer does not have to be (fictively) discovered, or proposed as an eschato-logical wager (supposing that the subject is in decline, what can be said of his future successor?). It is already given and in all our memories. We can even give it a date: 1789, even if we know that this date and the place it indicates are too simple to enclose the entire process of the substitution of the citizen for the subject. The fact remains that 1789 marks the irreversibility of this process, the effect of a rupture.

We also know that this answer carries with it, historically, its own justification: if the citizen comes after the subject, it is in the quality of a rehabilitation, even a restoration (implied by the very idea of a revolution). The subject *is not* the original man, and, contrary to Bossuet's thesis, men are not "born" "subjects" but "free and equal in rights." The *factual* answer, which we already have at hand (and about which it is tempting to ask why it must be periodically suspended, in the game of a question that inverts it) also contains the entire difficulty of an interpretation that makes of the "subject" a nonoriginary given, a beginning that is not (and cannot be) the origin. For the origin *is not* the subject, but man. But is this interpretation the only possible one? Is it indissociable from the fact itself? I would like to devote a few provisional reflections to the interest that these questions hold for philosophy—including when philosophy is displaced from the *subjectus* to the *subjectum*.

These reflections do not tend—as will quickly be apparent—to minimize the change produced by Kant, but to ask precisely in what the necessity of this change resides, and if it is truly impossible to bypass or go beyond (and thus to understand) it—in other words, if a critique of the representation of the history of philosophy that we have inherited from Kant can only be made from the point of view of a "subject" in the Kantian sense. The answer seems to me to reside at least partially in the analysis of this "coincidence": the moment at which Kant produces (and retrospectively projects) the transcendental "subject" is precisely that moment at which politics destroys the "subject" of the prince, in order to replace him with the republican citizen.

That this isn't really a coincidence is already hinted at by the fact that the question of the subject, around which the Copernican revolution pivots, is immediately characterized as a question of *right* (as to knowledge and as to action). In this question of right the representation of "man," about whom we have just noted that he forms the teleological horizon of the subject, vacillates. What is to be found under this name is not *de facto* man, subjected to various internal and external powers, but *de jure* man (who could still be called the man of man or the man in man, and who is also the empirical non-man), whose autonomy corresponds to the position of a "universal legislator." Which, to be brief, brings us back to the answer evoked above: after the subject (*subjectus*) comes the citizen. But is this citizen *immediately* what Kant will name "subject" (*Subjekt*)? Or is not the latter rather the reinscription of the citizen in a philosophical and, beyond that, anthropological space, which evokes the defunct subject of the prince even while displacing it? We cannot respond directly to these questions, which are inevitably raised by the letter of the Kantian invention once the context of its moment is restored. We must first make a detour through history. Who is the subject of the prince? And who is the citizen who comes after the subject?

III

It would be impossible to enclose the "subjectus" in a single definition, for it is a matter of a juridical figure whose evolution is spread out over seventeen centuries, from Roman jurisprudence to absolute monarchy. It has often been demonstrated how, in the political history of Western Europe, the time of *subjects* coincides with that of *absolutism*. Absolutism in effect seems to give a complete and coherent form to a power that is founded only upon itself, and that is founded as being without limits (thus uncontrollable and irresistible by definition). Such a power truly makes men into subjects, and nothing but subjects, for the very being of the subject is obedience. From the point of view of the subject, power's claim to incarnate both the good and the true is entirely justified: the subject is he who has no need of *knowing*, much less *understanding*, why what is prescribed to him is in the interest of his own happiness. Nevertheless, this perspective is deceptive: rather than a coherent form, classical absolutism is a knot of contradictions, and this can also be seen at the level of theory, in its discourse. Absolutism never manages to stabilize its definition of obedience and thus its definition of the subject. It could be asked, why this is necessarily the case, and what consequences result from it for the "surpassing" or "negation" of the subject in the citizen (if we should ever speak of sublation (*relève*) it is now: the citizen is a subject who rises up (*qui se relève*)!). In order to answer this question we must sketch a historical genesis of the subject and his contradiction.

The first question would be to know how one moves from the adjective to the substantive, from individuals who *are* subjected to the power of another, to the representation of a people or of a community as a set of "subjects." The distinction between independent and dependent persons is fundamental in Roman jurisprudence. A single text will suffice to recall it:

> *Sequitur de jure personarum alia divisio. Nam quaedam personae sui juris sunt, quaedam alieno juri sunt subjectae. Sed rursus earum personarum quae alieno juri subjectae sunt, aliae in potestate, aliae in manu, aliae in mancipio sunt. Videamus nunc de iis quae alieno juri subjectae sint, si cognoverimus quae istae personae sunt, simul intellegemus quae sui juris sint.* [We come to another classification in the law of persons. Some people are independent and some are subject to others. Again, of those persons who are dependent, some are in power, some in marital

subordination and some in bondage. Let us examine the dependent category. If we find out who is dependent, we cannot help seeing who is independent.][7]

Strangely, it is by way of the definition (the dialectical division) of the forms of subjection that the definition of free men, the masters, is obtained *a contrario*. But this definition does not make the subjects into a *collectivity;* it establishes no "link" *among them.* The notions of *potestas, manus,* and *mancipium* are not sufficient to do this. The subjects are not the heterogeneous set formed by slaves, plus legitimate children, plus wives, plus acquired or adopted relatives. What is required is an *imperium.* Subjects thus appeared with the empire (and in relation to the person of the emperor, to whom citizens and many noncitizens owe "service," *officium*). But I would surmise that this necessary condition is not a sufficient one: Romans still had to be able to be submitted to the *imperium* in the same way (if they ever were) as conquered populations, "subjects of the Roman people" (a confusion that points, contradictorily, toward the horizon of the generalization of Roman citizenship as a personal status in the empire).[8] And, above all, the *imperium* had to be theologically founded as a Christian *imperium,* a power that comes from God and is conserved by Him.[9]

In effect, the subject has two major characteristics, both of which lead to aporias (in particular in the form given them by absolute monarchy): he is a *subditus;* he is not a *servus.* These characteristics are reciprocal, but each has its own dialectic.

The subject is a *subditus*: this means that he enters into a relation of obedience. Obedience is not the same as compulsion; it is something more. It is established not only between a chief who has the power to compel and those who must submit to this power, but between a *sublimis,* "chosen" to command, and *subditi,* who turn towards him to hear a law. The power to compel is distributed throughout a hierarchy of unequal powers (relations of *majoritas-minoritas*). Obedience is the principle, identical to itself along the whole length of the hierarchical chain, and attached in the last instance to its transcendental origin, which makes those who obey into the members of a single body. Obedience institutes the command of higher over lower, but it fundamentally comes from below: as *subditi,* the subjects *will* their own obedience. And if they will it, it is because it is inscribed in an economy of creation (their creation) and salvation (their salvation, that of each taken individually and of all taken collectively). Thus the *loyal subject* (*fidèle sujet*) (he who "voluntarily," "loyally," that is, actively and willingly obeys the law and executes the orders of a legitimate sovereign) is necessarily a *faithful subject* (*sujet fidèle*). He is a Christian, who knows that all power comes from God. In obeying the law of the prince he obeys God.[10] The fact that the order to which he "responds" comes to him from *beyond* the individual and the mouth which utters it is constitutive of the subject.

This structure contains the seeds of an infinite dialectic, which is in fact what *unifies* the subject (in the same way as it unifies, in the person of the sovereign, the act and its sanctification, decision making and justice): because of it the subject does not have to ask (himself) any questions, for the answers have always already been given. But it is also what *divides* the subject. This occurs, for example, when a "spiritual power" and a "temporal power" vie for preeminence (which supposes that each also attempts to appropriate the attributes of the other), or more simply when knowing which sovereign is legitimate or which practice of government is "Christian" and thus in conformity with its essence becomes a real question (the very idea of a "right of resistance" being a contradiction in terms, the choice is between regicide and prayer for the conversion of the sovereign . . .). Absolute monarchy in particular develops a contradiction that can be seen as the culmination of the conflict between the temporal power and the spiritual power. A passage is made from the divine right of kings to the idea of their direct election: it is as such that royal power is made divine (and that the State transfers to itself the various sacraments). But not (at least not in the West) the *individual person* of the king: incarnation of a divine power, the king is not himself "God." The king (the sovereign) is *lex animata* (*nomos empsychos*) (just as the law is *inanimatus princeps*). Thus the person (the "body") of the king must itself be divided: into divine person and human person. And obedience correlatively. . . . [11]

Such an obedience, in its unity and its divisions, implies the notion of the *soul*. This is a notion that Antiquity did not know or in any case did not use in the same way in order to think a political relation (Greek does not have, to my knowledge, an equivalent for the *subjectus-subditus*, not even the term *hypekoos*, which designates those who obey the word of a master, who will become "disciples," and from whom the theologians will draw the name of Christian obedience: *hypakoè*). For Antiquity obedience can be a contingent situation in which one finds oneself in relation to a command (*archè*), and thus a commander (*archôn*). But to receive a command (*archemenos*) implies that one can oneself—at least theoretically—give a command (this is the Aristotelian definition of the citizen). *Or* it can be a natural dependence of the "familial" type. Doubtless differentiations (the ignorance of which is what properly characterizes barbarism) ought to be made here: the woman (even for the Greeks, and a forteriori for the Romans) is not a slave. Nevertheless these differences can be subsumed under analogous oppositions: the part and the whole, passivity and activity, the body and the soul (or intellect). This last opposition is particularly valid for the slave, who is to his master what a body, an "organism" (a set of natural tools) is to intelligence. In such a perspective, the very idea of a "free obedience" is a contradiction in terms. That a slave can *also* be free is a relatively late (Stoic) idea, which must be understood as signifying that on *another* level (in a "cosmic" polity, a polity of "minds") he who is a slave here can also be a master (master of himself, of his passions), can also be a "citizen." Nothing approaches the idea of a freedom residing in obedience itself, resulting from this obedience. In order to conceive of this idea obedience must be transferred to the side of the soul, and the soul must cease to be thought of as natural: on the contrary, the soul must come to name a supernatural part of the individual that hears the divinity of the order.

Thus the *subditus-subjectus* has always been distinguished from the slave, just as the sovereignty of the prince, the *sublimus*, has been distinguished from "despotism" (literally, the authority of a master of slaves).[12] But this fundamental distinction was elaborated in two ways. It was elaborated within a theological framework, simply developing the idea that the subject is a believer, a Christian. Because, in the final instance, it is his soul that obeys, he could never be the sovereign's "thing" (which can be used and abused); his obedience is inscribed in an order that should, in the end, bring him salvation, and that is counterbalanced by a responsibility (a duty) on the part of the prince. But this way of thinking the freedom of the subject is, in practice, extraordinarily ambivalent. It can be understood either as the affirmation and the active contribution of his will to obedience (just as the Christian, by his works, "cooperates in his salvation": the political necessity of the theological compromise on the question of predestination can be seen here), or as the annihilation of the will (this is why the mystics who lean towards perfect obedience apply their will to self-annihilation in the contemplation of God, the only absolute sovereign). Intellectual reasons as well as material interests (those of the lords, of the corporations, of the "bourgeois" towns) provide an incentive for thinking the freedom of the subject differently, paradoxically combining this concept with that of the "citizen," a concept taken from Antiquity and notably from Aristotle, but carefully distinguished from man inasmuch as he is the image of the creator.

Thus the *civis-polites* comes back onto the scene, in order to mark the quasi-ontological difference between a "subject" and a serf/slave. But the man designated as a citizen is no longer the *zôon politikon*: he is no longer the "sociable animal," meaning that he is sociable as animal (and not inasmuch as his soul is immortal). Thomas Aquinas distinguishes the (supernatural) *christianitas* of man from his (natural) *humanitas*, the "believer" from the "citizen." The latter is the holder of a neutral freedom, a "franchise." This has nothing in common with sovereignty, but means that his submission to political authority is neither immediate nor arbitrary. He *is submitted* as a member of an order or a body that is recognized as having certain rights and that confers a certain status, a field of initiative, upon him. What then becomes of the "subject"? In a sense he is more really free (for his subjection is the effect of a political order that integrates "civility," the "polity," and that is thus inscribed in nature). But it becomes more and more difficult to think him as *subditus*: the very concept of his "obedience" is menaced.

This tension becomes, once again, a contradiction under absolute monarchy. We have already seen how the latter brings the mysterious unity of the temporal and spiritual sovereign to the point of rupture. The same goes for the freedom of the subject. Insofar as absolute monarchy concentrates power in the unity of the "State" (the term appears at this moment, along with its "reason"), it dissolves all intermediate powers (at least ideally) and suppresses all subjections to the profit of one subjection. There is now only one prince, whose law is will, "father of his subjects," having absolute authority over them (as all other authority, next to his, is null). "I am the State," Louis XIV will say. But absolute monarchy is a *State* power, precisely, that is, a power that is instituted and exercised by law and administration; it is a political power (*imperium*) that is not confused with the property (*dominium*)—except "eminent" domain—of what belongs to individuals, and over which they exercise their power. The subjects are, if not "legal subjects (*sujets de droit*)," at least subjects "with rights (*en droit*)," members of a "republic" (a Commonwealth, Hobbes will say). All the theoreticians of absolute monarchy (with or without a "pact of subjection") will explain that *the subjects are citizens* (or, like Bodin in the *Republic,* that "every citizen is a subject, his freedom being somewhat diminished by the majesty of the one to whom he owes obedience: but not every subject is a citizen, as we have said of the slave").[13] They will not prevent—with the help of circumstances—the condition of this "free (*franc*) subject dependent upon the sovereignty of another"[14] from being perceived as untenable. La Boétie, reversing each term, will oppose them by defining the power of the One (read: the Monarch) as a "voluntary servitude" upon which at the same time reason of State no longer confers the meaning of a supernatural freedom. The controversy over the difference (or lack of one) between absolutism and despotism accompanies the whole history of absolute monarchy.[15] The condition of the subject will be retrospectively identified with that of the slave, and subjection with "slavery," from the point of view of the new citizen and his revolution (this will also be an essential mechanism of his own idealization).

IV

The *Declaration of the Rights of Man and of the Citizen* of 1789 produces a truth-effect that marks a rupture. It is nevertheless an intrinsically equivocal text, as is indicated by the dualities of its title and of its first line: rights of man *and* of the citizen, are born *and* remain, free *and* equal. Each of these dualities, and particularly the first, which divides the origin, harbor the possibility of antithetical readings: Is the founding notion that of *man,* or of *the citizen?* Are the rights declared those of the citizen *as man,* or those of man *as citizen?* In the interpretation sketched out here, it is the second reading that must take precedence: the stated rights are those of the citizen, the objective is the constitution of citizenship—in a radically new sense. In fact neither the idea of humanity nor its equivalence with freedom are new. Nor, as we have seen, are they incompatible with a theory of originary subjection: the Christian is essentially free *and* subject, the subject of the prince is "*franc.*" What is new is the sovereignty of the citizen, which entails a completely different conception (and a completely different practical determination) of freedom. But this sovereignty must be founded retroactively on a certain concept of man, or, better, in a *new* concept of man that contradicts what the term previously connoted.

Why is this foundation necessary? I do not believe it is, as is often said, because of a *symmetry* with the way the sovereignty of the prince was founded in the idea of God, because the sovereignty of the people (or of the "nation") would need a *human foundation* in the same way that imperial or monarchical sovereignty needed a *divine foundation*, or, to put it another way, by virtue of a necessity inherent in the idea of sovereignty, which leads to putting Man in the place of God.[16] On the contrary, it is because of the dissymmetry that is introduced into the idea of sovereignty from the moment that it has devolved to the "citizens": until then the idea of sovereignty had always been inseparable from a hierarchy, from an eminence; from this point forward the paradox of a *sovereign equality*, something radically new, must be thought. What must be explained (at the same time as it is declared) is how the concept of sovereignty and equality can be noncontradictory. The reference to man, or the inscription of equality in human nature is equality "of birth," which is not at all evident and is even improbable, is the means of explaining this paradox.[17] This is what I will call a hyperbolic proposition.

It is also the sudden appearance of a new problem. One paradox (the equality of birth) explains another (sovereignty as equality). The political tradition of antiquity, to which the revolutionaries never cease to refer (Rome and Sparta rather than Athens), thought civic equality to be founded on freedom and exercised in the determinate conditions of this freedom (which is a hereditary or quasi-hereditary status). It is now a matter of thinking the inverse: a freedom founded on equality, engendered by the movement of equality. Thus an unlimited or, more precisely, self-limited freedom: having no limits other than those it assigns to itself in order to respect the rule of equality, that is, to remain in conformity with its principle. In other terms, it is a matter of answering the question: *Who is the citizen?* and not the question: Who is a citizen? (or: Who are citizens?). The answer is: The citizen is a man in enjoyment of all his "natural" rights, completely realizing his individual humanity, a free man simply because he is equal to every other man. This answer (or this new question in the form of an answer) will also be stated, after the fact: *The citizen is the subject*, the citizen is always a *supposed subject* (legal subject, psychological subject, transcendental subject).

I will call this new development the citizen's becoming-a-subject (*devenir-sujet*): a development that is doubtless prepared by a whole labor of definition of the juridical, moral, and intellectual individual; that goes back to the "nominalism" of the late Middle Ages, is invested in institutional and "cultural" practices, and reflected by philosophy, but that can find its name and its structural position only *after* the emergence of the revolutionary citizen, for it rests upon the reversal of what was previously the *subjectus*. In the Declaration of Rights, and in all the discourses and practices that reiterate its effect, we must read both the presentation of the citizen and the marks of his becoming-a-subject. This is all the more difficult in that it is practically impossible for the citizen(s) to be presented without being determined as subject(s). But it was only by way of the citizen that universality could come to the subject. An eighteenth-century dictionary had stated: "In France, other than the king, all are citizens."[18] The revolution will say: If anyone is not a citizen, then no one is a citizen. "All distinction ceases. All are citizens, or must be, and whoever is not must be excluded."[19]

The idea of the rights of the citizen, at the very moment of his emergence, thus institutes an historical figure that is no longer the *subjectus*, and not yet the *subjectum*. But from the beginning, in the way it is formulated and put into practice, this figure exceeds its own institution. This is what I called, a moment ago, the statement of a hyperbolic proposition. Its developments can only consist of conflicts, whose stakes can be sketched out.

First of all, there exist conflicts with respect to the founding idea of equality. The absolutism of this idea emerges from the struggle against "privilege," when it appeared that the privileged person was not he who had *more* rights but he who had *less*: each privilege, for him, is substituted for a possible right, even though at the same time his privilege denies rights to the nonprivileged. In other words, it appeared that the "play" (*jeu*) of right—to speak a currently fashionable language—is not a "zero-sum" game: this is what distinguishes it from the play of power, the "balance of power." Rousseau admirably developed this difference, on which the entire argumentation of the *Social Contract* is based: a supplement of rights for one is the annihilation of the rights of all; the effectivity of right has as its condition that each has exactly "as much," *neither more nor fewer* right(s) than the rest.

Two paths are open from this point. Either equality is "symbolic," which means that each individual, whatever his strengths, his power, and his property, is *reputed* to be equivalent to every individual in his capacity as citizen (and in the public acts in which citizenship is exercised). Or equality is "real," which means that citizenship will not exist unless the *conditions* of all individuals are equal, or at least equivalent: then, in fact, power's games will no longer be able to pose an obstacle to the play of right; the power proper to equality will not be destroyed by the effects of power. Whereas symbolic equality is all the better affirmed, its ideality all the better preserved and recognized as unconditional when conditions are unequal, real equality supposes a classless society, and thus works to produce it. If a proof is wanted of the fact that the antinomy of "formal" and "real" democracy is thus inscribed from the very beginning in the text of 1789 it will suffice to reread Robespierre's discourse on the "marc d'argent" (April 1791).[20]

But this antinomy is untenable, for it has the form of an all-or-nothing (it reproduces *within* the field of citizenship the all-or-nothing of the subject and the citizen). Symbolic equality must be nothing real, but a universally applicable form. Real equality must be all or, if one prefers, every practice, every condition must be measured by it, for an exception destroys it. It can be asked—we will return to this point—whether the two mutually exclusive sides of this alternative are not equally incompatible with the constitution of a "society." In other terms, civic equality is indissociable from universality but separates it from the *community*. The restitution of the latter requires either a supplement of symbolic form (to think universality as ideal Humanity, the reign of practical ends) or a supplement of substantial egalitarianism (communism, Babeuf's "order of equality"). But this supplement, whatever it may be, already belongs to the citizen's becoming-a-subject.

Second, there exist conflicts with respect to the citizen's activity. What radically distinguishes him from the subject of the Prince is his participation in the formation and application of the decision: the fact that he is legislator and magistrate. Here, too, Rousseau, with his concept of the "general will," irreversibly states what constitutes the rupture. The comparison with the way in which medieval politics had defined the "citizenship" of the subject, as the right of all to be well-governed, is instructive.[21] From this point forward the idea of a "passive citizen" is a contradiction in terms. Nevertheless, as is well known, this idea was immediately formulated. But let us look at the details.

Does the activity of the citizen exclude the idea of *representation?* This position has been argued: whence the long series of discourses identifying active citizenship and "direct democracy," with or without reference to antiquity.[22] In reality this identification rests on a confusion.

Initially, representation is a representation *before* the Prince, before Power, and, in general, before the instance of decision making whatever it may be (incarnated in a living or anonymous person, itself represented by officers of the State). This is the function of the Old Regime's "deputies of the Estates," who present grievances, supplications, and remonstrances (in many respects this function of representing those who are administered to the administration has in fact again become the function of the numerous elected assemblies of the contemporary State).

The *representation of the sovereign* in its deputies, inasmuch as the sovereign is the people, is something entirely different. Not only is it active, it is the act of sovereignty *par excellence*: the choice of those who govern, the corollary of which is monitoring them. To elect representatives is to act and to make possible all political action, which draws its legitimacy from this election. Election has an "alchemy," whose other aspects we will see further on: as the primordial civic action, it *singularizes* each citizen, responsible for his vote (his choice), at the same time as it *unifies* the "moral" body of the citizens.[23] We will have to ask again, and in greater depth, to what extent this determination engages the dialectic of the citizen's becoming-a-subject: Which citizens are "representable," and under which conditions? Above all: *Who* should the citizens be in order to be able to represent themselves and to be represented? (for example: Does it matter that they be able to read and write? Is this condition sufficient? etc.). In any case we have here, again, a very different concept from the one antiquity held of citizenship, which, while it too implied an idea of *activity*, did not imply one of sovereign will. Thus the Greeks privileged the drawing of lots in the designation of magistrates as the only truly democratic method, whereas election appeared to them to be "aristocratic" by definition (Aristotle).

It is nonetheless true that the notion of a *representative activity* is problematic. This can be clearly seen in the debate over the question of the binding mandate: Is it necessary, in order for the activity of the citizens to manifest itself, that their deputies be permanently bound by their will (supposing it can be known), or is it sufficient that they be liable to recall, leaving them the responsibility to interpret the general will by their *own* activity? The dilemma could also be expressed by saying that citizenship implies a power to delegate its powers, but excludes the existence of "politicians," of "professionals," a fortiori of "technicians" of politics. In truth this dilemma was already present in the astonishing Hobbesian construction of representation, as the doubling of an *author* and an *actor*, which remains the basis of the modern State.

But the most profound antinomy of the citizen's activity concerns the *law*. Here again Rousseau circumscribes the problem by posing his famous definition: "As for the associates, collectively they take the name *people*, and individually they are called *Citizens* as participating in the sovereign authority and *Subjects* as submitted to the laws of the State."[24] The consequences of this follow immediately:

> It can be seen by this formulation . . . that each individual, contracting, so to speak, with himself, finds himself engaged in a double relationship . . . . Consequently it is against the nature of the political body for the Sovereign to impose upon itself a law that it cannot break . . . by which it can be seen that there is not nor can there be any sort of fundamental law which obliges the body of the people, not even the social contract . . . . Now the Sovereign, being formed only of the individuals who compose it, does not and cannot have an interest opposed to theirs; consequently the Sovereign power has no need of a guarantee toward the subjects, for it is impossible that the body wish to harm all its members . . . . But this is not the case for the subjects toward the sovereign, where despite the common interest, nothing would answer for their engagements if means to insure their fidelity were not found. In fact each individual can, as man, have a particular will contrary or dissimilar to the general will that he has as citizen . . . . He would enjoy the rights of a citizen without being willing to fulfill the duties of a subject; an injustice whose progress would cause the ruin of the political body. In order for the social pact not to become a vain formula, it tacitly includes the engagement . . . that whoever refuses to obey the general will will be compelled to do so by any means available: which signifies nothing else than that he will be forced to be free.[25]

It was necessary to cite this whole passage in order that no one be mistaken: in these implacable formulas we see the final appearance of the "subject" in the old sense, that of obedience, but metamorphosed into a *subject of the law*, the strict correlative of the citizen who *makes the law*.[26] We also see the appearance, under the name of "man," split between his general interest and his particular interest, of he who will be the new "subject," the Citizen Subject.

It is indeed a question of an antinomy. Precisely in his capacity as "citizen," the citizen is (indivisibly) *above* any law, otherwise he could not legislate, much less constitute: "There is not, nor can there be, any sort of fundamental law that obliges the body of the people, not even the social contract." In his capacity as "subject" (that is, inasmuch as the laws he formulates are imperative, to be executed universally and unconditionally, inasmuch as the pact is not a "vain formula") he is necessarily *under* the law. Rousseau (and the Jacobin tradition) resolve this antinomy by identifying, in terms of their close "relationship" (that is in terms of a particular point of view), the two propostions: Just as one citizen has neither more nor less right(s) than another, so he is neither only above, nor only under the law, but *at exactly the same level as it*. Nevertheless *he is not the law* (the *nomos empsychos*). This is not the consequence of a transcendence on the part of the law (of the fact that it would come from Elsewhere, from an Other mouth speaking atop some Mount Sinai), but a consequence of its immanence. Or yet another way: there must be an exact correspondence between the absolute activity of the citizen (legislation) and his absolute passivity (obedience to the law, with which one does not "bargain," which one does not "trick"). But it is essential that this activity and this passivity be *exactly* correlative, that they have exactly the same limits. The possibility of a metaphysics of the subject already resides in the enigma of this unity of opposites (in Kant, for example, this metaphysics of the subject will proceed from the double determination of the concept of right as freedom and as compulsion). But the necessity of an anthropology of the subject (psychological, sociological, juridical, economic, . . .) will be manifest from the moment that, in however small a degree, the exact correlation becomes upset in practice: when a distinction between *active citizens* and *passive citizens* emerges (a distinction with which we are still living), and with it a problem of the criteria of their distinction and of the justification of this paradox. Now this distinction is practically contemporary with the Declaration of Rights itself; it is in any case inscribed in the first of the *Constitutions* "based" on the Declaration of Rights. Or, quite simply, when it becomes apparent that to *govern* is not the same as to *legislate* nor even to execute the laws, i.e., that political sovereignty is not the mastery of the art of politics.

Finally, there exist conflicts with respect to the individual and the collective. We noted above that the institution of a society or a community on the basis of principles of equality is problematic. This is not—or at least not uniquely—due to the fact that this principle would be identical to that of the *competition* between individuals ("egotism," or a freedom limited only by the antagonism of interests). It is even less due to the fact that equality would be another name for *similarity*, that it would imply that individuals are indiscernible from one another and thus incompatible with one another, preyed on by mimetic rivalry. On the contrary, equality, precisely inasmuch as it is not the identification of individuals, is one of the great cultural means of legitimating differences and controlling the imaginary ambivalence of the "double." The difficulty is rather due to equality itself: in this principle (in the proposition that men, as citizens, are equal), even though there is necessarily reference to the *fact* of society (under the name of "polity"), there is conceptually too much (or not enough) to "bind" a society. It can be seen clearly here how the difficulty arises from the fact that, in the modern concept of citizenship, freedom is founded in equality and not vice versa (the "solution" of the difficulty will in part consist precisely of reversing this primacy, to make freedom into a foundation, even, metaphysically, to identify the originary with freedom).

Equality in fact cannot be limited. Once some x's ("men") are not equal, the predicate of equality can no longer be applied to anyone, for all those to whom it is supposed to be applicable are in fact "superior," "dominant," "privileged," etc. Enjoyment of the equality of rights cannot spread step by step, beginning with two individuals and gradually extending to all: it must immediately concern the universality of individuals, let us say, tautologically, the universality of x's that it concerns. This explains the insistence of the cosmopolitan theme in egalitarian political thought, or the reciprocal implication of these two themes. It also explains the antinomy of equality and society for, even when it is not defined in "cultural," "national," or "historical" terms, a *society* is necessarily *a* society, defined by some particularity, by some exclusion, if only by a *name*. In order to speak of "all citizens," it is necessary that somebody not be a citizen of said polity.

Likewise, equality, even though it preserves differences (it does not imply that Catholics are Protestants, that Blacks are Whites, that women are men, or vice versa: it could even be held that without differences equality would be literally unthinkable), cannot itself be *differentiated*: differences are close by it but do not come from its application. We have already glimpsed this problem with respect to activity and passivity. It takes on its full extension once it is a question of *organizing* a society, that is of instituting functions and roles in it. Something like a "bad infinity" is implied here by the negation of the inequalities which are always still present in the principle of equality, and which form, precisely, its practical effectiveness. This is, moreover, exactly what Hegel will say.

The affirmation of this principle can be seen in 1789 in the statement that the king himself is only a citizen ("Citizen Capet"), a deputy of the sovereign people. Its development can be seen in the affirmation that the exercise of a magistrature *excludes* one from citizenship: "The soldier is a citizen; the officer is not and cannot be one."[27] "Ordinarily, people say: the citizen is someone who participates in honors and dignities; they are mistaken. Here he is, the citizen: he is someone who possesses no more goods than the law allows, who exercises no magistrature and is independent of the responsibility of those who govern. Whoever is a magistrate is no longer part of the people. No individual power can enter into the people. . . . When speaking to a functionary, one should not say *citizen*; this title is above him."[28] On the contrary, it may be thought that the existence of a society always presupposes an organization, and that the latter in turn always presupposes an element of qualification or differentiation from equality and thus of "nonequality" developed *on the basis of equality itself* (which is not on that account a *principle* of inequality).[29] If we call this element "archy," we will understand that one of the logics of citizenship leads to the idea of anarchy. It was Sade who wrote, "Insurrection should be the permanent state of the republic," and the comparison with Saint-Just has been made by Maurice Blanchot.[30]

It will be said that the solution to this aporia is the idea of a contract. The contractual bond is in fact the only one that thinks itself as absolutely homogeneous with the reciprocal action of equal individuals,[31] presupposing only this equality. No other presuppositions? All the theoreticians are in agreement that some desire for sociability, some interest in bringing together the forces and in limiting freedoms by one another, or some moral ideal, indispensable "motor forces," would *also* be required. It will in fact be agreed that the *proper* form of the contract is that of a contract of *association*, and that the contract of subjection is an ideological artifact destined to divert the benefits of the contractual form to the profit of an established power. But it remains a question whether the social contract can be thought as a mechanism that "socializes" equals purely by virtue of their equality. I think that the opposite is the case, that the social contract *adds* to equality a determination that compensates for its "excess" of universality. To this end equality itself must be thought as something other than a naked principle; it must be justified, or one must confer on it that which Derrida not long ago called an *originary supplement*.

This is why all the theories of the contract include a "deduction" of equality as an indispensable preliminary, showing how it is produced or how it is destroyed and restored in a dialectic either of natural sociability and unsociability or of the animality and humanity in man (the extreme form being that of Hobbes: equality is produced by the threat of death, in which freedom is promptly annihilated). The Declaration of 1789 gives this supplement its most economical form, that of a *de jure* fact: "Men *are born and remain* . . . ." Then—as Michel Foucault saw beginning from other premises—the time of competing theories of human nature comes to an end. The time of man-the-subject (empirical and transcendental) can begin.

V

I think that, under these conditions, the indetermination of the figure of the citizen—referred to equality—can be understood with respect to the major alternatives of modern political and sociological thought: individual and collectivity, public sphere and private sphere. The citizen properly speaking is *neither* the individual *nor* the collective, just as he is *neither* an exclusively public being *nor* a private being. Nevertheless, these distinctions are present in the concept of the citizen. It would not be correct to say that they are ignored or denied: it should rather be said that they are suspended, that is, irreducible to fixed institutional boundaries which would pose the citizen on one side and a *noncitizen* on the other.

The citizen is unthinkable as an "isolated" individual, for it is his active participation in politics that makes him exist. But he cannot on that account be merged into a "total" collectivity. Whatever may be said about it, Rousseau's reference to a "moral and collective body composed of as many members as there are votes in the assembly,"[32] produced by the act of association that "makes a people a people,"[33] is not the *revival* but the *antithesis* of the organicist idea of the *corpus mysticum* (the theologians have never been fooled on this point).[34] The "double relationship" under which the individuals contract also has the effect of forbidding the fusion of individuals in a whole, whether immediately or by the mediation of some "corporation." Likewise, the citizen can only be thought if there exists, at least tendentially, a distinction between public and private: he is defined as a public actor (and even as the *only* possible public actor). Nevertheless he cannot be confined to the public sphere, with a private sphere—whether the latter is like the *oikos* of antiquity, the modern family (the one that will emerge from the civil code and that which we now habitually call "the invention of private life"), or a sphere of industrial and commercial relations that are nonpolitical[35]—being held *in reserve*. If only for the reason that, in such a sphere, to become other than himself the citizen would have to enter into relationships with *noncitizens* (or with individuals considered as noncitizens: women, children, servants, employees). The citizen's "madness," as is known, is not the abolition of private life but its transparency, just as it is not the abolition of politics but its moralization.

To express this suspension of the citizen we are obliged to search in history and literature for categories that are unstable or express instability. The concept of *mass,* at a certain moment of its elaboration, would be an example, as when Spinoza speaks of both the dissolution of the (monarchical) State and its (democratic) constitution as a "return to the mass."[36] This concept is not unrelated, it would seem, to that which in the Terror will durably inspire the thinkers of liberalism with terror.

I have presented the Declaration of Rights as a hyperbolic proposition. It is now possible to reformulate this idea: in effect, in this proposition, *the wording of the statement always exceeds the act of its enunciation [l'énoncé excède toujours l'énonciation],* the import of the statement already goes beyond it (without our knowing where), as was immediately seen in the effect of inciting the liberation that it produced. In the statement of the Declaration, even though this is not at all the content of the enunciation of the subsequent rights, we can already hear the motto that, in another place and time, will become a call to action: "It is right to revolt." Let us note once more that it is equality that is at the origin of the movement of liberation.

All sorts of historical modalities are engaged here. Thus the Declaration of 1789 posits that property—immediately after freedom—is a "natural and imprescriptible right of man" (without, however, going so far as to take up the idea that property is a condition of freedom). And as early as 1791 the battle is engaged between those who conclude that property *qualifies* the constitutive equality of citizenship (in other words that "active citizens" are proprietors), and those who posit that the universality of citizenship must take precedence over the right of property, even should this result in a negation of the unconditional character of the latter. As Engels noted, the demand for the abolition of class differences is expressed in terms of civic equality, which does not signify that the latter is only a period costume, but on the contrary that it is an effective condition of the struggle against exploitation.

Likewise, the Constitutions that are "based" on the principles of 1789 immediately qualify—explicitly and implicitly—the citizen as a *man* (= a male), if not as a head of the household (this will come with the Napoleonic Code). Nevertheless as early as 1791 an Olympe de Gouges can be found drawing from these same principles the *Declaration of the Rights of Woman and the Citizenness* (and, the following year, with Mary Wollstonecraft's *Vindication of the Rights of Woman*), and the battle—one with a great future, though not much pleasure—over the question of whether the citizen has a sex (thus what the sex of man as citizen is) is engaged.

Finally, the Declaration of 1789 does not speak of the color of citizens, and—even if one refuses to consider[37] this silence to be a necessary condition for the representation of the political relations of the Old Regime (subjection to the Prince and to the *seigneurs*) as "slavery," even as true slavery (that of the Blacks) is preserved—it must be admitted that it corresponds to powerful interests among those who collectively declare themselves "sovereign." It is nonetheless the case that the insurrection for the *immediate* abolition of slavery (Toussaint L'Ouverture) takes place in the name of an equality of rights that, as stated, is indiscernible from that of the "sans-culottes" and other "patriots," though the slaves, it is true, did not wait for the fall of the Bastille to revolt.[38]

Thus that which appeared to us as the indetermination of the citizen (in certain respects comparable to the fugitive moment that was glimpsed by Aristotle under the name of *archè aoristos*, but that now would be developed as a complete historical figure) also manifests itself as the opening of a *possibility*: the possibility for any *given* realization of the citizen to be placed in question and destroyed by a struggle for equality and thus for civil rights. But this possibility is not in the least a promise, much less an inevitability. Its concretization and explicitation depend entirely on an encounter between a statement and situations or movements that, from the point of view of the concept, are contingent.[39] If the citizen's becoming-a-subject takes the form of a dialectic, it is precisely because *both* the necessity of "founding" institutional definitions of the citizen and the impossibility of ignoring their contestation—the infinite contradiction within which they are caught—are crystallized in it.

There exists another way to account for the passage from the citizen to the subject (*subjectum*), coming after the passage from citizen to the subject (*subjectus*) to the citizen, or rather immediately overdetermining it. The citizen as defined by equality, absolutely active and absolutely passive (or, if one prefers, capable of auto-affectation: that which Fichte will call *das Ich*), suspended between individuality and collectivity, between public and private: Is he the constitutive element of a *State*? Without doubt the answer is yes, but precisely insofar as the State is not, or not yet, a society. He is, as Pierre-François Moreau has convincingly argued, a *utopic* figure, which is not to say an unreal or millenarist figure projected into the future, but the elementary term of an "abstract State."[40] Historically, this abstract State possesses an entirely tangible reality: that of the progressive deployment of a political and administrative right in which individuals are treated by the state *equally*, according to the logic of situations and actions and not according to their condition or personality. It is this juridico-administrative "*epochè*" of "cultural" or "historical" differences, seeking to create its own conditions of possibility, that paradoxically becomes explicit to itself in the minutely detailed egalitarianism of the ideal cities of the classical Utopia, with their themes of enclosure, foreignness, and rational administration, with their negation of property. When it becomes clear that the condition of conditions for individuals to be treated equally *by* the State (which is the logic of its proper functioning: the suppression of the exception) is that they also be equally entitled to sovereignty (that is, it cannot be *done for less*, while conserving subjection), then the "legal subject" implicit in the machinery of the "individualist" State will be made concrete in the excessive person of the citizen.

But this also means—taking into account all that precedes—that the citizen can be simultaneously considered as the constitutive element of the State and as the actor of a revolution. Not only the actor of a founding revolution, a *tabula rasa* whence a State emerges, but the actor of a *permanent* revolution: precisely the revolution in which the principle of equality, once it has been made the basis or pretext of the institution of an inequality or a political "excess of power," contradicts every difference. Excess against excess, then. The actor of such a revolution is no less "utopic" than the member of the abstract State, the State of the rule of law. It would be quite instructive to conduct the same structural analysis of revolutionary utopias that Moreau made of administrative utopias. It would doubtless show not only that the themes are the same, but also that the fundamental prerequisites of the individual defined by his juridical activity is *identical* with that of the individual defined by his revolutionary activity: he is the man "without property" (*der Eigentumslos*), "without particularities" (*ohne Eigenschaften*). Rather than speaking of administrative utopias and revolutionary utopias we should really speak of antithetical readings of the same utopia narratives and of the reversibility of these narratives.

In the conclusion of his book, Moreau describes Kant's *Metaphysics of Morals* and his *Anthropology from a Pragmatic Point of View* as the two sides of a single construction of the legal subject: on one side, the formal deduction of his egalitarian essence; on the other, the historical description of all the "natural" characteristics (all the individual or collective "properties") that form either the condition or the obstacle to individuals identifying themselves in practice as *being subjects* of this type (for example, sensibility, imagination, taste, good mental health, ethnic "character," moral virtue, or that natural superiority that predisposes men to civil independence and active citizenship and women to dependence and political passivity). Such a duality corresponds fairly well to what Foucault, in *The Order of Things*, called the "empirico-transcendental doublet." Nevertheless, to understand that this subject (which the citizen will be *supposed* to be) contains the paradoxical unity of a universal sovereignty and a radical finitude, we must envisage his constitution—in all the historical complexity of the practices and symbolic forms which it brings together—from *both* the point of view of the State apparatus and that of the permanent revolution. This ambivalence is his strength, his historical ascendancy. All of Foucault's work, or at least that part of it which, by successive approximations, obstinately tries to describe the heterogeneous aspects of the great "transition" between the world of subjection and the world of right and discipline, "civil society," and State apparatuses, is a materialist phenomenology of the transmutation of subjection, of the birth of the Citizen Subject. As to whether this figure, like a face of sand at the edge of the sea, is about to be effaced with the next great sea change, that is another question. Perhaps it is nothing more than Foucault's own utopia, a necessary support for the enterprise of stating that utopia's facticity.

Notes

1. Letter by Descartes to Elizabeth, 3 November 1645, *Oeuvres de Descartes*, ed. Charles Adam and Paul Tannery (Paris: J. Vrin, 1969), vol. 4, p. 333. Cited by Jean-Luc Marion, *Sur la théologie blanche de Descartes* (Paris: Presses Universitaires de France, 1981), p. 411.

2. *Oeuvres de Descartes*, 1:145.

3. I am aware that it is a matter of *opposing* them: but in order to oppose them directly, as the recto and verso, the permanence of a single question (of a single "opening") must be supposed, *beyond* the question of the *subjectus*, which falls into the ashcan of the "history of being."

4. Applying it to Kant himself if need be: for the fate of this problematic—by the very fact that the transcendental subject is a limit, even *the* limit as such, declared to be constitutive—is to observe that there always remains some substance or some phenomenality in it that must be *reduced*.

5. As Nancy himself suggests in the considerations of his letter of invitation.

6. Jacques-Bénigne Bossuet, *Politique tirée de des propres paroles de l'Ecriture sainte*, ed. Jacques Le Brun (Geneva: Droz, 1967), p. 53. Bossuet states: "All men *are* born subjects." Descartes says: There are *innate* ideas, which God has always already planted in my soul, as seeds of truth, whose *nature* (that of being eternal truths) is contemporaneous with *my nature* (for God creates or conserves them at every moment just as he creates or conserves me), and which at bottom are entirely enveloped in the infinity that envelops all my true ideas, beginning with the first: my thinking existence.

7. *The Institutes of Gaius*, trans. W. M. Gordon & O. F. Robinson (London: Gerald Duckworth & Co., Ltd., 1988), §48–50, p. 45.

8. Cf. Christian Bruschi, "Le droit de cité dans l'Antiquité: un questionnement pour la citoyenneté aujourd'hui," pp. 125–53 in *La citoyenneté et les changements de structures sociales et nationales de la population française*, ed. Catherine Wihtol de Wenden (n.p.: Edilig/Fondation Diderot, 1988).

9. Emmanuel Terray suggests to me that this is one of the reasons for Constantine's rallying to Pauline Christianity ("All power comes from God": cf. *Epistle to the Romans*).

10. On all these points, see, for example, Walter Ullman, *The Individual and Society in the Middle Ages* (Baltimore: The Johns Hopkins University Press, 1966), and *A History of Political Thought: The Middle Ages* (Harmondsworth: Penguin, 1965).

11. On all this, see Ernst Kantorowicz, *Frederick the Second, 1194–1250*, trans. E. O. Lorimer (New York: Ungar, 1957); *The King's Two Bodies* (Princeton: Princeton University Press, 1960); *Selected Studies* (New York: J. J. Augustin, 1965).

12. How does one get from the Roman *servus* to the medieval *serf*? Doubtless by a change in the "mode of production" (even though it is doubtless that, from the strict point of view of production, each of these terms corresponds to *a* single mode). But this change presupposes or implies that the "serf" also has an immortal soul included in the economy of salvation; this is why he is attached to the land rather than to the master.

13. Jean Bodin, *Les six livres de la République*, vol. 1, pt. 6 (Paris: Fayard, 1986), vol. 1, p. 114.

14. Ibid., 1:112.

15. Cf. Alain Grosrichard, *Structure du sérail: La fiction du despotisme asiatique dans l'Occident classique* (Paris: Editions du seuil, 1979).

16. Cf. the frequently developed theme, notably following Proudhon: Rousseau and the French revolutionaries substituted the people for the king of "divine right" without touching the idea of sovereignty, or "archy."

17. In the *Cahiers de doléance* of 1789, one sees the peasants legitimize, by the fact that they are *men*, the claim to equality that they raise: *to become citizens* (notably by the suppression of fiscal privileges and seigneurial rights). Cf. Regine Robin, *La société française en 1789: Semur-en-Auxois* (Paris: Plon, 1970).

18. Pierre Richelet, *Dictionnaire de la langue française, ancienne et moderne* (Lyon, 1728), s.v. "citoyen." Cited by Pierre Rétat, "Citoyen-Sujet, Civisme," in *Handbuch politisch-sozialer Grundbegriffe in Frankreich, 1680–1820*, ed. Rolf Reichardt and Eberhard Schmitt, vol. 9 (Munich: Oldenbourg, 1988), p. 79.

19. (Anon.), *La liberté du peuple* (Paris: 1789). Cited by Rétat, "Citoyen-Sujet, Civisme," p. 91.

20. Robespierre, *Textes choisis*, ed. Jean Poperen (Paris: Editions sociales, 1974), vol. 1, pp. 65–75.

21. Cf. Rene Fedou, *L'Etat au Moyen Age* (Paris: Presses Universitaires de France, 1971), pp. 162–63.

22. Cf. the discussion of *apathy* evoked by Moses I. Finley, *Democracy, Ancient and Modern*, rev. ed. (New Brunswick: Rutgers University Press, 1985).

23. Cf. Saint-Just, "Discours sur la Constitution de la France" (24 April 1793): "The general will is indivisible . . . . Representation and the law thus have a common principle." *Discours et rapports*, ed. Albert Soboul (Paris: Editions sociales, 1977), p. 107.

24. Jean-Jacques Rousseau, *Du contrat social*, I, 6, in *Oeuvres complètes*, ed. Bernard Gagnebin and Marcel Raymond (Paris: Gallimard, Bibliothèque de la Pléiade, 1964), vol. 3, p. 362.

25. Ibid., I, 7, in *Oeuvres completes*, 3:362–64.

26. During the revolution, a militant grammarian will write: "France is no longer a kingdom, because it is no longer a country in which the king is everything and the people nothing . . . . What then is France? A new word is needed to express a new thing . . . . We call a country sovereignly ruled by a king a kingdom (*royaume*); I will call a country in which the law alone commands a lawdom (*loyaume*)." Urbain Domergue, *Journal de la langue française*, 1 August 1791. Cited by Sonia Branca-Rosoff, "Le loyaume des mots," in *Lexique* 3 (1985): 47.

27. Louis-Sébastien Mercier and Jean-Louis Carra, *Annales patriotiques*, 18 January 1791. Cited by Retat, "Citoyen-Sujet, Civisme," p. 97.

28. Louis-Antoine de Saint-Just, *Fragments d'institutions républicaines*, in *Oeuvres complètes*, ed. Michele Duval (Paris: Editions Gérard Lebovici, 1984), p. 978. Cited by Rétat, "Citoyen-Sujet, Civisme," p. 97.

29. The Declaration of Rights of 1789, First Article, immediately following "Men are born and remain free and equal in rights," continues: "Social distinctions can only be founded on common utility." Distinctions are *social*, and whoever says "society," "social bond," says "distinctions" (and not "inequalities," which would contradict the principle). This is why freedom and equality must be predicated of man, and not of the citizen.

30. Maurice Blanchot, "L'insurrection, la folie d'écrire," *L'entretien infini* (Paris: Gallimard, 1969), pp. 323–42.

31. Instead of reciprocal action, today one would say "communication" or "communicative action."

32. *Du contrat social*, I, 6, *Oeuvres complètes*, 3:361.

33. Ibid., I, 5, *Oeuvres complètes*, 3:359.

34. I am entirely in agreement on this point with Robert Derathé's commentary (against Vaughan) on the adjective "moral" in his notes to the Pléiade edition of Rousseau (*Oeuvres complètes*, vol. 3, p. 1446).

35. Cf. Karl Marx, *Capital*, trans. Ben Fowkes (New York: Vintage Books, 1977), vol. 1, p. 292: "The product [of the worker's labor in his workshop] belongs to [the capitalist] just as much as the wine that is the product of the process of fermentation taking place in his cellar."

36. Cf. Etienne Balibar, "Spinoza, l'anti-Orwell—la crainte des masses," *Les temps modernes* 470 (September 1985): 353–94.

37. As Louis Sala-Molins does in *Le Code Noir ou le calvaire de Canaan* (Paris: Presses Universitaires de France, 1987).

38. Cf. Yves Benot, *La révolution française et la fin des colonies* (Paris: La découverte, 1988).

39. Let us note that this thesis is *not* Kantian: the accent is placed on the citizen and not on the ends of man; the object of the struggle is not anticipated but discovered in the wake of political action; and each given figure is not an approximation of the regulatory ideal of the citizen but an obstacle to effective equality. Nor is this thesis Hegelian: nothing obliges a new realization of the citizen to be superior to the preceding one.

40. Pierre-Franççois Moreau, *Le récit utopique: Droit naturel et roman de l'Etat* (Paris: Presses Universitaires de France, 1982).

4

Who?

Maurice Blanchot

Somebody looking over my shoulder (me perhaps) says, reading the question, *Who comes after the subject?*: "You return here to that far away time when you were taking your baccalaureate exam."—"Yes, but this time I will fail."—"Which would prove that you have, in spite of it all, progressed. Still, do you recall how you would have gone about it?"—"In the most traditional fashion, by asking about each word."—"For example?"—"Well, I would notice that the first word is *Who?* and not *What?* which postulates the beginning of an answer or a limitation of the question that does not go without saying; I would be expected to know that what comes after is someone and not something, not even something neutral, supposing that this term would let itself be 'determined,' whereas all along it tends to an indeterminacy from which nothing is exempt, no more the whomever than the whatever."—"That's not half bad, but it might irritate the examiner."—"Nevertheless I would still go on by asking how one should understand the meaning of 'come after.'—Is it a question of a temporal or even historical succession or of a logical relation (or both)?"—"You mean that there would be a time—a period—without subject or else, as Benveniste claims, and he was criticized for this, that the always personal 'I—you'—referring to a person—would lose its sovereignty, in the sense that it would no longer have the right to recognize itself in the 'it,' that which, in any language, cannot lay claim to anything personal, except inadvertently: it is raining, it is, it is necessary (to take a few simple, but of course insufficient examples). In other words, language is impersonal or it would be impersonal as long as nobody gets up to speak, even should it be to say nothing."—"It would seem that, as an examiner, you are answering for me, whereas I do not even know what question I am being asked. I therefore repeat the question: *Who comes after the subject?* And I repeat it in another form: What was there before the subject, which is of recent invention: the subject once again, but hidden or rejected, thrown, distorted, fallen before being, or, more precisely, incapable of letting Being or the

---

Translated by Eduardo Cadava

58

logos give it a place."—"But aren't you in an unwonted hurry to interpret the question as *Who comes after the subject?* and not as 'Who will come after the subject?' when really you are indulging yourself in seeking a time when the subject was not posited, neglecting the inaugural decision that, from Descartes to Husserl, privileged that instantiation (of the subject) that made us modern?"—"Yes, who comes after the subject? You are right, examiner, to turn me away from easy solutions, when I seem to be trusting ordinary temporality. The word 'comes,' I sensed from the start, is problematic—even understood as a present, it is only the imminence of a *je ne sais quoi* (as is indicated by the prefix 'pre' of *pre*sent, by means of which the present remains always ahead (of me), in an urgency that does not admit any delay and even increases from this absence of delay, which implies a belatedness, at least as long as my speech, in a statement or a conjuration, draws it, in the act of pronouncing it, toward the abyss of the present tense)."—"Then if I understand you correctly, the 'who comes' never comes, except arbitrarily, or has always already come, in accordance with some incongruous words that I remember having read somewhere, not without irritation, where reference is made to the coming of what does not come, of what would come without an arrival, outside of Being and as though adrift."—"The term 'adrift' is, in fact, appropriate here, but my halting remarks are not entirely useless, and they bring us back to an insecurity that no formulation could avoid. 'Who comes' has perhaps then always already come (according to the misfortune or fortune of the circle) and 'Who,' without claiming to once again put *the ego* into question, does not find its proper site, does not let itself be assumed by Me: the 'it' that is perhaps no longer the it of it is raining, nor even the it of it is, but without ceasing to be not personal, does not let itself be measured by the impersonal either, and keeps us at the edge of the unknown."—"It holds us there in order to engage us in it, whereas becoming engaged presupposes the disappearance of 'we,' as the perhaps infinite extenuation of the subject."—"But aren't we getting away from Western thought by taking refuge in the interpretation of a simplified Orient, leaving the I–subject for the self (the Buddhist emptiness) of peace and silence?"—"That's for you to decide, in the same manner that, returning to the question, I would suggest to you aloud a few of the answers that tacitly you do not dare to express, precisely in order to avoid making a decisive choice. I dare you to name: the overman, or else the mystery of *Ereignis*, or the uncertain exigency of the idle community, or the strangeness of the absolutely Other, or perhaps the last man who is not the last."—"Stop, tempter, this distasteful enumeration where, as in a dream, what attracts and what repels are mixed, neither existing without the other."—"Tempter, I agree, as is moreover any examiner, and I have the advantage over you of revealing myself and, in addition, of tempting you only to lead you away from temptation."—"Making of the detour then temptation itself."

And so on. I here end then this too easy dialogue, ending also my attempt to elucidate the question, without ignoring that I am vainly trying to avoid it, since it has not disappeared and continues to provide an uneasiness by its necessity. "Who then comes after the subject?" Understanding it and not understanding it, I take the liberty of borrowing from Claude Morali the title of one of his books and the citation from which he derives it: "As if that appeal had sounded, in a muffled manner, a nonetheless happy appeal, the cry of children playing in the garden: 'Who is me today?'—'Who is taking my place?' And the happy infinite answer: *him, him, him.*" Only children can create a counting rhyme (*comptine*) that opens up to impossibility and only children can sing of it happily.

So Let us be, even in the anguish and the heaviness of uncertainty, from time to time, these children.

5

The Freudian Subject, from Politics to Ethics

Mikkel Borch-Jacobsen

I have no conscience. The Führer is my
conscience. —Hermann Goering

When one has a sense of guilt after having
committed a misdeed, and because of it, the feeling
should more properly be called *remorse*. It relates
only to a deed that has been done, and of course,
it presupposes that a *conscience*—the readiness to
feel guilty—was already in existence before the
deed took place . . . But if the human sense of
guilt goes back to the killing of the primal father,
that was after all a case of "remorse." Are we to
assume that at that time a sense of guilt was not,
as we have presupposed, in existence before the
deed? If not, where, in this case, did the remorse
come from?—Freud, *Civilization and Its
Discontents*

It might seem strange that I have chosen to approach the notion of "the subject
in psychoanalysis" from the angle of politics and Freudian ethics. After all, isn't
the subject with which psychoanalysis deals—and treats—first and foremost the
individual, in all his remarkable resistance to the ethical and political prescriptions
of society? Why then, you may well ask, should we consider this irreducibly singular
subjectivity from the point of view of that which—as political power or moral
taboo—most often oppresses it, shackles it, or censures it? And is it not a fact that
the most intractable feature of the desiring subject is precisely its tendency to balk
at being reduced to that which Freud named the social "ego," the political "ego
ideal," the moral "superego"? Perhaps. We may still wonder, however, why Freud
himself, after having set up this immense antagonism between desiring subjectivity
and the various "egoist" forms of repression, then kept on trying to reduce it, either
by rooting the ego in the id, by analyzing the libidinal structure of the linkage of
political submission to the Ego-Ideal-Father-Leader, or even by revealing the
Oedipal origin of the moral superego. The question remains, in other words, whether
that which we stubbornly persist in calling the *subject* of desire or the *subject* of the
unconscious can really be so easily distinguished from what we no less stubbornly
persist in thinking of as its *Other*—namely, in no particular order, the symbolic
Father, Law, prohibition, society, power. . . .

Translated by Richard Miller

It is just as well to state at the outset that nothing seems more fragile than such a distinction. Indeed, everything in the Freudian text conspires to suggest the identity—the identification—of the desiring subject and this "Other" that at first glance would seem to be opposed to it, to alienate it, divide it, or separate it from itself. In short, and to anticipate the ultimate goal of my text, I might say that the Freudian subject *is* the other, it is *the same as* the other. The formulation is obviously ambiguous, and we must therefore employ it prudently, "literally and in all its senses." For, as must be clear by now, it involves two very different notions or "versions" of the subject, depending on the emphasis put upon it. Thus, either we understand that the Other is *the same as the subject,* in which case the latter, always identical to itself, triumphantly assimilates or absorbs into itself that otherness—this is the dialectical and, in Freud, the *political,* version of our formula. Or, on the contrary, we understand the subject to be the *same as the Other*—and at once the formula becomes more difficult to understand, at once we no longer know who or what this subject is that had just seemed so obvious, nor do we know if we are still dealing with a subject. I am not sure that we should, if we want to be rigorous, even contrast this second "version" with the first. To do so is to force it into a dialectical mold, whereas actually we need only put a different emphasis on that which is the *same* notion. And it does indeed exist in Freud, where it serves to indicate that which I call, for want of a better term, an *ethical* beyond of the subject. At least, that is what I should like to demonstrate here, convinced as I am that it is here, in this infinitesimal, imperceptible difference of emphasis, that Freud's notion of the subject is ultimately played out. For me, it also affords an opportunity to extend, while reorienting them somewhat, certain analyses I have previously published on this question of the "Freudian subject."[1]

Before we turn to the Freudian hesitation between a "politics" and an "ethics" of the subject, however, we ought to achieve some agreement on the significance and implications of this little—and apparently so obvious, so transparent—word: *subject.* Nowadays—I've just been doing it myself with comparative ease—we seem to have no difficulty with terms like *subject of desire, subject of the unconscious, subject of fantasy.* And yet, are we really sure that we always know what we mean by the word in such contexts? For example, do we know the history, the origin, the genealogy of the term? In this connection it might be useful to recall that it occurs fairly infrequently in Freud, who preferred to speak of the "ego," the "id," the "superego," or even of the "conscious" and the "unconscious." So we ought perhaps to begin by recognizing at the outset that the "subject" comes down to us, not from Freud himself, but from a certain interpretation of his work: it is from Lacan and his "return to Freud," begun in the early 1950s, that we must date the intemperate use of the word *subject* by French psychoanalysts.

Now, this word, as Lacan was well aware, is taken over from philosophy. We might even designate it as the key term of Western metaphysics. For the subject is not, first, the individual, and it is even less the psychological ego to which we nowadays so often find it reduced. Above all, it designates the *hypokeimenon*, the "underlying" or "subjacent" goal of basic, founding philosophical inquiry, the quest for which is posed, supposed, and presupposed in Book 7 of Aristotle's *Metaphysics: ti to on*, "What is being as being?" And, as Heidegger has demonstrated, it is only to the extent that it is the heir, in the form of the Cartesian *Cogito*, to this ultimate basic position, the *ultimum subjectum*, that the *ego* becomes a "subject" in the word's properly modern sense. Nor should this be understood in the sense of an *egoist* or *subjectivist* determination of being, but, rather, in the sense that being *qua* being is henceforth to be conceived of according to the initially Cartesian notion of the auto-foundation or auto-positioning of a subject presenting itself to itself as consciousness, in the representation or in the will, in labor or in desire, in the State or in the work of art.

Thus, it is this modern (and indeed, as can be precisely shown, actually Cartesian) concept of subject that Lacan has imported into psychoanalysis—with the success of which we are all aware. Since others have already done so, I shall not dwell here on the theoretical and institutional stakes involved in that operation, nor on the complex conceptual "corruptions"[2] to which it has given rise. I should merely like in a very preliminary way to draw attention to its fundamentally equivocal character. For obviously this appeal to the philosopheme of the subject (as well as to that of other concepts: "truth," "desire," "intersubjectivity," "dialectics," "alienation," etc.) should enable us to restore the trenchant quality of the Freudian text by ridding it of all psychologism or biologism. But why, in the end, has the word—and hence the concept—*subject* been retained, particularly when it was simultaneously being invested with all the Heideggerian de(con)struction of the "metaphysics of subjectivity"? Wasn't it rather more, as Lacan indicated in "The Mirror Stage as Formative of the Function of the I," a question of abstracting the psychoanalytic experience of the I "from any philosophy directly descendant from the *Cogito*"?[3] And, indeed, would Freud have been given a second's philosophical attention had he not precisely contributed, more than anyone else, to a requestioning of the notion of subject as *Ego*, subject present to itself in consciousness, in representation, or in the wish? Nor is it a question of overlooking the fact that the Lacanian subject is the originally divided, split subject of desire, the profoundly subjected subject of the signifier and of language—nothing, we can therefore say, like the transcendental and absolute subject of the philosophers or like its pale successor, the strong and autonomous ego of the ego psychologists. However, this infinitely decentered subject, reduced to only the desire for that part of itself that language simultaneously arouses and forbids it from rejoining, this subject is still a subject. For Lacan, very enigmatically, still retains the *word*—that is, at least the pure position of the subject. That such a position, from the very fact of its being linguistic, is tantamount to a de-position or dis-appearance does not apparently make much difference—a fortiori if the subject's *fading* or *aphanisis* occurs through what we persist in describing as an auto-utterance. Emptied of any substance, in all rigor null, the subject continues to subsist in the *representation* of its lack, in the closed combinative of signifiers in which it stubbornly continues to self-represent itself, always vanishing but always, upon its disappearance, reemerging.

It is not my intention here, however, to analyze in any detail this powerful ontology of the subject, the more powerful in that it is advanced in the guise of a kind of negative ego-logy avid to assail the "imaginary ego" and the "subject supposed to know." I have nevertheless made brief reference to it, first in anticipation of further analyses because today it represents both the horizon and the condition of possibility of any investigation of the "subject in psychoanalysis." Second, and above all, I have referred to it because it seems to me that it functions as a real *symptom*. For, if we really think about it, how are we to interpret this unexpected resurfacing of the subject smack in the middle of a discourse devoted to a critique of the authority of the consciousness and the illusions of the ego? Once the many conceptual "corruptions" Lacan has made of the Freudian text are taken into account, ought we not ask what, even in Freud himself, has brought about this surreptitious restoration of the subject? Must we not finally suspect the radicality and the depth of the break Freud made on behalf of the unconscious? In short, ought we not return to Freud, yes, but, with Freud, to his philosophical underpinnings, which alone can provide us with a key to the confused fate of psychoanalysis in France?

It is useless to conceal the fact that this is what I attempted to do in *The Freudian Subject*. I thought that it might be timely, that it was even urgent, to wonder if, behind the apparently radical contestation of conscience and ego, the schema of the subject was not continuing silently to command the theory and practice—and even the politics—of psychoanalysis. In short, I wanted to know the extent to which the "fundamental concepts" of psychoanalysis were still prisoners of, or, contrariwise, might have escaped the appeal of foundation—for that is always, in fact, what is at stake in the "subject."

And, indeed, once the question has been couched in those terms, is it not obvious that, in providing himself with an unconscious made up of "representations," "thoughts," "fantasies," and "memory traces," Freud had at the same time provided himself with a subject of representation, imagination, and memory—in short, with the material for a new *Cogito*, but merely conceived as being more basic and more subjectival than the conscious ego? For let us not forget that the subject of the moderns is first and foremost the subject of representation—we can even go so far as to say: the subject *as* representation and representation *as* subject. I would recall that it is by representing itself, by posing itself, in the mode of the *cogito me cogitare*, "with" all the representation it poses before itself, that the Cartesian ego establishes itself as the basis of all possible truth, i.e., as subjectum of the total being. Thus, we must take care not to reduce the subject to the ego. In reality, the latter is nothing outside the *cogitatio* within which it represents itself, conscientiously, con-scientifically, to itself, so that it is really rather the structure of representation as auto-representation that should be dubbed the true and ultimate subject. In this sense, in attempting to qualify this radical nonpresence to the self he dubbed "unconscious," Freud could scarcely have chosen a term more unfortunate than *representation (Vorstellung)*.[4] For to speak of unconscious "representations" was obviously to signal the existence of something beyond the subject, since I—I, the ego—was thus supposed to have thoughts (*Gedanken*) that could think without me. But, too, it had the inevitable consequence of reinstating in that 'beyond' another ego (always, of course, the same one), since there must necessarily be a spectator of that "other scene"—for such representations require a subject that represents them to itself as well as representing itself in them. This is the powerful constraint that brought Lacan to write, apropos of the linguistic "other scene," that "the signifier is what represents the subject for another signifier." And it is also what obliged Freud to substantize—in other words, to *subjectivize*—the unconscious with which he was dealing in an "unconscious," or an "id." The various topographies erected since the *Project* are testimony to this constant substratification of the psychoanalytic subject, always more fragmented, more broken down, and yet always more deeply led down to its own prebeginnings. The multiplication of topographic agencies and "personages" in this sense contravenes the subject's unity and identity much less than it supposes it: the subject can be divided only because it is *one* subject. Finally, neither the notion of some primary repression nor even that of some "after-shock" would have caused Freud to question his stubbornly held notion of a subject already given, already present (underlying) in its representations. And, in this connection, we can be sure that he would have found devoid of any meaning at all the notion so dear to Emmanuel Levinas of some "trauma" having affected the subjectivity anterior to itself, prior to any representation, to any memory, and, therefore, to any repression. According to Freud, the unconscious is memory, a storehouse of traces, inscriptions, remembrances, fantasies. And this memory must be underlaid, traumatic and fracturing as it may be, by a subject to which and in which it represents itself—the subject of fantasy, the backing for the inscription or the substance hospitable to nervous "facilitations."

Does calling this eternal representational subject "desire" change anything at all? Probably not. Desire, understood as libido, drive, or fantasmatic wish, is always a subject, at least insofar as it is described as desire for an object. Let such an object, indeed, be described as fantasmatic and even as "basically lost," it cannot be prevented from emerging, without mystery, as the object for a subject, before a subject. For us other moderns, the object is always the object of a representing (i.e., as the German so descriptively puts it, as a setting-before, a *Vor-stellen*), and this evidence continues to be valid when we understand it as the object of some desire, some libido, some drive. We may only wonder why, in Freud, the "drive" is accessible only through its objects: it is because he only conceives it as represented to or before the psyche—or: the subject. This latter must thus be presupposed to underlie the object in which it sets before itself its pleasure or its enjoyment and in which, simultaneously, it sets *itself* before itself, represents itself. From this viewpoint, by conceiving the object of desire as that "part" that language and representation deduct or remove from the subject, Lacan only confirms this basically auto-representative structure of desire. The "objet petit a" eludes the subject so totally only because the latter has first represented itself in it: thus, it subsists—breast or feces, gaze or voice—in the representation of its absence, of its lack-of-being-itself.

I do not, therefore, believe that it is in the direction of this objectival conception of desire that we should seek, in Freud, material for an in-depth solicitation of the schema of the subject. On the other hand, the same does not quite hold true if we turn to some other, much more problematic, aspect of Freud's theory of desire. This is the aspect that deals with desire of the ego, an expression we must here consider in all its genitive implications, subjective and objective. Indeed, we know that very early on Freud felt constrained to make room alongside the desire for the object that he discerned in sexuality for an "egoist" desire, a desire to be oneself or to be-an-ego, which he began by calling "egoistic" and then "narcissistic," and which he ended up attaching closely to the identification process. I shall not go into the details—they are well known to all—of the various stages of this clarifying process, via the themes of the "egoism" of dreams and fantasies, homosexuality, paranoia, or passionate love. Yet I must emphasize here the importance of that process, for we often really fail to appreciate in Freud the implications of this shifting and displacement of interest. Indeed, his emphasis on the violent passion that the ego conceives for (or devotes to) itself was not only to overturn the initially objectival definition of desire, and henceforth affect all the investigations into the repressing "ego," to which Freud, in a letter to Jung, confessed he had not paid sufficient attention.[5] It also—obscurely, problematically—called into question the subject of desire, the subject of the desiring representation, which he had so tenaciously posited hitherto.

Now, with what are we dealing here vis-à-vis this desire Freud described as "egoist" or "narcissistic"? First and foremost, with being an "I," a "self"—in other words, a subject: shut within itself, freed from all bonds, in this sense absolute. But if I *desire* to be (an) I, if I *desire* myself, it must, following elementary logic, be because I am not it. Thus, this singular desire, by and large, is the desire of no subject. When, for example, Freud wrote that the ideal of the narcissistic ego is "what we would like to be"[6] or, with regard to identification, that it is an "emotional tie with another person" whom one desires *to be* (in contrast to the object one desires *to have*),[7] he was clearly emphasizing the abyssal nature of narcissistic passion. For that ego-being (ego-ness, we might say, the essence and foundation of identity as *ego*), that being does not exist within me: it is elsewhere, in this other—always *alter*—Ego who fascinates me, in whom I love myself, in whom I kill myself. *Thus I am that other; ego sum alter huic.* Or, better, a more Freudian version of this other, very different, *Cogito*: "I am the breast."[8]

By the strangest and yet the most logical of paradoxes, with Freud the attention devoted to the ego's narcissism led to the question of the Other, of others. The question was to haunt him from then on, and more so in that this "other"—model or rival, homosexual figure or persecutor—always appeared to be becoming more and more like the ego, to the point of shattering the very opposition separating them. This is obviously why the great texts on the second topography are an inextricable mix of "ego analysis" and analysis of the culture or social tie: the other is no longer an object, an *Objekt*, whence the need to pay attention to nonerotic, "social" relationships, to others; and, inversely, the ego is no longer a subject, whence the need to inscribe this "sociality" in the ego itself, in the form of identification, superego, etc. Thus, since the ego was originally identified with others or the other principally assimilated to the ego, everything played a part, in a multiplicity of ways, in weakening the joint mutual position of subject and object, or, put another way, the position of the subject of the representation. For that is, in the end, the ultimate implication of the entire discourse on narcissism, the primary identification, and incorporation: if I am the other, then *I no longer represent him to myself*, since the exteriority in which he might have pro-posed himself to me—either as model or as object, *Vor-bild* or Ob-jekt—has faded away. And, at the same time, I have become unable to represent *me*, to present myself to myself in my presence: this other that I am no longer is and never was *before* me, because I have straightaway identified myself with him, because I have from the outset assimilated him, eaten him, incorporated him.

True, this That, this *Id*, which is nothing other than the ex- "subject of desire," is difficult to envisage, and in any event impossible to *represent*. But is it not toward that, that unrepresentable "point of the other," to which Freud was tending when he stated, for example, that the ego emerges through a "primary identification," adding that this primitive relationship to the object immediately amounts to its destroying incorporation? Or elsewhere, when he attempted to describe, under various names, such as "primary narcissism," "animism," "the omnipotence of thoughts," "magic," a type of mental operation that ignores the distinction between ego and others, between subject and object, between desire and its fulfillment? And is it not after all in the direction of this basically unrepresentable thought, the thought of no subject at all, that we should be seeking the ever-elusive "unconscious"?

I have just noted, however, that all this is difficult to think. I should quickly add that Freud himself had enormous trouble in dealing with this problem. For Freud also most frequently interpreted this narcissism, this desire-to-be-oneself that so radically disrupts any notion of a "self," as a desire of oneself *by oneself*—in short, as a subject's auto-affirmation, its auto-position, or its circular auto-conception. We need only recall, in "On Narcissism: An Introduction," the fascinating figures, totally enclosed within themselves, of the narcissistic Child and Woman. Or the theory of primary narcissism secondarily "granted" and "withdrawn" vis-à-vis objects: everything begins with and returns to Narcissus, who never loses himself in objects other than to find himself in them and represent himself in them mirrorwise, in *specula*-tion, *specula*-tively. It is this retrieval of the narcissistic ego in the specular other that Lacan has described by using the term *Imaginary*—but, of course, in order virulently to denounce the deception, the illusion. Yet by retaining, if not the ego, at least its *image*, he too has evidently allowed himself to be won over, in an apparent reversal, by the auto-representative structure of narcissistic desire. That the ego can imagine itself outside itself, imagine itself before itself in the mirror the other holds up to it, in no way, in fact, contravenes its auto-position, since it is precisely the principle of this auto-*ob*-position. . . . As for stigmatizing the "alienation" of the narcissistic ego within the imaginary "other self," that only serves to give some additional confirmation to the profoundly dialectic character of the process being described. For the Lacan of "The Mirror Phase," as for the Freud of "On Narcissism: An Introduction," the ego continues to *represent* itself—and thus, inevitably, to represent *itself*—in the specular mirror-image reflection in which it loves and desires itself.

It is my belief, therefore, that such Freudian or Lacanian interpretations of narcissism also require interpretation. They interpret narcissistic desire in the line of desire, they subscribe to a certain auto-interpretation of desire, whereas this latter is, clearly, a *desire to be a subject*, a desire to be oneself to oneself within an inalienated identity and autonomy. In this sense, the narcissism thesis does more than manifest, sometimes crudely and sometimes with more subtlety, the fascinated submission of psychoanalysis to the paradigm of the "subject." It also attests, in a turnaround, to the narcissistic character of that paradigm. Thus, when we say that psychoanalysis is in its essence deeply narcissistic and that, in a sometimes caricatural way, it reinstates the ancient and always new problematic of the "subject," we are saying one and the same thing.

Now, to get to the point, it is obviously in Freud's so-called "political" or "sociological" texts that this reinstatement is most flagrant, most massive. This is all the more striking in that the Freudian examination of culture and the social tie corresponds in the first instance, as I have said, to the constraining movement that has tilted the question of the narcissistic ego toward that of the other who inwardly haunts and obsesses it. And indeed, it was under the title of *der Andere* (the *Other*) that the great 1921 political text *Group Psychology and the Analysis of the Ego* opened: "In the individual's mental life the other is invariably involved," Freud began, "as a model, . . . as a helper, as an opponent; and from the very first, individual psychology . . . is at the same time social psychology as well."[9] An admirable statement, and one that does, by thus inscribing the other *in* the ego, appear to contain in embryo a whole nonsubjectival theory of the "subject" and "social relationship." Yet one need only read the text of *Group Psychology* to realize that the embryo does not develop and remains stillborn, stifled as it is by a problematic of the political Subject.

In short—since we do not have space to describe here in any detail the extraordinarily complex course of this essay—Freud, when it comes down to it, continually presupposes, in his attempt to explain the social relationship, a *subject* of the relationship, whether as an "individual" subject or as a supra-individual, political subjectivity. On the one hand, indeed, his analysis begins with the desire, the love, or the libido of individuals, who are consequently posited as preexistent to the various erotico-objectival relationships that link them together. And, on the other hand, once we recognize the fundamental fact that, in crowds, all subjectivity and all individual desire disappears, the analysis comes up with a kind of political super-Subject in the dual shape of a narcissistic chief and of the mass, the latter welded together by love of their Chief. We all recall the famous conclusion: society, Freud informs us, is a unanimous "mass" whose members have set up the same "object" (the "leader" or "*Führer*") in place of their ego ideal and who, as a result of so doing, identify, reciprocally and among themselves, with each other.

Having said that, we have first said that society—any society—is in essence *political*, because it depends totally upon the figure of a Chief, a sovereign head in which it represents itself and without which it would purely and simply fall apart. Yet we are also saying that society—any society—is fundamentally, basically, *totalitarian*. Not, I hasten to add, because State coercion or tyrannical violence would be essential to it. That trait is not confined to totalitarian societies, and Freud is clear that the reign of the *Führer* depends above all on the fiction of his love. No, if Freud's society is totalitarian in a strict and rigorous sense, it is because it is posited as an integrally political totality, as *ein totale Staat* knowing no division, unless it be minimal and intended solely to relate the social body to itself between the beloved Chief and his loving subjects. This is further borne out by the speculative biology underlying the description in *Group Psychology*, because that tends, on the grounds of "union" and erotic *Bindung*, to turn society into an actual organism, a real body politic. As Claude Lefort has shown in his expansion on Kantorowicz's work,[10] this is the totalitarian fantasy *par excellence*. It is the profoundly narcissistic fantasy of a single, homogeneous body proper recognizing no exteriority or otherness vis-à-vis itself other than in relation to itself. And it is thus the fantasy, the auto-representation of a subject: for Freud, society is a compact group, a mass, and that mass makes a single *body* with the Chief-Subject that embodies, *incarnates* it.

Of course, it is not a matter of declaring that this description is false. Too many examples in recent history confirm it for us to doubt its exactness and precision. From this viewpoint, I too am prepared to recognize, with Serge Moscovici,[11] the exceptional importance of Freudian "group psychology" for any understanding of the political and social facts of our time. But we must also recognize that Freud did not so much analyze this totalitarian fantasy as subscribe to it. For, contrary to what he is purported to have said here or there (and this was, inter alia, Lacan's thesis, or myth[12]), Freud never *criticized* "group psychology," convinced as he was, on the contrary, that it represented the very essence of society. Thus, he never questioned the primacy of the Chief, going so far as to write (to Einstein) the following terrifying sentence: "One instance of the innate and ineradicable inequality of men is their tendency to fall into the two classes of leaders (*Führer*) and followers. The latter constitute the vast majority; they stand in need of an authority that will make decisions for them and to which they for the most part offer an unqualified submission."[13]

We must look carefully at the historical and theoretical justification for this exacerbation of the role of "leader" of the masses. In the case of Freud, as in that of Le Bon or Tarde, in that of fascist ideologues as in that of the Bataille of the 1930s, it was based on the following observation—variously appreciated and exploited according to author, of course, but in the end always the same: modern man, the so-called *homo democraticus*, is in reality a "man of the crowds," a man of the "communal" masses, of "groups in fusion." And that anonymous man, brutally revealed by the retreat of the great politico-religious transcendences, is no longer a subject: he is the true "Man without Qualities," without personal identity, deeply panicked, de-individualized, suggestible, hypnotizable ("mediatized," as we would put it today) among "solitary crowds." Thus only an absolute Chief—"prestigious" and "charismatic," say Le Bon and Weber, "sovereign" and "heterogenous" in Bataille's words—can embody, reembody, in other words, give substantial consistency and subjective unity to, this magma of unanchored identities or imitations. In the texts of theoreticians as in the histories inspired by them, the figure of Chief-Subject thus emerges brutally, the more so in that it wards off what is perceived of as a radical de-subjectivization and alienation. In this connection it is probably not enough to say, as one so readily does today, that the twentieth-century totalitarianisms have politically realized the modern rationale and goal of the Subject in all its total ab-solution and immanence. It must be added that they have had greater success insofar as they have lucidly, cynically dealt with the de-liaison and dissolution of the subjects dually implicit in such a goal of immanentization. Briefly, the totalitarian Chief the more easily imposes the fiction or figure of his absolute subjectivity because he knows full well that it *is* a myth and that what he has before him is a mass of nonsubjects. So, in this connection, it is no mere chance that totalitarianisms have caused so many "new mythologies" and "personality cults" to flourish, nor that Bataille and his friends should have dreamed, lucidly and naively, of opposing fascism with an *other* "heterogeneous" and "acephalous" mythology. Inasmuch as the masses have no proper identity, only a myth can provide them with one by positing a fiction in which their unity is embodied, depicted—in short: in which they auto-envisage or auto-represent themselves as Subject. Henceforth, *the Subject is a myth*, because we know we are dealing with something fictional, with a *deus ex machina*, but it is also a myth because in that fiction it is reembodied and *massively* reinstated.

We find this same totalitarian myth of the Subject in *Group Psychology*, and here too, on the far edge of an investigation into the nonpresence of the self implicit in the social being. For just as Freud, on behalf of social identifications, emphasizes the radical alteration of so-called "subjects" assembled in crowds, just as he emphasizes the original character of such group psychology, so does he restore, reinstitute, despite everything, the full primacy and principality of an absolute

Subject. I would therefore recall that the investigation of *Group Psychology* concludes with an invocation of the "totally narcissistic" Father-Chief-Hypnotist. Here, this theme of "narcissism" and of the jealous "egoism"[14] of the primal Father is still decisive, because it is quite obviously only on condition that he be free of ties to anyone (to any "object," as Freud says) that the Chief is able to propose himself as a unique object to the admiring and awestruck love of the masses—in short, to create community where earlier there had been nothing but a chaos of reciprocal identification and suggestions. In other words, everything is locked onto this fascinating figure of a Narcissus or Egocrat sprung from nowhere—which makes moot the difficult question of a relationship or social tie anterior to the ego and makes room for a "scientific myth" that is at once the myth of the Subject's origin and the myth of the foundation of a Politics. The Subject self-proclaims itself Chief, and the Chief thereupon self-engenders himself as Subject.

It goes without saying that this myth remains for us to interrogate, both in its enigmatic resemblance to the totalitarian myth and because of its odd renewal of the figure of the Subject. Yet is it really fitting, in this case, to call it a mere *myth*? I do not think so, and I put even greater stress on this because it is, after all, just such a denunciation of myth that preoccupied me in *The Freudian Subject*. In that book I tried to show that the very violence with which Freud posited a Subject as the origin of Politics seemed to me to signal the failure of his attempt at foundation, at *instauratio*. And, in a way, I reveled in demonstrating that failure: I confined myself to drawing attention to Freud's inability to found the social tie—the relationship with others—other than by presupposing in mythic form a Subject founded in itself and based on itself. In short, I confined myself to revealing the innately unfounded, abyssal, nature of this constant, circular presupposition of a Subject-Foundation. Yet might not that very abyss—the abyss of relationship—be the source of some non-"subjective" notion of politics, of a non-"political" notion of the subject? Were we condemned, in accordance with the deeply ambiguous gesture of our post-Nietzschean modernity, to keep coming up with things like lack-of-foundation, obliteration-of-subject, loss-of-origin, collapse-of-principle? And this "an-archy" of the masses, *in extremis* warded off by the Chief-Subject myth, did it enable us *in extremis,* as it were, to achieve another and more essential understanding of the *archy* itself, the beginnings, the commandment?

For, in the last analysis, that is the formidable problem posed by the Freudian and, more generally, totalitarian Chief-Subject myth. Once its mythic character has been noted, we must still understand whence it derives its incredible *authority*. Because the myth works, whether we like it or not: everywhere, the masses group themselves around a Chief or Party supposed to represent them; everywhere, they convulsively sacrifice themselves on the altar of his or its myth. And that myth functions all the better, as we have seen, when it posits the radical lack of the very political subjectivity it creates. Whence, then, its awesome founding power? Whence does it derive its authority, since it is not from some subject? Since the subject—and this is the cynical lesson totalitarianism teaches us—is a myth?

Today we can no longer evade that question. And we can do so even less in that it is only through that question that we can—perhaps—find the means to resist the henceforth global domination of the "politics of the subject." For, in the end, *on behalf of what* should we reject totalitarianism? In the name of what notion of "subject" and "politics," if it can truly no longer be that of the Individual against the State, nor that of the Rights of the Human-Subject?

Perhaps, in spite of everything, the Freudian myth can provide us with the beginnings of an answer to that question. For we cannot, as I have done hitherto, rely on the version supplied by *Group Psychology*. That political version of the myth is already reinterpreting, reelaborating, an anterior version, a more properly *ethical* version, to which we must now return. We are familiar with this mother-form of the myth: it is the fable of the murder of the primal Father, as set forth in *Totem and Taboo*. And this fable, if we examine it closely, envisages quite another genesis for authority than does *Group Psychology* (I use *authority* in order to avoid the word *power*). For in *Totem and Taboo* the primal authority is not the Father-Chief-Hypnotist, that "Superman" Freud evoked following Nietzsche and before going on to call him, in *Moses*, the "great man." It is the *guilt-creating* Father, and guilt-creating because he is a *dead* Father. Therefore, we can already say—and herein lies the enigma—that such authority is not the authority of any person, in any case not of any man, and even less that of some absolute Narcissus.

True, Freud is still speaking of a murder of a primal "Father," and in so doing he appears once again to be using the language of myth. It is for this that all of our disenchanted modernity, from Lévi-Strauss to Girard, has criticized him: presupposing the authority of the Father rather than deducing it, *Totem and Taboo* does no more than provide us with a new myth of origins, a new myth of foundation. And yet that myth—which is a myth even in its auto-representation as a myth—is also the myth of the origin of the myth of the Father (indeed, we can say of *all* myth). Freud is well aware that the dominating and jealous male of the Darwinian tribe is no Father, and this is indeed why he feels the need, in his narrative, to have him murdered by his fellows: as his power is derived from strength alone, he still does not hold any properly paternal authority, and thus, according to this logic of the natural state, he must be someday overthrown. It is thus *after* the murder, *after* they have killed and devoured their tyrant, that his murderers submit to him, through an enigmatic guilt and obedience that are described as "retrospective" (*nachträglich*). The "Father," in other words, only emerges afterward, in the remorse felt by those who, in like wise, become for the first time in history, "brothers"— and brothers because they are guilty "sons." The "Father," then, does not appear in this strange Freudian myth other than as a myth—the myth of his own power and the power of his own myth. "The dead," Freud writes, "became stronger than the living had been."[15]

Now, this genesis of authority is extraordinarily interesting when viewed from the angle we are now taking, to the degree that it describes the primal authority as an "ethical," "moral" authority and not as a political authority. What the members of the tribe submit to—and because of which they form a community, an ultimately fraternal, human community—is no power, because the wielder of that power is now dead and perfectly powerless. As Freud insistently emphasizes, it is only out of the guilt feeling—the feeling of *moral* lapse, or sin—that the terrible figure that is to become the omnipotent Father, and later the God or the Leader, emerges. As he says in *Civilization and Its Discontents*, guilt feeling is not social anxiety (*soziale Angst*), the commonplace fear of being punished by some external power or censor. It is moral anxiety (or anxiety of conscience: *Gewissenangst*) vis-à-vis an "inner" authority that is as "imperative" as it is "categorical." It is this strange moral authority—even stranger, for that matter, because the subject submits to it by himself, autonomously—that Freud has earlier described as the "voice of conscience" (*Stimme des Gewissens*) and that he was later, after *Totem and Taboo*, to dub the "superego" or "ego ideal." And it is *in place of* that ego ideal that he will set up the *Führer* of *Group Psychology*, finally indicating that the essence of the community is "ethical" before being "political." What creates the community is not principally the fusional and loving participation of a collective Super-Subject or "Superman," but the always singular interpellation of a *Super*-ego that is strictly, rigorously, no one.

For I repeat: the primal authority—ethical authority—belongs to no one, and above all not to the Father-Chief-Narcissus, whose myth will emerge only afterward. Far from feeling guilt because of some anteriorially known and established law (which brings us back to the status of *soziale Angst*), his murderers become aware of the law of the Father—inexplicably, out of terror—through the sense of sin (through *Gewissenangst*): "They thus created," writes Freud, carefully underscoring the paradox, "*out of their filial sense of guilt* the two fundamental taboos of totemism."[16]! Freud does not, then, say that the murderers feel anxiety at having transgressed taboos laid down by the Father. He says—and this is even odder—that the Father's taboos, and, thus, human society, all spring from anxiety—about what? Nothing; nobody. In a wholly disconcerting way, it is when the powerful male is dead and no longer present to forbid anything that the alterity of duty and the debt of guilt, all the more unbearable, emerges. The Father emerges from his own death, the law from its own absence—literally *ex nihilo*. That, as a matter of fact, is why the Freudian myth is not, despite all appearances, a "twentieth-century myth," a new myth nostalgically reinstating the lost transcendence of myth (of the Father, of God, of the Chief). Freud does not deplore the death of the Father, nor does he attempt to alleviate the resultant "discontent of civilization." On the contrary, rooting civilization in the "discontent" of an a priori guilt anterior to any law and any Name of the Father, he offers us the myth of the *death* of myth—and of its tireless resurrection as well. For, finally, if the Father is dead (if his power is purely mythic), how is it that his murderers submit to him? Or, rather (for we are talking about ourselves, about the "killers of God"), if God is dead, how is it that we are so eager to reinstate him at the center and base of our societies, socialist mankind lying prostrate before the Stalinist "Little Father," the *Volk* or race bound together in a fasces behind its *Führer*?

Because we feel guilty for having killed him: this is Freud's—still mythic—response. The question, however, merely bounces back: Why do we feel guilty if no Father is any longer there, if he never was there, to punish us? That is the enigma of the myth—both of Freudian myth and of the mythic power it describes. To solve it, is it enough to evoke once again the love for the Father? Freud in fact writes that the murderers "hated their father, who presented such a formidable obstacle to their craving for power [*Machtbedürfnis*] and to their sexual drives; but they loved and admired him too. After they had got rid of him, had satisfied their hatred, and had put into effect their wish to identify themselves with him, the affection that had all this time been pushed under was bound to make itself felt."[17] Yet such "love" for the Father, as is all too obvious, is also a part of the myth. For it is only *after* they have eliminated the detested rival and when they are impelled by remorse that his murderers come to love him as a Father and to be united in that love. In order to love him, they thus had to begin by killing him. Society, a community of love, rests on a crime, and on the remorse for crime committed.

So, should we not seek the key to filial-fraternal "retrospective obedience" not so much in "love" per se as in the highly ambivalent, hate-filled and devouring side of its nature? The members of the tribe, as the myth makes clear, killed and *devoured* the male of whom they were jealous. Why is this so, if the only goal was to get rid of the retainer of exclusive rights over the females of the flock? The myth spells it out for us: because his murderers "loved and *admired* him." That singular "love" was admiring, identifying, envious, and it thus led inevitably to the cannibalistic incorporation of the model. As the narrative has it: "The violent primal father had doubtless been the feared and envied model of each one of the company of brothers: and in the act of devouring him they accomplished their identification with him, and each one of them acquired a portion of his strength."[18]

"Model," "identification," "devouring," "appropriating,"—all this is clear. Here the myth is not telling us about a love for an object, but about an indissolubly narcissistic and identificatory passion: it is to *be* the Father—*to be the Subject*—that the members of the horde kill and devour him. Not (or only secondarily) to *have* the women of the flock. Freud expresses it clearly when he speaks of the "need for power" and the "desire to identify with the Father": the murder is committed, not to gain possession of an object of desire or pleasure, but to acquire an identity. In this light, then, the murder of the Father is far less a mere animal struggle than it is the Freudian version of Hegel's "struggle for pure prestige." If desire leads to murder and devouring, it is because it is a desire to take unto oneself the other's being, a desire to assimilate his power (*Macht*), his strength (*Stärke*), in short, his mastery: his autonomy as Narcissus. My being is in the other, and it is for that reason that I can become "me," an ego, only be devouring him—*that* is what the Freudian myth is telling us, and in the end much less mythically than might seem. For what it treats of, by setting it in the mythic origins of the human community, is the primal relationship with others—"primal" because it is the relationship of no ego to no other, no subject to no object. And, thus, it is a relationship without relationship to another, an absolved tie: I am born, I, the *ego*, in assimilating the other, in devouring him, in incorporating him. Everything therefore begins, in the history of so-called "individuals" as well as in that of society, with a murderous and blind identification, the more so in that no ego is yet present to see or conceive anything at all, and the "envied" model it assimilates is immediately eradicated, eaten, swallowed up: "I am the breast," "I am the Father"—i.e., *no one.* In other words, everything begins with an identification without subject—and here the Freudian myth corresponds exactly to the status of panicked anarchical, acephalic masses without a Chief. The Father (but not a father, nor even a brother, but merely a counterpart, a fellow being) has been killed and there is therefore no subject at the foundation of the social tie, neither loving subjects nor beloved Subject.

Yet it is at this juncture that the myth of the Subject arises. The phantom of Father-Subject attacks the guilt conscience of the sons, who then attempt to atone for their sin through their love and submission. From where does this ghost, then, derive its vain, empty power? From the *failure* of the devouring act of identification. Freud puts it in a footnote, and it is ultimately to be the only explanation of the son's "retrospective obedience" he vouchsafes: "This fresh emotional attitude must also have been assisted by the fact that the deed cannot have given complete satisfaction to those who did it. From one point of view it had been done in vain. Not one of the sons had in fact been able to put his original wish—of taking his father's place—into effect. And, as we know, failure is far more propitious for a moral reaction than satisfaction."[19] Thus, none of the sons was able to become Subject and Chief by appropriating to himself the identity and glorious being of the Other. And what is, finally, the indomitable alterity that brings about the failure of the identificatory act of violence, the dialectical assimilation of the other? To return to and reverse Hegel's term, it can be nothing other than the "absolute Master," death. Death or the *dead man: der Tote*, says Freud.

In empirical reality there is nothing to prevent one of the tribe from taking in his turn the place of the dominant male by eliminating his competitors (indeed, Freud conceives of this solution in other versions of the myth[20]). So it must be something quite different, and not at all empirical, with which we are dealing here: namely the unoccupiable place of the dead, death being the absolute limit of identification. The myth, to be sure, does not state it so clearly, but it is the only way we can understand the retrospective power of death. *Der Tote* who is resurrected and lives on eternally in the guilty memory of his sons *represents* death, represents for them their own unrepresentable death. We must in fact imagine, at the myth's extremity, that the murderers, having devoured the other in order to appropriate his being, suddenly find themselves faced with "themselves"—in other words, with no one. The other was dead, *and therefore they themselves were dead.* The identifying incorporation brought them—brutally, dizzyingly—face to face with what is par excellence unassimilable: their own death, their own being-dead, with what escapes all appropriation. That is why "the dead became stronger than the living had been" and also why the "sense of guilt" is born of the anxious apprehension of death "beside the dead body of someone [we] loved," as Freud says in "Thoughts for the Times on War and Death."[21] "This dead man," his dazed murderers must have told themselves, "this dead man is me—and yet he is infinitely other, since I cannot envisage myself dead.[22] He is myself, and all the more other. And this All-Other, this All-Mighty who has escaped my power, how now can I appease His wrath?"

I have just used the language of the myth, following Freud's attempt to represent the unrepresentable, attempting *myself* to envisage this other that is me by setting it, once more, before myself. Of course, it is a myth, but the myth is inevitable, inescapable. And that, precisely, is its power: we cannot (but) represent the unrepresentable, we cannot (but) present the unpresentable. That is why, in attempting to represent this deep withdrawal of the subject, Freud could only write a new myth—powerful, like all myths, and one that also created a group, a community. Yet this myth—the myth of the death of myth, the myth of the inevitable power of myth—is no longer wholly a myth. A myth of the mythic emergence of the Subject, it is no longer wholly the myth of the Subject, and it is for that reason, lucidly confronting the vast power of the totalitarian myth, that it may perhaps enable us to elude it.

For, in the end, what is it telling us? First that we are submitting to nothing but ourselves—in that, of course, it is only repeating the totalitarian myth of Subject: State, Law, the Chief, the *Führer,* the Other in general are Me, always Me, always "His Majesty the Ego." And it is also quite true that Freud himself believed in this myth to a considerable degree, that he himself succumbed to its power. Yet by adding that this all-powerful ego is "the dead," *our* death, he also told us something quite different, something almost impossible to say and that he was therefore forced to utter in mythic terms: "I am death," "I am the other." In short: "I am not myself, I am not subject." What the members of the murderous horde submit to, what they assemble before, what unites them in a community, is *nothing*—no Subject, no Father, no Chief—other than their proper-improper mortality, their proper-improper finitude, their proper-improper powerlessness to be Absolute Subjects, "total Narcissus."

And, finally, that is why the enigmatic "retrospective obedience" of which Freud speaks is an ethical respect before it is a political submission, respect for others before being submission to oneself. It is obedience to what in the subject is beyond the subject, to what in me is above me, to the ego's superego. Or, and to return to the Freudian myth, adding *nothing*, it is obedience to what withdraws from the body social in its very incorporation and thereby—and only thereby—creates a "body politic" or a "mystical body": "This is my body. Behold here my death. Here behold your own."

Notes

This text first appeared in *October* 39 (winter 1986): 109–27.

1. Cf. *The Freudian Subject*, trans. Catherine Porter (Stanford: Stanford University Press, 1988).

2. The phrase is taken from Philippe Lacoue-Labarthe and J.-L. Nancy, *Le Titre de la lettre*. (Paris: Galilée, 1973.)

3. Jacques Lacan, *Ecrits*. (Paris: Seuil, 1966), p.93.

4. As Michel Henry has recently noted in *Généalogie de la psychanalyse* (Paris, Presses Universitaires de France, 1985); I shall have more to say elsewhere on this admirable and highly important book ("L'inconscient revisité," in preparation).

5. Sigmund Freud, C. G. Jung, *The Freud/Jung Letters*, ed. William McGuire, trans. Ralph Manheim. (Princeton: Princeton University Press, 1974).

6. Freud, *The Standard Edition of the Complete Psychological Works*, vol. 14, p. 90. ed. and trans. James Strachey. (London: Hogarth, 1953–74).

7. Ibid., 18:105.

8. Ibid., 23:299.

9. Ibid., 18:69.

10. Claude Lefort, "L'image du corps et le totalitarisme," in *L'invention démocratique* (Paris: Fayard, 1981); E. Kantorowicz, *The King's Two Bodies* (Princeton, Princeton University Press, 1959).

11. Serge Moscovici, *L'age des foules* (Paris: Fayard, 1981).

12. Lacan, *Ecrits*, pp. 474–475: "For our purposes we must begin with the remark, never to our knowledge made, that Freud had started the I[nternational] A[ssociation] of P[sychoanalysis] on its path ten years prior to the time, in *Group Psychology and the Analysis of the Ego*, he became interested in the Church and the Army, in the mechanisms through which an organic group participates in the crowd, an exploration whose clear partiality can be justified by the basic discovery of the identification of each individual's ego with a shared ideal image the mirage of which is supported by the personality of the chief. A sensational discovery, made prior to fascist organizations' making it patently obvious. *Made aware earlier of its effects* [emphasis mine] Freud would obviously have wondered about the field left open for dominance by the function of the *boss* or caïd in any organization that," etc. A remark that in turn gives rise to several others: (1) Freud's "basic discovery" in *Group Psychology* is not that *egos* are united in the same *identification* with the ego's Ideal-Chief, because he states, on the contrary, that they mutually self-identify because of their shared *love* for the "Object" that is set up "in place of" their Ego Ideal. Lacan's "remark" supposes, in fact, a reinterpretation of Freud's thesis and a reinterpretation probably dictated by implicit reflection on the fascist phenomenon. (2) Freud's "sensational discovery" "anticipates" the fascist mass organizations (as Bataille was to note as early as 1933, cf. *Oeuvres complètes*, 1:356) only because it broadly confirms a description of "crowd psychology," such as that of Gustave Le Bon, which fascist ideologues, led by Hitler and Mussolini, were to exploit deliberately (cf. R. A. Nye, *The Origins of Crowd Psychology: Gustave Le Bon and the Crisis of Mass Democracy in the Third Republic*, London, 1975, pp. 178–79). (3) "Made aware of its effects . . . "—in 1921 Freud felt absolutely no need to reorganize the analytical community on another model—and for good reason: as Lacan himself noted in the earlier version of his text (published as an Annex to *Ecrits*, p. 487), Freud insisted so much on his own function as Chief-Father because he never for an instant doubted the basic "inadequacies" of his "band" of disciples. The masses need a leader—isn't that what all the great "leaders" of this century have constantly reiterated, in public or in private, from Lenin to Mao by way of Mussolini or Tito? And is this not what Lacan himself is also saying in his way, when he heaps contempt on those attending his seminar or signs his contributions to *Scilicet* with

his proper name alone? In fact, nothing would have been done either by Freud or by Lacan to deal with what the latter called "the obscenity of the social tie" and substitute for it another, "cleansed of any group needs" ("*L'Etourdit*," in *Scilicet*, 4, Paris, 1973).

13. Freud, *Standard Edition*, 22:12.

14. Ibid., 18:123: "He, at the very beginning of the history of mankind, was the 'superman' whom Nietzsche only expected from the future. Even to-day the members of a group stand in need of the illusion that they are equally and justly loved by their leader (*Führer*), but the leader himself need love no one else; he may be of a masterful nature, absolutely narcissistic, self-confident and independent."

15. Ibid., 13:143 (translation slightly modified).

16. Ibid.

17. Ibid., cf. also, ibid., 21:132: "This remorse was the result of the primordial ambivalence of feeling toward the father. His sons hated him, but they loved him, too. After their hatred had been satisfied by their act of aggression, their love came to the fore in their remorse for the deed. . . . Now, I think we can at last grasp two things perfectly clearly: the part played by love in the origin of conscience and the fatal inevitability of the sense of guilt."

18. Ibid., 13:142. See also p. 82: "They not only feared and hated their father but also honoured him as a model, and . . . each of them wished to take his place in reality. We can . . . understand the cannibalistic act as an attempt to ensure identification with him by incorporating a piece of him."

19. Ibid., 13:143.

20. First and foremost in *Totem and Taboo*, in which Freud, as though frightened by his own paradox, has the father's murder followed by a fratricidal struggle—which brings Freud back to his point of departure and thus constrains him to fall back on the hypothesis (more classic and the one which the hypothesis of "retrospective obedience" was intended to avoid) of a "social contract" among the rival brothers. See also ibid., 23:82: "It must be supposed that after the parricide a considerable time elapsed during which the brothers disputed with one another for their father's heritage, which each of them wanted for himself alone." *Moses and Monotheism* describes the same scenario, the brothers struggling to take the father's place.

21. Ibid., 15:294–95: "What came into existence beside the dead body of the loved one was not only the doctrine of the soul, the belief in immortality and a powerful source of man's sense of guilt, but also the earliest ethical commandments. The first and most important prohibition made by the awakening conscience was "Thou shalt not kill." It was acquired in relation to dead people who were loved, as a reaction against the satisfaction of the hatred hidden behind the grief for them." The important thing in arousing the moral conscience is not, therefore, that the corpse be that of a father, nor that it have actually been murdered. The only important thing is that "primal man" be confronted with a *dead person with whom he identifies* in the ambivalent mode of devouring "love." For "then" in his sorrow he will experience the fact that he, too, can also die, and all his being revolts against the recognition of that fact; isn't each of the persons dear to him *a part of his well-beloved ego?*

22. Ibid., p. 294: "Man can no longer keep death at a distance because he had tasted it in his pain about the dead; but he was unwilling to acknowledge it, for he could not conceive himself as dead."

6

Voice of Conscience and Call of Being

Jean-François Courtine

It is the death of the other that is constituted
in the first place; it happens here just as with
the birth of others.—Husserl, ms. A VI 14a,
p.3.

That which, in the context of *Sein und Zeit*,
and there alone, was fore-thought under the
heading of *Sein zum Tode*, thought, that is, in
a fundamental ontological perspective, and
never in the sense of an anthropology or of a
world concept, is what no one has yet
foreseen or attempted to think-after.—
Heidegger, *Beiträge zur Philosophie*, (1936–
38)

If the Heideggerian critique of the metaphysics of subjectivity underlies the
enterprise of *Being and Time*, it rightly finds its first point of application in the
destruction of the *ego cogito, ego sum*, inasmuch as Descartes, in his quest for a
fundamentum inconcussum, institutes the *ego* as the ultimate subject for and of representation (Vor-stellung, Zu-stellung).[1] The destructive operation, here more
than elsewhere, and to the very extent that it is phenomenologically inflected, is
determined as a "return upstream"; it tends to revert to the near side of the subject,
directing itself, explicitly or not, to the following questions: What, originally, comes
before the subject and will always already have been ahead of it? Put another way:
From what has the determination of the subject's subjectivity been borrowed? At
the end of what narrowing-down has the subject found itself defined?[2]

We may point immediately to the principle of the answer, which it is the object
of this discussion to explicitate: At the origin of the subject is the voice. By
indicating the solicitation of the voice (*Stimmung*) as radical to subjectivity, or
better, as what *decidedly* comes before the subject, we do not mean simply to
"denounce" some phonocentrism consubstantial to metaphysics in general(?) or to
the metaphysics of presence, from which Heidegger might not have managed to
free himself. Indeed, we do not know what the voice is that we are concerned with
here, nor what it says, if it says anything. We do not, moreover, know whether it
calls and how it does so.

One of the guiding motifs of the critique formulated by Heidegger against the

---

Translated by Elisabeth Haar

Cartesian principle of the *ego cogito-sum* is the ontological indeterminateness of the *sum*. The mode of being of the *ego* in its specificity is not questioned as such. Or rather, if, without ever being expressly thematized, the mode of being of the *ego sum* constitutes in effect the cornerstone of that strange, bi-focal edifice that is the *Meditations*, this is because it concentrates in itself the ontological features of *Vorhandenheit*. To miss the Being of the *ego*, not to recognize its difference, which may be called ontological, is also and at once to confirm the obliteration of the temporal dimension of the *ego sum* or of *Dasein*. What is the meaning of the being of the *sum*? What is the temporality proper to that singular being that says: *cogito-sum*? The two questions are one and the same. But there is a point that commentary seems to have emphasized little, and it is that Heidegger, at least in the period of *Being and Time*, does not seriously call into question the Cartesian problematic of certainty, even though it is historically overdetermined.[3] Indeed, not only is the theme of *Gewissheit*, as we shall see further on, taken up again at the threshold of the second section of *Being and Time* (chapters 1 and 2), where the problem is to discover whether and how *Dasein* can *attest* to itself, of itself, and for itself, to its wholeness, its originary character, its authenticity, but it was already in the name of a *certainty* more absolute than that which Descartes had believed he was winning against the evil genius, that Heidegger engaged, in a course professed at Marburg in 1925, in the destruction of the metaphysics of subjectivity.

With regard to what unshakeable certainty could the Cartesian "foundation" reveal itself to be uncertain and ill-assured? With regard to death, of course! Not at all to the unerringly confirmed "fact" that "one dies." A proposition of the type "one dies" could not provide the principle of any certitude, not only because its subject is essentially indeterminate and rests on an anterior leveling, but because in truth *One* never dies, and a certain form of im-mortality might even represent one of the ultimate constituent features of the "They." If death does indeed confer a fundamental certainty (*Grundgewissheit*), it is solely inasmuch as it belongs rightfully and constitutionally[4] to *Dasein*, which is, each time, yours or mine. Hyperbolic doubt may ruin any assurance; it must nevertheless capitulate to "that certainty that I am myself." Not that I know who I am, or what my "identity" is. The certainty that I am myself (*ich selbst bin*) is not that of the *cogito-sum*. Such an utterance offers only an appearance (*Schein*) of certainty. The only authentic utterance in which *Dasein* finds expression, that which is consubstantial to *Dasein* itself and to its self-certainty, is rather: I shall die, I must die.[5] The subject of such a proposition—the first and fundamental proposition—is certainly always at every occurrence "mine." It is essentially ordered by the structure of the *Jemeinigkeit*. It remains nonetheless true that here the "subject," the *ego*, can be omitted or, as it is felicitously said, "under-stood," as, for example, in Latin. Heidegger proposes a double transformation of the central Cartesian proposition; it does not suffice to reduce the *ego cogito, ego sum* to its ontological core *ego sum*, it is still necessary to make explicit the *sum*, or the temporal being of the *sum* in *sum moribundus* and consequently have the *ego* "understood." Not in the sense that the latter would be always already presupposed as final substratum or "subject," but because it can never emerge in its egoity or its ipseity except along with, as its point of departure, the gerundive *moribundus*, a time-to-come opened up by the "coming to die" (*Sterbenwerden*) and as though reflected by it. The *Ego* does not put itself forward, does not institute itself as subject, not even in the grammatical acception of the term, unless it hears itself called as *mortal*.

(I) am—dead. *Sum moribundus*. Such is, as Heidegger clarifies it, the utterance that, far more than "I think, I am," can touch, concern, *Dasein* in its very being. Need it be said that "moribundus" does not characterize him whom we call "moribund," who, grievously wounded or afflicted with a severe, and precisely mortal illness, is going to die? It is inasmuch as I am *absolutely* and leaving aside any additional determination relative to health or sickness, to youth or age, that I am *moribundus*, "dying."

This is the principle of the answer to the initial question as to the meaning of being in the Cartesian *ego sum*: what gives proper meaning to the *sum* inasmuch as we are concerned with the being of *Dasein* that is mine or that I always am myself, is the *moribundus*. It is death that seals the meaning of the being of *Dasein*.

One will undoubtedly ask whether the utterance *sum moribundus* (or, to emphasize the circularity that binds each of the so-called "terms," *sum-moribundus*) does not reintroduce an indetermination analogous to that of *Man stirbt* ("one dies"), whose ambiguity, analyzed in *Being and Time*, has been recalled. Certainly the proposition *sum-moribundus* leaves entirely open the question of when I shall die, when the hour of death will come to me. But precisely such an indetermination belongs essentially to the certainty of (my) death. The "I am" of "I am—to die" must always be understood in the sense of an "I may die" *at any moment, at every instant*. The certainty of death that determines the meaning of my being is defined even strictly and solely in relation to this possibility—temporal possibility or, better, possibility of time.

Here the traditional conceptuality that grasps the possible as a potentiality susceptible or not of effective self-realization is revealed to be basically inadequate. The ontological relation (*Seinsverhältnis*) to whose possibility it is important here to gain access is not that of bringing to effect: on the contrary, possibility must be allowed to be as possibility. "A relation of being to the latter," states Heidegger, "must consequently be such that through it I am myself that possibility."[6] The being of the *ego: ego sum*, which must be uttered as *sum-moribundus*, may be said equally as: I am—possibility. Possibility, in the peculiar sense of possibility of death, is for *Dasein* the furthest reach or the utmost limit of possibility (*die äusserste Möglichkeit*). It defines a manner of being in which *Dasein* is referred back to itself and, as it were, thrust back on itself. The coming of death as essential possibility thrusts *Dasein* back and refers it to itself. This "retro-projection" (*Zurückwerfen*) is so absolute in its tearing that being-with (*Mitsein*), about which Heidegger nevertheless emphasizes that it co-belongs essentially to *Dasein*, becomes in its concretion irrelevant, impertinent. The mortal reflection (repercussion or reverberation) is not only absolute but in reality absolving: it unties all the bonds formed with the ambient world, the public space of the "They," the being-in-common one preoccupied with the other. One may thus rigorously argue that the possibility opened by being toward death, and the retro-projection that belongs to it essentially, is ab-solute possibility. Of course, Heidegger clarifies further that *Dasein* "remains, even in dying, essentially *being-in-the-world* and thus being-with others," but this is in order to stress immediately that in the light of the mortal possibility "being is transported (*verlegt*) now precisely and properly for the first time into the 'I am.' " I am in the full and absolute sense when I am—dead. "It is only in dying that I can say certainly and absolutely 'I am.' "

One could hardly affirm more clearly the strictly mortal meaning of the *ego sum*. In a first and obvious sense, death may be characterized as "extreme possibility of the 'I am,' " from the moment that the *exitus* precisely marks the end of my being and of being mine. It is nonetheless important to hear this utterance inverted, with the understanding that it is the mortal possibility and it alone, the possibility as possibility, or yet the possibility of death as such, that is the ultimate condition of possibility upon which *Dasein* can say, "I am."[7] I am inasmuch as I affect myself with my ultimate possibility. The affection here is auto-affection in the radical sense that it constitutes by the very fact and from the outset all ipseity.

In this same 1925 lecture, having recalled that for Descartes, in accordance with the canonical thesis of the *Principia*,[8] it was impossible to give credit to any affection of being as such, Heidegger characterized anguish doubtless still more neatly than in *Being and Time* as pure affection of being, taken as such or in the absolute. If anguish is indeed that which first reveals "the world as world," it is also, and more profoundly, "affection" (*Affektion, Stimmung*) attuned to the "marvel" that being is. The affection of the pure *quod*, apprehended in its nakedness,[9] must, if it allows itself to be explicitated through the affective tonality of anguish, also be able to sub-tend, through the experience of the coming-to-die (or just as rigorously through the mortal possibility as possibilizing of all experience), the basic ontological utterance (*die echte Daseinsaussage und Grundgewissheit des Daseins selbst*): I am in the sense of I am—dead.[10]

If, in order to determine its being and the mode of being peculiar to it, *Dasein* cannot utter *I am*, except on condition that it implicitly translate such a formula into an *I can die*, it is precisely because *Dasein is* not. This is why it would be vain, for example, to seek to oppose a fundamental ontological thesis, in the sense of the *Fundamental-Ontologie*, to the Parmenidean "esti gar einai." If *Dasein* is, its being is nothing other than *Möglichsein*, being-possible, given the extremity of the possible: death. "The *Dasein* that I myself am each time is determined in its being by this: that I can say of it, *ich bin* (I am), which is to say, I can die."[11] And not "one of these days," when the time comes, but truly "at any moment." To clarify "ich bin" as "ich kann (*sterben*)" is still insufficient. The "I am" must be understood still more radically in the sense of an "I am this 'I can,' namely, 'I can die at any moment.' " I am always already that exceptional possibility that is not properly my own except as the extreme of all possibility, precisely the possibility for me to be no longer there.[12] *My* possibility, the inappropriable possibility, of mineness and of all ownness, defines itself only in coming upon me from (my) death, as that instancing which underlies all temporalization.

The second section of the first part of *Being and Time* opens with a methodological reflection of greatest import, for the problem is indeed to determine what exactly is the "hermeneutic situation" of the existential analytics that has just been unfolded. The difficulty that first arrests our attention presents itself only formally in the guise of a "manifest contradiction." How is it possible to "read" (*ablesen*)[13] at the level of *Dasein* the meaning of being in general—for this is what is at stake in the project of fundamental ontology—if *Dasein* is that being that does not let itself be apprehended in its whole structure, its entirety (*ontologische Seinsganzheit*)?

How does *Dasein*, determined essentially as care, characterized by being-in-advance of itself, "being-not-yet," in a word, *possibility*, let itself be taken up again, *tel qu'en lui même enfin*"?[14] What is meant, when applied to *Dasein*, by the categories of ending, completion, being-at-end or at-the-end? Have they not lost all pertinence for that being to whose being waiting, reserve excess, and what-is-to-come belong?

Without being able to follow the Heideggerian analyses in their intricacy, let it suffice in the economy of this discussion to note that the guiding—methodologically decisive—question, as we enter this section, is that of unity, entirety, originariness (*Urspränglichkeit*) of *Dasein*. How are the determinations achieved up to this point to be brought back to unity? What can assure their structural uni-totality? And, above all, how may one clear a path to the giving source of such determinations, as a sole function of which it will become possible to discriminate between what is derived or "degenerate" and what is original or authentic, what is proper or improper. Such questions are far from rhetorical; upon the answer that may be given to them rests the validity of the project as a whole, if it is true, as Heidegger notes, that "one thing is sure at present: the existential analysis of *Dasein* developed until now cannot presume to be originary. It has never possessed as previously established anything but the inauthentic being of *Dasein*, apprehended moreover as *less* than a *whole* (*als unganzes*). If the interpretation of the being of *Dasein*, serving as foundation to the elaboration of the fundamental ontological question, must be originary, then it must formerly have elucidated existentially the being of *Dasein* in its possible *authenticity* and *totality*."[15]

To conceive *Dasein* in its entirety is to determine that it is in-ending, to arrest it with respect to or in regard to its end. But when it is "at the end," when it is dead, *Dasein* has ceased to be that very one that it is: "the being-there"—it is no longer. One is tempted to say: *Dasein* will only have been as living, inasmuch as it was *alive*. To be, for *Dasein*, is to live, in a sense that remains wholly to be determined existentially. Let us simply note that this underlying identity sharpens the "manifest contradiction" that consists in seeking to circumscribe *Dasein* in its total or completed structure, even while it is no longer alive.[16]

In order to explicitate the hermeneutic situation of the existential analytic, Heidegger takes as his guiding thread those concepts previously brought out in the study of "understanding": that which has been previously acquired (*Vorhabe*), foresight (*Vorsicht*), anticipation (*Vorgriff*).[17] What is the remaining import of his concepts for acceding to the originary uni-totality of *Dasein*, if, on the other hand, the basic feature of its being as brought out up to this point forbids, along with recapitulation, precisely, foresight, anticipation, the prae- of the previously acquired? The Heideggerian procedure here is remarkably aporetic or, better, diaporetic. The attempt whose failure is richest in instructive consequences is that which would consist in questioning the death of the other ("feeling the loss," "experiencing death"), in order to attempt to grasp *Dasein* mediately when it reaches its end. In effect, if none can say what the truth of it is, when it is finished, since acceding to entirety initially means for *Dasein* ceasing to be, and if the "deceased," the cadaver, cannot either teach us anything because of the radicality of the turn (*Umschlag*) by which we pass from life to death,[18] must we not envisage, since *Dasein* is essentially *Mit-dasein*, experiencing death through the death of the other? Is this not the only possible approach to "being-at-the-end" (*das Zu-Ende-Sein*), where *Dasein* is concerned? Is this not the only substitution (*Ersatzthema*) conceivable in order to pursue our enquiry?

Without lingering over the difficulties or phenomenological impossibilities of such an investigation, Heidegger immediately denounces the unacceptable expectations: such a procedure always rests upon the premise that "any *Dasein* may be substituted for another at random, so that what cannot be experienced in one's own *Dasein* is accessible in that of a stranger."[19] The underlying hypothesis, which has already condemned the undertaking to failure, is that of *Vertretbarkeit*, substitutability, representation or representativity. Now the relation to death—precisely the dying—is that in which none may take the place of another, be substituted for him or put in his place. Put differently, and positively this time, dying cleanly draws the absolutely unimpeachable line of division between what is my own and what is foreign. Death, if it is, is *my own*; it is uttered necessarily as *my* death, in entire and inalienable ownness. But this is also and at once to emphasize that (my) death is essentially and by principle unrelated to the disappearance of others (the "deceased," the "departed"). Doubtless *Vertretbarkeit*—replaceability, representability—has been first counted in the number of constituent possibilities of *Dasein* as *Miteinandersein*: it belongs in effect to being-there, in its being-in-community-with-others, to be able to be delegated to represent another, appear *in his name*, and in the *stead and place* of the other. But, as Heidegger remarks, the representation in cases of this kind always comes "*in und bei etwas*," in such and such a *case*, which precisely always belongs to the order of preoccupation, that is, in affairs in which a *Dasein* can, under certain conditions and within certain limits, take the place of others. However, the "coming-to-its-end" (*Zu-Ende-kommen*) marks the absolute and impassable limit of all possible representation (*Vertretung*).

"None can take from another his dying."[20] At most one may, in the extreme case of "sacrifice," go to death in the place of another, that is to say for him: to sacrifice oneself is to immolate oneself *for*, always in a determined matter and for a given "cause." But to sacrifice oneself for the other, to die to defend the fatherland, for example, does not in any way amount to delivering the other from the possibility of his death.[21] *Dasein* must always and each time assume for itself this singular dying that is its own. Insofar as it serves as a touchstone of the *Jemeinigkeit*, death represents a particularly significant existential phenomenon: it opens the space inside which the "They" may be checkmated, if it is true that the "They" is characterized by the general feature that it "unburdens [*entlastet*] *Dasein* in its everydayness."[22]

If it is thus impossible to gain access to the entirety of *Dasein* through the experience of the other's death, then the very signification of the "end" or of "ending" must be questioned, where *Dasein* is concerned (*daseinsmässiges Enden*). How may the existential meaning of the "end" and of the "entirety" be determined, if it is true that *Dasein* never simply perishes, does not merely stop living (*verenden*) in the sense that the animal that loses its life "collapses." Let us recall here the conclusion of Heidegger's analysis, which is always formally developed: To end, for *Dasein* (*Zu-Ende-Sein*), does not mean to-be-at-the-end, reach-one's-end, but to-be-face-to-face-with, for, or in relation to the end (*Sein-zum-Ende*). "In the same way as *Dasein is* constantly its not-yet, during all the time that it is, it is also always its end already." Now it is precisely this end that is properly named, in a manner wholly peculiar to *Dasein*, "death." Commensurate with *Dasein*, being means being constantly for-(toward-)-the-end. To die (*sterben*), inasmuch as it is carefully distinguished from all *Ableben* and from all *Verenden*, may thus be characterized as a "title" for the "mode of being in which *Dasein* is in *relation to* [*zu*] its end." This "end"—death as "imminence" (*Bevorstand*)—is that which, ahead of the "subject," will always already have made possible a being-ahead, a step beyond the given-present. The primordial relation to death as *one's* death very rigorously sustains the *relation to self*; it underlies generally all possibility to relate oneself-to-(*sich verhalten*).

The imminence (*Bevorstand*) in question here must in its turn receive a thoroughly determined meaning, inasmuch as the relation to self that it institutes necessarily obliterates being-in-common-with (*Miteinandersein*) which is nevertheless always implied in the other possible forms of imminence. Faced with this singular imminence, *Dasein* is turned back, reduced or rendered to itself; it is released from all the bonds that may unite it to others, as if exiled, banished, excluded from the "community."[23] The relation-of-self-to-self, a relation constituent of ipseity, which is opened to *Dasein* as *being-unto-death*, decisively disrupts all *Mitsein* or *Mitdasein*. Death, which is always being-for(to-ward)-death, as *the ownmost* possibility becomes the fundamental principle of absolutization and of bereavement or individuation (*Vereinzelung*) of *Dasein*.[24] Death in its unmatched imminence is thus the possibility that possibilizes all others; it constitutes what Heidegger characterizes, in an extraordinarily densified formulation, as *die eigenste, unbezügliche unüberholbare Möglichkeit*—as "*Dasein*'s ownmost possibility, non-relational . . . not to be outstripped."[25]

Thus we see how being-toward-death, to the extent that it institutes what may be called an *existential solipsism*, is present in the principle of possible differentiation between authenticity and inauthenticity, in that it radically separates the Self, ipseity, from the "They," which, precisely, multiplies on its side the subterfuges destined to hide that unmatched possibility and to insinuate a complete "indifference in the face of that extreme possibility of *Dasein*." One also understands why the concrete and complete figure of the "downfall" (*Verfallen*) is just this "flight before death." Here indifference consists in hiding from oneself "that which the certainty of death possesses specifically of its own (*das Eigentümliche*), namely that it is possible at every moment.[26] Now the *Dasein*, the moment it exists (this is the primary meaning of *exist*), is thrown into this possibility. Being-thrown (*Geworfenheit*) always reveals itself as being thrown in the direction of death, which is to say in the direction of possibility (*Geworfenheit in die Möglichkeit*). And this is also why the proper understanding of this being-thrown always implies the fundamental "affective disposition" that is anguish. Anguish that necessarily refers to anguish in the face of death, is in truth the principal auto-affection, the *Stimmung* in which the Self is constituted by the very fact that it is "claimed," "called,"[27] as an *individual* for its ownmost being-able, absolute and unsurpassable.[28]

As a principle of individuation, of absolutization, death is charged with a capital revelatory function: it opens *Dasein* to itself (*solus ipse*) as that which exists as being-thrown for and in relation to (*zu*) its end. Being-there is only *there* in order to exist as thrown into possibility, or inasmuch as it strikes out in that direction, anticipates it or goes ahead of it (*Vorlaufen*), and by so doing delivers it as such, making possibility possible. Death is not an expiration date with which *Dasein* will surely be faced one day or another, a possibility that hangs over its head and that will ultimately come true: it is not *possible* except as being itself essentially *possibilizing*, that is to say, as that instance always to come that allows *Dasein* to set out, going ahead, defining, or, better, indefining thereby the ontological possibility of its entire being-able-to-be. Such preceding (*Vorlaufen*), as preceding of possibility or in the direction of possibility, insofar as it institutes the relation to Self is also what reveals to *Dasein* its loss in the "They" and places it in the situation of being-able/having to choose: choose (or not) to choose *oneself*.

And yet—Heidegger expressly emphasizes this, returning to his methodological point of departure, at the opening of this section—"The fact that an authentic potentiality-for-Being-a-whole is ontologically possible for *Dasein* signifies nothing, as long as a corresponding ontical potentiality-for-Being has not been established evidently from *Dasein* it-self."[29] We must still show how this own potentiality-for-

Being belongs to *Dasein* as ontic possibility, phenomenally avowed. The question of being-whole proper to *Dasein* must be brought back to the *phenomenal ground* that alone may serve as a touchstone, if one wants to limit oneself to the "possible property of its being, *as it is attested by Dasein itself*."[30] To put it differently, it matters to see now "to what point *in general* and in what manner *Dasein* gives from its own potentiality-for-Being testimony to a possible authenticity (*Eigentlichkeit*) of its existence."

Here, clearly defined at the outset, are the function and import of the analysis of *Gewissen*: to show phenomenologically how, through the call of conscience, the ipseity of *Dasein* is constituted in the attesting of its authentic being-able-to-be. It is moreover the daily self-comprehension of the phenomenon that furnishes the point of departure of what has been called, since Kant[31] at least, "Stimme des Gewissens," "voice of conscience." The *Gewissen* is questioned as a *fact* that contributes to characterize facticial existence. What is remarkable in such a fact, for the question, here overriding, of the originary uni-totality of *Dasein*, given the integrality of its being-able-to-be, is that it gives us to understand or hear that it reveals, that it opens: "Analysis of conscience takes as its point of departure a character initially indifferent to this phenomenon: in one way or another, it gives something to be understood. Conscience discloses, and thus belongs within the range of those existential phenomena that constitute the *Being of the "There"* as disclosedness."[32] But the interpretation of conscience—Heidegger emphasizes this—does not simply extend the existential analytics, but aims to take hold again *more originally* of it, bringing it back to the possibility of a being-there proper. It is as a determined mode of speech—the call (*Ruf*)—that conscience opens and unveils. If the call is truly a singular determination of "discourse" or of discursiveness (*Rede*), conscience as "voice" (*Stimme*) may do perfectly well without any emission termed vocal, or any phonetic exteriorization. It calls in silence, addressing itself to a well-defined and corresponsive kind of listening. *Dasein*—Heidegger had noted while studying being-with—is always as being-there-with that understands as it listens to others. "Listening to . . . is *Dasein*'s existential way of Being-open as Being-with for others. Indeed, hearing (*das Hören*) constitutes the primary and authentic way in which *Dasein* is open for its ownmost potentiality-for-Being . . . ." And Heidegger continued in rather enigmatic fashion with this determination of comprehensive listening, radical to all psycho-physiological problematics of hearing, when he evoked listening to "the voice of the friend that every *Dasein* carries with it."[33] The possibility of listening to each other (*das Aufeinandern-hören*) indeed characterized the existential openness of *Dasein* inside of which being-with others, coexistence (*Mitdasein*) could be constituted. But, one will ask, must not the primordially opening listening cease, precisely, to be attentive to others, the moment we are concerned with the *Dasein*'s ownmost potentiality-for-

Being, that is, its potentiality-for-Being whole in the face of death as that possibility that suspends all relation to others? In fact, the *Dasein* listening to others is most often under obedience to the "They." And it is this regimen of standardized listening and/or small talk that comes precisely to disrupt the discovery of the possibility for *Dasein* to be *there* no longer, in the experience of "anticipation" and being-towards-death. The call silently sent out by conscience apprehending itself as voice, first has for effect the withdrawal of *Dasein* from listening to the "They." If it is true that anguish causes speechlessness,[34] the affect that gives its tone to the comprehensive opening of self to self, or that, more simply, accompanies the definition of the finite *and* mortal space of the Self, in turn leaves (one) speechless and even disconcerted. Here everything becomes a question of listening. It must not merely make itself sharper, but indeed change in nature. In its being-summoned *Dasein* is stricken by the call as if by a quake of great amplitude, from afar off: "The call resounds from afar towards the faraway."[35]

It is an analysis of the kind of call of conscience that must allow one to study, in its ontico-phenomenal *witnessing*, the constitution of ipseity.

Analysis of the call attempts first to gauge itself upon the general structure of discourse or of speech (*Rede*), as was established in paragraph 34. Where or from whom does the call come? What is literally called or touched by the call? *Upon what, exactly, does the call have bearing*? What is borne in such a call, what is transmitted by it? Actually, it becomes immediately apparent that none of these questions is truly pertinent, or rather that the logico-linguistics in function of which they are set out is basically inadequate and that it is therefore impossible to translate simply, in terms of call, utterances applicable to *Rede* in general. What the call touches, what it "immediately" encounters, is of course *Dasein*, but *Dasein* in the diminished sense that it always already possesses of itself in the midst of middling and daily preoccupation. The one who is called is indeed each time myself, but in the sense of a "they-self," since if it is incited to anything, it is always toward the Self, "with a view to oneself that is one's own." Conscience calls only to convoke *Dasein*, to itself, that is to say, to its ownmost potentiality-for-Being. Aside from this it says *nothing*.[36] The call (*Anruf*) towards the ownmost being-able-to-be is pro-vocation (*vor-rufen*): it projects *Dasein* towards the possibility of the self. But inasmuch as, by the calling, *Dasein* is torn from its native loss in the "They," to the extent that the call has always already gone ahead (*übergehen*) of the current and continuous (*zumeist—zunächst*) understanding of *Dasein*, starting from the world of care, the silent voice of conscience is also what makes *Dasein* essentially foreign to itself.

The foreignness corresponds to the essential indetermination of who/what calls: "The author of the call absolutely eludes all possible identification."[37] This indeter-minability, or, better, this disidentification, is a constituent feature of the call. It calls, or again, the call calls. The caller coincides with the call, as call made to—. Heidegger takes great care to disallow anything that could correspond to any transitive structure whatever of the call. The call does not seek to be listened to except as such: no transcendent sollicitation is seeking to open a path by means of it to the core of conscience. The call is not a calling of anything, and nothing is calling. Or rather something is! But the only conceivable answer is then the following: "The *Dasein* in conscience is calling itself." And this amounts to saying also that the question "Who/What calls?" merely repeats in another form the question that has, since paragraph 25, been the leading one: Who is *Dasein*? However, it is important to be particularly vigilant here: this proximity of the call and the one called—the call in the sense that *Dasein* calls itself—does not in any manner authorize the pure and simple identification of the caller with the one who is summoned. Indeed, one of the constituent features of the call being considered is precisely also that "it calls contrary to all expectation and even against our will."[38] The call is all-powerful; it allows none to elude it, even if the caller is impossible to identify by worldly criteria. If the call comes from me, it also comes as a falling upon me.[39] The voice that calls gives the figure or forewarning of the other in me; it is like "a foreign force surging up inside *Dasein*." Emphasizing the uncanny (*unheimlich*) character of what calls, Heidegger asks, "And what if *Dasein* rediscovering itself at the base of its own strangeness were the one who/which sends the call into the conscience?" The question, "Who is *Dasein*?" (asked in paragraphs 12 and 25) can now double up into the question of the essential indetermination of that which calls. The one who/which calls, determinable in its identity ("who?" "what?") by nothing that is of the order of the world, "is *Dasein* in its uncanniness, primordial, thrown Being-in-the-world as the 'not-at-home' (*das ursprüngliche geworfene In-der-Welt-sein als Un-zuhause*)—the naked 'that-it-is' thrown into the nothingness of the world."[40] The voice of conscience, even as it calls, is always "a foreign voice," be it that of the friend, if it is true that it reveals *Dasein* in its essential strangeness. And yet the voice addresses me; it so deeply concerns me that I can say, *I* am this foreign and/or friend's voice. Risen up from within and coming upon me from high above, the call is the voice of ipseity: the echo through which the Self is announced in its strangeness and its thrownness. If indeed the one who/which calls is nothing worldly, *no one/no thing*, this does not mean that, emanating from no particular individual, the call would impose itself upon all as a voice that "would place under universal obligation." Such an interpretation would rest upon a gross misapprehension: that which consists of making the call into an "injunction" from the "They." For it is of vital importance, as emphasized by Heidegger, that we not "mistake the thin partition,"[41] which completely separates the uncanny call from all the injunctions of the "They." Insofar as it always appeals to my own potentiality-for-Being, the call implies in its turn the structure of the *Jemeinigkeit. I am*—the One to whom the call is addressed. The voice of conscience addresses itself to me, it is *to me*, because it goes ahead of me in the direction of my potentiality-for-Being and comes from that being that I am each time myself.

Here let us posit, without being able to demonstrate it, that with the so-called *Kehre*, everything revolves around the voice and the listening to what is addressed to us—mankind—the "called." The lectures on Hölderlin, in the mid-1930s, as well as the *Beiträge zur Philosophie* (1937–38)—which sketch out the politically decisive determination of the "people" as "voice"—initiate a movement of thought that was to find particularly clear expression in the *Nachwort* of 1943, which was added to the inaugural lesson at Freiburg, *What is Metaphysics?* Heidegger indeed returns in them to anguish as the fundamental affective disposition, characterized from that time as "experience [*Erfahrung*] of being as of the other of all beings." Such an experience offers itself to us only if we are resolved and disposed to receive what nothingness *destines* to us (*zuschicken*), that is, if "we do not hide from the silent voice that disposes us to the fear of the abyss."[42] Essential anguish is, as in *Being and Time*, and as in the 1929 lecture, determined as *Stimmung*, "disposition," "affective tonality," related to being/nothingness; however, the disposition (*Stimmung*) must *understand* itself now as "die von jener Stimme gestimmte Stimmung": and this gives to the *Stimmung* its own determination and tone, the silent voice of being. It is part of the determination and destining of man that he should let himself be claimed by this voice. Touched by the voice of being, man can "experience the marvel of marvels: that being is." Thus exposed to the address of being, summoned to satisfy its "claim" (*Anspruch*), man is essentially *der Gerufene*: the called.[43]

The co-belonging of being and man (better, of the *Dasein* in man), first attested to in being-towards-death, the anticipation, the voice of conscience, may also be interpreted as "obedience" (*Zugehörigkeit*): situated within obedience to being, required by it, attentive to its calling, man is the one who responds to the call, who answers for it and by that fact allows being to unfold in presence. If to be (*sein*) means to enter and unfold in presence (*Anwesen*), the latter, as presence-to, presented- or addressed-to, is at base *Geheiss*, injunction, destiny.[44] To be man is now to hear the call, obey the injunction, belong to the *rufendes Geheiss*,[45] which is the condition that makes all listening possible. It is in the 1955 text *The Question of Being* that Heidegger dares to strike out—with a mark like the Cross of Saint Andrew—the name of being; this scratching out (b̶e̶i̶n̶g̶), which does not erase anything, but rather adds the sign of the fourfold (*Geviert*) to the most ancient "word" of philosophy, is also destined to draw all the consequences of the co-appurtenance "Being-Mankind." If being, thought through as *Anwesen, Geheiss, Stimme, rufendes Geheiss, . . .* , must be interpreted as "correspondence," "co-belonging" of a "call" and of a "listening" or an "obedience,"[46] then the name of being must be as resolutely abandoned as that of man. Now the name charged with saying the essence of man as *Dasein*, after being had itself been crossed out, is precisely the name inscribed on him by death: *mortal*.

The finitude that characterizes "mankind," properly speaking, in his relation to being: "man" is finite (he dies), because he has reference to being. This reference (*Bezug, Seinsbezug*), constituent of man as *Da-sein*, is first that of the "There must" (*Brauch, brauchen*),[47] which is to say the injunction as well as the call. To be *mortal* is not to have some day to cease to live, but to be claimed, to be touched by the injunction. In a passage included in the *Zollikoner Seminare*, Heidegger again emphasized in 1968 the centrality of what one may call the mortal difference: "The difference of being and of beings belongs to the reference that relates to being. But to experience this difference implies experiencing what is not beings [what is nothing of beings]. The fundamental experience of this 'not being' (*Nicht das Seiende*) is given in the stroke that relates to death (*Bezug zum Tode*), in mortality, if it is true that death is the dis-cease of beings (*Abschied vom Seiendem*)."[48]

This proximity of the difference (*Unterschied*) and of the dis-cease (*Abschied*) is only recalled here as the sign of a study still to be pursued: that of the strict articulation between the ultimate determination of language (or of the *Wesen der Sprache*) as "relation of all relations"[49]; and of death as recollection, reserve, sanctuary, holy of holies, where, sheltered and guarded, is found at the depths and as it were at the heart of *Verbergung*—occultation, concealment—the secret of deoccultation and of unsheltering: from *alèthéia* to the heart of *lèthè*.[50]

Notes

1. Cf. Heidegger, "Die Zeit des Weltbildes," in *Holzwege*, in *Gesamtausgabe* (Frankfurt: Klostermann, 1977), vol. 5, pp. 88ff and 106ff. [TN: a translation of this essay, "The Age of the World Picture," can be found in *The Question Concerning Technology and Other Essays*, trans. William Lovitt (New York: Harper and Row, Publishers, Inc., 1977), pp. 115–54]. On the debate with Descartes at the time of *Being and Time*, see J.-L. Marion, "L'*ego* et le *Dasein*: Heidegger et la destruction de Descartes dans *Sein und Zeit*," in *Revue de Métaphysique et de Morale*, no. 1 (1987).

2. On this Heideggerian determination of destruction as de-limitation, as determination of the narrowness of the phenomenal ground, see Rémi Brague, "La phénoménologie comme voie d'accès au monde grec," in *Phénoménologie et Métaphysique*, eds. J.-L. Marion and G. Planty-Bonjour (Paris: P.U.F., 1984), pp. 247–73, particularly p. 253.

3. Cf., among many others, T. Gregory, "Dio ingannatore e genio maligno: Nota in margine alle Meditationes di Descartes," *Giornale critico della Filosofia italiana*, vol. 4 (1969), and especially Anneliese Maier, "Das Problem der Evidenz in der Philosophie des 14. Jahrhunderts," in *Ausgehendes Mittelalter*, vol. 2 (Rome, 1967), pp. 367–418.

4. Cf. Heidegger, *Gesamtausgabe*, 20:435: "konstitutiv."

5. Ibid., p. 437.

6. Ibid., p. 439.

7. Ibid., p. 440.

8. *Principia philosophiae* I, 51: "Per substantiam nihil aliud intelligere possumus, quam rem quae ita existit, ut nulla alia re indigeat ad existendum"; I, 52: "Verumtamen non potest substantiam primum animadverti ex hoc solo, quod sit res existens, quia hoc solum per se nos non afficit."

9. Cf. *Gesamtausgabe*, 20:403: "Anguish is nothing other than the pure and simple experience of being, in the sense of being in the world. This experience can, but is not obliged to . . . show itself, make itself felt [*sich einstellen*] in an unparalleled way in death, or more exactly in the dying." Cf. also *Being and Time*, trans. John Macquarrie and Edward Robinson (New York: Harper and Row, 1962), §40, p. 232.

10. See *Gesamtausgabe*, 20:437: "This certainty, that it is I who is dying in my own death, is the fundamental knowledge of *Dasein* itself. It is the truth of *Dasein*, while the cogito sum is only a reflection thereof."

11. Ibid., p. 403.

12. Ibid., p. 433. Cf. also *Being and Time*, §50, pp. 293ff.

13. Cf. *Being and Time*, §2, p. 26, §56, pp. 279–80, and §49, pp. 292–93.

14. Stéphane Mallarmé, "Le Tombeau d'Edgar Poe," in *Oeuvres Complètes* (Paris: Bibliothèque de la Pléiade, 1956), p. 70: "As into Himself at last (eternity transforms him)."

15. *Being and Time*, §45, p. 276 (TN: whenever necessary, I have modified the available English translation).

16. On the predetermination of *Dasein* as life (*Leben*), cf. *Gesamtausgabe*, 60:85, part 3 of the analysis of "facticial life": "Leben = Dasein, in und durch Leben 'sein.' "

17. See *Being and Time*, §32, p. 191. [TN: Macquarrie and Robinson translate these terms as *fore-having* (*Vorhabe*), *fore-sight* (*Vorsicht*), and *fore-conception* (*Vorgriff*).]

18. *Being and Time*, §47, pp. 281–82.

19. Ibid., §47, p. 283.

20. Ibid., §47, p. 284.

21. Ibid. We can leave aside here the difficulties such an interpretation of sacrifice in its Christological application, for example, would entail.

22. Ibid., §27, p. 164.

23. *Being and Time*, §50, p. 294: "Death is a possibility-of-Being which *Dasein* itself has to take over in every case. With death, *Dasein* stands before itself in its ownmost potentiality-for-Being. . . . If *Dasein* stands before itself as this possibility, it has been *fully* assigned to its ownmost potentiality-for-Being. When it stands before itself in this way, all its relations to any other *Dasein* have been undone."

24. See *Being and Time*, §53, pp. 307–9. See also, already on the subject of anguish and its bereavement, §40, p. 232.

25. Ibid.,§52, p. 303.

26. Ibid., p. 302. Cf. also §51, pp. 298–99.

27. Ibid., §53, p. 308: "Death does not just 'belong' to one's own *Dasein* in an undifferentiated way; death *lays claim* [*beansprucht*] to it as an *individual Dasein* [*als einzelnes*]."

28. Ibid., §51, p. 298.

29. Ibid., §53, p. 311.

30. Ibid.

31. Kant, *Werke*, Akademie-Textausgabe (Berlin: de Gruyter, 1968), vol. 5, p. 98; vol. 6, pp. 186, 400–401, 438–39; vol. 10, p. 495. Fichte, *Sämmtliche Werke*, ed. J. H. Fichte (Berlin: Veit und comp., 1845–46), vol. 2, pp. 258ff., 298; vol. 4, p. 174.

32. *Being and Time*, §55, p. 315.

33. Ibid., §34, p. 206.

34. See *Was ist Metaphysik?* in *Wegmarken*, *Gesamtausgabe*, 9:112. [TN: a translation of this text can be found in *Martin Heidegger: Basic Writings*, ed. David Farrell Krell (New York: Harper and Row, 1977).]

35. *Being and Time*, §55, p. 316.

36. Ibid., §56, p. 318: " 'Nothing' gets called *to* (*zu*-gerufen) this Self, but it has been *summoned* (*aufgerufen*) to itself—that is, to its ownmost potentiality-for-Being."

37. Ibid., §57, p. 319.

38. Ibid., p. 320: "The call is precisely something which *we ourselves* have neither planned nor prepared for nor voluntarily performed, nor have we ever done so. 'It' calls, against our expectations and even against our will."

39. Ibid.: "On the other hand, the call undoubtedly does not come from someone else who is with me in the world. The call comes *from* me and yet *from beyond me and over me.*"

40. Ibid., §57, p. 321.

41. Ibid., p. 323.

42. *Wegmarken, Gesamtausgabe*, 9:306–7.

43. Ibid., p. 307: "Only men among all beings, called upon by the voice of Being, experience anything. Wonder of wonders: Beings *exist*. Whoever is, according to his essence, called into the truth of Being, is therefore always determined in an essential way."

44. Ibid., p. 408: "Anwesen ('Sein') ist als Anwesen je und je Anwesen zum Menschenwesen, insofern Anwesen Geheiß ist, das jeweils das Menschenwesen ruft. Das Menschenwesen ist als solches hörend, weil es ins rufende Geheiß, ins An-wesen gehört." In English, see *The Question of Being*, trans. William Kluback and Jean T. Wilde (New York: Twayne Publishers, 1958), p. 77: "Being present ('Being') as being present always is a being present for the essence of man, insofar as being present is a demand which at times summons the essence of man. The essence of man as such is in a state of hearing because it belongs in the summoning demand, belongs in its being present."

45. Ibid.

46. "Zusammengehören von Ruf und Gehör"—"Zugehörigkeit."

47. Cf. especially *What is Called Thinking?* trans. J. Glenn Gray (New York: Harper and Row, 1968), pp. 186ff; and *On the Way to Language*, trans. Peter D. Hertz (New York: Harper and Row, Publishers, 1971), p. 90.

48. *Zollikoner Seminare*, ed. Medard Boss (Frankfurt: Vittorio Klostermann, 1987), p. 230. Cf. also, in the commentary devoted to Trakl, the motif of the *Abgeschiedenheit*, in *On the Way to Language*, pp. 171ff.

49. *On the Way to Language*, pp. 72 and 83.

50. *Vorträge und Aufsätze*, 4th ed. (Pfüllingen: Neske, 1954), pp. 151, 177, and 256; *Der Satz vom Grunde* (Pfüllingen: Neske, 1958), pp. 186–87; *On the Way to Language*, pp. 107–8.

7

A Philosophical Concept . . .

Gilles Deleuze

A philosophical concept fulfills several functions in fields of thought that are themselves defined by internal variables. There are also external variables (states of things, moments in history), in a complex relation with the internal variables and the functions. This means that a concept does not die simply when one wants it to, but only when new functions in new fields discharge it. This is also why it is never very interesting to criticize a concept: it is better to build the new functions and discover the new fields that make it useless or inadequate.

The concept of subject does not escape these rules. It has for a long time fulfilled two functions, first, a function of universalization in a field where the universal was no longer represented by objective essentials, but by acts, noetic or linguistic. Thus, Hume marks one of the principal moments in a philosophy of the subject, because he calls upon acts that go beyond the given data (What happens when I say "always" or "necessary"?). The corresponding field, then, is not exactly the field of knowledge, but rather the field of "belief" as a new basis for knowledge. Under what conditions can a belief be considered legitimate, whenever I venture to say more than is given to me to know? Second, the subject fulfills a function of individuation in a field where the individual can no longer be a thing or a soul, but is instead a person, alive and sentient, speaking and spoken to (I–You). Are these two aspects of the subject, the universal "I" and the individual "me," necessarily linked? Even if they are, isn't there a conflict between them, and how might it be solved? All these questions actuate what has been called the philosophy of the subject, already with Hume, and also with Kant, who confronts an "I" as the determination of time and a "me" as determinable in time. Again with Husserl, similar questions will be asked in the last of the *Cartesian Meditations*.

Can we find new functions and variables able to bring about a change? Functions of singularization have invaded the field of knowledge, thanks to new variables of space–time. By singularity, we mean not only something that opposes the universal, but also some element that can be extended close to another, so as to obtain a connection; it is a singularity in the mathematical sense. Knowledge and even belief have then a tendency to be replaced by notions like "arrangement" or "contrivance" (in French, *agencement* and *dispositif*) that indicate an emission and a distribution of singularities. Such emissions, of the "cast of the dice" kind, constitute a transcendental field without subject. The *multiple* becomes a substantive—Multiplicity—and philosophy is a *theory of multiplicities* that refers to no subject as preliminary unity. What becomes important is not what is true or false, but the singular and the regular, the remarkable and the ordinary. The function of singularity replaces that of universality (in a new field in which there is no use for the universal). This can be seen even in law: the judicial notion of "case" or "jurisprudence" dismisses the universal to the benefit of emissions of singularities and functions of prolongation. A conception of law based upon jurisprudence does not need any "subject" of rights. Conversely, a philosophy without subject has a conception of law based on jurisprudence.

Correlatively, types of individuation that were not personal may have imposed themselves. We wonder about what makes the individuality of an event: *a* life, *a* season, *a* wind, *a* battle, 5 o'clock. . . . We can call ecceities or hecceities these individuations that no longer constitute persons or "egos." And the question arises: Are we not such ecceities rather than "egos"? Anglo-American philosophy and literature are particularly interesting from this point of view because they are conspicuous for their inability to find a sense to give to the word "me" other than that of a grammatical fiction. The events raise very complex questions about composition and decomposition, about speed and slowness, about latitude and longitude, about power and affect. Against all personalism, psychological or linguistic, they promote a third person, and even a "fourth person singular," the nonperson or *It* in which we recognize ourselves and our community better than in the empty exchanges between an I and a You. In short, we believe that the notion of subject has lost much of its interest on behalf of *pre-individual singularities and non-personal individuations*. But it is not enough to place concepts in opposition to one another in order to know which is best; we must confront the field of questions to which they are an answer, so as to discover by what forces the problems transform themselves and demand the constitution of new concepts. Nothing of what the great philosophers have written on the subject grows obsolete, but this is why, thanks to them, we have other problems to discover, problems that save us from a "return" that would only show our incapacity to follow them. Here, the position of philosophy is not fundamentally different from that of science or art.

8

"Eating Well," or the
Calculation of the Subject:
An Interview with Jacques Derrida

Jacques Derrida: From your question one might pick out two phrases: first, "Who comes after the subject?" the "who" perhaps already pointing toward a grammar that would no longer be subjected to the subject; and, second, "a prevalent discourse of recent date concludes with its [*the subject's*] simple liquidation."

Now should we not take an initial precaution with regard to the *doxa*, which in a certain way dictates the very formulation of the question? This precaution would not be a critique. It is no doubt necessary to refer to such a *doxa*, should it only be to analyze it and possibly disqualify it. The question "Who comes *after* the subject?" (this time I emphasize the "after") implies that for a certain philosophical opinion today, in its most visible configuration, something named "subject" can be identified, as its alleged passing might also be identified in certain identifiable thoughts or discourses. This "opinion" is confused. The confusion consists at least in a clumsy mixing up of a number of discursive strategies. If over the last twenty-five years in France the most notorious of these strategies have in fact led to a kind of discussion around "the question of the subject," none of them has sought to "liquidate" anything (I don't know moreover to what philosophical concept this word might correspond, a word that I understand more readily in other codes: finance, crime, terrorism, civil or political criminality; one only speaks of "liquidation" therefore from the position of the law, indeed, the police). The diagnostic of "liquidation" exposes in general an illusion and an offence. It accuses: they tried to "liquidate," they thought they could do it, we will not let them do it. The diagnostic implies therefore a promise: we will do justice, we will save or rehabilitate the subject. A slogan therefore: a return to the subject, the return of the subject. Furthermore, one would have to ask, to put it very briefly, if the structure of every subject is not constituted in the possibility of this kind of repetition one calls a return, and more important, if this structure is not essentially *before the law*, the relation to law and the experience, if there *is* any, of the law, but let's leave this.

Translated by Peter Connor and Avital Ronell

Let's take some examples of this confusion, and also some proper names that might serve as indices to help us along. Did Lacan "liquidate" the subject? No. The decentered "subject" of which he speaks certainly doesn't have the traits of the classical subject (thought even here, we'd have to take a closer look . . .), though it remains indispensable to the economy of the Lacanian theory. It is also a correlate of the law.

Jean-Luc Nancy: Lacan is perhaps the only one to insist on keeping the name . . .

JD: Perhaps not the only one in fact. We will speak later on about Philippe Lacoue-Labarthe, but we might note already that Althusser's theory, for example, seeks to discredit a certain authority of the subject only by acknowledging for the instance of the "subject" an irreducible place in a theory of ideology, an ideology that, *mutatis mutandis*, is just as irreducible as the transcendental illusion in the Kantian dialectic. This place is that of a subject constituted by interpellation, by its being-interpellated (again being-before-the-law, the subject as a subject subjected to the law and held responsible before it). As for Foucault's discourse, there would be different things to say according to the stages of its development. In his case, we would appear to have a history of subjectivity that, in spite of certain massive declarations about the effacement of the figure of man, certainly never consisted in "liquidating" the Subject. And in his last phase, there again, a return of mortality and a certain ethical subject. For these three discourses (Lacan, Althusser, Foucault) and for some of the thinkers they privilege (Freud, Marx, Nietzsche), the subject can be re-interpreted, restored, re-inscribed, it certainly isn't "liquidated." The question "who," notably in Nietzsche, strongly reinforces this point. This is also true of Heidegger, the principal reference or target of the *doxa* we are talking about. The ontological question that deals with the *subjectum*, in its Cartesian and post-Cartesian forms, is anything but a liquidation.

J-LN: For Heidegger, nevertheless, the epoch that comes to a close as the epoch of metaphysics, and that perhaps closes epochality as such, is the epoch of the metaphysics of subjectivity, and the end of philosophy is then the exiting of the metaphysics of subjectivity . . .

JD: But this "exiting" is not an exit, it cannot be compared to a passage beyond or a lapsing, even to a "liquidation."

J-LN: No, but I can't see in Heidegger what thread in the thematic or the problematic of the subject still remains to be drawn out, positively or affirmatively, whereas I can see it if it's a question of truth, if it's a question of manifestation, a question of the phenomenon . . .

JD: Yes. But two things: The very summary exposition that I have just ventured was a quick response, precisely, to whatever summariness there might be in this *doxa* that doesn't go to the trouble of analyzing, up close, in a differentiated manner, the differential strategies of all these treatments of the "subject." We could have chosen examples closer to us, but let's move on. The effect of the *doxa* consists in saying: all these philosophers think they have put the subject behind them . . .

J-LN: So it would now be a matter of going back to it, and that's the slogan.

JD: It's the effect of the slogan I was getting at. Second thing: what you called the "thread to be drawn" in Heidegger, perhaps follows, among other paths, that of an *analogy* (to be treated very cautiously) between the function of the *Dasein* in *Being and Time* and the function of the subject in an ontological-transcendental, indeed, ethico-juridical setting. *Dasein* cannot be reduced to a subjectivity, certainly, but the existential analytic still retains the formal traits of every transcendental analytic. *Dasein*, and what there is in it that answers to the question "Who?" comes to occupy, no doubt displacing lots of other things, the place of the "subject," the *cogito* or the classical *"Ich denke."* From these, it retains certain essential traits (freedom, resolute-decision, to take up this old translation again, a relation or presence to self, the "call" [*Ruf*] toward a moral conscience, responsibility, primordial imputability or guilt [*Schuldigsein*] etc.). And whatever the movements of Heideggerian thought "after" *Being and Time* and "after" the existential analytic, they left nothing "behind," "liquidated."

J-LN: What you are aiming at in my question then is the "coming after" as leading to something false, dangerous . . .

JD: Your question echoes, for legitimate strategic reasons, a discourse of "opinion" that, it seems to me, one must begin by critiquing or deconstructing. I wouldn't agree to enter into a discussion where it was imagined that one knew what the subject is, where it would go without saying that this "character" is the same for Marx, Nietzsche, Freud, Heidegger, Lacan, Foucault, Althusser, and others, who would somehow all be in agreement to "liquidate" it. For me, the discussion would begin to get interesting when, beyond the vested confusion of this *doxa*, one gets to a more serious, more essential question. For example, if throughout all these different strategies the "subject," without having been "liquidated," has been reinterpreted, displaced, decentered, re-inscribed, then, first: what becomes of those problematics that seemed to presuppose a classical determination of the subject (objectivity, be it scientific or other—ethical, legal, political, etc.), and second: who or what "answers" to the question "who"?

J-LN: For me, "who" designated a *place*, that place "of the subject" that appears precisely through deconstruction itself. What is the place that *Dasein*, for example, comes to occupy?

JD: To elaborate this question along topological lines ("What is the place of the subject?"), it would perhaps be necessary to give up before the impossible, that is to say, before the attempt to reconstitute or reconstruct that which has already been deconstructed (and which, moreover, has deconstructed "itself," an expression that encapsulates the whole difficulty) and ask ourselves, rather: What are we designating, in a tradition that one would have to identify in a rigorous way (let's say for the moment the one that runs from Descartes to Kant and to Husserl) under the concept of subject, in such a way that once certain predicates have been deconstructed, the unity of the concept and the name are radically affected? These predicates would be, for example, the sub-jective structure as the being-thrown—or under-lying—of the substance or of the *substratum*, of the *hypokeimenon*, with its qualities of stance or stability, of permanent presence, of sustained relation to self, everything that links the "subject" to conscience, to humanity, to history . . . and above all to the law, as subject subjected to the law, subject to the law in its very autonomy, to ethical or juridical law, to political law or power, to order (symbolic or not) . . .

J-LN: Are you proposing that the question be reformulated, keeping the name "subject," but now used in a positive sense?

JD: Not necessarily. I would keep the name provisionally as an index for the discussion, but I don't see the necessity of keeping the word "subject" at any price, especially if the context and conventions of discourse risk re-introducing precisely what is in question . . .

J-LN: I don't see how you can keep the name without enormous misunderstandings. But in lieu of the "subject," there is something like a place, a unique point of passage. It's like the writer for Blanchot: place of passage, of the emission of a voice that captures the "murmur" and detaches itself from it, but that is never an "author" in the classical sense. How might one name this place? The question "who" seems to keep something of the subject, perhaps . . .

JD: Yes.

J-LN: But the "what" is no better; what about "process," "functioning," "text" . . .

JD: In the case of the text, I wouldn't say a "what" . . .

J-LN: Can you be more precise?

JD: Yes, a little later, that can wait. I assumed, rather naively, that in our discussion here we would try to bypass the work that we have both done concerning the "subject." That of course is impossible; in fact, it's idiotic. We will refer to this later. Yes, it's idiotic. Moreover, one could put the subject in its subjectivity on stage, *submit* it to the stage as the *idiot* (the innocent, the proper, the virgin, the originary, the native, the naive, the great beginning: just as great, as erect, and as autonomous as *submissive*, etc.).

In the text or in writing, such as I have tried to analyze them at least, there is, I wouldn't say a place (and this is a whole question, this topology of a certain locatable non-place, at once necessary and undiscoverable) but an instance (without stance, a "without" without negativity) for the "who," a "who" besieged by the problematic of the trace and of *différance*, of affirmation, of the signature and of the so-called "proper" name, of the *je[c]t* (above all subject, object, project), as *destinerring* of missive. I have tried to elaborate this problematic around numerous examples.

Let's go back a little and start out again from the question "who?" (I note first of all in passing that to substitute a very indeterminate "who" for a "subject" overburdened with metaphysical determinations is perhaps not enough to bring about any decisive displacement. In the expression the *"question 'Who'?"* the emphasis might well later fall on the word "question." Not only in order to ask *who* asks the question or *on the subject of whom* the question is asked (so much does syntax decide the answer in advance), but to ask if there is a subject, no, a "who," before being able to ask questions about it. I don't yet know who can ask himself this nor how. But one can already see several possibilities opening up: the "who" might be there before, as the power to ask questions (this, in the end, is how Heidegger identifies the *Dasein* and comes to choose it as the exemplary guiding threat in the question of Being) or else it might be, and this comes down to the same thing, what is made possible by its power (by its being able to ask questions about itself (Who is who? Who is it?). But there is another possibility that interests me more at this point: it overwhelms the question itself, re-inscribes it in the experience of an "affirmation," of a "yes" or of an "en-gage" (this is the word I use in *De l'esprit* to describe *Zusage*, that acquiescing to language, to the mark, that the most primordial question implies), that "yes, yes"[1] that answers before even being able to formulate a question, that is responsible without autonomy, before and in view of all possible autonomy of the who-subject, etc. The relation to self, in this situation, can only be *différance*, that is to say alterity, or trace. Not only is the obligation not lessened in this situation, but, on the contrary, it finds in it its only possibility, which is neither subjective nor human. Which doesn't mean that it is inhuman or without subject, but that it is out of this dislocated *affirmation* (thus without "firmness" or "closedness") that something like the subject, man, or whoever it might be can take shape. I now close this long parenthesis.)

Let's go back. What are we aiming at in the deconstructions of the "subject" when we ask ourselves what, in the structure of the classical subject, continues to be required by the question "Who?"

In addition to what we have just named (the proper name in exappropriation, signature, or affirmation without closure, trace, *différance* from self, destinerrance, etc.), I would add something that remains required by both the definition of the classical subject and by these latter nonclassical motifs, namely, a certain *responsibility*. The singularity of the "who" is not the individuality of a thing that would be identical to itself, it is not an atom. It is a singularity that dislocates or divides itself in gathering itself together to answer to the other, whose call somehow precedes its own identification with itself, for to this call I can *only* answer, have already answered, even if I think I am answering "no" (I try to explain this elsewhere, notably in *Ulysse Gramophone*).

Here, no doubt, begins the link with the larger questions of ethical, juridical, and political responsibility around which the metaphysics of subjectivity is constituted. But if one is to avoid too hastily reconstituting the program of this metaphysic and suffering from its surreptitious constraints, it's best to proceed more slowly and not rush into these words . . .

J-LN: For me, the subject is above all, as in Hegel, "that which can retain in itself its own contradiction." In the deconstruction of this "property," it seems to me that the "that which," the "what" of the "itself" brings forth the place, and the question, of a "who" that would no longer be "in itself" in this way. A *who* that would no longer have *this* property, but that would nevertheless be a *who*. It is "him/her" I want to question here.

JD: Still on a preliminary level, let's not forget Nietzsche's precautions regarding what might link metaphysics and grammar. These precautions need to be duly adjusted and problematized, but they remain necessary. What we are seeking with the question "Who?" perhaps no longer stems from grammar, from a relative or interrogative pronoun that always refers back to the grammatical function of subject. How can we get away from this contract between the grammar of the subject or substantive and the ontology of substance or subject? The different singularity that I named perhaps does not even correspond to the grammatical form "who" in a sentence wherein "who" is the subject of a verb coming after the subject, etc. On the other hand, if Freudian thought has been consequential in the decentering of the subject we have been talking about so much these last years, is the "ego," in the elements of the topic or in the distribution of the positions of the unconscious, the only answer to the question "Who?"? And if so, what would be the consequences of this?

Henceforth, if we might retain the motif of "singularity" for a moment, it is neither certain nor a priori necessary that "singularity" be translated by "who," or remain the privilege of the "who." At the very moment in which they marked, let us say, their mistrust for substantialist or subjectivist metaphysics, Heidegger and Nietzsche, whatever serious differences there may be between the two, continued to endorse the question "Who?" and subtracted the "who" from the deconstruction of the subject. But we might still ask ourselves just how legitimate this is.

Conversely, and to multiply the preliminary precautions so as not to neglect the essential entanglement of this strange history, how can one forget that even in the most marked transcendential idealism, that of Husserl, even where the origin of the world is described, after the phenomenological reduction, as originary consciousness in the form of the ego, even in a phenomenology that determines the Being of beings as an object in general for a subject in general, even in this great philosophy of the transcendental subject, the interminable genetic (so called passive) analyses of the ego, of time and of the alter ego lead back to a pre-egological and pre-subjectivist zone. There is, therefore, at the heart of what passes for and presents itself as a transcendential idealism, a horizon of questioning that is no longer dictated by the egological form of subjectivity or intersubjectivity. On the French philosophical scene, the moment when a certain central hegemony of the subject was being put into question again in the 1960s was also the moment when, phenomenology still being very present, people began to become interested in those places in Husserl's discourse where the egological and more generally the subjective form of the transcendental experience appeared to be more *constituted* than *constitutive*—in sum, as much grounded as precarious. The question of time and of the other became linked to this transcendental passive genesis . . .

J-LN: Still, it was by penetrating *into* this Husserlian constitution, by "forcing" it, that you began your own work . . .

JD: It is within, one might say (but it is precisely a question of the effraction of the within) the living present, that *Urform* of the transcendental experience, that the subject conjoins with nonsubject or that the *ego* is marked, without being able to have the originary and presentative experience of it, by the non-*ego* and especially by the *alter ego*. The *alter ego* cannot present itself, cannot become an originary presence for the *ego*. There is only an analogical a-presentation [*apprésentation*] of the *alter ego*. The *alter ego* can never be given "in person," it resists in principle the principles of phenomenology—namely, the intuitive given of originary presence. This dislocation of the absolute subject from the other and from time neither comes about, nor leads *beyond* phenomenology, but, rather, if not in it, then at least on its border, on the very line of its possibility. It was in the 1950s and 1960s, at the moment when an interest in these difficulties developed in a very different way (Levinas, Tran Duc Tao, myself)[2] and following moreover other trajectories (Marx, Nietzsche, Freud, Heidegger), that the centrality of the subject began to be displaced and this discourse of "suspicion," as some were saying then, began to be elaborated in its place. But if certain premises are to be found "in" Husserl, I'm sure that one could make a similar demonstration in Descartes, Kant, and Hegel. Concerning Descartes, one could discover, following the directions of your own work,[3] similar aporia, fictions, and fabrications. Not identical ones, but similar ones. This would have at least the virtue of de-simplifying, of "de-homogenizing" the reference to something like The Subject. There has never been The Subject for anyone, that's what I wanted to begin by saying. The subject is a fable, as you have shown, but to concentrate on the elements of speech and *conventional* fiction that such a fable presupposes is not to stop taking it seriously (it is the serious itself) . . .

J-LN: Everything you have recalled here comes down to emphasizing that there is not, nor has there ever been any presence-to-self that would not call into question the *distance* from self that this presence demands. "To deconstruct," here, comes down to showing this distance at the very heart of presence, and, in so doing, prevents us from simply separating an outdated "metaphysics of the subject" from another thinking that would be, altogether, elsewhere. However, *something has happened*, there has been a *history* both of the thinking of the subject and of its deconstruction. What Heidegger determined as the "epoch" of subjectivity, has this taken place, or has the "subject" always been only a surface effect, a fallout that one cannot impute to the thinkers? But in that case, what is Heidegger talking about when he talks about subjectivity?

JD: An enormous question. I'm not sure that I can approach it head on. To the degree I can subscribe to the Heideggerian discourse on the subject, I have always been a little troubled by the Heideggerian delimitation of the epoch of subjectivity. His questions about the ontological inadequacy of the Cartesian view of subjectivity seem to me no doubt necessary but inadequate, notably in regard to what would link subjectivity to *representation*, and the subject-object couple to the presuppositions of the principle of reason in its Leibnizian formulation. I have tried to explain this elsewhere. The repudiation of Spinoza seems to me to be significant. Here is a great rationalism that does not rest on the principle of reason (inasmuch as in Leibniz this principle privileges both the final cause and representation). Spinoza's substantialist rationalism is a radical critique of both finalism and the (Cartesian) representative determination of the idea; it is not a metaphysics of the cogito or of absolute subjectivity. The import of this repudiation is all the greater and more significant in that the epoch of subjectivity determined by Heidegger is also the epoch of the rationality or the techno-scientific rationalism of modern metaphysics . . .

J-LN: But if the repudiation of Spinoza stems precisely from his having distanced himself from what was dominant elsewhere, does that not confirm this domination?

JD: It's not Spinoza's case that is most important to me. Heidegger defines a modern hegemony of the subject of representation or of the principle of reason. Now if his delimitation is effected through an unjustified repudiation, it is the interpretation of the epoch that risks becoming problematic. And so everything becomes problematic in this discourse. And I would graft on another remark at this point. We were speaking of dehiscence, of intrinsic dislocation, of *différance*, of destinerrance, etc. Some might say: but what we call "subject" is not the absolute origin, pure will, identity to self, or presence to self of consciousness but precisely this noncoincidence with self. This is a riposte to which we'll have to return. By what right do we call this "subject"? By what right, conversely, can we be forbidden from calling this "subject"? I am thinking of those today who would try to reconstruct a discourse around a subject that would not be predeconstructive, around a subject that would no longer include the figure of mastery of self, of adequation to self, center and origin of the world, etc. . . . but which would define the subject rather as the finite experience of nonidentity to self, as the underivable interpellation inasmuch as it comes from the other, from the trace of the other, with all the paradoxes or the aporia of being-before-the-law, etc. Perhaps we'll pick this up again later on. For the moment, since we're speaking of Heidegger, let me add this. I believe in the force and the necessity (and therefore in a certain irreversibility) of the act by which Heidegger *substitutes* a certain concept of *Dasein* for a concept of subject still too marked by the traits of the being as *vorhanden, and hence by an interpretation of time*, and insufficiently questioned in its ontological structure. The consequences of this displacement are immense, no doubt we have not yet measured their extent. There's no question of laying these out here in an improvised manner, but I simply wanted to note this: the time and space of this displacement opened up a gap, marked a gap, they left fragile, or recalled the essential ontological fragility of the ethical, juridical, and political foundations of democracy and of every discourse that one can oppose to national socialism in all its forms (the "worst" ones, or those that Heidegger and others might have thought of opposing). These foundations were and remain essentially sealed within a philosophy of the subject. One can quickly perceive the question, which might also be the task: can one take into account the necessity of the existential analytic and what it shatters in the subject and turn towards an ethics, a politics (are these words still appropriate?), indeed an "other" democracy (would it still be a democracy?), in any case towards another type of responsibility that safeguards against what a moment ago I very quickly called the "worst?" Don't expect from me an answer in the way of a formula. I think there are a certain number of us who are working for just this, and it can only take place by way of a long and slow trajectory. It cannot depend on a speculative decree, even less on an opinion. Perhaps not even on philosophical discursivity.

Having said this, whatever the force, the necessity, or the irreversibility of the Heideggerian gesture, the point of departure for the existential analytic remains tributary of precisely what it puts into question. Tributary in this respect—I am picking this out of the network of difficulties that I have associated with it at the beginning of *Of Spirit* (on the question of the question, technology, animality, and epochality)—which is intimately linked to the axiom of the subject: the chosen point of departure, the entity exemplary for a reading of the meaning of Being, is the entity that *we* are, we the *questioning* entities, we who, in that we are open to the question of Being and of the being of the entity we are, have this relation to self that is lacking in everything that is not *Dasein*. Even if *Dasein* is not the subject, this point of departure (which is moreover assumed by Heidegger as ontologico-phenomenological) remains analogous, in its "logic," to what he inherits in undertaking to deconstruct it. This isn't a mistake, it's no doubt an indispensable phase, but now . . .

J-LN: I'd like to point something out to you: a moment ago you were doing everything to dismiss, to disperse the idea of *a* "classic" problematic of the subject. Now you are targeting in Heidegger that which would remain tributary of the classical thinking or position of the subject. That seems a bit contradictory . . .

JD: I didn't say "there is no problematic of the subject," but rather that it cannot be reduced to a homogeneity. This does not preclude, on the contrary, seeking to define certain analogies or common sources, provided that one takes into account the differences. For example, the point of departure in a structure of *relation to self as such and of reappropriation* seems to me to be common just as much to transcendental idealism, to speculative idealism as the thinking of absolute subjectivity, as it is to the existential analytic that proposes its deconstruction. *Being and Time* always concerns those possibilities most proper to *Dasein* in its *Eigentlichkeit*, whatever the singularity may be of this "propriation" that is not, in fact, a subjectivation. Moreover, that the point of departure of the existential analytic is the *Dasein* privileges not only the rapport to self but also the power to ask questions. Now I have tried to show (*Of Spirit*, p. 129, n.5, sq) what this presupposed and what could come about, even in Heidegger, when this privilege of the question was complicated or displaced. To be brief, I would say that it is in the relation to the "yes" or to the *Zusage* presupposed in every question that one must seek a new (postdeconstructive) determination of the responsibility of the "subject." But it always seems to me to be more worthwhile, once this path has been laid down, to forget the word to some extent. Not to forget it, it is unforgettable, but to rearrange it, to subject it to the laws of a context that it no longer dominates from the center. In other words, no longer to speak about it, but to write it, to write "on" it as on the "subjectile," for example.[4]

In insisting on the *as such*, I am pointing from afar to the inevitable return of a distinction between the *human* relation to self, that is to say, that of an entity capable of conscience, of language, of a relation to death as such, etc., and a *nonhuman* relation to self, incapable of the phenomenological *as such*—and once again we are back to the question of the animal.[5] The distinction between the animal (which has no or is not a *Dasein*) and man has nowhere been more radical nor more rigorous than in Heidegger. The animal will never be either a subject or a *Dasein*. It doesn't have an unconscious either (Freud), nor a rapport to the other as other, no more than there is an animal face (Levinas). It is from the standpoint of *Dasein* that Heidegger defines the humanity of man.

Why have I rarely spoken of the "subject" or of "subjectivity," but rather, here and there, only of "an effect" of "subjectivity"? Because the discourse on the subject, even if it locates difference, inadequation, the dehiscence within auto-affection, etc., continues to link subjectivity with man. Even if it acknowledges that the "animal" is capable of auto-affection (etc.), this discourse nevertheless does not grant it subjectivity— and this concept thus remains marked by all the presuppositions that I have just recalled. Also at stake here of course is responsibility, freedom, truth, ethics, and law.

The "logic" of the trace or of *différance* determines this re-appropriation as an ex-appropriation. Re-appropriation necessarily produces the opposite of what it apparently aims for. Ex-appropriation is not what is proper to man. One can recognize its differential figures as soon as there is a relation to self in its most elementary form (but for this very reason there is no such thing as elementary).

J-LN: When you decide not to limit a potential "subjectivity" to man, why do you then limit yourself simply to the animal?

JD: Nothing should be excluded. I said "animal" for the sake of convenience and to use a reference that is as classical as it is dogmatic. The difference between "animal" and "vegetal" also remains problematic. Of course the relation to self in ex-appropriation is radically different (and that's why it requires a thinking of *différance* and not of opposition) in the case of what one calls the "nonliving," the "vegetal," the "animal," "man," or "God." The question also comes back to the difference between the living and the nonliving. I have tried to indicate the difficulty of this difference in Hegel and Husserl, as well as in Freud and Heidegger.

J-LN: For my part, in my work on freedom, I was compelled to ask myself if the Heideggerian partition between *Dasein*, on the one side, and, on the other side, *Vor-* or *Zuhandensein* would not reconstitute a kind of distinction between subject and object.

JD: The categories of *Vorhandenheit* and *Zuhandenheit* are also intended to avoid those of object (correlate of the subject) and instrument. *Dasein* is first of all thrown. What would link the analytic of *Dasein* with the heritage of the subject would perhaps be more the determination of *Dasein* as *Geworfenheit*, its primordial being-thrown, rather than the determination of a *subject* that would come to be *thrown*, but a being-thrown that would be more primordial than subjectivity and therefore [more primordial] than objectivity as well. A passivity that would be more primordial than traditional passivity and than *Gegenstand* (*Gegenwurf*, the old German word for object, keeps this reference to throwing, without stabilizing it into the stance of a *stehen*). I refer you to what I have said about the "*dé-sistance*"[6] of the subject in Philippe Lacoue-Labarthe. I am trying to think through this experience of the throwing/being-thrown of the subjectile beyond the Heideggerian protocols about which I was just speaking and to link it to another thinking of destination, of chance and of destinerrance (see again "My Chances,"[7] where I situate a (repudiated) relationship between Heidegger and a thinking of the Democritean type).

Starting at "birth," and possibly even prior to it, being-thrown reappropriates itself or rather ex-appropriates itself in forms that are not yet those of the *subject* or the *project*. The question "who" then becomes: "Who (is) thrown?" "Who becomes— 'who' from out of the destinerrance of the being-thrown?" That it is still a matter here of the trace, but also of iterability (cf. my "Limited Inc."[8]) means that this ex-appropriation cannot be absolutely stabilized in the form of the subject. The subject assumes presence, that is to say sub-stance, stasis, stance. Not to be able to stabilize itself *absolutely* would mean to be able *only* to be stabilizing itself. Ex-appropriation no longer closes itself; it never totalizes itself. One should not take these figures for metaphors (metaphoricity implies ex-appropriation), nor determine them according to the grammatical opposition of active/passive. Between the thrown and the falling (*Verfallen*) there is also a possible point of passage. Why is *Geworfen-*

heit, while never put into question, subsequently given to marginalization in Heidegger's thinking? This is what, it seems to me, we must continue to ask. And ex-appropriation does not form a boundary, if one understands by this word a closure or a negativity. It implies the irreducibility of the relation to the other. The other resists all subjectivation, even to the point of the interiorization-idealization of what one calls the work of mourning. The non-subjectivable in the experience of mourning is what I tried to describe in *Glas* and in *Memoires (for Paul de Man)*. There is, in what you describe in your recent book[9] as an experience of freedom, an opening that also resists subjectivation, that is to say, it resists the modern concept of freedom as subjective freedom.

J-LN: In what you are calling ex-appropriation, inasmuch as it does not close in on itself and *although* it does not close in on itself (let us say in and in spite of its "passivity") is there not also necessarily something on the order of *singularity*? It is in any case something on the order of the singular that I was getting at with my question *who*.

JD: Under the heading of *Jemeinigkeit*, beyond or behind the subjective "self" or person, there is for Heidegger a singularity, an irreplaceability of that which remains nonsubstitutable in the structure of *Dasein*. This amounts to an irreducible singularity or solitude in *Mitsein* (which is also a condition of *Mitsein*), but it is not that of the individual. This last concept always risks pointing towards both the ego and an organic or atomic indivisibility. The *Da* of *Dasein* singularizes itself without being reducible to any of the categories of human subjectivity (self, reasonable being, consciousness, person), precisely because it is presupposed by all of these.

J-LN: You are getting around to the question "Who comes after the subject?" reversing its form: "Who comes before the subject? . . .

JD: Yes, but "before" no longer retains any chronological, logical, nor even ontologico-transcendental meaning, if one takes into account, as I have tried to do, that which resists the traditional schema of ontologico-transcendental questions.

J-LN: But I still do not understand whether or not you leave a place for the question "Who?" Do you grant it pertinence or, on the contrary, do you not even want to pose it, do you want to bypass every question . . . ?

JD: What troubles me is what also commands my thinking here: it involves the necessity of locating, wherever one responds to the question "Who?"—not only in terms of the subject, but also in terms of *Dasein*—conceptual oppositions that have not yet been sufficiently questioned, not even by Heidegger. I referred to this a moment ago, and this is what I have been aiming at in all my analyses of Heidegger.[10] In order to recast, if not rigorously re-found a discourse on the "subject," on that which will hold the place (or replace the place) of the subject (of law, of morality, of politics—so many categories caught up in the same turbulence), one has to go through the experience of a deconstruction. This deconstruction (we should once again remind those who do not want to read) is neither negative nor nihilistic; it is not even a pious nihilism, as I have heard said. A concept (that is to say also an experience) of responsibility comes at this price. We have not finished paying for it. I am talking about a responsibility that is not deaf to the injunction of thought. As you said one day, there is a duty in deconstruction. There has to be, if there is such a thing as duty. The subject, if subject there must be, is to come *after* this.

After: not that it takes the rather improbable end of a deconstruction before we can assume responsibilities! But in order to describe the origin, the meaning, or the status of these responsibilities, the concept of subject still remains problematic. What I find disturbing is not that it is *inadequate*: it is no doubt the case that there neither can be nor should be any concept adequate to what we call responsibility. Responsibility carries within it, and must do so, an essential excessiveness. It regulates itself neither on the principle of reason nor on any sort of accountancy. To put it rather abruptly, I would say that, among other things, the subject is also a principle of calculability— for the political (and even, indeed, for the current concept of democracy, which is less clear, less homogenous, and less of a given than we believe or claim to believe, and which no doubt needs to be rethought, radicalized, and considered as a thing of the future), in the question of legal and human rights (including the rights of man, about which I would repeat what I have just said about democracy) and in morality. There has to be some calculation, and this is why I have never held against calculation that condescending reticence of "Heideggerian" haughtiness. Still calculation is calculation. And if I speak so often of the incalculable and the undecidable it's not out of a simple predilection for play nor in order to neutralize decision: on the contrary, I believe there is no responsibility, no ethico-political decision, that must not pass through the proofs of the incalculable or the undecidable. Otherwise everything would be reducible to calculation, program, causality, and, at best, "hypothetical imperative."

It is therefore a certain closing off—the saturating or suturing—of identity to self, and a structure still too narrowly fit to self-identification, that today gives the concept of subject its dogmatic effect. Something analogous perhaps occurs, it seems to me, with the concept of *Dasein*, but at a distance that must never be neglected. In spite of everything it opens up and encourages us to think, to question, and to redistribute, *Dasein* still occupies a place analogous to that of the transcendental subject. And its concept, in *Being and Time*, is determined, it seems to me, on the basis of oppositions, that remain insufficiently interrogated. Here once again we find the question of man. The possibility for the indeterminate "who" to become subject, or, more originarily, to become *Dasein* and *Dasein* thrown (*geworfene*) into the world, is reserved for man alone. This possibility, which in sum defines man for Heidegger, stands in opposition to every other form of self-relation, for example, what one calls the living in general, a very obscure notion, for the very reasons we have indicated. As long as these oppositions have not been deconstructed—and they are strong, subtle, at times mainly implicit—we will reconstitute under the name of subject, indeed under the name of *Dasein*, an *illegitimately* delimited identity, illegitimately, but often precisely under the authority of rights!—in the name of a particular kind of rights. For it is in order to put a stop to a certain kind of rights, to a certain juridico-political calculation, that this questioning has been interrupted. Deconstruction therefore calls for a different kind of rights, or, rather, lets itself be called by a more exacting articulation of rights, prescribing, in a different way, more responsibility.

It is thus not a matter of opposing another discourse on the same "things" to the enormous multiplicity of traditional discourses on man, animal, plant, or stone, but of ceaselessly analyzing the whole conceptual machinery, and its interestedness, which has allowed us to speak of the "subject" up to now. And the analysis produces always more and something other than an analysis. It transforms; it translates a transformation already in progress. Translation is transformative. This explains the nervous distrust of those who want to keep all these themes, all these "words" ("man," "subject," etc.), sheltered from all questioning, and who manipulate an ethico-political suspicion with regard to deconstruction.

If we still wish to speak of the subject—the juridical, ethical, political, psychological subject, etc.—and of what makes its semantics communicate with that of the subject of a proposition (distinct from qualities, attributes viewed as substance, phenomena, etc.) or with the theme or the thesis (the subject of a discourse or of a book), it is first of all necessary to submit to the test of questioning the essential predicates of which all subjects are the subject. While these predicates are as numerous and diverse as the type or order of subjects dictates, they are all in fact ordered around being present (*étant-present*), presence to self—which implies therefore a certain interpretation of temporality: identity to self, positionality, property, personality, ego, consciousness, will, intentionality, freedom, humanity, etc. It is necessary to question this authority of the being-present, but the question itself neither offers the first nor the last word, as I have tried to show for example in *De L'esprit*, but also everywhere I have spoken of the "Yes, yes," of the "Come" or of the affirmation that is not addressed first of all to a subject.[11] This vigil or beyond of the question is anything but precritical. Beyond even the force of critique, it situates a responsibility as irreducible to and rebellious toward the traditional category of "subject." Such a vigil leads us to recognize the processes of *différance*, trace, iterability, ex-appropriation, and so on. These are at work everywhere, which is to say, well beyond humanity. A discourse thus restructured can try to situate in another way the question of what a human subject, a morality, a politics, the rights of the human subject are, can be, and should be. Still to come, this task is indeed far ahead of us. It requires passing through the great phenomeno-ontological question of the *as such*, appearing as such, to the extent that it is held to distinguish, in the last analysis, the human subject or *Dasein* from every other form of relation to the self or to the other *as such*. The experience or the opening of the *as such* in the onto-phenomenological sense does not merely consist in that which is lacking in the stone or the animal; it equally involves that to which one *cannot and should not* submit the other in general, in other words the "who" of the other that could only appear absolutely *as such* by disappearing as other. The enormity involved in questions of the subject, as in the questions of right, ethics, and politics, always lead back to this place.

If we go back to the semantics of throwing or of the "subjectile" that has instituted the concept of subject, we should note that the *Geworfenheit* (thrownness) of *Dasein*, even before being a subjectivity, does not simply characterize a state, a fact, as in being-thrown into the world at birth. It can also describe a manner of being thrown, delivered, exposed to the call (*Ruf*). Consider the analysis of *Gewissen* and originary *Schuldigsein*. Heidegger shows in particular what is insufficient, from the anthropo-logico-ontological point of view, about both the "picture" (*Bild*) of the Kantian "court of justice" and any recourse to psychical faculties or personal actions (*Being and Time*, p. 271) in order to describe the call and "moral conscience." But the translation remains equivocal. *Gewissen* is not yet the "moral conscience" it renders possible, no more than *Schuldigsein* is a culpability: it is rather the possibility of being guilty, a liability or an imputability. I would be tempted to relate this call to what Heidegger says enigmatically and elliptically about the "voice of the friend," and particularly in terms of "hearing" this voice that every *Dasein* "carries within it" (*Being and Time*, p. 163). I treat this elsewhere.[12] But for the moment I would already say this much: the "who" of friendship, the voice of the friend so described, belongs to the existential structure of *Dasein*. This voice does not implicate just one passion or affect among others. The "who" of friendship, as the call (*Ruf*) that provokes or convokes "conscience" and therefore opens up responsibility, precedes every subjectal determination. On the indefinite openness of this question I would be tempted to read to you from your *The Inoperable Community* or from Blanchot's *The Unavowable Community*, or else these few lines from his *L'amitié*: "And when we ask the question: 'Who has been the subject of this experience?' this question is perhaps already an answer, if, for the one who introduced it, it was affirmed through him in this interrogative form, substituting for the closed and unique 'I' the openness of a 'Who?' without answer. Not that this means that he simply had to ask himself: 'What is this me that I am?' but much more radically he had to seize hold of himself and not let go, no longer as an 'I?' but as a 'Who?,' the unknown and sliding being of an indefinite 'Who?.' "[13]

The origin of the call that comes from nowhere, an origin in any case that is not yet a divine or human "subject," institutes a responsibility that is to be found at the root of all ulterior responsibilities (moral, juridical, political), and of every categorical imperative. To say of this responsibility, and even of this friendship, that it is not "human," no more than it is "divine," does not simply come down to saying that it is inhuman. This said, in this regard it is perhaps more "worthy" of humanity to maintain a certain inhumanity, which is to say the rigor of a certain inhumanity. In any case, such a law does not leave us any choice. Something of this call of the other must remain nonreappropriable, nonsubjectivable, and in a certain way nonidentifiable, a sheer supposition, so as to remain *other*, a *singular* call to response or to responsibility. This is why the determination of the singular "Who?"—or at least its determination as subject—still remains problematic. And it *should* remain so. This obligation to protect the other's otherness is not merely a theoretical imperative.

J-LN: In that respect, indeed, the determination of "who" is problematic. But in another respect, is not the interrogative "Who?"—the one I used in my question— determinative? By which I mean that it predetermines—as every question predeter- mines the order of response—a response from some*one*, from some *one*. What is predetermined—which is also to say, what is called—is a *respondent*. It seems to me that this would link up with the guiding threat of your response. But I would note that with a single gesture, or at least in this same interview, you are keeping at a distance, under suspicion, the question "Who?" while you also increasingly validate the "Who?" You validate it by suppressing that which, a priori, would limit the question to humanity.

JD: Yes, I would not want to see the "who" restricted to the grammar of what we call Western language, nor even limited by what we believe to be the very humanity of language.

J-LN: An incidental remark. In Heidegger's seminar, to which you alluded in reference to the animal, there is all the same something strange, if I remember correctly: toward the end of the analysis of the animal, Heidegger attributes to it a *sadness*, a sadness linked to its "lack of world." With this single remark, does not Heidegger contradict part of what he said before? How could sadness be nonhuman? Or rather, how would such a sadness fail to testify to a relation to a world?

JD: The Heideggerian discourse on the animal is violent and awkward, at times contradictory. Heidegger does not simply say "The animal is poor in world [*weltarm*]," for, as distinct from the stone, it has a world. He says: the animal *has* a world in the mode of a *not-having*. But this not-having does not constitute in his view an indigence, the *lack* of a world that would be human. So why this negative determination? Where does it come from? There is no category of original existence for the animal: it is evidently not *Dasein*, either as *vorhandene* or *zuhandene* (Being cannot appear, be, or be questioned as such [*als*] for the animal). Its simple existence introduces a principle of disorder or of limitation into the conceptuality of *Being and Time*. To come back to your remark, perhaps the animal is sad, perhaps it appears sad, because it indeed has a world, in the sense in which Heidegger speaks of a world as world of spirit, and because there is an openness of this world for it, but an openness without openness, a having (world) without having it. Whence the impression of sadness—for man or in relation to man, in the society of man. And of a sadness determined in its *phenomenology*, as if the animal remained a man enshrouded, suffering, deprived on account of having access neither to the world of man that he nonetheless senses, nor to truth, speech, death, or the Being of the being as such. Heidegger defends himself in vain against this anthropo-teleological interpretation, which seems to me to derive from the most acute aspect in his description of having-in-the-mode-of-not-having-a-world. Let us venture, in this logic, a few questions. For example, does the animal hear the call that originates responsibility? Does it question? Morever, can the call heard by *Dasein* come originally to or from the animal? Is there an advent of the animal? Can the voice of the friend be that of an animal? Is friendship possible for the animal or between animals? Like Aristotle, Heidegger would say: no. Do we not have a responsibility toward the living in general? The answer is still "no," and this may be because the question is formed, asked in such a way that the answer must necessarily be "no" according to the whole canonized or hegemonic discourse of Western metaphysics or religions, including the most original forms that this discourse might assume today, for example, in Heidegger or Levinas.

I am not recalling this in order to start a support group for vegetarianism, ecologism, or for the societies for the protection of animals—which is something I might also want to do, and something which would lead us to the center of the subject. I feel compelled to underscore the *sacrificial* structure of the discourses to which I am referring. I don't know if "sacrificial structure" is the most accurate expression. In any case, it is a matter of discerning a place left open, in the very structure of these discourses (which are also "cultures") for a noncriminal putting to death. Such are the executions of ingestion, incorporation, or introjection of the corpse. An operation as real as it is symbolic when the corpse is "animal" (and who can be made to believe that our cultures are carnivorous because animal proteins are irreplaceable?), a symbolic operation when the corpse is "human." But the "symbolic" is very difficult, truly impossible to delimit in this case, hence the enormity of the task, its essential excessiveness, a certain unclassifiability or the monstrosity of that *for which* we have to answer here, or *before* which (whom? what?) we have to answer.

Keeping to original, typical possibilities, let's take things from another angle: not that of Heidegger but of Levinas, for whom subjectivity, of which he speaks a great deal in a new, forceful, and unusual way, is constituted first of all as the subjectivity of the *hostage*. Rethought in this way, the hostage is the one who is delivered to the other in the sacred openness of ethics, to the origin of sacredness itself. The subject is responsible for the other before being responsible for himself as "me." This responsibility to the other, for the other, comes to him, for example (but this is not just one example among others) in the "Thou shalt not kill." Thou shalt not kill thy neighbor. Consequences follow upon one another, and must do so continuously: thou shalt not make him suffer, which is sometimes worse than death, thou shalt not do him harm, thou shalt not eat him, not even a little bit, etc. The other, the neighbor, the friend (Nietzsche tries to keep these two values separate in *Zarathustra*, but let's leave that, I'll try to come back to it elsewhere), is no doubt infinitely remote from transcendence. But the "Thou shalt not kill" is addressed to the other and presupposes him. It is destined to the very thing that it institutes, the other as man. It is by him that the subject is first of all held hostage. The "Thou shalt not kill'—with all its consequences, which are limitless—has never been understood within the Judeo-Christian tradition, nor apparently by Levinas, as a "Thou shalt not put to death the living in general." It has become meaningful in religious cultures for which carnivorous sacrifice is essential, as being-flesh. The other, such as this can be thought according to the imperative of ethical transcendence, is indeed the other man: man as other, the other as man. Humanism of the other man is a title in which Levinas suspends the hierarchy of the attribute and the subject. But the other-man is the subject.

Discourses as original as those of Heidegger and Levinas disrupt, of course, a certain traditional humanism. In spite of the differences separating them, they nonetheless remain profound humanisms *to the extent that they do not sacrifice sacrifice.* The subject (in Levinas's sense) and the *Dasein* are "men" in a world where sacrifice is possible and where it is not forbidden to make an attempt on life in general, but only on the life of a man, of other kin, on the other as *Dasein.* Heidegger does not say it this way. But what he places at the origin of moral conscience (or rather *Gewissen*) is obviously denied to the animal. *Mitsein* is not conferred, if we can say so, on the living in general, no more than is *Dasein,* but only on that being-toward-death that also makes the *Dasein* into something else, something more and better than a living [thing]. As justified as it may be from a certain point of view, Heidegger's obstinate critique of vitalism and of the philosophies of life, but also of any consideration of life in the structure of *Dasein* is not unrelated to what I am calling here a "sacrificial structure." This "sacrificial structure," it seems to me (at least for the moment, this is a hypothesis that I am trying to relate to what I call elsewhere the "phallogocentric" structure) defines the invisible contour of all these reflections, whatever the distance taken with regard to ontology in Levinas's thinking (in the name of what he calls metaphysics) or in Heidegger's with regard to onto-theological metaphysics. Going much too quickly here, I would still try to link the question of the "who" to the question of "sacrifice." The conjunction of "who" and "sacrifice" not only recalls the concept of the subject as phallogocentric structure, at least according to its dominant *schema*: one day I hope to demonstrate that this *schema* implies carnivorous virility. I would want to explain *carno-phallogocentrism,* even if this comes down to a sort of tautology or rather hetero-tautology as a priori synthesis, which you could translate as "speculative idealism," "becoming-subject of substance," "absolute knowledge" passing through the "speculative Good Friday": it suffices to take seriously the idealizing interiorization of the phallus and the necessity of its passage through the mouth, whether it's a matter of words or of things, of sentences, of daily bread or wine, of the tongue, the lips, or the breast of the other. You will possibly want to object: there are ethical, juridical, and political subjects (recognized only quite recently, as you well know), full (or almost full) citizens who are also women and/or vegetarians! But this has been admitted in principle, and in rights, only recently and precisely at the moment when the concept of subject is submitted to deconstruction.

Is this fortuitous? And that which I am calling here *schema* or image, that which links the concept to intuition, installs the virile figure at the determinative center of the subject. Authority and autonomy (for even if autonomy is subject to the law, this subjugation is freedom) are, through this schema, attributed to the man (*homo* and *vir*) rather than to the woman, and to the woman rather than to the animal. And of course to the adult rather than to the child. The virile strength of the adult male, the father, husband, or brother (the canon of friendship, I will show elsewhere, privileges the fraternal schema) belongs to the schema that dominates the concept of subject. The subject does not want just to master and possess nature actively. In our cultures, he accepts sacrifice and eats flesh. Since we haven't much time or space here, and at the risk of provoking some screaming (we pretty much know from which quarter), I would ask you: in our countries, who would stand any chance of becoming a *chef d'Etat* (a head of State), and of thereby acceding "to the head," by publicly, and therefore exemplarily, declaring him- or herself to be a vegetarian?[14] The *chef* must be an eater of flesh (with a view, moreover, to being "symbolically" eaten himself—see above). To say nothing of the celibate, of homosexuality, and even of femininity (which for the moment, and so rarely, is only admitted to the head of whatever it might be, especially the State, if it lets itself be translated into a virile and heroic schema. Contrary to what is often thought, the "feminine condition," notably from the point of view of rights, deteriorated from the fourteenth to the nineteenth century in Europe, reaching its worst moment when the Napoleonic code was inscribing the positive right of the concept of subject we are talking about).

In answering these questions, you will have not only a scheme of the *dominant*, of the common denominator of the dominant, which is still today of the order of the political, the State, right, or morality, you will have the dominant schema of subjectivity itself. It's the same. If the limit between the living and the nonliving now seems to be as unsure, at least as an oppositional limit, as that between "man" and "animal," and if, in the (symbolic or real) experience of the "eat-speak-interiorize," the ethical frontier no longer rigorously passes between the "Thou shalt not kill" (man, thy neighbour) and the "Thou shalt not put to death the living in general," but rather between several infinitely different modes of the conception-appropriation-assimilation of the other, then, as concerns the "Good" (*Bien*) of every morality, the question will come back to determining the best, most respectful, most grateful, and also most giving way of relating to the other and of relating the other to the self. For everything that happens at the edge of the orifices (of orality, but also of the ear, the eye—and all the "senses" in general) the metonymy of "eating well" (*bien manger*) would always be the rule. The question is no longer one of knowing if it is "good" to eat the other or if the other is "good" to eat, nor of knowing which other. One eats him regardless and lets oneself be eaten by him. The so called nonanthropophagic cultures practice symbolic anthropophagy and even construct their most elevated socius, indeed the sublimity of their morality, their politics, and their right, on this anthropophagy. Vegetarians, too, partake of animals, even of men. They practice a different mode of denegation. The moral question is thus not, nor has it ever been: should one eat or not eat, eat this and not that, the living or the nonliving, man or animal, but since *one must* eat in any case and since it is and tastes good to eat, and since there's no other definition of the good (*du bien*), *how* for goodness sake should one *eat well* (*bien manger*)? And what does this imply? What is eating? How is this metonymy of introjection to be regulated? And in what respect does the formulation of these questions in language give us still more food for thought? In what respect is the question, if you will, carnivorous? The infinitely metonymical question on the subject of "one must eat well" must be nourishing not only for me, for a "self," which, given its limits, would thus eat badly, it must be *shared*, as you might put it, and not only in language. "One must eat well" does not mean above all taking in and grasping in itself, but *learning* and *giving* to eat, learning-to-give-the-other-to-eat. One never eats entirely on one's own: this constitutes the rule underlying the statement, "One must eat well." It is a rule offering infinite hospitality. And in all differences, ruptures and wars (one might even say wars of religion), "eating well" is at stake. Today more than ever. One must eat well—here is a maxim whose modalities and contents need only be varied, *ad infinitum*. This evokes a law of need *or* desire (I have never believed in the radicality of this occasionally useful distinction), orexis, hunger, and thirst ("one must," "one must [eat] well"), respect for the other at the very moment when, in experience (I am speaking here of metonymical "eating" as well as the very concept of experience), one must begin to identify with the other, who is to be assimilated, interiorized, understood ideally (something one can never do absolutely without *addressing oneself to the other* and without absolutely limiting understanding itself, the identifying appropriation), speak to him in words that also pass through the mouth, the ear, and sight, and respect the law that is at once a voice and a court (it hears itself, it is *in us* who are *before it*). The sublime refinement involved in this respect for the other is also a way of "Eating well," in the sense of good eating but also doing well to eat. The Good can also be eaten. And it must be eaten well. I don't know, at this point, who is "who," no more than I know what "sacrifice" means; to determine what this last word means, I would retain this clue: need, desire, authorization, the justification of putting to death, putting to death as denegation of murder. The putting to death of the animal, says this denegation, is not a murder. I would link this denegation to the violent institution of the "who" as subject. There is no need to emphasize that this question of the subject and of the living "who" is at the heart of the most pressing concerns of modern societies, whether they are deciding birth or death, including what is presupposed in the treatment of sperm or the ovule, pregnant mothers, genetic genes, so-called bioethics or biopolitics (what should be the role of the State in determining or protecting a living subject?), the accredited criteriology for determining, indeed for "euthanastically" provoking death (how can the dominant reference to consciousness, to the will and the cortex still be justified?), organ transplant, and tissue grafting. (I might recall in passing that the question of the graft in general has always been—and thematically so from the beginning—essential to the deconstruction of phallogo-centrism).

Let's go back a little: In relation to whom, to what other, is the subject first thrown (*geworfen*) or exposed as hostage? Who is the "neighbor" dwelling in the very proximity of transcendence, in Heidegger's transcendence, or Levinas's? These two ways of thinking transcendence are as different as you wish. They are as different or as similar as being and the other, but seem to me to follow the same schema. What is still to come or what remains buried in an almost inaccessible memory is the thinking of a responsibility that does not stop at *this* determination of the neighbor, at the dominant schema of this determination. One could, if one so wished, show that the problems or the questions that I am raising here concern not only metaphysics, onto-theologies, and certain claims to go beyond them, but also the ethnology of the religious domains in which these thinkings "presented" themselves. I have tried to suggest, notably in *Of Spirit*, that in spite of many denegations, Heidegger was a Judeo-Christian thinker. (However, an ethnology or a sociology of religions would only be up to these questions if it were no longer itself dominated, as regional science, by a conceptuality inherited from these metaphysics or onto-theologies. Such an ethnology would in particular have to spend quite some time in the complex history of Hinduist culture, which perhaps represents the most subtle and decisive confirmation of this schema. Does it not, precisely, set in opposition the political hierarchy—or the exercise of power—and the religious hierarchy, the latter prohibiting, the former allowing itself, indeed imposing upon itself the eating of meat? Very summarily, one might think of the hierarchy of the *varna*, if not of the castes, and of the distinction between the Brahman priests, who became vegetarians, and the Kshatriya warriors, who are not . . .

J-LN: I must interrupt you, for in the time remaining I want to ask you some more questions. Beginning with this one: in the shift, which you judge to be necessary, from man to animal—I am expressing myself very quickly and crudely—what happens to language?

JD: The idea according to which man is the only speaking being, in its traditional form or in its Heideggerian form, seems to me at once undisplaceable and highly problematic. Of course, if one defines language in such a way that it is reserved for what we call man, what is there to say? But if one reinscribes language in a network of possibilities that do not merely encompass it but mark it irreducibly from the inside, everything changes. I am thinking in particular of the mark in general, of the trace, of iterability, of *différance*. These possibilities or necessities, without which there would be no language, *are themselves not only human*. It is not a question of covering up ruptures and heterogeneities. I would simply contest that they give rise to a single linear, indivisible, oppositional limit, to a binary opposition between the human and the infra-human. And what I am proposing here should allow us to take into account scientific knowledge about the complexity of "animal languages," genetic coding, all forms of marking within which so-called human language, as original as it might be, does not allow us to "cut" once and for all where we would in general like to cut. As you can see, in spite of appearances, I am speaking here of very "concrete" and very "current" problems: the ethics and the politics of the living. We know less than ever where to cut—either at birth or at death. And this also means that we never know, and never have known, how to *cut up* a subject. Today less than ever. If we had been given more space, I would like to have spoken here about AIDS, an event that one could call *historial* in the *epoch* of *subjectivity*, if we still gave credence to *historiality*, to *epochality*, and to *subjectivity*.

J-LN: Second question: since, in the logic you have deployed, you foresee for a long time hence the possibility of coming back to or coming at last to interrogate the subject of ethical, juridical, political responsibility, what can one say of this or these responsibilities now? Might one not speak of them under the heading of a "provisional morality"? What would this mean? And I would add to this the question of what is today perhaps recognized as "the" question, or as "the" figure of responsibility, namely, Auschwitz. There, where an almost general consensus recognizes an absolute responsibility and calls for a responsibility so that it might not be repeated, would you say the same thing—provisionally or not—or would you say that one must defer the answer to this question?

JD: I cannot subscribe to the expression "provisional morality." At the very least, an exacting responsibility requires not trusting blindly the axioms of which we have just spoken. These limit still more the concept of responsibility within frontiers that the axioms refuse to answer for, and they constitute, in the form of provisional schemas, the very models of traditional morality and right. But for this surplus of responsibility that summons the deconstructive gesture or that the deconstructive gesture of which I am speaking calls forth, a waiting period is neither possible nor legitimate. The deconstructive explication with provisional prescriptions might ask for the indefatigable patience of the recommencement, but the affirmation that motivates the deconstruction is unconditional, imperative, and immediate—in a sense that is not necessarily or only Kantian, even if this affirmation, because it is double, as I have tried to show, is ceaselessly threatened. This is why it leaves no respite, no rest. It can always upset, at least, the instituted rhythm of every pause (and the subject is a pause, a stance, the stabilizing arrest, the thesis, or rather the hypothesis we will always need), it can always trouble our Saturdays and Sundays . . . and our Fridays. . . . I'll let you complete this monotheistic sentence, it's a bit wearying.

J-LN: Would you think, then, that Heidegger's silence concerning the camps—this almost total silence, as distinct from his relative silence about his own Nazism—would you think that this silence might have come from such a "deconstructive explication," at once different but comparable, that he might have been trying to carry out in silence, without managing to explain himself on it? (I could ask this question about others, about Bataille, for example, but let's stick to Heidegger for today.)

JD: Yes and no. The surplus of responsibility of which I was just speaking will never authorize any silence. I repeat: responsibility is excessive or it is not a responsibility. A limited, measured, calculable, rationally distributed responsibility is already the becoming-right of morality; it is at times also, in the best hypothesis, the dream of every good conscience, in the worst hypothesis, of the small or grand inquisitors. I suppose, I hope you are not expecting me simply to say "I condemn Auschwitz" or "I condemn every silence on Auschwitz." As regards this last phrase or its equivalents, I find a bit indecent, indeed, obscene, the mechanical nature of improvised trials instigated against all those whom one thinks one can accuse of not having named or thought "Auschwitz." A compulsion toward sententious discourse, strategic exploitation, the eloquence of denunciation: all this would be less grievous if one began by stating, rigorously, what we call "Auschwitz" and what we *think* about it, if we think something. What is the referent here? Are we making a metonymical usage of this proper name? If we are, what governs this usage? Why this name rather than that of another camp, of other mass exterminations, etc. (and who has answered these questions seriously)? If not, why this forgetful and just as grievous restriction? If we admit—and this concession seems to me to be readable everywhere—that the thing remains unthinkable, that we still have no discourse equal to it, if we recognize that we have nothing to say about the real victims of Auschwitz, the same ones we nonetheless authorize ourselves to treat by metonymy or to name *via negativa*, then let's stop diagnosing the alleged silences, forcing avowals of the "resistances" or the "unthought" in everyone indiscriminately. Of course, silence on Auschwitz will never be justifiable; nor is speaking about it in such an instrumental fashion and in order to say nothing, to say nothing about it that does not go without saying, trivially, serving primarily to give oneself a good conscience, so as not to be the last to accuse, to teach lessons, to take positions, or to grandstand. As for what you call Heidegger's "infamous silence," I think that in order to interpret or to judge it—which is not always the same thing—it would be necessary *at least* to take into account, and this is not easy to circumscribe and would require more space and time, what we have said here about the subject, about man, about the animal, but also about sacrifice, which means also about so many other things. A necessary condition, which would already call for lengthy discourse. As for going beyond this necessary but insufficient condition, I would prefer that we wait for, let us say, another *moment*, the occasion of another discussion: another rhythm and another form.

Notes

1. CF. *Spurs: Nietzsche's Styles*, trans. B. Harlow (Chicago: University of Chicago Press, 1979); "Préjuges" in *La faculté de juger* (Paris Minuit, 1984); *Ulysse Gramophone* (Paris, Galilée, 1987);

Of spirit: Heidegger and the Question, trans. G. Bennington and R. Bowlby (Chicago, 1989). On the "yes, yes," cf. note 11 here.

2. Cf. for example *La voix et le phénomène* (Paris, PUF, 1967), p. 94, n. 1—*Speech, and Phenomena*, trans. David B. Allison, (Northwestern University Press, 1973), p. 84, n. 1. This note develops the implications of Husserl's sentence: "We can only say that this flux is something which we name in conformity with what is constituted, but is nothing temporally 'objective.' It is absolute subjectivity and has the absolute properties of something to be denoted metaphorically as 'flux,' as a point of actuality, primal source-point, that from which springs the 'now,' and so on. In the lived experience of actuality, we have the primal source-point and a continuity of moments of reverberation [*Nachhall-momenten*]. For all this, names are lacking." The note ends with: "There is no constituting subjectivity. The very concept of constitution must be deconstructed."

3. Cf. *Ego Sum* (Paris, Flammarion, 1975).

4. Cf. "Forcener le subjectile" in *Antonin Artaud: Portraits et Dessins* (Paris, Gallimard, 1986).

5. Cf. *Of Spirit*, pp. 27–75, sq. and *Psyché*, p. 415 sq.

6. Cf. *"Desistance"*, preface to the American translation of Philippe Lacoue-Labarthe's *Typography*, ed. C. Fynsk (Harvard University Press, 1989).

7. Cf. "My Chances" in *Taking Chances*, trans. A. Ronell and I. Harvey (Johns Hopkins University Press, 1984).

8. Cf. *Limited Inc.*, trans. Samuel Weber (Northwestern University Press, 1988).

9. *L'expérience de la liberté* (Paris, Galilée, 1988).

10. Cf. also, for example, *The Truth in Painting*, trans. G. Bennington (The University of Chicago Press, 1987), p. 286: "Unless Heidegger ignores (excludes? forecloses? denies? leaves implicit? unthought?) an *other* problematic of the subject, for example in a displacement or development of the value "fetish." Unless, therefore, this question of the *subjectum* is displaced *otherwise*, outside the problematic of truth and speech which governs *The Origin*."

11. On the question, cf. *Of Spirit: Heidegger and the Question*, passim; on the "yes, yes," cf. "Otobiographies," trans. A. Ronell in *The Ear of the Other*, ed. C. McDonald (Lincoln: University of Nebraska Press, 1989), and "A Number of Yes," trans. B. Holmes in *Qui Parle*, vol. 2, no. 2 (Berkeley, 1988), pp. 120–33; on "viens," cf. "Psyché: Inventions de l'autre" in the volume of the same name (Paris: Galilée, 1989), pp. 11–62, and *Parages* (Paris: Galilée, 1988).

12. Cf. "The Politics of Friendship," trans. G. Motzkin in *The Journal of Philosophy* (1988) pp. 632–44.

13. M. Blanchot, *L'amitié* (Paris: Gallimard, 1971), p. 328. Cf. also Jean-Luc Nancy, *The Inoperative Community*, trans. P. Connor (Minneapolis: University of Minnesota Press, forthcoming), and M. Blanchot, *The Unavowable Community*, trans. P. Joris (New York: Station Hill Press, 1988).

14. Hitler himself did not offer his vegetarian practices as an example. This fascinating exception, moreover, can be integrated into the hypothesis I am evoking here. A certain reactive and compulsive vegetarianism is always inscribed, in the name of denegration, inversion or repression, in the history of cannibalism. What is the limit between coprophagy and Hitler's notorious coprophilia? (See Helm Stierlin, *Adolf Hitler, psychologie de groupe familial* [Paris: PUF, 1975], p. 41). I refer the reader to René Major's valuable contribution (*De l'élection* [Paris: Aubier, 1986], p. 166, n. 1). JD.

9

Apropos of the "Critique of the Subject" and of the Critique of this Critique

Vincent Descombes

Until recently, French philosophy had given the impression of having invested the best part of its energy in the enterprise of the "critique of the subject." It was necessary to put an end to what we call the "philosophy of the subject" or the "metaphysics of subjectivity." This conviction was shared by the two rival schools: authors of "structuralist" inspiration (known in the United States under the label of "post-structuralism") and authors of Heideggerian inspiration. Lately, several philosophers have recommended a return to one or another version of the philosophy of the subject (a return, of course, illuminated and informed by the results of the critique). Some return to phenomenology. Others to Kant and to Fichte.[1]

I

I should begin by confessing a first embarrassment. I find it difficult to get used to this locution, so frequent in contemporary French authors, of the "critique of the subject" or the "death of the subject." I find it no less difficult to get used to the closely related locution of a critique or destruction "of subjectivity." What is, then, a critique of the subject? When we speak of the "critique of power," we well understand by this a critique of persons in power, a critique of the way in which power is exercised, or else again a more general denunciation of the wrongs we are subjected to, perhaps because of an ineradicable power. Similarly, the "critique of money" is, it seems, the critique of the exaggerated or pernicious role that money plays within our lives. In the same way, the critique of the subject ought to be the critique of persons who take themselves for subjects. And the critique of subjectivity ought to be the critique of those persons who give proof of subjectivity. However, if we consider the developments presented under the heading of a *Critique of the Subject*, we find not so much a censure of persons as the denunciation of an illusion. What we call the critique of the subject is in fact the critique of the *concept* of

Translated by Eduardo Cadava

subject (or of the *concept* of subjectivity). This critique bears upon the content of the concept, upon its possible applications, upon its validity. According the this critique, it is an illusion—an illusion ascribable to a "metaphysics of subjectivity"—to believe that a lover is the subject of his desires, that a thinker is the subject of his thoughts, that a writer is the subject of his writing, that an agent is the subject of his action, and so on.

There is a strange hesitation here between two kinds of critique. On the one hand, we reproach the spirit of our times as much as the "metaphysics of subjectivity" for strongly encouraging persons to think of themselves as subjects. Each person would be more or less under the injunction of having to say to himself: I am the subject of my thoughts, of my desires, of my actions, etc. But we could never reproach persons for succumbing to this appeal if they were not able, with some success, to figure themselves as "subjects." On the other hand, we claim that the concept of subject is chimerical: it is an illusion to believe in the thinking subject, in the desiring subject, in the writing subject, in the militant subject, etc.

Upon reflection, the hesitation that marks the summary phrase *critique of the subject* is instructive. It would be mere intellectual confusion to found in a single critical discourse the critique of morals and the critique of the concept if this concept was not destined to play a role in our lives. In other words, this "philosophy of the subject" implies both a theoretical element and a practical element. As *theory of the subject*, it assigns to the concept of the subject a fundamental role in the explanation of a host of other concepts. (What other concepts? "Structuralists," on account of their interests, think more of the concepts used in the human sciences. "Heideggerians," more versed in metaphysics, claim that it is instead a question of all our concepts, those of the sciences, natural as well as historical, those of modern technology, those of our politics, of our urbanism, of our aesthetics, etc.) As *ethics of the subject*, the "philosophy of the subject" assigns to the concept of the subject the function of rendering possible an ethical and political thinking. We cannot pose ethical questions (*What is good or bad? Is it honorable or shameful?* etc.) if we cannot be guided by the ideal of free subjectivity. *To be* a subject is here understood as the very definition of the moral ideal. To work to *become* always more (of) a subject, such is here the principal of a moral life.

If we leave it at this, the quarrel that opposes critics of the subject and defenders of the same seems to have the following content. For the critics, the philosophy of the subject is invalid in terms of its theoretical aspect, therefore vain or even disastrous in terms of its practical aspect. On the side of *theory:* it is not true that man is a subject (or, to speak the essentialist idiom of philosophers: *that man is subject*) and it is not true that he can ever become one. On the side of *practice*, the ideal of subjectivity, being profoundly false, is at best useless and at worst harmful. As for the defenders of the subject, they seem to assert the "primacy of practical interest" in philosophy. For them, the "philosophy of the subject" cannot be totally invalid in its theoretical aspect since it is valid in its practical aspect. If we no longer had the possibility or the right to consider ourselves, even if only partially, as subjects, we could no longer pose ethical questions. We could no longer differentiate between an oppressive political regime and a regime of liberty: if we were not at least a little right in believing ourselves to be subjects, the only thing we could see would be a different distribution of existing forces. We could no longer differentiate between a tyrant and a man who resists this tyrant: these are only different "points of view." The concept of subject should therefore be maintained and its justification found in its (surely unrealizable) function as regulating ideal.[2]

Such is therefore the *Querelle* of the subject in French philosophy today. It is a typically philosophical quarrel, that one can compare to the ancient controversy over skepticism. The skeptical philosopher denies the existence of an external world, but the *man* who finds himself protected by his corporeal envelope, *this* skeptical philosopher holds the greatest regard for the external world in his practical decisions: in order to leave, he passes through the door; on the way, he stays on the road, keeps from falling in the well, etc. (cf. Aristotle, *Metaphysics*, IV, 4, 1008b). Similarly, the philosopher critical of subjectivity thinks that man is not a subject. He can then be reproached for this: the man with whom this philosopher coincides still continues to make arguments, objections, value judgments, as if he were a subject.

Throughout this quarrel, we note this: The *critics of the critique of the subject* comprehend, it seems, the arguments and distinctions presented in the critique of the subject. As for the *critics of the subject*, they comprehend, according to all appearances, the accounts of the philosophy of the subject. But what can be said of that *philosophy of the subject*? Are we so sure that we understand it? It is nevertheless what ought to define the property of "being a subject." What do we affirm when we say that the writer, for example, *is the subject* of his writing? What do we deny when we say that he *is not?* Thus, the analysis of the predicate *being a subject* governs the entire discussion.

II

I should now take into account a *second* embarrassment. In the remarks that are exchanged during the quarrel of the subject, no clear distinction is drawn between the ordinary use of the word *subject* and the properly philosophical use of this same word. We might even sometimes wonder, in reading some author, if he thinks that the distinction is too well known to be gone over again, or else if he sees no real difference between the nonmetaphysical subject of which we have the occasion to speak in grammar, in logic, in psychology, etc., and the metaphysical subject of metaphysicians (examples of which would be the Cartesian *ego*, the Kantian transcendental self-consciousness, the Heideggerian *Dasein*, Sartrean nothingness, etc.). This remark leads me to defend the following two theses:

(a) *Apropos of the critique of the theory of the subject:* if it is a question of the subject of the philosophers, we can say that the critique of this concept has not yet really begun. It remains as yet entirely undone, at least in philosophy of the French language. (It is true, as I will maintain later on, that it has been done, and with the greatest success, *elsewhere*.)

(b)   *Apropos of the ethics of the subject*: if we deprive ourselves of the philosophical concept of subject, the philosophy of ethical and political questions, far from becoming impossible, is thereby facilitated. In fact, morals and politics have nothing to do with the subject of philosophers (a subject that they distinguish from the particular and "strictly empirical" person of someone). They have to do with particular persons insofar as these persons are subjects of action. And here the word *subject* does not have the especially philosophical sense used a moment ago, but an ordinary sense. *Practical philosophy does not require a thinking of the (philosophical) subject, but a thinking of the suppositum.*

My entire argument presupposes, then, that there is an important difference between what we ordinarily understand by the word *subject* and the meaning that this word has finally taken in philosophy. This difference is of course completely misunderstood if we content ourselves with a few philological observations on the history of the word *subject* and on its ancestors (*subjectum, hypokeimenon*). Historical philology can indeed show that the word was used by philosophers, then became diffused, via the teachings of grammarians, into everyday usage. But what interests us is rather the logic of the concept of subject, a logic that cannot be drawn from etymological or historical considerations.

The ordinary notion of the subject comprises part of the elements of grammar that are instilled in us in elementary school. In the sentence *Romeo loves Juliet*, we have the verb *to love*. In grammar class, we learn to ask: Who loves Juliet? Who is loved by Romeo? The subject of the verb is the proper name *Romeo*, the object of the verb is the proper name *Juliet*. By extension, we can easily say that Romeo is the subject of the love of Juliet (and we speak here of the person named *Romeo*, as well as of a certain love, the love of Juliet, the words *of Juliet* constituting an "objective genitive"). We can also say that Juliet is the object of the love of Romeo (the words *of Romeo* offer a case of "subjective genitive"). As long as we hold onto this notion of subject, we never have occasion to ask ourselves if the lover is or is not the subject of his amorous desire. There is no reason to pose the question. For by saying that Romeo is the subject of a love for Juliet, we do not attribute to him a new property of subjectivity. We are content with emphasizing that, in the sentence with which we are concerned, the love of Juliet is attributed to Romeo. Thus, the question of modern philosophers—is the lover the subject of his love?— has no meaning, no possibility of being asked, unless we decide to introduce a new concept of subject. This new concept is what I call here the properly philosophical concept (since it can only result from a philosophical reasoning). If we make use of the philosophical concept, the question of the subject (*Who?*) takes on a different meaning: it becomes conceivable that Romeo, for example, is amorous without his being the subject of his love. We come, then, to a definition of the "philosophy of the subject": it is the exposition of an argument destined to sustain, in some cases, the distinction between the *person* (understood here not in an especially Kantian or "personalist" sense, but in the sense of a human being, therefore of a body living a human life) and the *subject*.

In order to explain this point, it is perhaps best to return to the argument of the *cogito* in Descartes. When Descartes set out in search of an absolutely certain truth, he comes to a stop with: *Ego sum, ego existo*. This existence is certain, but of what is it the existence? The following question therefore bears upon the *ego ille*, upon the *self*. This is the case in speaking of a question of the subject. Who is it, that of whom it is true that he thinks and he exists? One point at least appears clear, whatever reading we might give to the second *Meditation:* The Cartesian argument requires that we do not understand the pronoun *I* (in the cases when it is used by Descartes) and the name *Descartes* as mutually substitutable terms. For us, the word *Descartes* is the name of a particular person, born into a family from Poitiers, in 1596, in La Haye, etc. This name, like all human names, refers to an individual identifiable by his body. On the contrary, within the Cartesian argument, the word *I* of the *I think* ought to refer to a subject of thinking and only to a subject of thinking. We should in no way say: Descartes is certain that Descartes thinks, but Descartes is not certain that Descartes exists, nor that Descartes is Descartes. We must say instead: Descartes is certain of a truth that he expresses to himself by saying "I am, I exist," but Descartes is not certain that there is, beyond that, a person named Descartes. Thus, the philosophy of the subject, in Descartes, uses the method of *skeptical doubt* in order to establish a difference between the person (or the man) and the subject. Descartes then determines this subject as *res cogitans* or soul. Other doctrines employ other methods and end at the same time with other determinations of the subject. We will cite three of these. The method of *presupposition* poses a subject distinct from any empirical given as the condition of all the conditions of possibility of experience and science. The method of *phenomenological experience* does not want the subject to be posed: it should be experienced, presented to itself in an experience. It is therefore a question in this method of describing certain special experiences in the course of which the subject who is living the experience—that which appropriates this experience to itself—has the impression of being unable to recognize itself in any of the traits that characterize its person (its ties and links, its roles and its obligations, its biography, etc.). We must finally mention the method used by the recent critics of the "critique of the subject": the method of *postulation*. Here, the notion of a subject distinct from the person is no longer a metaphysical concept (permitting the description of a being inaccessible to naturalist observation), nor a phenomenological concept (permitting the description of lived experience, our impression of something). This notion is now an *idea*, in the sense of a guiding or regulating idea. We must postulate that each of us is not only a person (this living body), but also a subject, failing which we can no longer maintain our conviction that there is a difference between liberty and servitude (and that it is shameful not to want liberty rather than servitude).

The Cartesian *ego* is the first in a long series of philosophical subjects. It is still today the paradigmatic case in this series. What should a critique of the philosophical subject entail? One might think that it would bring about a counterargument, so as to be able to deny that it would be possible to differentiate between the person of Descartes and the thinking subject of the *ego cogito*. But we are surprised to discover that the critics of the subject agree, on one point at least, with the defenders of the subject. The philosophy of the subject, through one or another of the methods advocated in the various schools, wishes to establish that Descartes is justified in saying "I am not Descartes" (in a sense such that this declaration is neither a lie, nor a symptom of amnesia or mental confusion). That is, in the third person: Descartes is justified in saying that Descartes is not the subject to which we should attribute the thoughts that we attribute, in our prephilosophical manner of speaking, to Descartes (and without this coming down to accusing Descartes of plagiarism). But this is precisely what also bears out the critics of the subject: Descartes is not the subject of his thoughts. We must not say: *Descartes thinks*. We must say: *it thinks in Descartes*. We must not say: *Descartes writes his books*. We must say: *the books of Descartes write themselves under the pen of Descartes*. And so on. Contrary to what we might expect, the thinking that passes itself off as a critique of the philosophy of the subject has not at all sought to restore the identity of Descartes's person and of the subject to whom we should attribute Descartes's thoughts. Quite the contrary. It has sought to accentuate this difference. The critique of the subject was not the critique of the philosophical subject, but rather a protest against the tendency to confuse subjectivity (defined by methods of doubt, of presupposition, of experience or postulation) with a person's mental life. The critique of the subject has nothing to reproach the philosophy of the subject for, unless it is that the difference between the subject in the ordinary sense and the subject in the philosophical sense has not been traced in a radical enough way. The *ego* in Descartes designates a *res cogitans*. But this thinking thing resembles too much a human person. Under the name of subject, the "philosophies of consciousness" of the Cartesian tradition persist in seeking a *being* (whose ontological traits are those of the body), a being endowed with a temporal *continuity* (comparable to the physical continuity of a material thing), with an *identity* (analogous to personal identity). The critics of the Cartesian subject want the difference to be more vigorously marked. Generally, the critique of the philosophy of the subject had remained the critique of timidity in the thinking of the subject. The subject resembles too closely that from which we wish to distinguish it. The Cartesian mind is still too corporeal. The transcendental self is still too close to the empirical self. The absolute as subject is too easily taken for an absolute of the substantial type. *Dasein* always risks being confused with a being whose mode of presence would be that of things.

In short, whether one supports a doctrine of the subject or whether one attacks it, one thing remains indisputable: When the thought *Ego sum, ego existo* is expressed, it is not in any case Descartes who thinks this thought. The classical philosophers of the subject, taking the word *subject* in a sense where it only applies to *that which thinks* in Descartes, say that it is spirit, or consciousness, that acts as the thinking subject in Descartes. As for the critics of the philosophical subject, they find that the word *subject* is dangerous: this word, because of its familiar nonphilosophical use, appears to authorize the transfer of certain attributes of the person to *that which thinks* in the person. But the true subject should be opposed to the human subject. Or else, then, through a reversal of vocabulary that changes nothing in the conceptual situation, if we cannot keep from giving human traits to what we call *subject*, we must now say that Descartes, since he is a human subject, is not *that which thinks* in Descartes. Whether we speak of "true subject" or of "nonsubject" is a difference in terminology but not in thinking. Descartes is a man: the true thinking subject (or *that*—the "nonsubject"—which thinks) must therefore be inhuman. Descartes is a person: the true subject will be impersonal. Descartes, like all persons, is identifiable thanks to the individuality of the body that constitutes him: the true subject escapes identification. Descartes has a history, a face, can be described: the true subject is ineffable. And so on.

This is why there is no paradox in saying that the critique of the philosophical subject has still never occurred in French philosophy. It has occurred, it is true, elsewhere. But it is remarkable that French philosophers, whether they have been influenced by linguistics or by the reading of Heidegger, have never manifested much interest in the most profound critique of Cartesian thought that has ever been offered. I wish to speak, of course, of the critique that we find in Wittgenstein and his students.[3]

III

Here as elsewhere, the method followed is that of "philosophical grammar": it teaches us to pass "from a latent non-sense to a manifest non-sense" (*Philosophical Investigations*, §464). In the case that interests us here, the latent non-sense is rendered manifest by a remark upon the meaning of the question *Who?*, or the question of the subject. The philosophical notion of a subject distinct from the person is reached by using the question *Who?* in a way that no longer responds to the ordinary conditions in which we posit this question. When we pose the question outside of philosophical reasoning, we know what we are asking because we know what kind of response we can expect. Who wrote the *Metaphysical Meditations?* The answer is René Descartes. There is nothing wrong in extending the use of the word *subject* from grammatical analysis (where the subject is a "part of speech," for example, a proper name) to logical analysis (where the subject will be that which receives the predicate, consequently an individual and no longer a word in the sentence). In doing so, we did not leave ordinary usage behind. And if we were to say here that Descartes did not write the *Meditations* (or that Descartes was not the subject of the process of the writing of the *Meditations*), we would mean quite simply that they were written by someone else, by another person. We pass from the ordinary subject to the philosophical subject when we no longer expect a proper name (designating a person) in answer to the question concerning the subject. The conditions of meaning for the question in its familiar use are no longer met. The ground upon which we understand what we are speaking of when we speak in the ordinary sense has been closed to us. But, strangely, no other ground has been opened for us. The new conditions of meaning for the question of the subject have not been specified. This is perhaps why we tend to return surreptitiously to the familiar ground of persons in order to give a meaning to our question *Who thinks?*. The critique of the subject deplores this, judging it to be a relapse into a mode of "substantialist," "dogmatic," "materialist," "ontic" thinking. On this point we must grant its lucidity: it is true that the philosophical subject, as soon as it is given a definite face, dangerously resembles the familiar nonphilosophical subject. This family likeness betrays an illicit generation. The philosophical subject, in the thoughts of the subject, is only the nonsubject (the person) disguised as a pure thinking subject. That is to say, in the inversed idiom of the critiques of the subject: there where we seek to find something other than the familiar human subject (the person), we find this human subject, disguised as impersonal and anonymous power, but no longer masked by personal traits.

One could raise the following objection to what I have said. Does not the method of doubt in fact succeed in proving that it is possible to decide that one is a thinking subject without having to decide as well that one is a human person? The difference between the two is conceivable, and this is all that a philosophy of the subject requires. This objection has no validity. It would first have to pose the minimal question of the subject concerning the phrase "I think." In the Latin text of the *Meditations*, Descartes accentuates this presence of the subject by prefixing the pronoun: *"Ego sum, ego existo."* What is the function of the pronoun here? Does the pronoun, in these phrases, introduce a reference to a subject of whom all we know for certain at this point is that it is thinking? Not at all! The question of the subject is not posed here because there is no point in asking *of whom* a certain predicate is affirmed. This question of the subject finds its meaning in the predicate form of the declarative proposition, a form by virtue of which the proposition is true if the name that is figured there refers to the individual of whom the predicate is true, false in the contrary case when the name does not refer to the individual of whom the predicate is true. The pronoun *I* can of course have this referential function in the case of the dialogue. It is then used in conditions wherein it contrasts with other pronouns (*Who thinks that? It is I, and not you, nor him*, etc.) But when Descartes, in his soliloquy, declares "I think" or else "I am," the predicative proposition that he expresses does not bear upon a referent that would be Descartes himself. The word *I*, pronounced by Descartes in his soliloquy, does not function to help Descartes to know of whom the predicates *think, am, exist* are true. The word *I* does not have here, in effect, any referential function. The celebrated propositions *Cogito* and *Ego sum,* looking at them more closely, are not predicative propositions. They cannot be translated into the third person. These propositions express "thoughts without a subject,"[4] not of course in the sense of thoughts that would be nobody's thoughts, but in the sense in which these thoughts (whose proper mode is the soliloquy) include nothing that permits the question of the subject to be posed.

We have seen how the Quarrel of the subject has turned around the possibility of finding an acceptable meaning for the proposition: *I am not René Descartes.* This proposition has a meaning, but a trivial meaning, if it implies: *I am another person than Descartes.* (It is moreover true if it is uttered by someone other than Descartes.) Does it still have a meaning when it says: *I am another, the thinking subject named "I" is other than the person called Descartes?* One does not see how it would have a meaning in this second interpretation. In fact, to those who would claim this, we would have the right to ask: another *what?* Not another *person* (since we would then come back to the trivial meaning). Nor another *subject,* since René Descartes is not exactly a subject in the new sense that had to be introduced here. What's left perhaps: another *being,* another *thing.* This last answer is precisely the Cartesian solution. But it envelops a non-sense. It is incontestable that Descartes is (among other aspects of his person) a *res extensa.* We can say in fact which *res extensa* is Descartes (or at least, is the living person of Descartes, his contemporaries could say). But we cannot say which *res cogitans* is the subject of the thought. We cannot distinguish one thinking thing from another thinking thing. We do not know, in the case where two persons share the same opinion, whether one or two thinking subjects are involved. We have no idea of what constitutes the identity of a thinking thing. But the question *Who?* loses all meaning when points of reference are so lacking. We know how to distinguish an ordinary subject from an other ordinary subject. The philosophers of the subject act as if we know, in the same way, how to distinguish a philosophical subject (as a thinking thing) from all the rest, from everything that is not this philosophical subject. We have here the essence of the chronic crises that agitate the philosophy of the subject. If there is an answer to the question of the subject of thinking, it is that we have assigned to this subject an inadequate status: we have assimilated it to an individual susceptible of being designated, identified, distinguished, etc. But if we do not assign this inadequate status to the subject of thinking, the very question of the subject of thinking can no longer be posed. There is no conceivable response to the question, for we do not really know what we are asking. The philosophical subject discovered in the *cogito* is a pseudo-subject because the question of the subject, posed in terms of the *cogito,* is a psuedo-question.

IV

If I have mentioned this argument that one can draw from Wittgenstein against every philosophy of the subject, it is in order better to bring out what a true critique of the (concept of) philosophical subject would have been. In reality, the entire Quarrel of the subject has taken place, in France, inside of the philosophy of the subject. It is, finally, a scholastic quarrel. In appearance, the "critics of the subject" are opposed to the use of this concept whenever we speak of human affairs, whereas the "defenders of the subject" wish to restore this concept to a central role. In fact, the quarrel concerns something entirely different. Nobody asks: Is there a subject (*ego* or *id*) distinct from the person by virtue of the subject to whom we attribute human operations? Nobody asks this because this point is already accepted by everyone. But the Quarrel concerns the point of knowing whether it is appropriate to humanize or dehumanize this philosophical subject. The "critics of the subject" are instead then critics of the *human subject*. They in no way refuse to differentiate between the human person (the "physical" or "empirical" entity, that which we can name, locate, etc.) and the true subject of human operations (such as thinking, willing, desiring, etc.). What they refuse is the possibility that the human being can identify himself as the source of operations that he believes, insofar as he is naive (or mystified by the ideologies of subjectivity), to be his.

Between the "critics of the subject" and its "defenders," there is therefore only an age difference from the point of view of the evolution of the doctrine of the subject. The defenders wish to return to the good old days of the middle period, whereas the critics belong to the last period of the doctrine. We can in fact distinguish three periods of the philosophy of the subject.

(I)   First version ("dogmatic"): There is a difference between *the human being* and *the subject*, and each of us can say *"ego cogito*, I think." In other words, it is *I* who think: I am, when I think, not a human being, but a thinking subject.

(II) Middle version ("critical"): There is a difference between *the human being* and *the subject*, whence results a division of that which says *I* between the human being ("empirical consciousness," natural self) and the subject ("transcendental consciousness," self as subject of the act whereby it freely determines itself). In other words, it is *I* that thinks: however, what I am when I think is in no way a given, in no way immediately understandable, except in terms of a pure act of thinking that I have yet to produce. A tension appears between the individual who finds himself there, produced by his race, and the true subject who must construct himself.

(III) Last version ("paradoxical"): There is a difference between *the human being* and *the subject*, and this is why I am not the true subject of my thoughts, nor of my desires. In other words, it is not *I* who thinks or who desires: the true source of these operations does not resemble a human person. However, all that we invoke as a subject to whom we attribute a thought or a desire ends up resembling a person. In order to avoid having the subject be taken for a double of the person, the word *subject* will now be abandoned. According to this critique of the humanism of the subject, the error of earlier versions of the doctrine was to conceive the philosophical subject upon the model of the system of personal pronouns (*I, you, him, her*). In order to conceive of the philosophical subject in a nonanthropomorphic fashion, we must instead think according to impersonal uses of the third person. We should say, no longer "I think," but "it thinks in me," "it thinks," "there is thinking," "thinking happens to us," etc.

V

The preceding will allow me to briefly mention another point in the Quarrel of the subject, namely, the question of knowing whether an ethical and political thinking is possible without recourse to a (concept of) subject.

If the concept of a philosophical subject is a pseudo-concept, all is said. A pseudo-concept can certainly not guide us in our reflection upon practical questions. A non-sense cannot miraculously be changed into a regulating idea under the pretext that we are passing from the terrain of logic (namely, the logic of the argument of the *cogito*) to a different terrain, that of practical urgencies.

Unless the concept of philosophical subject is not purely and simply empty of meaning. Unless it is instead a concept *still* empty of meaning insofar as we have not proceeded to the true terrain of its use, the terrain of reflection upon practical questions. If this was it, the Quarrel of the subject would not be the scholastic quarrel I have already signaled above. It would be a true question for all of philosophy. We would be unable to avoid an engagement with an argument of pure philosophical grammar.

But this is exactly what we seem to be told by the authors who use, in order to rehabilitate the concept of the subject, the argument of *postulation*. This concept of the subject, they say, is the *sine qua non* condition of all practical philosophy. To eliminate this concept would amount to saying that there is no way to pose the question of the subject in its properly philosophical sense. In practical terms, the question of the subject in the ordinary sense is, for example: Who has done this? To whom do we attribute this work or this incident? The question of the subject in its specifically philosophical sense will be therefore: Is that which is the subject of this action in the ordinary (or, if you will, "empirical") sense equally the subject in the philosophical sense? Is it *truly* this person that we must hold responsible for the works of which he is, in the ordinary sense, the author?

Here, the "critique of the subject" appears in fact paradoxical, since it ends by saying that we shouldn't really attribute to someone his acts and gestures, unless by way of a kind of conventional fiction. But if we can never point to a human subject when it is a matter of answering the question *Who?*, it is, philosophically speaking, no longer possible to take practical questions seriously. The philosophical subject in its paradoxical version, if it is consistent, will stop short of developing a reflection upon the practical. Here it is important to emphasize the difference that separates the abovementioned philosophical argument from a purely rhetorical argument that would say that the "critics of the subject" promote immoral ideas or risk corrupting the young. The argument that I wish to examine is philosophical: it does not aim in fact at preventing the examination of a particular *logos* by reason of its consequences, even if they are repugnant or unpleasant; on the contrary, it aims at bringing to light the until now unperceived consequences of the *logos* in question. It is a question, then, of better understanding this *logos* (through an examination of its consequences), in such a way as to then be able to return to the reasons that we have for taking the aforesaid *logos* as an acceptable proposition.

Here we should make a distinction between the subject of action (the suppositum) and the Cartesian-Kantian-Fichtean subject of the philosophy of the subject in its first two versions. It is clear that the philosophy of action is not possible if it is at bottom inadmissible to attribute actions to persons. Now the "critique of the subject" gives various philosophical reasons that tend to withdraw our right to seriously attribute an action to someone. According to this critique, actions are never *attributed*, in the manner of an ontological attribution, to persons. They are in fact *assigned*, in the manner of a purely "performative" attribution, to people who will henceforth be *held responsible*, with all the legal and social consequences that this implies, for what is done. Of course, such a doctrine cannot present a philosophy of action, only a critique of the vulgar view of action.

However, is the *subject of action* that a philosophy of action needs really the autonomous subject of the philosophy of the subject? It is here that we need a terminological difference, otherwise the in many ways revolutionary thesis of the philosophy of the subject will turn into a trivial tautology. It is convenient to borrow from the old scholastic vocabulary the term *suppositum* in order to designate a subject of action. According to the old adage, which Leibniz repeats, *actiones sunt suppositorum*.[5] In other words, the attribution of a predicate of action makes no sense in a proposition unless its logical subject is a being that belongs to the category of suppositum. This is what Wittgenstein would call a grammatical remark. It is a matter of adjusting each of two grammatical categories (or sets of mutually substitutable terms in a proposition without the logical form of the proposition being affected): on the one hand, the category of verbs that signify an action, on the other, the category of designations for individuals susceptible of being considered, in an intelligible fashion, as subjects of action.

I cannot develop here a theory of suppositums. It is important, however, to sketch out the kind of problems that such a theory would allow us to consider.[6] Let us begin with the case of an action verb requiring the possibility of an ordinary complement: for example, *to write a word with a quill pen*. The philosophical problem of the suppositum, or subject, of this action will be here that of knowing what kinds of things can be named so as to form an intelligible phrase. What can write a phrase with a quill pen? We can imagine, as acceptable answers: a human person (for example, *Napoleon*) or a personal organ corresponding to the means of the action (for example, *Napoleon's hand*). Now let us consider the same action, but under a different description, which could be, for example: *to sign a peace treaty with Austria*. This time, an acceptable suppositum for such an action is Napoleon, whereas the relation between Napoleon's hand and the action of signing the treaty is no longer as clear. Let us move finally to a third description of the same action, namely: *to reconcile with Austria*. For this description, Napoleon's hand is no longer a conceivable suppositum, whereas other entities now appear in the field of acceptable responses, for example: *the French Empire*.

The philosophy of the subject, in its usual "humanist" version, declares that the only conceivable suppositum of a "properly human" action is the being that identifies itself, not with the empirical person that it also is, but with the autonomous subject. Not the individual, taken up as he is in the tissue of the world, but a being capable of positing itself as *ideally* (or ultimately) different from everything that history has made, from everything that society has conditioned, from everything that institutions have fixed, from all the futures that past events have already marked or cleared the way for. But also the being that has decided to conduct itself in such a way that it can think of itself, at the end of an infinite effort, as the author of all its worldly determinations.

In light of the distinction between a suppositum and a subject of the Cartesian or post-Kantian type, the practical doctrine of the philosophy of the subject appears incoherent. For we know at least this: the subject of a *worldly action* should be a *worldly suppositum*. It cannot be a transcendent *ego*. If certain actions performed in the world should be recognized as "properly human" actions, that is to say, as actions that are open to examination and rational critique, it is necessary that these actions, freely performed in this world, be attributed to suppositums of this world. Now the transcendent subject assumed by doctrines of "self-positing" appears capable of accomplishing, at most, one act and only one: that of mystical contemplation (or "intellectual intuition"). This act does not require any worldliness on the part of the suppositum. On the contrary, only a worldly suppositum can have a *grasp* on things, so as to modify the source of things in a way that will appear, upon a rational examination, reasonable, inept, or mad.

The doctrine of the philosophical subject as the true suppositum of human action therefore falls into "idealism," in the sense that it forgets the idealization that enters into its definition of an autonomous subject.

In order that political questions can be posed so as to constitute the object of a rational (and finally philosophical) examination, it is not enough that we recognize the existence of free human subjects to whom we can attribute actions. It is still necessary that we recognize the existence of *political actions*. For as long as political actions are not performed, the question *Who?* cannot be posed. But in what case can we consider human actions as political actions? It is necessary that they be taken into consideration by a collective process of *deliberation* upon decisions to be taken, upon compromises to be considered, upon an order of priority to be established among possible projects *from the point of view of a given group* that has, under one form or another, an organ of deliberation. Now there has never been a philosophy of the subject that has been able to produce this group, this "global society" of sociologists. This is not because it hasn't been tried. However, the efforts to derive the group in terms of the subject, whether by virtue of the result arising from the encounter between free wills, or by virtue of a condition presupposed by the self's affirmation of a consciousness, have never ended in anything but ideal cities. (It would be appropriate here to examine what has in fact been proposed for *philosophies of nationality*.)

We can make analogous remarks concerning ethical questions. What is required for the positing of moral questions is not only the existence of subjects disposed to assuming their responsibilities. What is required is also the existence of *responsibilities to assume*. Now the philosophy of the subject is incapable of deriving these responsibilities solely from the position of a pure moral conscience, or from a "categorical" form of ethical exigency. For what is at stake is the assumption of responsibilities that consist in certain functions, or "offices," which fall upon such and such a person in the world because of the state of the world and of the order of things. But the philosophy of the subject, by positing that the suppositum of a free action must necessarily be the autonomous subject of a pure will, has begun by excluding from ethical reflection all consideration of the order of the world, all observation of ends proper to the worldly (or "empirical") suppositum of these human actions.

The quarrel of the subject is therefore, when all is said and done, a scholastic quarrel.

Notes

1. See the work of Luc Ferry and Alain Renaut in *La pensée 68, essai sur l'anti-humanisme contemporain* (Paris: Gallimard, 1985).

2. Ferry and Renaut write, for example: "It in no way goes without saying that, in order to prove that man is not really (*here and now*) autonomous (that he opens onto his other), it is necessary to take away from the idea or the ideal, in short, from the Idea itself of autonomy all meaning and all function." Or again: "The entire contribution of the *Critique of Judgment* lies in its trying to show that, if the metaphysics of absolute mastery is devoid of all meaning whenever we attribute to it the status of a truth, it can still, as a regulating principle of reflection, constitute a *horizon of meaning* for human practice, as much in the scientific order as in the ethico-political order" (*La pensée 68*. pp. 266 and 281).

3. See Ludwig Wittgenstein, *Philosophical Investigations*, trans. G.E.M. Anscombe (Oxford: Blackwell, 1968), §§410–11; Peter Geach, *Mental Acts* (London: Routledge & Kegan, 1957), chapter 26: "The Fallacy of 'COGITO ERGO SUM' "; Elizabeth Anscombe, "The First Person" (1975), reprinted in *Collected Philosophical Papers* (Minneapolis: University of Minnesota Press, 1981), vol. 2, pp. 21–36. In French, the best account of this argumentation remains the work of Jacques Bouveresse, *Le mythe de l'intériorité; Expérience, signification et langage privé chez Wittgenstein* (Paris: Editions de Minuit, 1976). See also: Ernst Tugendhat, *Selbstbewusstsein und Selbstbestimmung* (Frankfurt: Suhrkamp Verlag, 1979).

4. See E. Anscombe, "The First Person," p. 36.

5. See *Discourse on Metaphysics*, trans. Peter G. Lucas (Manchester: Manchester University Press, 1961), §5

6. I am indebted here to Elizabeth Anscombe's article "On Brute Facts" (1958), in *Collected Philosophical Papers*, 3:22–25. The object of this article is, moreover, not the nature of the subject of action (or of the *suppositum*, a term that, to my knowledge, Anscombe never uses), but the validity of the passage from a factual statement to a normative one (from "is" to "ought").

10

Being and the Living
Didier Franck

Who are we? What essence do we bear, and whence is this essence determined? Do we still have an essence, or have we become the provisional figure for the decaying of essence? Are we as much as ever, or almost as much, as we say, the rational animal? But are animality or rationality, body, soul, or mind, adequate to our being? In other words, has not the metaphysical interpretation of man as a rational animal reached its limit in that absolutization of human subjectivity that demarcates the end of philosophy by opening onto the truth of Being? Is it not through a constraint on Being itself that our essence is originally constituted? And how might we arrive at this Being, how might we properly be that which we have to be without destroying the history of that long error about ourselves—the history of ontology?

But to destroy is not merely to return to the things themselves, it is also to take account of a tradition by starting out from what made the tradition possible. It is thus just as necessary to define the essence of man as *Dasein*, while ceasing to understand it against the horizon of subjectivity, as it is to endorse, albeit in a restricted way, the concept of the rational animal. Since man's rationality is the distinctive mark of his animality, the specific trait of his life, we cannot take the name of *Dasein* and assume the tasks that this name imposes upon us without first examining if and how our life, life as it manifests itself in us, can acquire an existential meaning.

Let us return to the context in which this problem first emerges. Having established that a fundamental ontology must follow the path of an analytic of *Dasein*, and having sketched out its guiding lines and set in place its cardinal concepts, Heidegger secures the originality of such an analytic with regard to all those disciplines with which it might be confused. In Section 10 of *Being and Time*, in order to distinguish his phenomenology of existence from a philosophy of life or a general biology that would include the fields of anthropology and psychology, he

---

Translated by Peter T. Connor

affirms that "life, in its own right, is a kind of Being; but essentially it is accessible only in *Dasein*. The ontology of life is accomplished by way of a privative interpretation; it determines what must be the case if there can be anything like mere-aliveness [*Nur-noch-leben*]. Life is not a mere Being-present-at-hand [*Vorhandensein*], nor is it *Dasein*."[1] This thesis is taken up again in Section 41, which Heidegger devotes to the determination of the Being of *Dasein*, and where he shows that care cannot be brought back to elementary drives that, on the contrary, are ontologically rooted in it. He goes on to point out that "this does not prevent willing and wishing from being ontologically constitutive even for entities that merely 'live'," and that "the basic ontological state of 'living' is a problem in its own right and can be tackled only reductively and privatively in terms of the ontology of *Dasein*."[2] The same stance reappears finally in Section 49, which aims at rejecting any medical characterization of death. If Heidegger acknowledges that "death, in the widest sense, is a phenomenon of life" and that "life must be understood as a kind of Being to which there belongs a Being-in-the-world," it is only to add right away that "we can fix its character ontologically only if this kind of Being is oriented in a privative way to *Dasein*," whereas biology and physiology can always treat *Dasein* as a theme by considering it as pure life on the same basis as animals and plants. While admitting that *Dasein* is also a living being since life is accessible in it, and conceding that *Dasein* can have a physiological death "co-determined by its primordial mode of Being,"[3] Heidegger nonetheless argues for the priority of the existential concept of death over any science or ontology of life.

These brief references dealing with the Being of life raise a number of difficulties. These concern *Dasein* itself and, beyond this, fundamental ontology in its entirety. Certainly, *Dasein* does not begin as a living being to which existence is subsequently added on, but rather, in the manner of everything that lives, it is born, reproduces, and dies.[4] How then can death, as the phenomenon of a life that does not exist, be co-determined by the primordial mode of *Dasein:* ecstatic temporal existence? And conversely, in what way can death, as the supreme possibility of existence, be co-determined by a life whose mode of Being is different? In short, is the life in *Dasein*, the life of *Dasein*, compatible with its existence? How can something ontologically foreign to *Dasein* be ostensible, thanks to *Dasein*, and in *Dasein*? How can existence be reduced to life? What significance can be granted to the phenomenological method, according to which access to a being is governed by its Being, if in order to grasp living and "life" one must proceed privatively, starting with a being that is ontologically other? Supposing this privative channel to be practicable, what pre-understanding of life would guide its trajectory? Wherein would this pre-understanding find its legitimacy and pertinence if understanding is precisely a structure of *Dasein*, an *existential*? More generally, against what horizon of meaning of Being and of negation can it be said that "life is not Being-present-at-hand nor *Dasein*" if universal phenomenological ontology is shared between these two modes of Being that have their possibility in two temporalities, one of which is derived from the other, and if the meaning of negation depends on the meaning of Being?

Are life and living phenomena forever at a remove from the clearing of Being, refractory to all ontology, "phenomena" that time cannot constitute, that have no temporal meaning, absolutely incomprehensible? As disconcerting as this question might be, it has been if not exactly asked then at least formulated by Heidegger himself when, having described the temporality of feeling and disposition, he ends Section 68b of *Being and Time* with this strange reservation: "It remains a problem in itself to define ontologically the way in which the senses can be *stimulated* or *touched* in something that merely has life, and how and whether the Being of animals, for instance, is constituted by some kind of 'time.' "[5]

But can the temporal constitution of life and the living be considered a separate, that is to say, in the end, a secondary problem? From the moment Being is understood in terms of time, does not the ontological analysis of animality assume on the contrary a decisive role? Is it not liable to disconnect Being from time, opening up once again the issue of the determination of the essence of man as *Dasein*, and shattering the very ground of fundamental ontology? Indeed, if the being of an animal were to be excluded from time, Being itself would thereby lose the exclusivity of its temporal meaning, and, if we live only by being incarnate in a body that testifies to our kinship with the animal,[6] the ontological detemporalization of the animal would imply that the living incarnate that we are is existentially inconceivable, and that we must abandon the name of *Dasein*.

The interpretation of animality and of life is in part the topic of a course given in the winter semester of 1929–30, entitled *The Fundamental Concepts of Metaphysics (Die Grundbegriffe der Metaphysik)* and dealing with the concept of world. Having described in *Being and Time* the worldly character of the being with which we daily enter into relation, and having retraced, in *The Essence of Reason (Vom Wesen des Grundes)*, the history of the word "world" along with the various meanings that have been attributed to it, Heidegger takes the path of a "comparative consideration," whose guiding thread is furnished by the following three theses: "The stone is without world, the animal is poor in world, man is formative of world." If each of these theses determines the essence of the stone, the animal, and man, it is not a matter, regarding the second thesis, of understanding animality from the standpoint of the world and its impoverishment, but of understanding poverty-in-world from the standpoint of animality. And to conceive the essence of animality, says Heidegger, is "to conceive the essence of life in general."[7]

The phenomenology of the living must first of all make sure of its theme by answering the question of knowing whether or not we can have access to the animal. For this possibility to be offered to us, it is necessary that the animal itself relate to something other than itself. Now whereas the stone does not enter into any relation with the Earth that supports it, whereas the stone is without world, the animal that stalks its prey or builds its nest is essentially open to its surroundings. The animal itself, therefore, points to a possible sphere of access. But an animal is not *Dasein*, and is thus not primordially constituted by being-with, and we cannot both share the same rapport to being. If world is the condition for any rapport to being, the animal has a world because being is open to it, but it has no world because this opening is foreclosed. To have and not to have a world is to be poor-in-world in the sense of a privation, for only a being capable of having a world can be deprived of one.

What is this poverty-in-world that characterizes animality, and how can one define it positively if not by carrying out an ontological analysis of life oriented around the animal? And where might this hermeneutic begin if not with the fundamental proposition of zoology, according to which everything that lives is an organism? What then is an organism? It is that which has organs. What does "organ" mean? The term comes from the Greek ὄργανον: tool. An organism then, following Wilhelm Roux's formula, is a complex of tools. But conceived in this way, is not the organism similar to a machine, and are the organs nothing but tools? Notwithstanding that a machine is not purely and simply an arrangement of tools, if the eye serves to see and the hammer to hammer, this similarity should not be allowed to cover up more definitive differences. Whereas several people can use the same hammer, a living being sees only with its own eyes. "The organ is therefore a tool built into the user."[8] Such a definition supposes, however, that the organ is still understood as a tool, i.e., misunderstood. Where then is the essence of the organ to be sought? Generally speaking, that which can be used for something opens up a possibility for something else. To do so, that which is useful must, as such, be in possession of a possibility that constitutes its Being. In other words, to establish the difference between an organ and a tool, or more generally between an organ and an item of equipment, the difference must be defined right down to what it is they are capable of doing, to the mode of being and the ontological distinction of their possibility.

A hammer is used to hammer, and the making of it is complete when it can fulfil this function, when it is end-ready. Being ready for something (*Fertigkeit für etwas*) defines the constitutive possibility of the item of equipment as such. The hammer, however, will never be capable of hammering in the way the eye is capable of seeing. Being capable of something (*Fähigkeit zu etwas*) defines the constitutive possibility of the organ as such, that is, in its appurtenance to the organism. It is therefore the organism that possesses the capacity of seeing to which the ocular organ then belongs, and hence it is the capacity that is endowed with an organ, and not the organ that is endowed with a capacity.

What is the link between the capabilities of an organism and the organs assigned to them? Which organ might bring out this link most concretely? Heidegger chooses to describe not the complex organism of a higher animal but that of a lower, protoplasmic, single-cell animal that, since it seems to have no organs, is likely to reveal to us the essence of this link more clearly. Protoplasmic animalcules have no fixed form and have to create for themselves the necessary organs, which they afterward destroy. "Their organs are instantaneous organs (*Augenblicksorgane*)."[9] In infusoria, for example, the prehensile organs and the organs for movement remain in place when those used for nutrition come into effect. "Around each mouthful, observes J. V. Uexhüll, "there forms a pocket which becomes at first a mouth, then a stomach, then the intestines and finally an anus."[10] The nutritional capacity is thus prior to the nutritional organs, whose appearance and disappearance it moreover regulates.

At this stage in the analysis Heidegger raises an objection and points out a problem. If one acknowledges that an organism produces its organs, is one not surreptitiously admitting that these are its equipment? Certainly, in the case of the infusoria, the very instantaneity of the organ precludes making it into an item of equipment; but one cannot distinguish between an organ and an item of equipment on the basis of their duration since a number of animals have permanent organs. Heidegger then adds: "It is also clear that *the organ and the item of equipment differ precisely and fundamentally in their relationship to time,* and this marks an essential difference between their modes of being."[11] This brief allusion indicates that the organ and the item of equipment must each have their mode of temporalization through which, in accordance with the main principle of fundamental ontology, their respective modes of being can take on meaning. Conversely, it is only when their appropriate temporalities have been exposed that it will be possible and legitimate to distinguish the Being of an organ from that of an item of equipment, the organism from the world, life from existence or from Being-present-at-hand. Thus it is solely the determination of the rapport of the organism and the organs to time that will in the end decide the ontological meaning of life.

We shall leave open the question of the temporal constitution of the living to take up the elucidation of the link between the organ and the organism, and to tackle the objection mentioned above. If the item of equipment is end-ready, if it is a finished product, the organ, subject to vital processes, knows nothing of this finishedness. This means that the organ remains assigned to the organism as capacity. The following fact is proof of this: in order to move, pseudopodes produce something that they then reabsorb by amalgamating it into the remaining protoplasm. But when this protoplasmic prolongation comes into contact with another microorganism, this latter will not absorb it. The organ is thus held in place by the very capacity that alone can annihilate it. The organ is retained in the service of the capacity, it is in its service. But how can the capacity make possible such a subservience if not by itself having primordially the property of service? The eye serves to see and could not do so were the capacity of seeing not itself in the service of the organism. It is not the eye that sees but the organism, and, in giving rise to the organ, the capacity gives itself over to itself, practices, advances toward that of which it is properly capable.

Can we, still in contrast to the utility of the item of equipment, illuminate this subservience of the organ and the capacity which founds it? Equipment is usable according to its "directions for use," a prescription that is not given with or by its Being-end-ready-for . . . since it springs from that which has presided over its fabrication. "By contrast, *that which is capable* is not subordinated to any prescription but *brings its own rule with it* and *rules* itself. It *propels itself* in a specific way

in its *being capable of.* . . . This self-propelling and this being-propelled toward
that of which it is capable [*sein Wozu*] is only possible, for that which is capable,
if being-capable is in general a drive-activity [*triebhaft*]. There is capacity only
where there is drive."[12] It is therefore because the capacity of the organ—the mode
of constitutive possibility of its Being—is impulsive that the organ is ontologically
distinct from the item of equipment. There is nothing impulsive in the readiness to
hammer of a hammer; everything is impulsive in the being-capable-of seeing of an
eye.

If with the drive (*Trieb*) we have arrived at the essence of capacity, which is to
say the essence of the organ in its appurtenance to the organism, it should now be
possible to gain access to the Being of the organism itself. Being-capable-of . . .
is to be self-driven toward that of which the capacity is capable: toward itself.
Capacity therefore implies a relationship to self that one finds in the concepts of
self-regulation and self-preservation by which the organism is customarily defined.
How is this "self" that is implied in the capacity to be thought? In function of the
capacity alone, and without having recourse to an entelechy or any sort of vital
force. To say that the capacity drives itself toward that of which it is capable is not
to say that it turns away from itself to expend or lose itself in something else: on
the contrary, in this drive-movement, the capacity itself never stops appropriating
itself (*sich zu eigen*), never ceases to be in the process of its own appropriation of
itself. The fundamental trait of capacity is property (*Eigentümlichkeit*), which here
obviously has no significant or categorical attribute, but which denotes a mode of
being as irreducible to existence as it is to Being-present-at-hand, that division that
runs through and sustains all of fundamental ontology. The drive's self-appropriation
takes place without reflection, and this is why Heidegger refuses to speak of an
ipseity of the capacity or the organism. "We reserve," he writes, "the expressions
'self' and 'selfhood' to characterize *the specifically human property, its* being-in-
appropriation-of-itself, and for this reason we say: everything which has the nature
of a self, of a being which, in a general sense, has the character of a person
(everything which is personal) is property, but not all property has the nature of a
self or of an I."[13]

We are still far from having arrived at a sufficient concept for the organism, for
we have left aside that of which the capacity is capable, that "for which" or in view
of which (*wozu*) there is capacity. Capacity is, for example, capable of seeing. But
what is vision here? The worm sees the mole; this means: it flees before the mole,
it behaves in a certain way toward the mole. Being-capable-of . . . is thus capable
of a behavior (*Benehmen*). To ascertain the behavior we must proceed from what
we have already learned, namely the instinctual property of the capacity and of the
organism. By propelling itself toward that of which it is capable, the capacity doesn't
dwindle away in self-expropriation. There is consequently in this appropriation
something held back that cannot fail to affect the behavior. In behaving amidst that

which surrounds it an animal does not expulse itself outside of itself; on the contrary, it withdraws into itself, absorbed in and by its drive. "Behaviour as a general mode of being is only possible on the basis of *the being absorbed* [*Eingenommenheit*] in itself of the animal. We characterize *the being-alongside-itself specific to the animal*—which has nothing to do with an ipseity of man behaving as a person—we characterize this being-absorbed in itself of the animal which makes any behaviour possible, as *captivation* (*obnubilation: Benommenheit*)."[14] In the same way that being-in-the-world is fundamentally constitutive for *Dasein*, captivation is the essential structure of animality and must be explicated in terms of the animal's behavior, its drive-capacity.

How does this captivation manifest itself in behavior? Following Heidegger, let us borrow an observation from entomology. A bee is set in front of a bowl with enough honey so that it cannot take it all in at one sitting. It begins to eat and then, a moment later, stops and flies away, leaving the remainder. What has happened? The bee has noticed that there was too much honey, that it could not suck it all up and it has therefore terminated its drive activity. This explanation is unacceptable. In effect, the following experiment has been carried out: if, while the bee is sucking in the honey, its stomach is carefully cut open, the bee continues to suck in while the honey runs off behind it. This proves that the bee had not noticed the abundance of honey—nor moreover the disappearance of its abdomen—and that it continues to persist in its drive. Absorbed in and by this, it does not have the opportunity to en-counter the honey in order to ascertain its presence. Why then does the bee stop taking in the honey when it is not deprived of its abdomen and remains organically whole? Because it is satisfied, and the satiation inhibits the drive. But the fact that the satiation is necessarily linked to the food in no way implies that it is connected to the bee's having noticed the abundance of food. Strictly speaking, the drive is not directed toward an object, it has no object; it is a behavior relating to something that is never perceived as such. In our example the drive is captivated by the honey, and, when it becomes inhibited, the bee flies off to the hive.

This new behavior is just as captivated as the first. How does the bee find its way back? Thanks to experiments conducted by Bethe, Radl, in his *Investigations into the Phototropism of Animals* of 1905, is able to offer an explanation. A hive is set up in a meadow. The bees become used to it. The hive is then moved back several meters. Now, when returning to the hive, the bees first head for the spot that now stands empty, and only return to their colony after having looked all around. Why? What draws them in that direction if neither the scent around the hive nor even the landmarks on the ground can direct them on their way since the bees' territory ranges over several kilometers? How does the bee return to its dwelling? It takes its cue from the sun. When it flies away, the bee has the sun behind it at a certain angle. Given that little time elapses between the bee's departure and its return, the position of the sun barely changes at all, and so it finds its way back to the hive by positioning itself in front of the sun at the same angle. Another experiment confirms this interpretation: if one captures a bee at the spot where it has come to gather honey and encloses it in a box long enough for the sun to change position, then when it is released it flies off at an angle identical to the one it made when it left the hive.

What is happening in this behavior and what does it teach us about captivation? The bee does not, in one way or another, take its bearings in order to orient itself, for, absorbed in its drive, it is given over to the sun as to a structural element of that drive. The bee never apprehends the sun *as* sun. The animal's captivation signifies this impossibility of apprehending a being as being and this impossibility is the condition of possibility of its absorption in and by the drive. To state that captivation is the essence of animality is to say that the animal is not self-sustained in the manifestation of the being as such. Propelling itself from drive to drive, it is essentially at a remove from the revelation of Being, and this is why "the animal is so to speak suspended between itself and its environment without either of these being experienced *as* being."[15] In short, the drive does not understand the *as*.

The animal nevertheless has access to that toward which it behaves. How might we describe this openness specific to captivation, and also that to which the animal is open and which nevertheless cannot be present to it in its being? The drive that absorbs the bee in the movement toward the hive is in the service of the nutritional drive. Each drive is thus in itself pushed toward or by other drives, and this drive from drive to drive keeps the animal within a circle (*Ring*) of drives that it cannot get out of. Encircled by its drives, the animal is, however, open to something else. In what way? In the mode of a setting aside. The behavior of the drive always has the character of a setting aside (*Beseitigung*). Exemplary in this respect is the sexual behavior of certain insects. After copulating, the female devours the male. Thus for the female the male is not simply a living fellow creature but a sexual partner or her prey, and the one excludes the other. "The behaviour 'sets aside,' that is to say it is in relation to . . . but in a way such that the being as being can never essentially manifest itself."[16] The animal is open to something else only in a repulsive mode thanks to which it can be absorbed in the drive proper.

Having defined the openness characteristic of captivation, it is now possible to determine the essence of that to which the animal relates in its drive behavior. The animal does not relate to its environment as to a manifest surrounding world, nor is it associated with it in a mechanical way. Inasmuch as it is capable of . . . , the animal opens onto something else in such a way that this other thing can play a role in the drive capacity. The bee is open to the sun as to a beacon, as to that which sets in motion and disinhibits its drive. But why must the drive be disinhibited? Let us consider the drive itself, leaving aside the behavior to which it gives rise. It possesses an "internal ex-tension [*innere Gespanntheit*],"[17] a tense restraint, an accumulated load, a constriction, an inhibition that needs to be lifted in order to become a behavior. This means that the drive must be a priori open to a disinhibiting factor that will never be manifest to it since it is what allows the behavior, and therefore the animal, to appropriate its "self." Encircled by its drives, the animal is thus necessarily open to a circle of disinhibition, and this "self-encircling is not an encapsulating but precisely the *drawing open* of a surrounding [*ein öffnendes Ziehen eines Umrings*] within which any disinhibiting factor can disinhibit."[18]

We are now in a position to establish the conditions of possibility for the excitability in terms of which certain physiologists have defined "living matter," and to answer the question of how the senses of a being that is merely alive can be *stimulated* and *affected*. Excitation and reflex occur only whenever there is disinhibition. That which is merely alive must first be open to whatever is likely to concern it, and "it is only when this *preliminary relation of the excitable* to that which can excite has already the character of a drive and of the drive encounter (*Entgegen*) that something like the release of excitation is possible in general."[19] We can also understand why different species of animal do not react to the same stimuli; they are not constituted by the same circle of disinhibition for, among other reasons, they do not all live in the same milieu. Whatever the intensity of a sensory stimulation may be, for example, it can still remain without effect. The lizard that hears the slightest rustling in the grass does not hear a rifle discharged in its nearest vicinity, a noise that makes even a distant bird flee.

Let us recapitulate before proceeding. The phenomenology of the living and of the organism began with a comparison between the organ and the item of equipment, and was developed by advancing the organism as the constitutive capacity of the organ, and ended up by emphasizing behavior as the mode of being of the organism and captivation as the condition of possibility of the drive behavior. The organism is thus as such neither a complex of tools nor a collection of drives or reflexes but "the capacity of behaviour in the unity of captivation."[20] It cannot be reduced to the body, and the relation to an environment belongs to its very essence. The organization of the organism is not a morphological fact but must be conceived in function of the circle of possible disinhibition. To F.J.J. Buytendijk's argument that "the link between the animal and its environment is almost as intimate as unity of body," Heidegger rightly rejoins that "the animal's unity of body is founded, as unity of the animal body, in the *unity of captivation*, that is the *self-encircling by the circle of disinhibition* within which, for the animal, the environment can unfold. Captivation is the fundamental essence of the organism."[21]

Should not this last proposition now replace the second of our guiding theses? Is not the captivation of the animal more essential than its poverty-in-world? In light of what has been learned, let us return to the initial determination of animality. If world means having access to being, then the animal has a world since it is open to something else, but if the world means having access to being *as* being, then the animal does not have a world since it is captivated. Hence can one still speak, using the word in its fullest sense, of the *poverty* of the world of an animal whose openness to that which disinhibits the drives forecloses the *as*? Is not to qualify the animal as poor in world to tacitly understand it as a modification of ourselves and not the way it is in itself? Must not the thesis that the animal is poor in world be abandoned on account of its phenomenological inauthenticity? If this were the case, one would have to conclude that captivation, as the essence of the animal but separate from it, situates the poverty-in-world as an expression of our own rapport to the animal. Is this not however a premature conclusion? Apart from the fact that the concept of world has not been adequately elaborated, the objection Heidegger makes here against his own thesis presupposes that the retreat of being outside of manifestation constitutes the totality of captivation and that the essence of the organism has been entirely constructed. But the expulsion of the animal outside of the manifestation of being as such is only a moment in captivation, and the foregoing analysis of the organism is incomplete. Only an exhaustive characterization of the organism will allow us to decide if the primordial principle of animality consists in captivation or in poverty-in-world.

We can now assess the importance that the interpretation of the merely alive assumes in universal phenomenological ontology. This is not a problem of local or secondary interest. The irreducibility of life to being and to time would be of little significance if *Dasein* were not alive and could be thought without organs. Now it is essential—although this necessity was something that Heidegger never took into account—that *Dasein* have hands so that, all metaphors aside, the being of the being that it is could be named being-at-hand. And as indispensable as it may be to distinguish between organ and equipment, the being of the equipment as being-at-hand presupposes the being of the hand, something that nothing in the hermeneutic gives us to understand since the ecstatic constitution of existence cannot be reconciled with its incarnation.[22]

Is this to say, however, that the being that we are must posit the name of *Dasein* in order to be able to echo the life that is incarnate in it? Can the necessity of such a mutation be truly established when it stems from the being-at-hand or close-at-hand that we are not? In brief, for incarnate life to prompt the designation of our being as *Dasein*, it does not suffice that we be alive; it is above all necessary that *Dasein* itself witnesses that the life that does not exist is "more essential" to it than existence. And where might such a witnessing take place if not there where *Dasein* properly appears to itself: in anxiety?

It is hardly necessary to go over in detail the analysis of anxiety that assumes such a cardinal methodological function in the existential hermeneutic. At the end of Section 40 of *Being and Time*, after having justified the privilege of anxious disclosure, Heidegger makes an odd remark, which he goes on to comment on in an even odder way. "Anxiety," he notes, "is often conditioned by 'physiological' factors." Of course, this is indeed a descriptive moment, but in view of the context within which it is inscribed it cannot fail to surprise. Having made this observation, Heidegger adds: "This fact, in its facticity, is a problem *ontologically*, not merely with regard to its ontical causation and course of development. Only because *Dasein* is anxious in the very depths of its Being, does it become possible for anxiety to be elicited physiologically."[23] Why does this etiology of anxiety pose, as Heidegger emphasizes, an *ontological* problem? If anxiety can have an organic cause, this means that the very affect of freedom[24] is subject to conditions, and that life belongs to the being proper of *Dasein*. Now it is possible, except for the major ontological contradiction, that the anxious freedom of *Dasein* is a conditional freedom and that life, which is captivation, is profoundly rooted in *Dasein*, which is understanding of Being. Where is the source of this contradiction to be located if not in the *Being* of the being that anxiety reveals? We have already seen that the physiological release of an excitation cannot come about without that which is excitable first being open, in the form of the drive and the drive encounter *(l'encontre pulsionnel)*, to that which can excite. Consequently, the *Dasein* whose anxiety is physiologically conditioned could never reveal itself to itself, in the truth of its existence,[25] if it is not firstly a living driven being *(un étant pulsionnel vivant)* whose meaning is neither ecstatical nor categorical. On the other hand, a life drive will never release anxiety, which is essentially Being-toward-death, if it is not first to some extent linked to anxiety. And how would it be so without being a death drive working on the principle of a life drive? Anxiety thus has its origin in the intertwining of the death and life drives, and this is precisely where the elucidation of the organism stumbles, and incarnate life is "more essential" than existence because it precedes the truth of existence. Therefore, resoluteness being motivated by the drive, we must stop understanding ourselves as *Dasein* and temporality and think ourselves as living, driven flesh [*chair pulsionnelle vivante*], a property on the basis of which drive, path, and thought must henceforth be interrogated.

But does this resignation of existence enable us *ipso facto* to think our incarnate relationship with the animal? What does "to stop understanding ourselves as *Dasein*" mean? Nothing less and nothing other than ceasing to make the ontological difference. Formulating this idea for the first time, Heidegger declared: "The distinction *is there*, that is to say, it has the mode of being of the *Dasein*: it belongs to existence. Existence means, as it were, "to be in the performance of this distinction. Only a soul that can make this distinction has the aptitude, going beyond the animal's soul, to become the soul of a human being. *The difference between being and beings is temporalized in the temporalizing of temporality.*"[26] What does this mean if not that in the operation of ontological difference—and this operation is its whole existence—*Dasein* institutes the abyss that separates it from the animal or, the other way around, that only the relegation of ontological difference can render our bodily animality thinkable. And since temporality exclusively constitutes the meaning of the Being of *Dasein*, or already of subjectivity, is this not also to say that life is incarnate without either Being or time? This last proposition means, first, that the mobility of that which is alive is ungraspable within the vulgar or ecstatic horizon of concepts of time, and, further, that in order to think incarnate life one must either construct a new concept of time—but why persist in calling *time* something that has never been conceived in that way?—or else one must go back to that property of which time is only a mode among other possible modes.

It is therefore necessary to cease to determine the essence of man as *Dasein* if due consideration is to be given to its incarnation and to its life. This necessity cannot, however, be taken as established and assured in its possibility as long as *Dasein* has not once more and by itself witnessed, in short as long as it has not renounced, so to speak spontaneously, the understanding of Being. And where might this happen if not, once again, in anxiety? Now what does anxiety include and disclose? "It discloses *the world as world.*"[27] But is this statement comprehensible if the two meanings of the *as*, the hermeneutic and apophantic, as these are distinguished and articulated in the analysis of understanding and the statement, presuppose the disclosure of the world? The world *as* world, the a priori of all understanding, is incomprehensible if one takes existential understanding as one's measure; and if the *as* designates the truth of Being itself,[28] then anxious *Dasein,* giving rise to a life of drives that is refractory to existence, ceases to relate to Being by demitting its own Being [*en se démettant de son être*]. Therefore the incarnate life drive that is ignorant of the *as* can never become, as Heidegger once wrote, "the other echo [*Widerklang*] of *Da-sein,* 'indeed' the beginning of overtness [*die beginnliche Eröffnung*] of the being in view of being."[29]

This is no doubt the reason why Heidegger held the phenomenon of body to be "the most difficult problem."[30] Indeed, since we *are* incarnate, the body ought to be rooted, in the manner of everything that results from our Being, in existence, but as *alive* it cannot be so. Body, which presents itself as outside of Being in the heart of that which is only through Being, constitutes then the greatest difficulty in a thinking of Being that it exposes to its limits. The ecstatic determination of man's essence implies the total exclusion of his live animality, and never in the history of metaphysics has the Being of man been so profoundly disincarnated. If it might be necessary, in order to pose the question of Being and to understand our Being in this question, to reduce that which the traditional definition of man as rational animal concedes to captivation, it nonetheless remains that the disappearance of the body is *the phenomenological price* of the appearance of Being.

Notes

1. *Being and Time,* trans. John Macquarrie and Edward Robinson (New York: Harper and Row, 1962), p. 50. Page references are to the pagination of the German edition, as indicated in the margins of Macquarrie and Robinson's edition.

2. Ibid., p. 194

3. Ibid., pp. 246 and 247.

4. Cf. ibid., pp. 374 and 385 concerning "generations."

5. Ibid., p. 346. We are quoting from the text of the earlier editions here.

6. Cf. *Letter on Humanism,* in *Basic Writings of Martin Heidegger* (New York: Basic Books, 1976), p. 206.

7. *Die Grundbegriffe der Metaphysik,* in *Gesamtausgabe* (Frankfurt am Main: Klostermann, 1986), vol. 29/30, p. 303.

8. Ibid., p. 321.

9. Ibid., p. 327.

10. Quoted by Heidegger, ibid.

11. Ibid., p. 328.

12. Ibid., pp. 333–34.

13. Ibid., p. 340.

14. Ibid., p. 347.

15. Ibid., p. 361.

16. Ibid., p. 368.

17. Ibid., p. 370.

18. Ibid.

19. Ibid., p. 373.

20. Ibid., p. 375.

21. Quoted by Heidegger, ibid., pp. 375–76.

22. Cf. my *Heidegger et le problème de l'espace* (Paris: Minuit, 1986).

23. *Being and Time*, p. 190.

24. Cf. Ibid., p. 266.

25. Cf. Ibid., p. 307.

26. *The Basic Problems of Phenomenology*, trans, A. Hofstadter (Bloomington: Indiana University Press, 1982), p. 319.

27. *Being and Time*, p. 187.

29. Cf. ibid., §33.

29. *Beiträge zur Philosophie*, 1936–38.

30. *Heraclitus*, seminar, 1966–67.

11

Who Comes after the Subject?

Gérard Granel

If one did not know that, in history, there are in fact *actual* subjects; that it is
indeed a question (probably even a necessity) of trying to discern their forms; and
finally that through what is coming to an end something else may be searching for
itself, which already calls for actual subjects other than all those we have known
up to now: if one did not know or believe all of this, one would simply have rejected
the question "Who comes after the subject?"—a question whose formulation seems
calculated to render it foreign to philosophical interrogation. "Who comes?" is a
messianic question, and probably, more specifically, a catholic one.

First of all, there is a presupposition, perhaps unintentional, in the given formulation, according to which the "subject" would already have been a "who." However,
whether it is understood as transcendental *subjectivity* or as the historical *subjectum*
of modernity, the subject has never been a "who," it has always been a "what." In
the first sense—that is, as *Ego cogito cogitata mea*—the subject *in its text* has
never been a someone (a René, for example, "in his bed"). Unless one mistakes
Descartes for Montaigne. Descartes instead took himself for Ausonius and *witnessed*
his own thinking as something sent to him in a dream by the Holy Spirit. Or else
he viewed it as a fable, the making of an automaton the size of the world, the
baroque machine generalized—including the theoretical device of the *Cogito* (the
hyperbolic fulcrum of an infinite Archimedean lever) as well as that of the "divine
veracity" (veracity rather than truth, word rather than discourse: a word outside of
discourse in order to seal discourse). Descartes, the Jesuit.

Now if, on the one hand, the *Cogito* was never a somebody, if it was—and,
according to me, deliberately—an ontological puppet, whose inventor at the same
time sketched a new figure of the philosopher as transcendental-talking ventrilo-
quist, on the other hand, the historical *subjectum* that characterized Modern Times
[*Les Temps Modernes*], more ancient and more profound than the alleged subject of
philosophers, was not something that could be inscribed under the heading "who."

Translated by Eduardo Cadava and Anne Tomiche

On the contrary, this *subjectum* was inscribed by Marx under the figure of Capital and by Heidegger under that of the essence of modern technology. As such, it is a matrix for all practice, a Sending of Being, that must be considered as much a logic of the general equivalent as a logic of "Gegenstand" and "Bestand." This Grand Form *fabricated* the "subject," as rational and productive subject, as political and literary subject, as psychological and creative subject—and, finally, from Colbert to all the Bouvards and Pécuchets of yesterday, today and tomorrow, as an indefinitely repeated element of the grand bourgeois "They."

Second, one must find out in which sense the question is admissible, by eliminating all the senses in which it is not:

(a)   by eliminating the false-who of the (human) "person," the person who, since 1781, is no more than the metaphysical hypostasis of the logical identity of the "Ich Denke";

(b)   by eliminating the false-who of the speculative and rational God, where the relation between a principle and its concepts is taken for an intelligible reality;

(c)   by eliminating the false-who of the Christian God. For if one takes away from him all that simply belongs to the ideal of pure reason, what remains is either nothing but the clerical swindle of the "resurrection" that transformed a prophet into a new god or something Jewish and not Christian;

(d)   by eliminating the false-who of what one calls "the gods," which are forms of the world, forms of the "what";

(e)   finally by eliminating (and this elimination is the inverse of all the previous ones) from the unfigurable figure of the "true god" (granted that such a possibility ought to be left open) all the characteristics of the "who," that would immediately make it a false-god. For the "who" is the *je meines* of *Dasein;* it is essentially finite (mortal in the Greek sense), and is always conceived in the form of the "they"; in short, it is absolutely unworthy of the "true god." Apart from such characteristics, we think strictly nothing under the word "who," that is, under the word *Dasein*. There is a limit to a thinking whose two sides do *not* communicate, or rather that does not have *two* sides at all, but only one: the limited side. The gesture of negative theology is thus inexorably impious, and cannot leave the universe of meaning, even though it desires (and believes itself able) either to drive it beyond any limit or to "empty" it. We do not repeat such an operation in our last elimination: in an absolutely savage and particularly superstitious gesture, we put down a gift of milk and fruits on the threshold (it doesn't matter where) of the grand animal that is stronger than we are. After which, we must run away, laughing.

The only "who" is thus the one, the actual (we mean historical) one, who comes from the fact that *Dasein*'s form is the "*je meines*"—who immediately poses the question of knowing whether he is two or one (or else "dual") inasmuch as the "mine" is "each time" that of a singular and *individual* existence (this is obviously not the right term, but a designative marker that essentially belies what it designates) and inasmuch as this singularity nevertheless always proceeds from a *being with* (*Mit-sein*).

There is, however, a truth that is older than this question of the individual or common character (or: the individual *and* common character, for the "dual" case envisaged above is certainly the effective case) of the "each time mine" of *Dasein*. What has to be established is certainly not that existence would in any case belong to a "me." The deduction is precisely the opposite: existence is older than any "me" (this is why elephants are venerable monumental and quietly crumpled images of the immemorial) and it is what makes a me: hence not a "me," but the form (of the) "each time mine"—a pure form. If the question "who" is that of unicity or ipseity, then it must be recognized (in both senses of the term: to recognize and to acknowledge—each as difficult as the other) that the *unus ipse* is itself *received:* it is given to us and then taken away, that is all we may know with any certainty. And all we may know, again with any certainty, is that it wouldn't make sense to want to know, or rather that it would be a misinterpretation to simply imagine any consistency or subsistence to this form that existence gives itself before us and without us, and that we call "us."

The only admissible question that remains is that of the actual "who"—what the French call "the bourgeoisie" and what Hume calls "the middle rank of men."

In what sense is the who a "subject"? On the one hand, he is caught in the system of justificative illusions constituted by the *logic of the proper:* he represents himself (to himself) as the origin, the motor, and the end of knowledge, of power and possession. He wishes *himself* to be in the moral law, he gives *himself* political law, he posits *himself* at the foundation of scientific idealities, he sets *himself* to work, he develops *himself* in wealth, he realizes *himself* in culture. On the other hand, he is caught in the system of *effective impropriety:* his morality is not his own but rather the majesty of a moral law that is only his when it increases either his debt or his fault (his moral *unworthiness*). Politics escapes him as political *game,* political *class, politicking* politics, that is to say, whenever it is actual politics— about which he only knows two things (and both things *at the same time*, although they contradict each other): that "everything is political" and that "one must not politicize" (such or such question, such or such field, and finally any question and any field). Similarly, work escapes him at both ends: either because, as the mere execution of one or another task, it is not a work in which the subject can recognize himself, or because, as the means to wealth, it is not a work but an entire series of substitutes: lack of pleasure, risk, "overall responsibility," control. However, culture does not any less elude the bourgeois, since arts, sciences, and literature have become practices reserved for various categories of specialized sorcerers, practices for which the middle rank of men nourishes at the same time feelings of the reverential fear due to the sacred and the contempt that is deserved, according to its innermost conviction, by any activity that leaves the ground of "realities."

The actual subject would thus be in real trouble if it were not for one exception: *political economy*. It, and it alone, bridges the science/reality gap, for it is precisely the science of what the modern bourgeois subject conceives as *the* reality: production as the production of wealth. As far as political economy depends on "abstract considerations" (such as value, price, etc.), as globally as it conceives its object (in terms of the interdependencies of macroeconomy), or, at the other extreme, as carefully as it conducts its microanalysis, and no matter what quantificational form its method takes (statistics, econometry), Political Economy always has its origin, its end and its center in the *Firm [l'Entreprise]*. And *there*, the middle rank of men is not "less" but is as much or more than the scientist. He is the one who practices that which the latter endlessly approaches. In the *Firm*—which thus rightly deserves a capital letter—lies banality and *its* mystery. There knowledge itself yields to the contractor's will.

But the Firm does much more still: it is (apparently) overcoming the opposition between work and property by the creation of *valorized* (and valorizing) *occupations*, whose particularized competence is a still unanalyzed historical novelty, as well as by the transmutation of property into *management*, the specific form of a master's work that exceeds Hegelian oppositions. Both born within the Firm, the valorized occupation and management are two different—but nevertheless complementary and even interpenetrable—modes of material technicity, which the firm extends and progressively (recently at a galloping speed) applies "outside," that is, in all the social activities that are not immediately productive and in the political sphere itself. In the process, the Firm incorporates into itself all the effective means of an ultimately "serious" morality, for it has discovered the art of containing within the limits of production the "realization" of the individual, the "security" of the socius, and the "responsibility" of the State. It dominates the progress of sciences by its seizure of research and of the University, it reforms the school apparatus in order to adapt it to the tool of production, it transforms intellectual life into cultural industry, it reduces the young to a clientele through the sponsorship of sports and the organization of a set of products and of specific "services," and, finally, it homogenizes the expression of any liberty and the formulation of any question within *its* sterilized pluralism: newspapers, radios, TVs, and even books. In an amazing dialectical sublation centered on the Firm, a finite world is thus perpetuated. *There* is the true actual subject: in this "form" under which Capital has managed to hire mankind.

We have thus also reached the point from which the question "who" and the question of the "after" can be posed. First and foremost, one must describe (as richly as possible) the "phenomenon"—whose most important and essential feature, because the newest and least questioned, is to be based on what we have called "material technicity." Like all *techné*, it is a certain knowledge: a *knowledge of how to find one's bearings*. It thus consists in discovering forms, in outlining the dependency of these forms among themselves, and in drawing from there a protocol for their use.

It is enough to do housework [*le ménage*] in place of the housekeeper [*la femme de ménage*] in order to realize that this can only be done in a certain way, that is, in a certain order that stems from certain principles. It is thus a matter of a technique because it is a matter of a *series* of actions based on *knowledge*. However, the knowledge here does not go any further or any higher than mere "know-how"—because the considered principles are themselves strictly limited, or, more precisely, are *dead-end* principles. The questioning about the forms (which may indeed occur in order to improve the technique being used) is actually in no way a free questioning: it is not opened by the resolution to question alone, by the desire "to reveal" alone. It is only opened to a certain extent, to the extent that it also ends (or to the extent on which it closes itself), which is *evidence of a reality*. To do housework [*faire le ménage*] indeed assumes opening the window before sweeping, sweeping before mopping, sorting out the laundry, the clothes, and all kinds of objects before cleaning them or putting them away, etc. But all of this is organized within the evidence that belongs to the master-words: "to clean," "putzen," "mettre de l'ordre." What, on the contrary, never comes into question is the housework [*le ménage*] itself: it is *done*, but not *questioned*.

The sign of the dead-end character of such a *techné* (which is what we mean when we call it "material") is that (as always) such a *techné* remains deaf to its own word. *What* must be "taken care of" [*ménager*] in housework [*le ménage*]? What then, in the housework [*le ménage*], is being treated with consideration [*ménagement*] (that is, with the caution and the care due to something both essential and fragile)? What possibility for existence does housework [*le ménage*] provide [*ménage*]? For an *existentiale* must indeed be at stake for the man and the woman, in the conjugation of their "tun und treiben," to be named by this word in particular: a "household" [*un ménage*] and for the French to say, with no need for any explanation: "a young household" ["*un jeune ménage*"], "their household [*leur ménage*] has its problems," etc.

What is at stake here is nothing less than what antiquity called *oikonomia*, in a sense of the word that was preserved until Rousseau. *Oikonomia* is the law of the sojourn, which indeed *also* includes the rule of acquisition and spending but can by no means be reduced to "economic" categories. Like the "garden" for the Persians, the house is rather a kind of model of the world. Neither order, nor cleanliness, nor furniture (nor the absence of furniture in the Japanese case), nor the layout of the rooms, their allocation to such and such a function, the way to go from one to the other, nor even the relationship of the inside to the outside (of the "house" to "nature") are the same everywhere. All of this varies in its idea, and thus in the material systems and arrangements, according to the variety of worldly-configurations at stake for each civilization, and, within each of them, according to the provincial, familial, and individual variations that make up so many singular developments of the common theme—which enrich it, reveal it to itself in specific forms, make it evolve, shift it, and sometimes shatter it upon one or another of its limits.

The name of the housekeeper [*la femme de ménage*], as the woman who takes care of [*qui ménage*] a figure of the world in the *oikos*, was first "Estia" (related to the Latin "Vesta")—a name in which the verb "to be" [*être*] can be heard directly. When *techné* is thus understood in architectonic terms (less in terms of a construction "by principles" than in terms of a construction that is the work and the manifestation of the "*archai*" themselves), it never closes itself on the evidence of a real: it instead always opens itself to the furtive appearance of a world-of-being. As an Appearance, it immediately disappears, but it is commemorated by an entire disposition of forms with neither beginning nor end. Thinking ("to take care of" [*ménager*] something is an exercise of thought) is, as technicity that thus moves on from form to form, a *formal* technicity. It breathes and circulates freely in itself, retracing the goddess's footsteps (methodus *investigandae* veritatis). It is a dance of logic—and, for the community as well as for each person within the community, it is immediately a ritual.

This was an example—meant to set the stage for a counterexample, that of the dead-end technique, under its two aspects of the promotion of "modern occupations" and of the universalization of "management."

A modern occupation is a set of activities organizing a particularized aspect of production, which appears when the development of production, at the crossroad of technological possibilities and the rate of the turnover of capital, suddenly makes it feel necessary. It may happen that this modern occupation is grafted onto older occupations (those that have their limit in themselves and thus constituted "practices" before belonging to production, or were not even a part of it at all), but it is then to transform them in their essence and in all their effective modalities under the thin semblance of a social and historical continuity that is now no more than a misleading image. Such is the case, which has become canonical since Heidegger used it as an example, with the transformation of the farmers' "hegen und pflegen" (which made of peasantry a "state of life"—*Lebenstand*) into a new occupation, in which what is organized is only a particularized aspect of the food and farming industry, that of the "small farmer." Such is perhaps also already the case, although much more hidden (or rather: *kept* hidden for obvious reasons), of entire sections of the ancient occupations of writers, artists, and even scientists and philosophers. What part of such practices, whose greatness lay in the fact that they had in themselves the principle of their movement, being so to speak directly and constantly exposed to their foundations and changed by them, what part survives only in appearance, when each of these practices has actually become an entirely new occupation, a particularized aspect of cultural industry, from which it receives not only (which is more and more the case) its means of subsistence and success, but also the at least implicit definition of the limits of its liberty and of the outline of its task? It is very likely that this "part" may have for a long time already been the largest part, in any case the dominant part. And that the ancient free and proud subjects of the letter, the line, the touch, the hypothesis, and the symbol, the subjects that *fell prey* to their art, may almost all be transmuted, beneath the apparent continuity of the products (don't we still have "paintings," "books," "research," "debates," and more and more of them?), and thanks to the consolations provided by an easier "social recognition," into professionals of cultural organization, of ideologico-moral sound effects, of the progress of a science based on results, and, brocaded upon the rest, of the eternal supplement of the soul. Such jobs make of these subjects, in spite of their mischiefs, which are tolerated, and in spite of the money they are given for jam or the rattles that are distributed to them, the very humble and very obedient subjects of production for the sake of production.

But the true modern subject, he who develops in all his newness,[1] is the one who brings to the level of competence, that is, to the level of a knowledge that is no more than a *skill*, a set of tasks drawn "somewhere" along the way from one or several productions, tasks that can never be torn from their merely executory (or in any case subordinated) character; similarly, no essential unity presides over the grouping of these tasks, which is entirely due to the conveniences of making and selling. All this gives birth to a race of *trained servants*, who take their servitude for the liberty and dignity conferred on them by their "qualifications" (this is at least what they are told) and who are, of course, unaware of the principally formless character of their "formation."

However, the same goes for these new generations of occupations as for the generations of products and of ways to produce in view of which they have been instituted: they are essentially ephemeral, either because *what* is produced has shifted and the job suddenly dries out in a "branch" as suddenly as a well whose phreatic water has run off, or because new *ways* to produce (what learned barbarism calls new *technologies*) have made obsolete all the savoir-faire up to now constitutive of a given "formation." So that the employment must learn something more than what it had learned with so much hope: it must learn to be *flexible* (mobile, re-classifiable, de-classifiable, etc.), that is, to submit, and it must learn to learn again (to enter into the cycle of re-cycling and retraining by means of new "formations"). In this process, dignity, more and more diminished, and liberty, more and more illusory, generate behaviors that all—except for absolute servility—meet with an internal contradiction, but that can only take on the unbearable features of an external obstacle. Hence those whom the communist party alone still calls "workers," but who, trained and qualified, have become the *new workers* and form a sort of infrabourgeoisie of synthesis, an establishment of survival,[2] hang on to "save the firm" abandoned by the development of capital, or to perpetuate the "acquired benefits" that no surplus-value permits the payment of any more, as if labor had, for a while, stopped being the mere expenditure of the labor force that finds the conditions of its use in the dead labor it faces. This internal contradiction is then denied, in an entirely non-Marxian manner, by the populist statement: "the bosses can pay." And indeed *Capital* is not short of capital, but what this capital *can* pay (that is, the labor force that it can buy for itself *because* its use guarantees the return-to-itself of an increased Capital) has shifted or has taken different forms.

Sometimes (especially nowadays, in France, where socialist pedagogy has put into people's heads the idea that the Firm was the buffer of all reality and the limit of all possibility), the awareness of the internal character of this contradiction becomes widespread (or at least the pragmatic form of such awareness does: the resignation to a phenomenon that is not understood, but about which one has nevertheless understood that it could not be shifted *in this way*). Unfortunately, this only happens in order to try to shift it in several other ways, which are only apparently other and therefore stumble against the same contradiction. One of these ways consists in exorcising it (in exteriorizing it once again as pure "obstacle"), appealing to the evidence of the *national* frame of production: "Let's produce French" was and still is its slogan, as if the nation had not been for ages the mere pseudo-political dressing of a productive body that is only some part or other of world production. In order to change something, the political should be steeled in its *rupture* from the world market: nobody today dares suggest even the shadow of such an idea. It is only clear that the theologians of the Communist Party keep nurturing such a hope "among the initiated," without, however, understanding that it is incompatible with its pseudo-realist disguise in "economic" and "social" terms. Either class collaboration gets the upper hand, or lies hit everyone over the head. So that communist Secretaries are dragging out at the Cabinet while for a long time already the Cabinet has demonstrated its decision to "break with the rupture" (besides, this was foreseeable from the start), or so that one sabotages the French car industry at the very moment when one stands up for a chauvinism of production. The only consistency that the Communist Party line still has (and one is mistaken in thinking that this line "zigzags along" as if it had no directions, when it actually *oscillates* with the regularity of an electrocardiogram around the straight contradiction that gives it its pulse) is that of the "moral point of view," which it shares with Catholics, *or* that of the "radical populism" that it shares with the voters for Le Pen, *or* a mixture of both. A sad ending.

In its pure wavering, this line nevertheless testifies to more courage than all the attitudes that are the products of the "social treatment of unemployment" and of the "division of labor." The Communists at least present the image of a community that obstinately keeps watch over the corpse of an Idea, whose death they do not know they have caused themselves by dint of making it at the same time serve *outside* the real and *inside* the real. With Marx, on the contrary, the analysis of forms was a conceptual analysis that, if it indeed brings out the a priori form of the real with which it is concerned, only does so precisely because it comes neither from a sky of ideas nor from a reflection of contents. In other words, the bite of Marx's thought (I mean that by which it actually bites at realities) lies entirely in the philosophical character of his method, inasmuch as this philosophical character

156 / Gérard Granel

itself finds its rule in a reliable logical instinct. It is thus still from Marx's thinking—provided that this instinct is elevated as much as possible to the level of a certain knowledge, to a certain degree of elucidation (one never without remainder) of what makes it *reliable*, hence with the help of works ("travails")[3] undertaken on textual bodies other (but neither "totally other" nor "simply other") than the Marxian corpus, some older (such as, at least, Kant) and others more recent (such as, prominently, Heidegger and Wittgenstein), hence also with a critique of the translations, in Marx himself, of this logical instinct into a mere reversal of metaphysical knowledge—it is thus still from this thinking that the understanding of a future for history itself may come, an understanding other than the indefinitely rehashed management of the un-historical as such.

One should not think too quickly that an ultimate version of the "if philosophers are kings, or kings philosophers . . ." is peeping through here. For we are not saying that the future itself, but only the *understanding* of the future, will depend (in the future) on the future that philosophy (if it does not renounce itself) will be able to give itself from the conjunction of the thoughts that we have just mentioned. The actual subjects "who come" (if any are coming) will, of course, be peoples, such as they emerge from the efforts of humanity (if it consents to such efforts) to exist otherwise than mankind now exists, i.e., otherwise than as a people of production (understood as a people that Production *has given to itself*). It remains to say that these efforts comprehend themselves, and up to what point and in what way they do so is also part of the form they will give themselves, and this also decides of their fortune.

Notes

1. Newness is itself emphasized by the neologisms that signal their fields, parts of words manufactured in a very peculiar way: either with a "tic" ending (as [Engl.] "robotic", [French] "bureautique", etc.) that imitates (apart from one barbarism—the adding of a "t") the *ike* ending of Greek adjectives (*phusikè*, *logikè*) qualifying a *technè*; or through the importation of the felicities of the American language: soft-ware, marketing, etc.

2. There is survival when one wastes one's life to make a living, however "decent" this living may be.

3. I say "travails," leaving "travaux" to the academics, in the same way that painters say "ciels" [skies], leaving "cieux" [heavens] to Christian preachers.

12

The Critique of the Subject
Michel Henry

The critique of the subject is taken for the principal lesson of the philosophy of the second half of this century—and already, to a large extent, of the first half. To each of the different forms it has assumed, a precise historical expression can be assigned. Indeed, so widespread is it that one would have to draw up a list of almost all contemporary movements of thought in order to take stock of its numerous but convergent formulations. We will restrict ourselves here to citing, on the one hand, its philosophical rootedness in Heidegger and, on the other, its extra- or para-philosophical origin in the human sciences, notably in Marxism and Freudianism, which were to be crowned by structuralism—to say nothing of linguistics.

As diverse as these movements may be in their explicit aims and their qualities—meaning the level of reflection at which they are situated—they have a common outcome, namely the critique of the subject, which is to say, in the end, the critique of man conceived as a specific and autonomous reality.

But it is this specificity and this autonomy that must be understood according to the meaning bestowed upon them in the philosophy of the subject. Man identified as the subject (let us use for the moment this passive phrasing that occludes precisely what has to be illuminated) is not only a very particular and superior reality, but also one homogeneous with others. He is granted an exorbitant privilege in that there is in the end no Being nor being except in relation to him, for him and through him, and this insofar as he constitutes the a priori condition of possibility for all experience and thus for all that is and can be, at least for us.

It is inasmuch as he is identified as this subject that man appears as a super-being to whom everything that is has entrusted its Being, a Being that the subject henceforth has at his disposal and that he can make use of, not as he sees fit (in which case he might just as well not make use of it at all, or respect it, fear it, etc.), but rather as that which is in its principle subjugated to him by way of its

Translated by Peter T. Connor

ineluctable and unsurmountable ontological condition, as an ob-ject whose Being is the Subject.

The reader will be spared further repetition of these famous descriptions, except for the inclusion of one remark. These descriptions are those of our world—of the ravaging of Earth by Technology. Technology consists in the unconditional subjugation of the Whole of being, which becomes the Ob-ject, to man, who becomes the Subject—the Ob-ject of the Subject, then, dis-posed before him and disposed of by him, at his disposal therefore, having no other end than this being at the disposal of, subject to tallage and corvée as the serf of this new Lord.

We will not ask here how an illusion can have such power. How can the illusion by virtue of which man takes himself for the Subject and Master of things determine these things globally and in their effective reality, how can it confer its being on everything that is? Other, more urgent questions require our attention.

The common trait of all the critiques of the subject just mentioned lies not in attributing to the illusion of the Subject the extravagant capacity to change the face of the Earth (this completely illusory conception of the illusion is peculiar to Heidegger; the other critiques of the subject see in it nothing but an illusion, unaccompanied by any effects, or having purely illusory effects, "ideological" effects, as they put it); more seriously, it lies in not knowing anything about the being of this subject that is to be cut into pieces, or, in the best of cases, in being totally mistaken about it. Two questions must therefore be asked here:

(1) What is the Being of this subject that has to be eliminated, "evacuated," from the problematic?

(2) Who, contesting at once the right and the existence of such a subject—the right of man to identify with it—goes about its elimination?

At least twice in the history of modern thought the subject has been the theme of an explicit problematic. The two philosophers who should be named at this point, Descartes and Kant, are precisely the two greatest, the two whose influence has been decisive and who have given such a rigorous meaning to the concept of subject that any critique leveled against the subject that does not proceed by the light of the foundational analyses of the *Meditations* and the *Critique of Pure Reason* would be meaningless. For various reasons, one of which will be mentioned in a moment, we will begin with the second.

How can one not be struck by this extraordinary conceptual situation: it is precisely with Kant, who relates the Being of all beings to the Subject, that the Subject becomes the object of a radical dispute that denies it all possible Being. Or, to put it another way: it is at the very moment when philosophy sees itself clearly as a philosophy of the subject that the foundation on which it explicitly and thematically bases itself, and which it systematically endeavors to elaborate, escapes it and, slipping from its grasp, tips over into the void of inanity.

One cannot forget in effect how the rich developments of the Analytic end up, like a torrent that suddenly dries up, lost in the desert of the Dialectic. Now this peculiar turning of the positive into the negative happens when the Being of the subject itself comes into question, when it is a matter of knowing if such a subject exists and, if so, what it might be. *The Critique of the Paralogism of Rational Psychology* in fact radically critiques the Being of this subject in such a way that anything one might advance about this Being includes a paralogism, so that if, in spite of everything, it must be spoken about, one can say only that it is an "intellectual representation."

Which means that "I think" (since we are dealing here with the *cogito*) is equal to "I represent to myself that I think." Which means that the Being of the subject is classed as the object of a representation, an object that, on the one hand, presupposes this subject and, on the other, never contains by itself, insofar as it is represented, any *reality*—just as to represent to oneself a thaler does not imply that one has one in one's pocket. Thus the foundation of any conceivable Being is stricken with a profound ontological indigence that prevents us from attributing to Being itself any kind of Being. Like it or not, it is the philosophy of the subject itself that has raised the most serious objection to the subject, to the point of rendering its very existence problematic. Kant may not eliminate the subject from the problematic, like the braggarts of today, but he reduces it to "a simple proposition" and allows us, at the very most, and without furnishing the slightest reason to do so, the right to pronounce it.

We must now turn our attention more closely to our two questions: which subject finds itself thrown out of existence, and by whom? The subject thrown out of existence is the subject of representation. These two terms, "subject" and "representation," are tautological. "Subject of representation" does not denote something that would have the additional faculty of being able to re-present to itself (whatever it might be). That the subject is not something, according to the critique of paralogisms, that it is not a being among others, as privileged as it may be, means this: it is nothing but representation itself, the pure fact of setting forth as the opening up of an Outside, an Outside that is the world as such. The subject is not the opposite of the object, it is the opposite of the being. It is that which makes being into an ob-ject, something that is set-forth, re-presented. The subject is the being re-presented as such, the fact of being represented—not being but being in its condition as ob-ject, objectivity as such, its unfolding. The subjectivity of the subject in the philosophy of the subject is the objectivity of the object. The proof is that Kant's analysis of the structure of this subject is nothing other than the analysis of the structures of objectivity (space, time, causality, etc.).

Why then does the subject unfold the Outside of Objectivity, of representation, why does it bring the being into the condition of an ob-ject, a being-represented? So that it shows itself, and is something rather than nothing, in order to make it into a phenomenon. Representation is the essence of phenomenality. This is what Kant calls consciousness, the *I think* experience, i.e., pure experience, the condition of all possible experience. For Kant, therefore, *I think* = pure manifestation

= pure consciousness = pure experience = representation. If it is experience that gives Being to all things, representation is the essence of Being.

The subject thrown out of existence, out of Being, is the essence of Being itself understood as the structure of representation. By whom is this subject thrown out of Being? By itself. This is what the whole of the *Critique of Pure Reason* demonstrates. Insofar as the subject draws its essence, its Being, from the structure of representation, and is identified with it, it is impossible to confer on it any kind of Being. In fact, the structure of representation is, on the one hand, intuition, on the other, the concept, and, according to the explicit statements of Kant, we have no intuition of the *I think* and no concept of it either, such that we cannot know anything about it. This means that it is not a phenomenon for us and cannot be one. The deconstruction of the subject by the philosophy of the subject is a self-deconstruction, a self-destruction. By applying its own presuppositions to the essence of the subject, to the essence of Being, the philosophy of the subject no longer finds any subject, any Being.

The historical self-destruction of the philosophy of the subject has been set forth here, however briefly, only because it implies this decisive consequence: that the essence of the subject, that is to say, of Being itself, cannot consist in representation, because representation does not rest upon itself and cannot ground itself in itself, because to be does not mean to be represented if we are dealing with a being that actually exists in all its concreteness, that truly is. What then does "being" mean? Is there an essence of the subject that does not succumb to its own presuppositions, that is not given over in its very principle to nothingness? Or, to put it another way, this time from an epistemological point of view: Is there a philosophy of the subject capable of thinking a subject other than representation, one whose being therefore would not destroy itself?

The founder of the philosophy of the subject and thus, it is said, of modern thought, is Descartes. Descartes's problematic of the subject is characterized by two decisive traits, the full significance of which we are now in a position to see. The first is that it is a determined effort to contest the Being of the subject, to unsettle it and even to deny it—an attempt that is unparalleled, unprecedented, and unrepeated. With the first two *Meditations* it is therefore the Being of the subject, and hence Being itself, that is most properly in question. All interpretation that aims to reduce the full ontological significance of the Cartesian problematic, to assimilate the Being of this subject to a being, indeed to a super-being, is nonsensical. For Descartes does not first of all ask himself what sort of Being he is dealing with as regards the subject, the cogito, but, purely and simply, *if* it is, and then how it is: he questions the how of any possible Being in general and, consequently, its pure essence.

The second feature of the Cartesian problematic of the subject is that the foundation of the Being of the subject, that is to say the recognition of *that through which this Being is*, presupposes as an incontrovertible condition that representation be ruled out [*mise hors jeu*], which means, first of all, ruling out everything that is represented or capable of being represented, and, second, ruling out the structure of representation itself. For I can only doubt universally everything that is represented or representable, the sensible world and the intelligible world, to the extent that representation in general is itself dubious. It is the domain of representation as such, it is the light in which I represent to myself everything that I represent, the things of this world as well as eternal truths, that is fallacious *if* what I see as quite evident in it—that $2 + 3 = 5$ or that "if I think then I must be," etc.—can and must be deemed false, as Descartes deemed it.

The Cartesian problematic of the subject appears to us then to be a reduction. It is a question of knowing what can sub-sist, that is to say; what can still be when representation in its entirety has been blocked, when "being" is neither the whole nor the part of the represented or the representable, nor representation itself— when being is not through representation. This block placed on representation, we might say in passing, brings us back to the situation encountered in the analysis of the paralogism of psychology, meaning now Kant's paralogism and not the one attributed to Descartes. For if representation, when we begin to ask questions about it—about the Being of the subject—hovers in the void, if it merely is a pure form without content, a simple expression, not even a concept, according to Kant's own terms, this is precisely because it *is* not through representation, through itself, but only on the basis of its anti-essence—of the anti-essence of representation that is the essence of the subject. Let us see then how in Descartes the anti-essence of representation is posited as being precisely the essence of the "subject."

Such a position is reached, in abrupt but indisputable fashion, in Article 26 of the *Passions of the Soul*. Once again Descartes suddenly practices the radical *epoche* of the world. He imagines the situation of a sleeper lost in his dream. If he is dreaming, everything he represents to himself in his dream is illusory, *is* not. But if in this dream he experiences sadness, anguish, any sort of feeling, this feeling *is* absolutely, even though it is still a dream, *even though the representation is false*. This feeling, therefore, occurs not through representation but independent of it. Which means: without being set forth, without being represented and—if representation is false—*on condition of not being so*.

How then is it set forth? It is precisely that it is not set forth, if to set forth is to set forth as a representation sets forth, by a kind of action that inscribes itself within the dehiscence of a first Outside that also renders it possible. It is because feeling is not set forth that Descartes calls it a passion, determining its Being at the outset as a submission that is extraneous to any action but above all to any Outside. What is this submission that is no longer submission to some other reality, to an exteriority, that is the submission of and to the self—*feeling?* How does feeling submit to its own Being in such a way as to be definitively and indisputably possible? *In and through its affectivity*.

But if affectivity, the self's submission to itself, the self's immediate and undistanced experience of itself, defines the Being of feeling—in this case the Being of all being that subsists, that still is after the reduction, after illusory representation has been eliminated—then this affectivity, this pathos, let us say, through which all Being is primordially and unconditionally, is equally the essence of the subject, its subjectivity, and the essence of all possible Being. It is only when, as happens at one moment in Descartes, the philosophy of the subject returns to this original essence of subjectivity and Being that the "subject" can become the theme of a philosophical discussion. Is it necessary to emphasize here what we briefly evoked at the beginning of this study; namely, that the critique of the subject, across the various historical forms it has assumed for a century, has been elaborated in almost complete ignorance of that about which it speaks or thinks it speaks?

The most striking misunderstanding is Heidegger's, who explicitly and repeatedly identifies the "I think" as an "I represent myself to myself." One might argue that any great thought has the right to interpret in its own way those that precede it, that this is indeed its contribution, and that, as inappropriate as it may be in regard to the Cartesian cogito, the critique of representation nonetheless has considerable value as a critique of representation in itself, i.e., of what dominates Kantianism and, through it, the whole of modern idealism. But our point is that the Being of the subject, and the Heideggerian problematic that will subsequently lead to all contemporary critiques of the subject and serve as their foundation (acknowledged or not), has nonetheless lost, as far as the Being of the subject is concerned, all possible philosophical meaning.

As concerns representation itself, however, one could equally well question the pertinence of such a critique. It is really the structure of representation that is put into question, truly attacked in this critique? Yes, in the sense that it contests the right of a subject that sets itself up as the Subject to reduce, by that act, all of being to the state of an ob-ject for it, cast before it, by it, then cast back to itself, placed at its disposal, and exploitable to the point of being nothing other than the object of this exploitation, as occurs in modern technology.

But this op-posing casting forth of the being as the object of the Subject does not come about *ex nihilo*, it must be possible, it must *be*. What Being, by which we mean what sort of Being, gives it leave to come about, to set forth before it, to op-pose and thus represent to itself everything that it re-presents to itself? What Being if not the Heideggerian Being itself, the transcendence of *Being and Time*, the ekstatic Dimensional of the "Letter on Humanism," the *Ereignis* of the late philosophy? A Being, in any case, whose Being, whose coming into Being, whose being brought into Being, consists in the original unfolding of exteriority and is identical with it. And this is because to be means to appear, and appearing appears in and through unfolding, as the exteriorization of exteriority, the Openness of the Open, which is the light of the world and the world itself. Only representation fulfills itself within this opening and does so precisely as *one of its modes of fulfillment*; its light *is* the light of the world, its ob-ject *is* the Greek phenomenon, that which shines in this light and presents itself to us as this shining and in it alone. The essence of representation is the essence of Being as Heidegger understands it; the critique of the philosophy of the subject is here nothing more than its simple repetition.

One might object here that the Greek being *is* neither in the representation nor through it. But the Greek being is through the same Being as the one through which representation will be (and hence everything represented in it). The Greek man does not represent to himself an object (*Gegenstand*), he does not cast it before him as a possession of this Subject that he is not. The Greek belongs to the Whole of being and lets it come to him as that which advenes, as that which is "counter" (*Gegenüber*) to him. But in the *Gegenüber* there prevails the same *gegen* as the one on the basis of which representation establishes itself—the *gegen* that makes possible the *Gegenstand*.

All of Heidegger's philosophy acknowledges this ultimate essence of Being, and surely not its representation but its essence; it is, indeed, an explicit affirmation of it. The philosophy of the subject is the metaphysics of representation, which is itself inscribed in the history of Western metaphysics. But the history of metaphysics is the history of Being itself. It is the Being that is destined for us, here as the *phusis* of the Greeks, there as the *idea* of Plato, or again as the *perceptio* of Descartes, the representation of Leibniz or that of Kant, the will to power of Nietzsche or of modern Technology. It is not that the philosophy of the subject misunderstands itself, it is rather that Being induces it into this misunderstanding. The Heideggerian critique of the subject, reduced to the subject of representation and hence simply to representation, not only misses the true Being of the subject inasmuch as it can only be thought against representation, against all Difference, it is further absurd, doubly absurd, because it has nothing to oppose to the Being of the subject it contests if not the very Being of this subject, because if there is after all a misunderstanding about the true nature of this Being and therefore about Being in general, this misunderstanding is precisely the doing of Being itself—one of its "tricks" which it delights in playing on us or which it plays on itself.

With Freud, the critique of the subject remains naive, but turns out to be more useful, capable of opening up new paths. In a sense it also consists in a simple repetition. The subject that Freud critiques is the subject of representation—what he calls "consciousness," and rightly so if the structure of representation is that of phenomenality, its essence, and if consciousness designates nothing other than this pure essence, i.e., not what is conscious but the fact of being conscious, the quality of being conscious or, to use Freud's terms, *Bewußtheit*. It is remarkable that in order to justify what will become the first given of all his analyses—"the fact of being conscious . . . is the point of departure for all our analyses"—Freud calls explicitly on the philosophical tradition, and on what this tradition understands by "consciousness": "There is no need to explain here what we are calling consciousness, which is the same as the consciousness of philosophers and of everyday usage." Something that is stated with equal clarity is that what tradition (i.e., modern philosophy, as well as, for Freud, more distant philosophies) understands by consciousness is, precisely, representation: "Let us call 'conscious' the representation which is present to our consciousness and of which we are aware, and let this be the only meaning of the term 'conscious.' "[1]

Even the most cursory reading of this text from 1915 reveals that

(1) It contains the foundation upon which the philosophy of the unconscious explicitly grounds itself. That there is an unconscious is indisputable because there is such a thing as the nonrepresented: there are memories of which I am not thinking right now. The unconscious is posited in reference to consciousness understood as representation. It is in reference to phenomenality, understood as the opening of an Outside, that nonphenomenality can claim to substitute itself for phenomenality thus understood, so as to define in its place the law of Being. It is the subject consisting of the "I represent to myself" that is edged out of the problematic, which in other words can no longer claim to reduce its whole being to its phenomenality, its "consciousness," its "I represent myself to myself," precisely because in its Being there is a host of things that it is not representing to itself (all its childhood memories, etc).

We said that this subject is excluded from the problematic: this is imprecise. It is rather maintained by it; it is to the extent that I understand my Being as the "I represent myself to myself," and thus as the "I represent to myself what I am," that I must confess to the contrary that I do not represent to myself everything that I am, that my consciousness is not coextensive with my being, that there is an unconscious part of me, that I am not master of my own house. The philosophy of the unconscious is here a sequel to the metaphysics of representation, it belongs to it. This will become clearer when we make our second point:

(2) Whatever is not conscious, in that it is not represented, is capable of becoming conscious, in that it is representable—as for example with childhood memories. The unconscious still designates only the virtuality of what, in its actuality, would be conscious, i.e., would be representation. The unconscious is not the opposite of representation, it rather names it as the law of everything that is, as its indefeasible phenomenality. It simply happens that under this law, in such a conception of the phenomenality of the subject, almost everything that has escaped the subject, that has escaped this particular phenomenality, is "unconscious."

The concept of psychoanalytic therapy is based on this metaphysics of representation; it is a question of *taking cognizance* [*prendre conscience*], of bringing to the actuality of representation something nonconscious that is secretly homogeneous with representation and that can, for this reason, change into it—an unconscious constituted by "unconscious representations," i.e., those that are not yet represented and that, ontologically if not existentially, are only asking to be. Classical thought calls out for the coming of psychoanalysis.

It is another subject that comes to light with the idea that the unrepresented is also unrepresentable, that the original Being of this subject is no longer representation but its anti-essence. Freud in his turn runs up against such a subject, half perceived by Descartes, when he finds himself in the presence of an unconscious that is no longer provisional, no longer one phase in the history of representation, capable of completing itself in itself, in the actualization of its full essence. *The history of our representations refers back to a force that allows them precisely to actualize themselves or that forbids them to do so. It is only this force itself that is irreducible to any representation.* This force collapses in on itself in an immediation that is so radical, and in this immediation is submerged into itself in such a way that there is no room in it for any Difference, no distantiation thanks to which it would be possible for it to perceive itself, to represent itself—*to be conscious in the mode of representation.*

It is at this point, at this decisive difference with the metaphysics of representation, at the very moment when he is divulging the most original dimension of Being—the unrepresented and unrepresentable force that secretly directs all representation, the affect that constitutes the phenomenological given of this force—that Freud succumbs once again to the presuppositions of this metaphysics and that, since they cannot be represented, force and affect return once again to the unconscious.

Thus the subject is led back to its true Being, to the Being that signifies appearing and that exhausts itself in it—for, as Nietzsche states, "What can I say about any Being that does not come down to listing the attributes of its appearance"[2]—only to find itself forthwith removed from its own Being and from that which in general could confer a meaning on its concept. For the subject is nothing other than this: that which in making appearance appear, in this same gesture, makes be everything that is.

The intent of the critique of the critique of the subject is not to promote its return, like the return of a past reality that, tired of being neglected, would aspire to play once again a role on the philosophical stage. The critique has shown us that the Being of the subject has never been recognized; it is not its "return" that is announced in this critique, but its first coming.

One question cannot now be avoided: with Descartes, had not the Being of the subject been perceived, half-perceived as we have said, in its peculiarity, as an anti-essence of representation? How can all of philosophy after Descartes (or almost all) have been—as was Heidegger in the final analysis—so completely mistaken about the *cogito*? Or did this mistake arise in Descartes himself, by a stroke of bad luck, or else for perhaps more essential reasons?

Philosophy is an approach to reality that habitually takes itself for reality itself, confusing the processes of thought with those of reality. In what we call "the cogito," we must discern this process of thought that in the first two *Meditations* is realized in the form of a series of implications, of propositions, in the form of a text leading to the evident fact [*évidence*] that if I think then I must be. The *cogito* then passes for an evident fact, that is, for the completed form of representation. *I think* means "I think that," I represent to myself that I think, "that I represent to myself," etc.

As an evident fact the *cogito* designates the first truth and at the same time the prototype for all truth. When Descartes himself, before the end of the second *Meditation* and then explicitly in what follows it, enters into this kind of problematic that aims to found knowledge [*connaissance*] and, through it, all science [*science*], without marking the rupture with what has gone before, he is not a little responsible for all the blunders that ensue. All the same there is something vaguely uneasy in this transcendental theory of knowledge that will rule over modern thought: how can the *cogito*, which results from the radical critique of all evidentiality, be an evident fact itself, and, moreover, "certain," in such a way that everything rests upon it? It remains only to consider the cogito as a text, to submit it to a logical or historical analysis destined to uncover its faults or unconscious presuppositions, and to assess its difficulties.

Considered as designating reality itself and not its approach or the knowledge of it, the cogito has nothing to do with thought processes and nothing to do with thought itself, and has even less to do with the text of the *Meditations*. *Cogito* means everything, except *I think*. *Cogito* designates that which appears to itself immediately in everything that appears, or rather in pure appearing (what Descartes calls thought). *Subjectivity* is the pathetic immediation of appearing as auto-appearing, such that, without this pathetic grasp of appearing in its original appearing to itself, no appearing—notably the aesthetic appearing of the world—would ever appear. Thus for example I can only see (whatever it might be) in that I re-present it to myself on the basis of the *ek-stasis* of the World. But this ecstatic opening itself would not appear if it did not auto-affect itself in the very movement of its ecstasy. This auto-affection of *ek-stasis* is fundamentally different from its affection by the world: the latter consists in the Difference that the former excludes. *Sentimus non videre*, says Descartes against hyperbolic doubt. But this can only be understood—sight being notoriously doubtful—if there is, in the originary feeling through which sight senses itself seeing and experiences itself not seeing. Sight is—appears—only under the condition of a non-seeing.

It is in the face of the positive phenomenality of this non-seeing that Descartes draws back. Whereas everywhere—in passion, in sensation, in sight itself—affectivity is named as immediation, as the original essence of subjectivity, Descartes interprets it to the contrary as a disturbance brought into subjectivity by some foreign agent. Why? Because thought is light, the light of representation, the light of the world, the light in which things and their geometric shapes shine—Greek light. It is at its beginning, in its birth, that the aborted philosophy of the subject carries inscribed within it the defect that all critiques of the subject were to develop and bring to an extreme point: absolute objectivism, whether it be the naive objectivism of the sciences, notably the human sciences, or the *ek-stasis* of Being that, unbeknownst to them, serves as their foundation.

Such in any case is the lesson given to us in the critique of the subject, in the simple repetition of what it critiques. As soon as this repetition is perceived and understood, the philosophy of the subject becomes possible. The philosophy of the subject need not blush at its past, it need even less turn to it in nostalgia: it has no past. It draws its work and its tasks from itself; they remain before it.

Notes

1. Respectively: *The Unconscious*, in *The Complete Psychological Works of Sigmund Freud*, (London: Hogarth, 1953–74), vol. 14, p. 172; *An Outline of Psychoanalysis*, in ibid., vol. 23, p. 159; "A Note on the Unconscious in Psycho-Analysis," in ibid., vol. 12, p. 260.

2. *The Gay Science*, trans. Walter Kaufmann (New York: Vintage, 1974), p. 116 (translation modified).

13

Love Between Us

Luce Irigaray

Marx defined the origin of the exploitation of man by man as the exploitation of woman by man, and he affirmed that the first human exploitation stems from the division of labor between man and woman. Why did he not devote his life to resolving this exploitation? He perceived the root of the evil but he did not treat it as such. Why? The answer is to be found partly in the writings of Hegel, in particular in those chapters where he addresses love, Hegel being the only Western philosopher to have broached the question of love as labor.

To ask a woman philosopher [*une philosophe*] to speak to you of love is thus an entirely pertinent request. It corresponds to the necessity for you and for me to think and to practice that which Marxist theories and practices have left in the shadows up until now, giving rise to partial economic and cultural revolutions with which we cannot today be satisfied. I will give three examples or symptoms: the fate of the earth as a natural resource; the problems concerning the liberation of women; and the worldwide crisis of culture exemplified by the student revolts that have been born and reborn here and elsewhere since 1968. Moreover, it is in the same melting-pot of revolution that the struggles of students, of the feminism of difference, and of ecological movements have repeatedly found their impulse in our countries. The stakes of these programs persist, stakes often subjected to repression, even among us, by powers blind to their objectives or by militants who misunderstand the profundity and radicalism of what is involved in these struggles. Indeed, it is not a matter of changing such and such a thing within a horizon already defined as human culture, it is a matter of changing the horizon itself. It is a matter of understanding that our interpretation of human identity is theoretically and practically incorrect.

It is the analysis of the relations between women and men that can help us change this situation. Unless we pose the questions there where they are posed most radically, we fall or relapse into an infinity of secondary ethical tasks, as Hegel

Translated by Jeffrey Lomonaco

writes in Chapter 6 of *The Phenomenology of Spirit* while treating the flaw tainting our entire culture. This flaw concerns the lack of ethical relations between the sexes. And the countless ethical tasks, which are multiplied in proportion to the complexity of our civilizations, do not accomplish the work that imposes itself today: to remove the exploitation existing between the sexes in order to allow humanity to continue the development of its History.

I will thus start out from Hegel again in order to explain the motives for this exploitation and to indicate some remedies for it.

At several points in his work, at several moments of his life, Hegel reflects on the question of the love between the sexes, which he analyzes notably as labor. How does Hegel define the love between men and women? He defines it as it is most often practiced in our epoch, but also as it is defined by patriarchal, monotheistic religions or, apparently at another extreme, by theories of sexuality, the Freudian one being an example. He defines it as it is still for the most part our custom and our duty to live it, in private and in public. He defines it as that which exists within a culture of the patriarchal type, without managing to resolve the lack of spirit and ethics that he perceives. He also defines it in accordance with his method. This means that in order to resolve what he calls natural immediacy within the family, Hegel has recourse to pairs of opposites. He is therefore obliged to define man and woman as opposed and not as different. But is it not still most often in this way that the masculine and feminine genders are interpreted?

Man and woman are in opposition, then, in the labor of love, according to Hegel. This labor is defined within the family that they form, insofar as they are a couple (of opposites). Outside the context of the family, Hegel is preoccupied little with endowing each gender with an identity, in particular a juridical one, even though he affirms that the status of a human person is tributary of this recognition by civil law. A sexed/gendered [*sexué*] law would therefore be solely familial in his perspective. There would not be a sexed/gendered [*sexuée*] identity for the citizen.

It is still so for us today. There are still no civil rights proper to women and men.[1] This is particularly evident as it concerns women, since the existing law is adapted more to men than to women insofar as the former have for centuries been the model for citizenship, the woman citizen being abusively defined by an equality of rights that do not satisfy her needs. In all rigor, even today there is no civil law that makes human persons of men and women. Inasmuch as they are sexed/gendered, they remain in natural immediacy. Furthermore, this means that there still are no rights of real persons because only women and men exist—not neuter individuals. The rights of these abstract citizens are more or less copied or deduced from religious, and above all patriarchal, duties or rights. Whence the difficulty in distinguishing between these domains. We still lack a civil law concerning real persons, and first and foremost women and men. In the absence of such rights, our sexuality relapses to a level of barbarity at times worse than that of animal societies.

How then, for Hegel, are the relations between woman and man in the family organized? The woman is wife and mother. But this function, for her, corresponds to an abstract duty. She is therefore not *this* particular woman, irreducible in her singularity, wife of *this* particular man, himself irreducible, and she is no more *this* particular woman, mother of *this* particular child or *these* particular children. This singularity is left to her only from the point of view of the man, for whom she remains bound to natural immediacy. For her, it is a matter of being wife and mother insofar as these functions represent a task vis-à-vis the universal that she performs by renouncing her singular desires.

Love is therefore not possible on the part of woman, Hegel writes, for love is labor of the universal, in the sense that she must love man and child without loving *this* particular man or *this* particular child. She must love man and child as generic members of the human species dominated by mankind. She must love them as the ones who are able to achieve the infinite of humankind, unconsciously assimilated to the masculine, in disregard of her gender and her relationship to the infinite. In other words, the woman's love is defined as familial and civil duty. She does not have the right to singular love nor to love for herself. She is therefore not able to love but is rather subjected to love and to reproduction. She must be sacrificed and must sacrifice herself to this task, disappearing within it as this particular woman alive right now. She must also disappear in terms of desire, unless it be as abstract desire: desire to be wife and mother. This effacement of herself in a function tied to the family is her civil task. For the man, on the contrary, the love of the woman represents the repose of the citizen in the singularity of a home. He must thus love this particular woman insofar as she is singular nature, on the condition that she remain bound to this singularity and he can therefore exchange her while remaining faithful to his relationship to the universal.

The universal for the woman is therefore reduced to a practical labor included within the horizon of the universal defined by the man. Deprived of the relation to the singularity of love, the woman is also deprived of the possibility of a universal for herself. Love, for her, corresponds to a duty—and not a right—that defines her role within humankind, where she appears as the servant of the man.

As for the man, he surrenders himself to the singularity of love as a regression to natural immediacy. Love with a woman in his home represents the repose that complements his labor as a citizen. Insofar as he is a citizen, he is supposed to renounce his sexed/gendered singularity in order to accomplish a universal task in the service of the community. In the name of this supposed universality, he would therefore have the right and the duty to represent all of humankind [*l'espèce humaine*] in the city.

Love, for the man, is thus a permissible lapse into natural immediacy. His wife or another woman must devote herself to granting him this regression on account of the difficult labor of the universal that he assures in other ways. But she must also send him back to this task, distance him from her, unceasingly engender him as the craftsman of universal spirit. The redemption of the man's fall into singularity is found in his consequent capacity to resume his labor as citizen, in the child who, once conceived, deprives the man of the possession of his *jouissance* as his own, and also in the acquired goods supposedly possessed in equality by the two sexes, goods that represent the *for itself* of the union of the man and the woman in the family. The finality of love for the two spouses is finally to acquire a familial capital. The family would thus be a privileged birthplace of capitalism.

Clearly, the self-renunciation demanded of the woman is coupled with the loss of identity of the man as citizen. The woman is made to bend to the lack of forms and norms of the masculine desire that perhaps defines itself *against* incest, *against* the mother, that other who is unpossessable in her singularity—but nevertheless does not define itself *as* masculine desire, unless one were to think that this desire wants only enslavement to death.

In fact, for centuries in the West, marriage has been an institution that chains the woman to a universal duty—the becoming of the spirit of the man in the community—and that chains the man to a regression to the natural in order to assure, in other ways, the service of the State. Insofar as there are no two juridical, sexed/gendered persons, there are, in fact, no nuptials. They are both enslaved to the State, to religion, and to the acquisition of goods. Furthermore, this absence of two in the couple necessitates the intervention of other limits tributary of the work of the negative in accordance with the culture of the man: death as the assembling-place of sensible desires; the real or symbolic dissolution of the citizen in the community; the enslavement to capital or property.

This division of tasks between home and city cannot be perpetuated without depriving the woman both of her relationship to the singular in love and the necessary singularity in her relationship to the universal. The home—couple or family—must be a place of the singular *and* of the universal for each sex, as must be the life of the citizen, be it man or woman. This signifies that the order of cultural identity, and not only natural identity, must be realized for both sexes within the couple, the family, the State. Without a cultural identity adequate to the natural identity of each sex, nature and universal are separate, like earth and sky—infinitely distant from each other and no longer married to one another. The division of tasks between earth and sky—suffering and labor here below, reward and felicity beyond—begins during an epoch of our culture described by mythology and inscribed in philosophy and theology, themselves separated from then onwards, something that is often not the case, as in most far Eastern traditions, for example.

In effect, this conception of the world does not in any way correspond to other cultures where the body is spiritualized as body and the earth as earth, the heavens being the manifestation of our degree of spiritualization here and now. I am thinking of certain cultures of yoga that I know a little, cultures where the body is cultivated as body not solely in the muscular-sportive, competitive-aggressive dimension that we know only too well and that (as sole dimension) bodes no good. In these cultures, the body is cultivated to become both more spiritual and more carnal at the same time. An ensemble of alimentary and gestural practices, an attention to breath in respiration, a respect for the rhythms of day and night, for the seasons and years as the calendar of the flesh [*la chair*], the world and History, an education of the senses toward perception that is correct, pleasant, and concentrated, all train the body little by little to be reborn, to give itself a proper birth, carnally and spiritually, each day at each instant. The body is therefore no longer simply a body engendered by parents, it is also the one I give back to myself. In the same way, immortality is no longer restricted to the beyond, and its condition is no longer determined by someone other than me. It is acquired by each in his or her respect for life and its spiritualization. The universal—if this word can still be used here—consists in the flourishing of life and not in the submission to death, as Hegel would have it. The gathering of the multiple, and the remedy for the dispersion linked to singularity, for the distraction by desire of all that is perceived, encountered, produced, are found in the training of the sensible toward concentration. It is thus a question not of renouncing the sensible, of sacrificing it to the universal, but rather of cultivating it until it becomes spiritual energy. Thus the Buddha's gazing upon the flower is not a distracted or predatory gaze, it is not the lapse of the speculative into the flesh, it is the at once material and spiritual contemplation that provides an already sublimated energy to thought.

This contemplation is equally an education in finding pleasure in the respect for that which does not belong to me. In effect, Buddha contemplates the flower without picking it. He gazes upon this other than him without removing it at its roots. Moreover, what he gazes upon is not just anything—it is a flower, which perhaps offers us the best object for meditation on the adequation of form to matter.

The Buddha's gaze at the flower can serve us as a model. And so can the flower. Between us, we can train ourselves to be at once contemplative gaze and beauty adequate to our matter, the spiritual and carnal flourishing of the forms of our bodies. Continuing to reflect a little on this simultaneously natural and spiritual meditation of a great sage of the East, I would say that the flower most often has a pleasing scent. It sways according to the wind, without rigidity. It also evolves within itself—it grows, blooms, is reborn. Certain flowers—the most engaging to my taste—open with the rising sun and close up in the evening. Each season has its flowers. The most vivacious among them, the least cultivated at the hand of man, yield blossoms while preserving their roots—they move ceaselessly between the appearing of their forms and the resources of the earth. They survive bad weather, winter. These are perhaps the ones that can best serve us as a spiritual model.

Certainly we are spirit, we have been told. But what is spirit if not the means by which matter flourishes in its proper form, its proper forms. What is spirit if it bends the body to an abstract model that does not suit it? This spirit is already dead, is already death. Illusory ecstasy in the beyond. Capitalization of life in the hands of a few who demand this sacrifice of the many. In particular, capitalization of the living by a masculine culture that oppresses the feminine by giving itself death as its only horizon. Dialectic of master and slave, then, between the sexes, a dialectic that compels the woman to engender life in order to bend it to the demands of a universal bound to death. And that requires the woman to mother her children in order to submit them to the condition of citizens abstracted from their singularity, cut off from their unique identity by their conception and birth, both genealogical and historical—consequently, as adolescents or adults exposed either to real death for the city or to spiritual death for culture. The woman herself becomes then an agent of ambivalence in love, contrary to her singular desire. Educated for love, familiar with this intersubjective dimension by the fact of having been born daughter of a woman, the woman finds herself obligated to sacrifice this love, except as abstract labor of *jouissance*, of engendering, of mothering. Where she was expecting to achieve her identity, she finds only self-sacrifice. If it remains for the man to be able to move on to another woman, another singularity, to work toward the accumulation of goods for the family or the community, to return to his citizenship, nothing remains for the woman except the duty to be available for coupling, to suffer childbirth, to mother her children and her husband. Love between mother and daughter is even forbidden, in the sense that it recalls to the daughter, to the woman, the singularity of the feminine gender that she must renounce except as abstract desire imposed on her by a culture that is improper for her. The daughter has no other motive for being than to become wife and mother. On this account, her mother represents for her this abstract function, just as she does for her mother. They are two functionaries of the universal, of a universal inappropriate to their singular nature, and consequently they are strangers to each other. The daughter is the child of the universal in her mother.

The most radical loss of human singularity entails the effacement within the universal, or within the holocaust of spirit, of this relation between mother and daughter. This abduction of one from the other as it pertains to the feminine gender is a crime that humanity perpetuates unconsciously and without being able to mourn it. We know from mythology that it can bring about the sterility of the earth.[2] In deciphering the mystery of our decline, we know that it can bring about the end of the human species, sacrificed to an abstract universal: absolute spirit.

How then to emerge from this abstract duty, from this sacrifice of sexed/gendered identity toward a universal defined by the man whose master is death, for lack of having known how to open out life as universal? How can we discover for us, between us, the singularity and the universality of love as the natural and spiritual achievement of human identity? This must proceed through the evolution, the revolution of the relations between the man and the woman, and first and foremost in the couple, before any family. The changes to be brought about in the relations between mothers and daughters are linked to a mutation of the relationships between the two genders of the human species that necessitates the passage to another culture irreducible to a single gender, and also irreducible to a sexed/gendered dimension that is simply genealogical, in other words, to a patriarchy or matriarchy.

Concretely, this means that each woman will no longer love her lover as *man* in general, that each man will no longer love his lover as *one* woman (who can be substituted by another). The task of the passage from the singular to the universal remains then the task of each person in his or her unique singularity, and, in particular, the task of each sexed/gendered person in the at once singular and universal relationship that he or she maintains to him- or herself and to the person of the other sex. Each woman will therefore be for herself the woman in becoming [*la femme en devenir*], model for herself as woman and for the man whom she needs, just as he needs her in order to ensure the passage from nature to culture. In other words, to be born woman demands a culture, particular to this sex and to this gender, which it is important for the woman to achieve without, however, renouncing her natural identity. She must not submit herself to a model of identity imposed by anyone else: not by her parents, her lover, her child, the State, or religion, nor by culture in general. This does not signify that she may fall into caprice, dispersion, the multiplicity of her desires, and the loss of identity. She must, on the contrary, gather herself within herself in order to achieve the perfection of her gender for herself, for the man whom she loves, for her children, but equally for civil society, the world of culture, and a definition of the universal corresponding to reality. With regard to this task, to desire to be equal to the man is a serious ethical error, for in so doing the woman contributes to the effacement of natural and spiritual reality in an abstract universal at the service of a sole master—death. In so doing, in addition to her own suicidal loss of identity, she also deprives the man of the possibility of defining himself naturally and spiritually as man, that is, as a sexed/gendered person. In fact, each man must remain a man in becoming [*homme en devenir*]. He himself must accomplish this task of being both *this* particular man that he is by birth and a model for humanity, a model at once corporeal and spiritual. He must not leave the cultural-maternal care of himself to his wife, all the more so because she cannot take charge of it herself, not being him. He must become man all by himself, grow without her and without opposing himself to her. He must be capable of sublimating his instincts and his drives himself. Not only his partial drives but also his genital drives. The defense of the preoedipal as the liberation from the genital sexual norm brings with it all the caprice or immaturity of a desire exercising itself to the detriment of becoming-human *qua* genus [*genre*], *qua* two genders [*deux genres*]. And to those who cite the preoedipal against Freud, it is easy to respond that the sublimation of the pregenital *is* present in Freud's work, but that the sublimation of genitality—which is reduced to reproduction— is not.

Now reproduction does not use all the drives of the desire between the sexes. Thus, if reproduction appears as the sole sexual value, the drives corresponding to this attraction are therefore neutralized and diverted toward the service of the family, the community, and the State, without being sublimated as desire between the sexes. I mean by this that masculine desire must become desire *for itself* as man and *for the other*—the woman. Sexed/gendered desire, sexual desire, must not have its end, its effectivity, in the family as such, nor in the State or religion, for it then perverts the truth, and the spirit, of the community. Sexual desire must have an effectivity appropriate to its matter, its nature. Therefore, it must keep its privileged place in the body proper and in the couple that the man forms with the other sex—woman. This couple forms the elementary social community. It is there that sensible desire must become potentially universal culture. It is there that the genders of the man and the woman must become models of masculine or feminine humankind while remaining tied to the singular task of being *this* particular man or *this* particular woman. In realizing this passage from nature to culture, from the singular to the universal, from sexual attraction to the effectuation of gender, the couple that the man and the woman form assures the well-being of the community and of nature, the two together. It is not only their pleasure that is at stake but also the order of the becoming spirit of the entire community and the safeguarding of nature as macro- and microcosm, as species and humankind. The attraction between the sexes is therefore not left without a *for itself*, this having become (in Hegel's perspective, for example) the child, the family goods, or the service of a masculine community and culture dominated by death as the guarantor of the universal. Sexual pleasure does not blindly or cynically become social power of a patriarchal or matriarchal type as practiced in the house or the city. Nor is desire left uncultivated, impulsive, making of the couple a place of debauchery (a natural place, Hegel would say) alternative to the order of citizenship. Desire and pleasure are cultivated by and for each sex so as to achieve the perfection of the genders. The man trains his instincts and drives so as to fully become man, and the woman acts likewise in order to achieve the perfection of her gender. The man and the woman can then form a human couple. Sexuality finds in the couple its effectivity, its achievement, an *in itself* and a *for itself* that correspond to the necessary poles of the perfect incarnation for each one of his or her humanity. This task is realized separately and together.

This aspect of the labor of love, as Hegel calls it, is one we do not know or no longer know. And the order of culture forbids it. We must interpret and go beyond this order insofar as it represents a human alienation for both sexes and for all of humanity, an alienation that leads the human species to its ruin. Love would have to remain a natural unhappiness without possible redemption other than the authoritarian spiritual element of a community dominated by a father patriarch. Of love we know only the singularity of sensible desire deprived of a *for itself*, the pangs of the attraction for the other, the burden of the error and the price to pay for our redemption. We know the solitude of desire, the despair of the refusal or the impossible, the pathological derangements of the drives, the dereliction of separation. We also know the passionate rebirths of desire for such and such a man or woman, a singular desire for the one who feels it, but unspeakable, irrational in its end, without language for the one who inspires it and therefore without possible reciprocity in the attraction, unless it be for the blind and annulling reciprocity of the spirit there at work. We also know the shame of desire, its sinking into the loss of identity, its chaos, its drug, and the disillusioned mornings after. We do not yet know the salvation that love brings, the individual and collective salvation.

In our cultures, this salvation has been presented to us for centuries as genealogi- cal at best. Salvation would be tied to the family, a family of masculine genealogy, a family in the restricted or in the generalized sense, a family in which the woman remains bound to nature and has as a task to make the natural pass into the universal while renouncing her proper desire and her feminine identity. This salvation perhaps had a sense at one epoch of History. But did this sense not already represent a regression in relation to other stages of culture? In any case, we are failing to accomplish History—or at least to continue it—as the salvation of humanity as composed of women and men. This task is ours. In accomplishing it, we work at the becoming of History by bringing about more justice, truth, and humanity in this world. This task is the task of our epoch (unless it is the task *once again* of *renewing* ties with repressed, forgotten, covered-over traditions). This task belongs to each of us [*à chacun(e)*]. No one is foreign to it, no one is by nature master or slave, poor or rich. We are all, women and men, sexed/gendered. Our primary task is to pass as such from nature to culture, to become women and men while remaining faithful to our genders. This task for all, men and women, must not be confused with that of reproduction. The latter represents another task. It can be accomplished correctly only through a respect for the first one. Only women and men dignified in their human gender, concerned with achieving it spiritually within the couple and in society, can engender children with dignity. Reproduction cannot be reduced to an order coming from an absent master or his omnipotent mediators. It must be the fruit of love cultivated between woman and man. Otherwise it is the lapse of humanity from its spiritual task and, in particular, the enslavement of the woman to her natural destiny in order to assure a partial, unjust, and abstract culture of humankind dominated by a masculine that does not know itself as a singular gender.

Engendering a child must be understood in the same measure as the engendering of society, of History, of the universe. The child must be the natural and spiritual fruit of the labor of love in each couple at any given moment of the History of the world. Engendering a child cannot be separated from the engendering of the natural and spiritual site that is able to receive it. Without this concern, having a child relapses into uncultivated instinct. This gesture becomes an error corrupting all of humanity.

Sanctified desire—to take up the words of Hegel—does not consist in the engendering of children, since children represent the *for itself* of the *in-itself* of the parents' desire, desire for death, therefore, but not sanctified in its natural substance. Nor does sanctified desire correspond to the possession of family goods common to both sexes, as Hegel (and many others!) would have it; it can be understood rather as the passage for each gender from the natural to the spiritual, from nature to culture. In this consists the most holy work of the couple: to spiritualize humankind in its sexed/gendered members, the man and the woman. In effect, sexual desire is not satisfied by labor in general, it has a particular labor to perform. It must cultivate itself for its own becoming. It has its end in itself. Sexual desire is not to be sacrificed to the labor of the community. Sexual desire is moreover not satisfied by this labor. As the personal good of one or the other sex it becomes impoverished. And it is unjust to affirm that the good reverting from it to the family in the form of money, capital, or property, can be an adequate recompense for the expenditure of desire. For the so-called common good, often acquired by the man and according to the economy of his world, cannot correspond to an immediately spiritual possession, as Hegel writes, for it is an inanimate object and we are incommensurable with it. This object can eventually serve as mediation, but this mediation better suits the exchanges between men, as women prefer intersubjective relations. Furthermore, money as mediation represents the loss or the alienation of singularity in an abstract universal of the natural without adequate spiritualization of the latter and with no return to self possible.

To taste the substance of the other inasmuch as it is already spiritual while remaining sensible—this is what a mediation between the sexes might be. This gesture seems impossible to Westerners who no longer know love in its simultaneously corporeal and spiritual dimension. But the reading of certain texts concerning yoga, for example, can teach us that spiritual substance exists and that it is experienced otherwise than as a good that is exterior to the self. In other words, the interior or interiority of the body is cultivated and is not reduced to the obscurity of the natural. Love as objectivity can be known as sexed/gendered love and lovers can be contemplated as subjects and objects of love. Certain traditions of India are still close to this contemplation of the objectivity of a love that is subjected to a rigorous corporeal and spiritual apprenticeship. In the tradition of yoga, for example, to make love does not signify to return to a zero degree of tension but rather to raise the energy of the lowest *chakras* (*chakras* are supposed to be nervous centers simultaneously physical and spiritual) to the highest *chakras,* or more exactly to make the energy circulate between the lowest and the highest *chakras.* To love carnally in this way means to cultivate together one's instincts, to make love circulate between the *chakras* of the belly, those of the heart, of the throat, of the head while using breath as mediation (without forgetting their return to the lowest centers, situated in the feet).

Love is not contemplated, then, in the child who is an Other easy to produce sexually and who represents the sacrifice of the lovers to genealogy. Love is contemplated in the lovers who love each other in a more or less accomplished manner.

It seems that our culture still tends to make us relapse into the most base love, with morality supporting it, and notably by reducing the finality of love to procreation. One coitus is enough to engender a child. Sublimating one's amorous energy is a much more subtle and sublime task. And blissful are the children freely conceived in the sublimated energy of the lovers. Blissful are the children of lovers spiritualized in their flesh. From birth, they are by nature already spiritual for they are not conceived in the lapse of love, in the simple mixing of seeds resulting from a more or less successful coupling. They are rather the children of a couple spiritual enough to share its treasure—subjective and objective, natural and cultural—with a third. They are children announced in love and awaited. They are the sons or the daughters who find spiritual bodies—which remain carnally living and happy all the while—to welcome them, to cradle them, to nourish them, to love them, to speak to them. They are the children of the parents' speech [*la parole*] as much as of their flesh. For the lovers' culture of sexuality proceeds through their speech, even if it is silent gesture. For such children, the body, the house, the city, are habitable places. One passes into the other without imperative. Body, house, and city are a common work built by men and women for the present and the future, and out of respect for ancestors. The objectivity of love in this case is no longer solely the child or the familial or collective goods but rather the natural and cultural world engendered by women and men at a moment of History.

Notes

Editor's Note: This text is a translation of "L'amour entre nous," first given as an address in Italian, 3 September 1989, at the national festival of *Unita*, the daily of the Italian Communist Party, at the invitation of the *F.G.C.I.* (the Federation of Young Italian Communists), and then given in French, 19 October 1989, as the introductory lecture of Irigaray's seminar at the *Collège International de Philosophie*. Certain modifications of the text were made while working on the translation in consultation with the author. It remains unpublished in French.

1. Tolerance of abortion, when it exists, clearly does not constitute a real civil right. It is only a very rough sketch of one.

2. This is a reference to the myth of Demeter and Persephone/Kore. Irigaray treats this myth and its significance more extensively in "Le mystère oublié des généalogies féminines" in *Les Temps de la différence* (Paris: Le Livre de Poche, 1989).

14

Descartes Entrapped

Sarah Kofman

"Let us be more prudent than Descartes, who remained caught in the trap [*Fallstrick*] of words. *Cogito*, to tell the truth, is only a single word, but its meaning is complex. (There is no lack of complex things that we seize brutally, believing in good faith that they are simple.) In this famous *cogito* there is: (1) it thinks; (2) I believe that it is I who thinks; (3) but even admitting that this second point is uncertain, being a matter of belief, the first point—"it thinks"— also contains a belief: that "thinking" is an activity for which one must imagine a *subject*, if only "it"; and the *ergo sum* signifies nothing more. But this is a belief in grammar: one supposes "things" and their "activities," and this puts us far from immediate certainty. Let us therefore set aside this problematic "it" and say *cogitatur*, in order to record a state of fact free from articles of faith. But this is to delude ourselves once again, for even the passive form contains articles of faith and not only "states of fact"; *when all is said and done*, it is precisely the state of fact that does not let itself be laid bare; "belief" and "opinion" are found in *cogito* or *cogitat* or *cogitatur*.

"Who guarantees us that thanks to the *ergo* we will not gain something from this belief and this opinion, such that there remains something more than this: "Something is believed, therefore something is believed"—vicious circle! Finally, one would have to know what "being" is in order to get the *sum* from the *cogito*; one would also have to know what "knowing" is: one starts from belief in logic—in the *ergo* before all else— and not uniquely from the position of a fact! Is "certainty" possible in knowledge? Isn't immediate certainty perhaps a *contradictio in adjecto?* What is knowing in relation to being? For whoever brings to all these points a ready-made belief, Cartesian prudence no longer has meaning; it comes too late. Before coming to the problem of "being," one would have to have resolved the problem of the value of logic.—Nietzsche, *Nachgelassene Fragmente* (1885)

With Descartes, we pass from the scene of antiquity to the scene of modernity. Philosophy has always wanted this to be the passage from childhood to adulthood.

Translated by Kathryn Aschheim

Having reached maturity, sure of his means, the now dogmatic philosopher thinks he can conquer, in all certainty, woman-truth. But "what is certain is that she has not let herself be won," for the means used by the dogmatic philosophers were "awkward and very improper for winning a woman's heart": in aspiring indecently to strip truth of her veils, they gave proof not of maturity but of a loss of virility of their instincts.[1]

Between the philosopher and woman-truth a primitive scene is enacted, observed in a perverse way by the spoiled child of philosophy; suspicious, he watches, so as to ridicule the false steps of these pseudo-adults that make them fall into those very traps that, in their imprudence and seriousness, they claimed to have avoided by forging *rules of method*. But their prudence always arrives too late, and behind the dogmatic seriousness there hides "a noble childishness and a stuttering."

Questions of Method

Descartes does not do what he says and exhorts one to do in his own rules of method: he is entirely lacking in prudence. This contradiction is worth underlining and interrogating in the case of a philosopher who affirms—this is one of his imprudences—the value of truth, of reason, and of his logic. It is therefore appropriate—placing oneself on the same terrain as Descartes, that of logic—to begin by denouncing the internal contradictions of his system, by making a "philosophical critique" of them, and, pushing it to its limit, by turning his own method against him.

Confusing the hierarchical oppositions that command the entire Cartesian itinerary—mind and body, reason and imagination, maturity and childhood, philosophy and common sense—Nietzsche, like a malicious child, makes fun of this "mature" man, this prisoner of childhood prejudices—common prejudices he claims to denounce and master, believing that he is using only the inspection of his mind at the very moment when he is the victim, like the common people, of what he calls "imagination."

Thus the *cogito*—this indubitable truth that would resist radical and hyperbolic doubt, the hypothesis of the evil demon; this first truth, clear and distinct, the only truth to get by without the divine guarantee; this *cogito* famous in the entire history of philosophy, the foundation of idealism, refuted only to reappear in another, better form (whether in Kant, Hegel, or Husserl), declared only recently by Sartre to be an "unsurpassable truth," the starting point of all philosophy—this "famous *cogito*" would be only a pure and simple word. Descartes, despite his rule of prudence, would have fallen into the snare (*Fallstrick*) of language, would have been trapped like a child, worse, like an animal abandoned by the most elementary prudence: its very instinct of preservation. So that if the itinerary followed by Descartes is, as he declares, rational, this would prove only that "reason" is a more deficient organ than instinct and that to want to trust it, the *ratio*, is to make a bad calculation indeed.

In fact, the *cogito* could not be a rational truth, an immediate certainty, for it implies a series of mediations that separate me always already from myself and that are so many beliefs, opinions, prejudices, "articles of faith," imaginative fictions. To speak of immediate certainties is a contradiction in terms, or, as the logicians say, a *contradictio in adjecto*; the *cogito* is a product not of reason but of "imagination"—a "supposition," a fiction, an invention, an illusion.

In order to denounce and solicit these "articles of faith," Nietzsche introduces a series of interrogations neglected by Descartes, and, pushing doubt and prudence to their extreme limits, asks unheard-of questions that had never occurred to the philospher of "radical" doubt. Even supposing, Descartes, that your *cogito ergo sum* were an irrefutable truth—and it is not—one would still have to ask: why did you *want* to find an irrefutable, grounded truth, "firm and constant," escaping all doubt? Why did you *want* certainty rather than uncertainty? What is the value of the value of truth? And if you transgressed the rules of your own method to the point of letting yourself be trapped, what is hidden by the will to truth and certainty that you proclaim so loudly? At bottom, does it not conceal an entirely other will, the will to be deceived, deluded, to let yourself be trapped? And what do you *want* in letting yourself fall into a trap? Is it to protect yourself against a more formidable trap, such that your imprudence would be the height of prudence? The only means, perhaps, for you to preserve your life and continue to affirm your power?

If, O philosophers! you neglect to ask these genealogical questions and you remain at the level of "critique," at least you should be able to denounce Descartes's contradictions and theoretical imprudences. But you will be unable to decipher behind this imprudence the supreme prudence and wisdom of a living man, his last recourse for preserving his life.

Descartes's Imprudence and Precipitousness

Nietzsche exhorts us therefore to be more prudent than Descartes, who has nonetheless raised prudence to a rule of method. One must be more prudent than Descartes because the prudence he displays has no meaning: it comes too late, at a moment when he already has been too imprudent and his invitations to a methodical prudence serve only to mask an actual imprudence. At the very moment that he preaches a radical and hyperbolic doubt, he relies on unshakeable "articles of faith" that deprive his doubt of radicality and seriousness. Descartes, in wanting to proceed too quickly, breaks the rules of his method—the rule of having to avoid precipitousness and having to conduct one's thoughts in orderly fashion—and turns out to have been influenced by the most naive, the most common prejudices. In vain did he declare that he had waited to reach an age so mature that he was unable to "hope for another after it" before undertaking, with all the seriousness that it merits, the methodical enterprise of doubt. Everything looks as if he were not mature enough for such a task or, even, that he is one of those people who, believing themselves to be more skillful than they are, would do better never to doubt, for "they cannot prevent themselves from precipitating their judgement nor do they have enough patience to conduct all their thoughts in order: from which it follows that if they had once taken the liberty to doubt the principles that they received and to leave the common path, they would never be able to keep to the path that one must take in order to advance more directly, and would remain lost their entire lives."

And what if this suspicion were verified, what if Descartes had remained lost his entire life? That would be most surprising for a philosopher who had resolved to proceed so slowly and to use so much circumspection in all things that "if [he] did not advance very far, at least [he] would guard [himself] against falling."[2]

For in spite of his hopes, his method did not in fact prevent him from *falling*; and from falling into a trap (*Fallstrick*) woven by language. Like a clumsy animal, he remained caught in this trap, and never escaped from it.

And yet! Did he not very quickly give proof of the utmost suspicion with respect to language? Did he not dream of a universal language that would substitute for natural language, that would be "very easy to learn, pronounce and write, and that, most important, would aid judgement, representing all things to it so distinctly that it would be impossible for it to be deceived"? And this because "our words have always only confused meanings, to which the minds of men became accustomed over time; this is the reason they understand almost nothing perfectly."

Such a universal language, by means of which "peasants would be better able to judge the truth of things than philosophers do now," is possible, and yet it would be utopian ever to hope to see it in use: "This presupposes great changes in the order of things, and would require that all the World be a terrestrial paradise, which is only conceivable in the land of fictions [*le pays des romans*]."[3]

Because we are therefore neither in paradise nor in a fictional universe produced according to the rules of our desire (of our reason), we must deal with a language—a source of obscurity and confusion for knowledge—of which it is best to be wary.

Like the entire metaphysical tradition, Descartes distinguishes the idea—the conception (the signified) that a pure and attentive mind could grasp "without speaking," the rational intuition—from the word (the signifier), a pure emission of sound that implies the union of the soul and the body and that is necessary only for communication. Descartes makes it a rule to direct all his attention to the idea so as not to be deceived by the word, and this rule is prudent because men spontaneously give more attention to words than to the things that they designate. One of the principal causes of our errors and misunderstandings (the fourth) is that we attach our thoughts to words that do not express them exactly:

> Because we attach our conceptions to certain words in order to express them verbally, and because we remember words rather than things, we are hardly able to conceive a thing so distinctly as to be able to separate entirely that which we conceive from the words chosen to express it. In this way men give their attention to words rather than to things, and this is why they often give their agreement to

terms which they do not understand, either because they believe that they have understood them or because it seemed to them that those who taught them the terms knew their signification, and that they learned it the same way.[4]

In the *Second Meditation*, after the famous analysis of the piece of wax, Descartes pretends to be blocked in his demonstration and constrained to put his results in doubt because of an objection that would arise from considering the "terms and speech forms of ordinary language" to which he is led by force of habit and which are found to contradict the truth that was grasped, without speech, by the pure inspection of the mind:

> However I could not be more astonished when I consider how great is the weakness of my mind and the force which carries it insensibly into error, for even if *without speaking I consider all this in myself, words stop me nevertheless* and I am almost deceived by the terms of ordinary language. For we say that we see the same wax if it is presented to us, and not that we judge it to be the same because it has the same color and shape: from which I would almost want to conclude that one knows the wax by the vision of the eyes and not by the sole inspection of the mind. . . . A man who tries to raise his knowledge above the average should be ashamed to find an occasion for doubt in the forms and terms of vulgar speech.[5]

Descartes therefore affirms it himself: he would have been ashamed to let himself be caught in the trap of language, a trap that is fine for the common people but not for a philosopher who is attempting to situate himself above them and who trusts only in his reason.

And yet! What if it was only a presumption that made him neglect to give enough attention to language to perceive that reason itself was simply one of its categories.

The "fourth principal cause of our errors" comes from an excessive attention to the word to the detriment of the idea; but included in one of the "four great errors" is the belief in reason and its categories—the subject, substance, cause and effect, etc. Descartes's imprudence was not to have doubted language radically enough, to have been unable to carry out the complete enumeration of errors of which it is the source, thus transgressing the fourth rule of his method. And therefore to have let himself be well and truly trapped.

The example of the *cogito* proves that Descartes *confused* an idea and a word; that he therefore did not "grasp" this "truth" by a pure inspection of his mind, but rather "seized" it with all the violence, confusion, and obscurity that characterize a mind always already united with a body—in other words, the will to power. Believing therefore that he has "grasped" an idea, he has—breaking his second rule of method—confused the fictive unity of the word with the simplicity of the clear and distinct idea, the simple with the complex.

If the *cogito* is therefore the "first truth" on which the entire system rests, then the entire system rests only on a word and the common prejudices that it contains. This is Nietzsche's suspicion. Despite his vigilance, Descartes fell into the trap set by language, for in pursuing clarity and distinctness he was attentive only to dissipating the lure of obscurity and confusion. He therefore perceived a minor trap that concealed from him a major trap: the old metaphysical inheritance incorporated in language and grammatical categories.

But Descartes could not have avoided this trap, inasmuch as he needed metaphysics: for to believe in reason, cause, effect, the subject and the predicate, to believe in all these grammatical categories inherent to language, is the very essence of metaphysical thought, of thought itself.

Descartes's naïveté is to have believed that he could "think" without language, that he could "rid himself" of language in favor of reason, at the very moment he was obeying the unsurpassable constraints of language, at the very moment he was interpreting things according to a schema inherent to language—a schema belonging not to a pure mind but indispensable to a living man determined to appropriate the world and affirm his power.

"We believe in reason: this, however, is the philosophy of gray *concepts*. Language depends on the most naive prejudices. We introduce dissonances and problems into things because we can *think* only in the forms of language—and because we believe consequently in the "eternal truth" of "reason" (for example, the subject, the predicate, etc.).

We cease to think when we refuse to do so under the constraint of language, we hardly manage to doubt that this limit is a real limit.

Rational thought consists in interpreting things according to a schema which we cannot reject."[6]

From this old metaphysical inheritance incorporated in language, from all this mythology that it is so difficult to rid ourselves of—even assuming we can get rid of that "which returns always by a kind of all-powerful regression" and which seems indispensable to us because we believe that if we renounced it we would cease to think—from all these naive prejudices Descartes could not and did not want to free himself for he was unaware of them as such, responding as they did to his deepest need. Because he needed metaphysics *and* he criticized language as a source of obscurity and confusion *and* he relied on it blindly believing that he was relying on the sole light of reason. Admitting, thereby, in all naïveté, that the fundamental concepts and categories of reason—whose source is language—belong by nature to the empire of metaphysical certainties, and admitting reason "as a fragment of the metaphysical world itself."

Seduced by the "fallacious magic of words,"[7] by the fundamental errors of reason that have become frozen in language,[8] Descartes was therefore not prudent enough, broke the rules of his own method—thus obeying an entirely different method that commands subterraneously and sovereignly, a method that requires of the living man that he preserve his life.

A Word-Trap

Parodying the Cartesian method of analysis, Nietzsche takes hold in his turn of the word-trap *cogito* in order to undo the tangled knots that constitute the tissue of its web and to reveal not an eternal truth, a simple, clear, and distinct idea, but a set of beliefs woven together by instinctive evaluations. Carrying "the analysis" to the end so as better to denounce its validity, Nietzsche shows that, if it is truly serious, the analysis never arrives at a simple element. In vain will you remove one by one the clothes that cover Woman-Truth, never will she appear naked before you, stripped of every veil. In vain will you undo one by one the knots of the "cogito" trap, never will you attain the nudity of a brute fact, but only beliefs, interpretations referring *ad infinitum* to other interpretations.

In parodying Descartes, Nietzsche not only gives proof of a greater prudence: he plays with the father of the *Discourse on Method*. In "deconstructing" the famous rule of analysis, he invalidates its truth value and the value of its claim to truth; he also underlines its "indecency."

He takes hold of the word *cogito* and discovers first that it is not an "idea" but a pure word, for it refers to no reality: *cogitare*, to think, is a fictive thing, a pure abstraction, an act that never took place.

An entire series of fictions derives from this first fiction, including that of the *thinking subject*.

" 'Thinking,' as epistemologists define it, is a thing that never happens: it is an arbitrary fiction, which one arrives at by emphasizing one element from the process and ignoring all the others; it is an artificial arrangement for the purpose of rendering facts intelligible. . . .

" 'Spirit,' *the thing that thinks*: if possible, even absolute, immaculate pure, spirit—this conception is a second consequence derived from a false self-observation, which believes in 'thinking'; here only, one imagines an act that never takes place, the act of 'thinking' and, second, one imagines a subject-substratum in which each of the acts of this thinking, and these acts only, take their origin: this is to say that *the deed and the doer are fictive*."[9]

Nietzsche discovers next that the simplicity of the word *cogito* is also, like all simplicity, fictive ("everything that is simple is purely imaginary, is not 'true.' But that which is real, that which is true is not one nor is it reducible to unity"). The simplicity of a word, in conformity with the nature of language, always covers a complex meaning: the word "is a way of gathering many images under a single reality which is not concrete but audible." To reduce the complex to the simple: this is the project of a mastering of language that violently "grasps" (*greifen*) the real in order to submit it to the measure of unity. "To grasp": this is the activity inherent in the will to power that is formative of the concept (*Begriff*). The etymology of this word is symptomatic of the brutality of this mastering project and reveals the illusion of a pure, innate, a priori idea, of an eternally "simple" truth, sheltered from historical violence. "Simplicity" is the red-iron brand of the concept that suppresses differences and singularities—a change to the benefit of an empty abstraction that disfigures reality and that is in the service of the allied forces of morality and religion.[10]

In affirming the innateness of simple ideas, Cartesian philosophy conceals the fact that it too is part of these living forces that work with violence and brutality to master the real. If Descartes was caught in the trap of words, he was caught in his "own" trap, the one woven by his instincts in order to enclose and dominate the real.

To show that any "simple" idea is composed of a complex meaning is therefore to decipher in the philosophical, conceptual, "analytic" activity of a "pure and attentive mind" the impure activity of the will to power: this is Nietzsche's perennial gesture in response to the philosophers' no less perennial gesture of mastery. It is always a matter of denouncing the illusion of simplicity, of unity, which rests simply on the common prejudice of the unique word, for everywhere you find complicated things that have unity only as a word.[11] And if, in the manner of the philosophers, you dissect this unique word, you will always discover in it various hidden "ingredients."

The "cogito" thought as a simple idea is a product of the philosophers' "cuisine," and the *Discourse on Method* is perhaps only a recipe book for this cuisine. Nietzsche lays out all its secrets, displaying one by one the ingredients composing this famous *cogito*.

The Ingredients of the Cogito

If you remove from the *cogito* its tissue of simplicity, if you unravel it and cut it up, you will find a certain number of elements that are so many concealed beliefs.

First: a postulate grafted onto the previous fiction of a thinking activity: "it (*es*) thinks." Then a second postulate: this *es* is an *Ich*, I believe that it-is-I-who-thinks.

To this belief, this superstition, it is easy to oppose the following *fact*, namely, "that a thought comes when 'it' wishes, and not when 'I' wish, so that it is a falsification of the facts of the case to say that the subject 'I' is the condition of the predicate 'think.' *It* thinks; but that this 'it' is precisely the famous old 'ego' is, to put it mildly, only a supposition, an assertion, and assuredly not an 'immediate certainty.' "[12]

You are prepared to admit, Descartes, that this second "ingredient" is uncertain, is only a belief, when you push your doubt so far as to imagine the hypothesis of an evil demon, as clever as he is powerful, who would employ all of his energy to deceive you, and to imagine that you would have nothing—not these hands, nor these eyes, nor this flesh, nor this blood, nor these senses that you believe yourself to have, that the only certainty remaining to you therefore would be the certainty of believing yourself to possess them. Certainly, let him deceive you as much as he likes! There is no doubt that *you* are if he deceives *you*.

"Let him deceive me as much as he likes, he will never bring it about that I am *nothing* as long as I think that I am some*thing*."[13]

But what is this *you* that you are when you believe that you are something? It is not "nothing," it is a "something": this is the only certainty that the evil demon leaves you, and not that this "something" is a "self." "I" am, "I" exist—you will acknowledge—must only be understood as "*that* exists that thinks and for as long as *it* thinks."

The immediate certainty would therefore not be "I think therefore I am" but "it thinks therefore it exists." But here as well, Descartes, you are too imprudent, you advance too far even in saying only "it thinks": "even the 'it' contains an *interpretation* of the process, and does not belong to the process itself."[14]

You are quite imprudent, Descartes. And you, Lacan, you seem to have misread Nietzsche and even Descartes when you think that you are emphasizing some kind of deconstitution of the subject with the formula "it thinks" or "it speaks."

For to say *es denkt* or "it thinks" implies the belief that thinking is an activity requiring a subject, if only a very small subject, reduced to the size of two letters: *es*, *it*. *Es* is not nothing, it is a something that reveals, Descartes, your Aristotelianism, your belief in a substance/cause of an activity that would be its effect. The *ergo sum* that you proclaim after the *cogito*—what else is it if not the substantiality of the subject that you affirm behind the act of thinking and that you display as an immediate certainty, when all you are doing is concluding according to grammatical habits?

It is, indeed, the grammar immanent to language that obliges you to imagine the fiction of a fixed subject, identical to itself, cause of the activity indicated by the verb. "Thinking is an activity; consequently, every activity requires an agent": such is your implicit "reasoning."[15]

The *ergo* of the *ergo sum* does not translate therefore the necessity of a logical conclusion but only the necessity of a very strong belief raised to a veritable article of faith: the belief in the subject and the predicate, that is, the belief in identity, in fixity, in the whole of Aristotelian logic founded only on grammar.[16]

"There is thought," therefore "there is a thinking subject": this is the upshot of all Descartes's argumentation. But this amounts to positing as true, a priori, our belief in the concept of *substance*; to say that if there is thought there must also be "something that thinks" is a formulation of our grammatical habits that presupposes an acting subject behind every act. In short, here already one *constructs* a logical and metaphysical postulate, *one does not simply record it*. . . . By the Cartesian path one does not reach an absolute certainty but only the fact of a very strong belief.

If one reduces the proposition to "there is thought, therefore there are thoughts," one obtains a pure tautology, and fails to reach precisely that which is in question— the "reality of thought"; in this form, indeed, it is impossible to get beyond the phenomenalism of thought. Now what Descartes wanted is that thought would have not only an apparent reality, but a "reality in itself."[17]

It is appropriate at this point to ask what need underlies the necessity of such a belief, a belief so strong that it subsists always, even when one passes from the "venerable self" to this small *it*, this small *es*, this small "terrestrial remainder" to which the "self" is finally reduced.[18] This belief is symptomatic of the "atomistic need" that survives tenaciously and reappears where one expects it least and in an even more harmful way in the form of a "soul atomism."[19] This need is typical of metaphysics: it is what haunts Descartes when he seeks at least "one point that would be fixed and secure" in order to escape the untenable position in which he finds himself after having doubted everything and before having arrived at some sort of certainty, namely, the position of a swimmer who has fallen into very deep water and who can neither steady his feet on the bottom nor swim to stay on the surface.

Nietzsche declares a "war of knives and without mercy" against this "atomistic need" in all its forms, for the old and the new atomism rely on the same apparatus: in a mythological fashion, they separate force from the effects of force; to the force that acts they join "that lump of matter in which force resides and out of which it operates—the atom."[20]

Now this atomistic apparatus is complicit with the morality of free will and of merit—the most common morality there is, the one necessary to the preservation of the weak. If the belief in the subject seems unshakeable, if it seems to constitute a veritable article of faith, this is because it is necessary for the majority of men, in order to preserve their lives and triumph over the strong, to hold their very weakness to be a liberty and a merit; because such a belief is necessary for the "lamb" to defend itself against what it calls the "meanness" of the bird of prey:

"For just as the popular mind separates the lightning from its flash and takes the latter for an *action* (*Tun*), for the operation (*Wirkung*) of a subject called lightning, so popular morality also separates strength from expressions of strength, as if there were a neutral substratum behind the strong man, which was *free* to express strength or not to do so. But there is no such substratum; there is no 'being' behind doing, effecting, becoming; 'the doer' is merely a fiction added to the deed—the deed is everything. . . . All its coolness, its freedom from emotion notwithstanding, our entire science still lies under the misleading influence of language and has not disposed of that little changeling, the 'subject' (the atom, for example, is such a changeling, as is the Kantian 'thing-in-itself') . . . This type of man [*the weak man*] *needs* to believe in a neutral independent 'subject,' prompted by an instinct for self-preservation and self-affirmation in which every lie is sanctified. The subject (or, to use a more popular expression, the *soul*) has perhaps been believed in hitherto more firmly than anything else on earth because it makes possible to the majority of mortals, the weak and oppressed of every kind, the sublime self-deception that interprets weakness as freedom, and their being thus-and-thus as a *merit*."[21]

The strongest, most unshakeable belief—the belief in grammar, the belief in the subject—is for this very reason the *greatest stupidity*: a veritable undemonstrable act of faith, a dogma with the deepest, most unconscious origins, sheltered from reason.

" 'It is faith that saves': good! at least sometimes. But faith, in fact, leads in all cases to stupidity, even in the more unusual case where it is not stupid *in itself*, where it is in principle an intelligent faith. Any long-standing belief eventually *becomes* stupid; which amounts to saying, in the precise language of our modern psychologists, that its motives sink 'into the unconscious'—they disappear into it. Henceforth they rest no longer on reasons but on emotions. . . . Given that one could discover the strongest, oldest, most uncontested, most honest belief there is, one may suppose with a high degree of likelihood that it is also the deepest, the stupidest, the most 'unconscious,' the best sheltered from reasons, the faith that reasons have abandoned for the longest time. . . . Man is before all else an animal *that judges*; but it is in judgment that our most ancient, most constant belief resides; any judgment contains a fundamental affirmation and belief, the certainty that something is like this and not otherwise, that man really 'knows.' . . . That we have the right to *distinguish* between the subject and the predicate, the cause and the effect, is our strongest belief: at bottom, the belief in cause and effect, in the *conditio* and the *conditionatum*, is itself only a particular case of the first and more general belief, our original belief in the subject and the predicate (as an affirmation that any effect is an activity, and that the conditioned supposes a conditioner, activity an actor, in short, a subject). Should not this belief in the concepts of the subject and the predicate be a great stupidity?"[22]

The force of this belief in no way guarantees its truth value. For however indispensable the fiction—that of the subject, for example—this does not change the fact that it is imaginary, and that, although necessary to life, it may be false.[23]

Descartes's *ergo sum?* It is the pretension of affirming the logical value of this "stupidity" in order better to conceal these "illogical," unconscious origins. Descartes's imprudence is not to have interrogated the value of logic, the value of this *ergo*, proclaimed like a cry of victory. It is to have been unable to decipher this *ergo* as a symptom, for *ergo* does not give the affirmation a demonstrative truth value but signifies only the necessity of believing in a subject. The "logic" of reason both betrays and masks the logic of the living man, only the rules of which are imperative.

To this, Descartes would object that the *cogito* is an immediate certainty grasped by rational intuition and not the conclusion of a syllogism:

"When we perceive that we are things that think, this is a primary notion which is not derived from a syllogism; and when someone says: 'I think, therefore I am, I exist' he does not conclude his existence from his thought through a syllogism, but as a thing known in itself; he sees it by a simple inspection of his mind. Because if he had deduced it from a syllogism, he would have had to know beforehand the major premise: *everything that thinks is or exists*. But on the contrary, it is taught to him by the fact that he feels in himself that he cannot think if he does not exist. For it is proper to our mind to form the general propositions of knowledge from particular ones."[24]

The *ergo* would intervene therefore only at the moment when Descartes would pass from the truth grasped in silence, by the simple inspection of the mind, to its "verbal expression" in the *exposition*. But, beyond the fact that it is futile, as we saw, to distinguish between "reason" and language, it certainly seems that Descartes was unable to forego the victory cry that proclaims the assurance of a living man who has finally been rescued from the deep water into which he fell, has finally found a fixed and stable point on which to stand. If he does not deduce his existence through the force of some explicit syllogism, at least *ergo* betrays that there is an implicit reasoning founded on our grammatical habits, of the type: "Thinking is an activity; every activity requires an agent; consequently, . . ." It is therefore the force, if not of a syllogism, at least of the logic immanent to our grammar that alone assures substantial existence, and this alone can confirm it in everyone's eyes. For the people would only be able to believe in a "demonstrated," "logical" truth.

"The true is that which can be demonstrated." This is an arbitrary definition of the word "true"; *this definition cannot be demonstrated*. . . . The underlying motive is that this understanding of the concept of truth is useful; for the demonstrable appeals to what is most common to minds—logic; consequently it is nothing more than a utilitarian norm in the interest of the greatest number.

"True," "demonstrated"—these words signify "deduced by reasoning" only if the judgments one reaches in conclusion are already true (that is, *generally admitted*). Thus the true is that which can be assimilated to generally recognized truths, according to general procedures of reasoning. *This signifies* that the axiom "that which can be demonstrated is true" presupposes "*truths given in advance*."

To add *ergo sum* to *cogito* is simply to confirm the people's belief in logic. It is to add the most common of supplementary ingredients to the composition of the *cogito* without having analyzed it sufficiently.

To decipher the *ergo* as a symptom is to remove all the fictive supplements, the metaphysical remnants, the netherworlds that hide the text of *homo natura*; it is to show that the *cogito* could not have the nudity of a brute fact but is "fabricated," "composed" by the activity of forces attempting to affirm their power. It is to display in broad daylight the presumption and the imprudence of Descartes who, seeking to doubt all the opinions that he had been given to believe previously in order to find something firm and constant,[25] only repeats this "immediate certitude" in which he finally finds the same prejudices, the same beliefs, the same articles of faith. He who thought he was trusting only the natural light of Reason remains a victim of the same fetishism, the same magical mysticism as that of primitive peoples. He continues, in any case, to believe in God, at the very moment when he affirms that he has found a truth that could get by without the divine guarantee, a condition of any demonstration of the existence of God.

For to believe in grammar is to believe in God, as only the people above whom he tried to raise himself still do. The people? Governesses? . . . Some cook perhaps? Or maybe that wayward servant whom he seduced and with whom it is said he had a natural child?

Could he have been seduced, he as well, by this "governess," charmed by her, caught in her trap to the point of falling in the trap of grammar?

"Except for governesses who still believe today in grammar as in a *veritas aeterna* and, consequently, in the subject, the predicate and the complement, there is no one innocent enough to posit, as Descartes does, the subject 'I' as the condition of the verb 'think.' "[26]

And if he was able to be seduced by a governess or a servant, maybe it is because he had first been charmed by some old woman magician, some old woman who was even more deceptive . . . the maternal tongue?

"In its origin language belongs in the age of the most rudimentary form of psychology. We enter a realm of crude fetishism when we summon before consciousness the basic presuppositions of the metaphysics of language, in plain talk, the presuppositions of reason. Everywhere it sees a doer and doing; it believes in will as *the* cause; it believes in the ego, in the ego as being, in the ego as substance, and it projects this faith in the ego-substance upon all things. . . . In the beginning there is that great calamity of an error that the will is something which is effective, that will is a capacity. Today we know that it is only a word. . . . Indeed, nothing has yet possessed a more naive power of persuasion than the error concerning being, as it has been formulated by the Eleatics, for example. After all, every word we say and every sentence speak in its favor. Even the opponents of the Eleatics still succumbed to the seduction of their concept of being: Democritus, among others, when he invented his atom. 'Reason' in language—oh, what an old deceptive female she is! I am afraid we are not rid of God because we still have faith in grammar."[27]

A Tissue of Lies

If one recognizes therefore that the *cogito*, composed of fictive and fallacious ingredients, could never be an immediate certainty, and if one nevertheless wants to assure oneself of a fixed and firm point and to reach the nudity of a fact stripped of all interpretation, of every article of faith, is one sure to succeed by abandoning this small "terrestrial remainder," this *es*, this *it*, which is still problematic, and by affirming not *cogito* but *cogitatur*?

But does one truly renounce this last remainder, this *es* and all its stupidity, when one passes from the active to the passive voice? For whether one says *cogito*, *cogitat*, or *cogitatur*, whether one changes the voice or the person, the substantialist postulate remains, covering with its illusory lie the supposed immediate certainty. The passive is simply the inverse of the active and presupposes as well an agent who is the cause of acts, a *subject* separated from its activity.

"To interpret an event either as active or as passive (every act being at the same time suffered) is to say: every change, every becoming-other, presupposes an author of the change and a patient in whom one changes something."[28]

" 'Cause' and 'effect': accounted for in psychological terms, this is a belief that expresses itself in the *verb*, the active and the passive, the doing and the suffering.

This is to say, in the division of the fact into active and passive, the hypothesis of an agent preexisted. Underneath lies the belief in the doer of the deed; as if *the 'doer' could subsist by himself apart from his deeds!* It is always our representation of the self: all that has been done is interpreted as doing, thanks to a mythology that creates a being corresponding to the 'I.' "[29] Descartes states it at the beginning of the *Treatise on Passions*: "What is passion in regard to a subject is always action in some other regard. . . . Although the agent and the patient are often quite different, action and passion are always a single thing which has these two names, because of the two different subjects to which it can refer."

You are therefore under an illusion if you think that it suffices to change the voice to reach, finally, the nudity of the brute fact and free yourself of your illusions. For this illusion at least would subsist: your belief in the existence of "brute facts," your conception of truth as unveiling. Because your desire is to strip, in all indecency, Woman-Truth of her last veil, your effort remains destined to failure, for Woman, at the risk of losing all modesty, does not let herself be denuded.

It is in a completely improper way, Descartes, that you manipulated your famous piece of wax, that you stripped it of its exterior forms in order to grasp its essence, as if—you say it yourself—you had removed her clothes in order to consider her "completely naked." And is it really only without a human mind that you could not consider her in such a way? In this entire "voyeurist" enterprise, is it really "mind" that is in question?

And if you believed that you "saw" the wax—by the pure inspection of your mind—completely naked, it was because your sight was neither penetrating nor intrepid enough to perceive in nudity itself yet another veil. A veil woven in silence by instincts not virile enough to dare to affirm the veil, "the appearance" as such. You lacked the audacity of Oedipus, and this is why you falsified and hid the original text, *homo natura*, with a tissue of lies, the tissue of nudity.[30]

It's what you always wanted to do, to lay bare by purifying: to lay bare the mind by stripping it of the prejudices of childhood that perverted it; to lay bare extension by stripping it of the sensible and imaginative clothes that denatured it. And in this way you arrived at two pure residues, two clear and distinct substances, radically separate—proper and naked, no longer able to contaminate each other, so pure that you were never able to put them together again, to mix them . . .

In believing that you could stop at these two small "remainders," you let yourself be trapped by what you call imagination (by the will to power), which was able to fabricate this veil of nudity the better to seduce and deceive you, you who, in your stupidity, sought to let yourself be caught in its web. And when you cried "*ergo!*" what was this if not the victory cry of the male who believes he has finally conquered the inaccessible woman? But this very need to proclaim it, to demonstrate it, signifies perhaps that you were lacking in certainty, in assurance.

If from *cogito, cogitat, cogitatur*, you want to draw some "logical" consequence, then you can only extract from a tissue of beliefs another belief, and arrive at a simple tautology: "Something is believed, from which it follows that something is believed." In this your "mathematical" method will hardly have been less sterile than the formal logic of the scholastics whom you claim to oppose.[31]

You cannot escape from your tissue of lies and your tautological circle except by guaranteeing the truth value of your opinions and beliefs and the value of truth value. Only a truthful and good God could guarantee that you are not concluding one belief from another belief; only the "divine guarantee" could deliver you from the phenomenalism of belief.

"It is wrong to call Descartes's recourse to the truthfulness of God frivolous. In fact it is only if one grants a God analogous to ourselves in moral terms that the 'truth' and the search for truth continue to have a meaning and a hope of success. Without this God, it is permissible to wonder whether to be tricked is not among the very conditions of life."[32]

"Descartes had the notion that in a Christian and moral philosophy that believes in a *good* God as the creator of things, only God's truthfulness *guarantees* to us the judgements of our senses. Outside of a religious sanction and guarantee granted to our senses and to our reason, where will we find the right to trust existence?"[33]

But if you cannot demonstrate the existence of a truthful and good God before having found a first certainty—that of the *cogito*—once again you are caught in a vicious circle.

In Which the More Stupid of the Two is Not Whom One Thinks

To all the imprudences that you commit when you dare to affirm in all immediate certainty *cogito ergo sum*, we must also add that you transgress the rule that consists "in following one's thoughts in order": you would not have had the right to get "sum" from *cogito* unless you already knew beforehand what "being" and also "knowing" were, what certain knowledge is and whether it isn't a *contradictio in adjecto*.

Descartes seems to respond to this critique in advance: it is not necessary to define "being," "knowing," "certainty," "thinking," for these are common notions evident to everyone, innate notions, just as it is evident that "he who thinks cannot fail to be or to exist while he thinks."

To want to define common notions would be to obscure them. And it is to be quite stupid, more stupid than the most stupid, not to understand the meaning of such simple notions:

"There are notions so clear in themselves that one obscures them by defining them in the manner of the scholastics; they are not acquired through study but are born with us.

"I do not explain here several other terms which I have used already and which I intend to use in what follows; for I do not think that among those who will read my writings there will be any so stupid that they cannot understand by themselves what these terms signify. I have noticed that philosophers, in trying to explain by the rules of their logic things which are *clear* in themselves, have done nothing but obscure them; and when I said that the proposition 'I think therefore I am' is the first and most certain proposition which presents itself to he who conducts his thoughts in order, I did not deny however that it was necessary to know beforehand what thought, certainty, and existence are, and that in order to think it is necessary to be, and other similar things. But because these are notions so simple that by themselves they do not give us knowledge of anything that exists, I did not think that they ought to be enumerated here."[34]

Unless it was Descartes who gave proof of stupidity, simplicity, and innocence in admitting the existence of simple, clear, and distinct, innate notions; in letting himself be trapped by the pseudo-clarity and simplicity of words.

Who is the more stupid of the two? Nietzsche or Descartes? And is it so "bad" to be stupid? Isn't it because Descartes refused to be stupid, wanted to "play the angel," that he was stupid [*a fait la bête*]? Wasn't his stupidity to have denied the stupidity [*la bête*] within himself and to have therefore let himself be caught in the trap like a stupid and imprudent animal [*une bête*]?

Minimal prudence demanded that he submit to questioning that which seemed evident even to the most "stupid."

It is Nietzsche who substitutes for ready-made evidences a series of interrogations destined to unsettle them; interrogations that seem philosophical, "critical," Kantian, about the conditions of possibility of knowledge, about the relations of knowledge to being. But the responses brought to these questions change the very nature of the interrogation. If Kant was indeed more prudent than Descartes in making Being itself a category of the knowing subject—in no longer concluding, therefore, that the subject "I" was the cause of the verb to think, since it is thought that would be the cause and condition as much of the "subject" as of the "object"—perhaps he committed only an inverse error[35] that still depends on the belief in grammar and its categories, in logic, even if he conceives the latter no longer as a logic of being but as a transcendental logic.

No more than Descartes, Kant did not "know" how to see that Being is neither a "reality" nor even a transcendental category, but a category that belongs to the optic of a living man who does without it on pain of death. "Being," "substance," the "subject," the "cause" and the "effect," the "thing in itself" and the "phenomenon," "the doing and the suffering," are not facts, but necessary—because conservative—interpretations (all going in the direction not of truth but of the will to power).

The inventive force that imagined the categories worked not in the service of truth but in the service of the need for security: thought invented the schema of "being" or of substance because it contradicted the world of becoming—the changing, intolerable, unassimilable world as such. If one interrogates the value of logic (which Kant, like Descartes, imprudently failed to do); if one displays the value judgements that determine logic, such as "the certain is worth more than the uncertain," "thinking is our highest function"; if behind every conclusion one knows how to read the feeling of triumph inspired by the imperative quality of judgement[36]; then one can no longer deny that the value of logic lies not in its "truth" but in its aptitude for falsifying the "real," for imposing the necessity of a "Being," of a "substance" uncontaminated by becoming and evolution. The logic of substance—that of Aristotle, that of our grammar—is the fictive product of an instinct that orders, simplifies, introduces distinctions and identities, for ends not of truth but of mastery. Logic is a conquest of the world of becoming, which one can suppose with Plato to be "false," contradictory, unknowable. It transforms this world into an intelligible world, a world of stable identities, available to knowledge:

"In order to think and infer, it is necessary to *admit the existence of being*; logic has formulas only for that which remains identical to itself. This is why this belief would not be proof of reality: 'being' belongs to our perspective. The 'self' as 'being' (unaffected by becoming and evolution.)

"The *fictive* world of the subject, of substance, of 'reason,' etc., is *necessary*: there is in us an organizing, simplifying, falsifying power, a maker of artificial distinctions. 'Truth' is the will to master the multiplicity of sensations, to organize phenomena into definite categories. If we start from a belief in the 'in itself' of things (we admit phenomena as *real*).

"The character of the world of becoming is that it cannot be *formulated*; it is 'false,' 'contradictory.' Knowledge and becoming are mutually exclusive. 'Knowledge' must therefore be something else; the will to render the world knowable must preexist it; a kind of becoming must itself create the *illusion of being*."[37]

Since "Being" is therefore only a fictive category indispensable to the knowledge and mastery of a living man, to his logic, one would not be able to conclude the "being" of thought before having posed the problem of the value of logic: the value of that which remains eternally similar to itself, opposed "to the value of the briefest and most ephemeral, the seductive flash of gold which glitters on the belly of this serpent, life [*der Schlange, vita*]."[38]

Out of naïveté, Descartes failed to push his doubt as far as this radical, "genealogical" interrogation, the condition of the seriousness of any other interrogation: he did not know how "to conduct his thoughts in order."

Such that—even if *cogito ergo sum* was irrefutable from a logical point of view, even if it did not rest on "illogical" postulates, vicious or tautological circles, and a *contradictio in adjecto*—one would still wonder why Descartes believed the certain to be worth more than the uncertain, why he believed in the value of logic.

And if to opt for the value of logic is to refuse to let oneself be seduced by this serpent, life (and all *vita* is *femina*), to refuse to be charmed by this veil "interwoven with gold, a veil of beautiful possibilities, sparkling with promise, resistance, bashfulness, mockery, pity, and seduction," to refuse to be conquered by the charm of woman, for—"ah yes, life, life is a woman,"[39] then to opt for logic is to give proof of a lack of virility of the instincts, and it is, definitively, to opt for a truth that is *inertia*, to opt for death.

Such is Descartes's ultimate imprudence, the trap into which, as a stupid animal, he let himself fall, having lost even his instinct of preservation.

But this imprudence was also the height of prudence, the last recourse of instincts in the process of losing their virility for affirming once again their power, "the powerlessness of a power."

What would therefore have been trapped, definitively, was not the animal-Descartes, who "knew" well what he was doing, but the pure "mind" to which Descartes believed he was able to reduce himself (at least during a few *Meditations*) at the very moment when the body—understood not as an extended substance but as a "collectivity of many souls"—was directing the entire enterprise.

Descartes's illusion is to have believed that he was taking the mind and not the body as his guiding thread . . . and to have therefore let himself, as "mind," be trapped by the "body."

"Pure mind, pure lie": this is at least posited clandestinely in Descartes's "text," more powerful than Descartes himself. Indeed, if we follow the metaphors in the text—and they abound—those, among others, of the house, of the necessity of destroying the old house and of building another whose *foundations* would be more secure; the necessity also of building a provisional house where one can at least live comfortably while one is working on the new one; the metaphor of the swimmer who has fallen into very deep water to describe the uncomfortable, aporetic position of doubt, before the acquisition of a fixed point—of a small terrestrial remainder—on which one can establish oneself; above all the metaphor of *method*, this *path* that, allowing one to advance slowly and prudently, ought to prevent this man who walks alone in the dark from falling and losing his way; all these metaphors (to which one must clearly add at least the metaphor of truth as light) indicate that "Descartes" (but what in him? "the pure and attentive mind" or something completely other?) "knew" (with a "certain" knowledge) that his (and the) search for truth and certainty is inseparable from the search for security and the preservation of life. To search for truth—the "text" declares it—is always definitively to attempt to avoid "falling." Into a trap? . . . *Cave ne cadas (Fear lest you fall)*: such is the rule of the rules of method.

Notes

This text first appeared in *Nietzsche et la scène philosophique* (Paris: U.G.E., 1976; rpt. Galilée, 1986). The quote that opens the essay is in Nietzsche, *Sämtliche Werke: Kritische Studienausgabe in 15 Bänden*, ed. Giorgio Colli and Mazzino Montinari (Munich: Deutscher Taschenbuch Verlag, 1980), vol. 11, pp. 639–40.

1. Nietzsche, *Beyond Good and Evil*, trans. Walter Kaufmann (New York: Random House, 1966), "Preface," p. 2.

2. Descartes, *Discours de la méthode*, pt. 2, in *Oeuvres philosophiques*, ed. Ferdinand Alquié (Paris: Granier, 1988), vol. 1, p. 584. All subsequent references to Descartes are from this edition and will be cited by volume number and page number. TN: All translations of Descartes are my own.

3. Descartes, Letter to Mersenne, 20 November 1629, *Oeuvres philosophiques*, 1:232.

4. Descartes, *Les Principes de la philosophie*, §74, *Oeuvres philosophiques*, 3:143.

5. Descartes, *Les Méditations: Méditation Seconde* in *Oeuvres philosophiques*, 2:426–27.

6. Nietzsche, *The Will to Power*, trans. W. Kaufmann and R. J. Hollingdale (New York: Random House, 1968), §522 (1886–87). TN: Whenever possible, I have used this edition and translation for Kofman's citations from Nietzsche's posthumous fragments. When Kaufmann has not selected the particular passage that Kofman is interested in, I then refer to Nietzsche's *Sämtliche Werke*. In the latter case, the translations are my own; in the former case, I have at times modified the translation slightly.

7. Nietzsche, *Beyond Good and Evil*, §16, p. 23.

8. Cf. Nietzsche, *On the Genealogy of Morals*, trans. W. Kaufmann and R. J. Hollingdale (New York: Random House, 1974), pt. 1, §13.

9. Nietzsche, *The Will to Power*, §477.

10. Cf. Nietzsche, *Das Philosophenbuch/Le Livre du philosophe*, ed. and trans. Angèle K. Marietti (Paris: Aubier, 1969), and my *Nietzsche et la métaphore* (Paris: Payot, 1972).

11. Cf. Nietzsche, *Beyond Good and Evil*, §19, on the subject of will.

12. Ibid., §17, p. 24.

13. Descartes, *Méditation Seconde* in *Oeuvres philosophiques*, 2:415.

14. Nietzsche, *Beyond Good and Evil*, §17, p. 24.

15. Ibid.

16. Cf. "Les présupposés de la logique" in Kofman, *Nietzsche et la scène philosophique*, pp. 137–64.

17. Nietzsche, *The Will to Power*, §484.

18. Cf. Nietzsche, *Beyond Good and Evil*, §17.

19. Ibid., §12, p. 20.

20. Ibid., §17, p. 24.

21. Nietzsche, *On the Genealogy of Morals*, pt. 1, §13, pp. 45–46.

22. Nietzsche, *Sämtliche Werke*, 12:181–82.

23. Cf. Nietzsche, *The Will to Power*, §488.

24. Descartes, *Réponses aux secondes objections* in *Oeuvres philosophiques*, 2:564–65.

25. Cf. Descartes, *Première Méditation* and the second part of the *Discours de la Méthode*.

26. Nietzsche, *Sämtliche Werke*, 11:637.

27. Nietzsche, *The Twilight of the Idols* in *The Portable Nietzsche*, trans. W. Kaufmann (New York: Viking Press, 1954), "Reason in Philosophy," §5, pp. 482–83. Cf. my discussion of Baubô in "Baubô, preversion théologique et fétichisme," in *Nietzsche et la scène philosophiques*, pp. 263–304.

28. Nietzsche, *The Will to Power*, §546.

29. Nietzsche, *Sämtliche Werke*, 12:249–50.

30. Cf. Nietzsche, *Beyond Good and Evil*, §230 and my "Généalogie, texte, interprétation" in *Nietzsche et la métaphore*.

31. Cf. the second part of the *Discours*.

32. Nietzsche, *Sämtliche Werke*, 11:563.

33. Nietzsche, *The Will to Power*, §436.

34. *Les Principes de la philosophie* in *Oeuvres philosophiques*, vol. 3, §10, pp. 96–97.

35. Nietzsche, *Sämtliche Werke*, 11:637–38.

36. Nietzsche, *The Will to Power*, §539.

37. Ibid., §517.

38. Ibid., §577.

39. Nietzsche, *The Gay Science*, trans. W. Kaufmann (New York: Viking Press, 1954), §339, p. 272.

15

The Response of Ulysses

Philippe Lacoue-Labarthe

To Avital Ronell

"Who comes after the subject?"

The temptation is great to answer this question with the response of Ulysses to Polyphemus—the one aptly named, in terms at least of current "philosophical" idle talk concerning the subject—"No one" ("*Personne*"). And following an old schoolboy stereotype that has not altogether lost its resonance, the temptation is also great to play as well upon the *persona* or the *hupokrites*. One can imagine the "scene." The unique and powerful but henceforth blinded eye of metaphysics (this eye that Nietzsche evoked in the *Birth of Tragedy*, explaining that it had destroyed all stages, precisely, in its function as "the eye of Socrates,"), incapable of "theorizing," at the moment of its escape, the former subject that it thought to have fixed, in full light, like Being itself. In lieu of and for want of this stage: a theater of shadows, pretenses and ghostlike presences, the play of language games: *mimesis* unchained, which is to say that no stage (no theater) will henceforth contain it.

But the staging is too simplistic: replayed a hundred times within the tradition of an "as if" (*als ob*), a tradition soon to mark its bicentenary, it has been a hundred times more or less skillfully reset in all the forms of the "post." This suffices, or should suffice (after all, in the language that today dominates, following the example of what was once Latin, the anagram of *post* is quite simply *stop*). To act as if the subject no longer existed, or as if the question is no longer being raised, is possibly as vain as supposing—as if nothing were going on—a "renewed" problematic of the subject (of law, ethics, communication, etc.) to be sufficient and consistent. It is in any case to forget that nihilism, which on the one hand one follows—gaily or not—and which on the other hand one claims to combat, belongs, metaphysically, to the subject. This, whether one declares it to be passé or proclaims its return, has not, for a moment, since the beginning of modern times (*les Temps modernes*), ceased to reign and does not cease, even today, to confirm its reign—though, to be sure, this takes place less and less in the form of the grand subject that Europe, during the last two centuries, has variously promised for historical effectuation,

Translated by Avital Ronell

emancipation, or domination (the progress of humanity, nations or peoples, working or productive man, race(s), the community of the oppressed, etc.). But the contours of the promise were shaped by traits of an individual *psukhè*, of an "I-me" on the way to universalization (the subject of desire as consumer subject), to which humanity is necessarily reduced, which means, in the first place, Western humanity, from the moment that technology itself—which, in and of all of this, is the true subject—took on the profile of what Marx called political economy and others that followed, aggravating the diagnostic, "spectacle-market society" (i.e., the Situationists, TN).

(To concern oneself with assuring this "little subject" its rights is by no means demeaning, and in any case thousands of examples indicate every day that it is a matter of urgency to do so. From there to decree that this constitutes the essential is a completely different matter. Political economy itself recognizes that democracy, or that which it interprets as such, is, all things considered, the form that is most readily conducive to its current deployment. This is cheering. But should one let loose, around this motif, a grandiloquent philosophical combat?)

The response of Ulysses, in any case, if one were to dwell upon it momentarily, proves to be perfectly enigmatic: have we noted for example that when Ulysses responds "No One" (in Greek, *outis*, or *oudeis*), it is his proper name (*Odusseus*) that he only slightly deforms? The ruse (which one may well consider exaggerated or "infantile") runs the risk, through a faulty (or overly correct) pronunciation, of avowing his real name, or at the very least of uttering a name. And a name that itself is neither more nor less "significant" than mythic names are in general. To the question of Polyphemus, "Who?" Ulysses appears to respond negatively with a "what" (no one: not nothing, but no being of the human realm). But in responding "No one," he certainly intends to answer the question "Who?" or indeed to take it upon himself—a bit like, and much closer to us, the Portuguese poet who signed his books with the name of Pessoa. In other words, at this playful (and vertiginous) point, the ruse is only a ruse because it offers a response that confuses, by pure recourse to a *Witz* (would this be the matrix of the entire *Odyssey*?), the two instances of *what* and *who*: of *was* and *wer*. But, at the same time, in this fluttering from one to the other, the question of existence trembles—or a certain question of existence, one, possibly, that has never been thematically formulated by philosophy itself, but perhaps always mutely present in philosophy, at least since philosophy became "the philosophy of the subject": why is there someone rather than no one?

Such a question overtakes the question, exceeding it: who is it of whom I ask "Who are you?" or "Who goes there?" What is his name, that is to say, that which constitutes him *as* this one or the other? The question is overtaken for the simple reason that, posed in the mode of *who*, it withdraws at least one of its possibilities (namely, from that which renders it possible as *this* question), a response in the mode of *what*, which in turn can be understood as in the mode of *who*. It is the simultaneous unhinging of *what* and *who* that is responsible for an overtaking—if the word is appropriate, or if it is not necessary to imagine a sort of internal flooding at the boundaries of both questions— that can be considered identical or at least analogous to Heidegger's reworking, from the most buried foundation of philosophy, of *Dassheit* (*quodditas*) on the *Washeit* (*quidditas*), of the *oti estin* upon the *ti estin*.

I propose, for lack of a better inflection, to call this question: the question of *Werheit*.

The question of "whoness," like that of *Dassheit*, "thatness," implies a question of existence *as* a question of being. In this sense, it gestures toward *Dasein* and its inessentiality, towards the *Das Wesen des Daseins liegt in seiner Existenz*.

But it entails yet another thing that one need not hastily view as deriving merely from the ontic order; this involves, namely, the question of *identity*. Not of identity already constituted or given (which simply supposes that the *who* is always already folding in on the *what*), but under the impact of the always possible response: no one (or No One), which bars any hold on the *what* or on the *who*, of an identity not yet established or not yet related to itself, not even in the mode of its potentiality. Or of an originary identity, if one prefers, and for lack of a better term, one that is natively stumped since, on this very basis, the question arises concerning the cognition that there is some *one* or, more generally, concerning the possibility of a "there is someone." Why is there someone rather than no one?

One must obviously concede that the inessentiality of *Dasein* is, as they say, also its "absence of identity." This is so at least potentially, and for two contradictory reasons: at once because *Jemeinigkeit* constantly threatens to concede that it "is" (but this absence of identity is in the mode of the loss of identity, of the fall into the "inauthenticity" of the "they," etc.) and, especially, because it is thrown, that is—I am condensing possibly to the point of abuse—because *Jemeinigkeit* is nothing itself, in my own death, but the impossibility of my ownmost possibility. But precisely, the question of identity (we have no other word), as I want to pose it, is not the question of death, even if it is within infinitely (imperceptibly) close proximity to it. For it does not ask questions, down the road, about a disappearance (though it can *always* take this form), but it does so going upward, on the chance— or not—of an apparition: of a being there. It questions, rather—this is an indication of "tragic wisdom" according to Nietzsche, that is to say, of the experience of pain ("Better not to be born")—in the direction of birth. It culminates in astonishment (not amazement, always too easily ontic) before the "that there is someone"—"me," if one so wishes.

(I say: " 'me,' if one so wishes," because if it is the feeling that I exist that carves the bottomless pit of the experience of pain, to the extent indeed that it is marked indissociably as revelation of the *né*-ant, of being as the nothing of the being; there is, in the experience of love that one can call ecstatic, surpassing amazement, the sheer astonishment before the "that he or she exists," a feeling that *you* exist at least as stunning as the sentiment that I exist—and that in itself, moreover, is accompanied by the retreat of the sentiment of my own existence. This allows for the experience of love—and it is in no way a matter of a "romantic theme"—to count among the paradoxical experiences of death, and derives very particularly from what Bataille called "the practice of joy in the face of death.")

To the degree that literature proceeds from (or by) questions, this clearly becomes a question of literature, if not the question of literature. It even defines most particularly, though not exclusively, that which one calls lyricism. This explains why the question does not appear in what is properly defined as philosophy, and certainly not in what has been located as "philosophy of the subject." Which does not mean that it is prevented from haunting that philosophy, and above all "the philosophy of the subject." Quite the contrary.

The thinking organized around the subject will always have responded to the question "What?" that is to say, in its ontological and canonical form: "What is?" More precisely, in return for what Heidegger, under the heading of the advent of modernity, asserted as the subjugation of (Platonic) truth by certitude, and under the predominance achieved by mathematics, it will always have been oriented by the search of an *ens verum* (*certum*), equaled to being, of an assured being whose foundation would permit the deployment and construction, the articulation of the (systematic) totality of knowledge *as* the jointure of being itself in totality. Whatever the ensuing historical declension of this being-Being could then have been, it will have always proceeded from the *ego cogito* as the self-established guarantee of knowledge, that is to say, of *tekhne*. This is the case until the Marxian and Nietzschean reversals, even extending to the appearance of the will of willing. It is clearly the case that, within these limits, the thinking that has enveloped the subject absolutely prohibited the question of the "Who" from ever being posed.

Even so, nothing forced Descartes for example to commit to writing the autobiographical narration of the *Discourse* nor even to the relative "fiction" of the *Meditations*, as nothing forced the (systematic) thinker Pascal, even within the register of faith and of the "logic of the heart," to base himself on the Augustinian model (which he subsequently bequeaths to the thinker Rousseau) nor to lose so much energy in the debate with the "literary hack" Montaigne who, for his part, seized hold *in extremis* of the example of Socrates. In the same vein—and, as could be shown, in a hardly detected blueprint—nothing forced the metaphysics of the subject from Kant to Nietzsche to look to a figure (*Gestalt*) for the emblematic resources of a systematic *Darstellung* (and it turns out that in Kant as with Nietzsche it concerns the same figure: Zoroaster or Zarathustra); just as nothing forced Schelling, before he envisaged the great philosophical myth of the *Ages of the World* to present—everything obliges me to mention it here—the *System of Transcendental Idealism* as "the Odysseus of the conscience." By which he *also* evoked, on the grounds of a rigorous nostalgia, the return of knowledge to its original homeland: poetry. Nothing therefore forced philosophy, nor certainly this philosophy (the one of the systematic age), to compromise, with forms whose essence it brought to light, the name of "literature," if not the mute "presence," under the subject, of a unique existence—whether this "presence" consisted of just one, several, or all. It becomes crucially necessary to interpret the metaphysics of the subject, from the *cogito* to the will to power, as a pure ontology in its philosophical form—and consequently in the "Let's leave Mr. Nietzsche out of this." The subject will have been quite simply the place, and the name, of the last theses on being, and in this sense *nothing* comes after the subject if no thesis on being is any longer possible beyond the will to will (that is, if all possibles of philosophy are as such exhausted). But if it be imposed upon us to "leave Mr. Nietzsche out of this," it is just as imposing to hear the resonance, under the name of "Mr. Nietzsche" and in his name, of the "Who are we?" (we latecomers, good Europeans, harbingers of the future, etc.) resounding into the pathetic (*and* comic) and "Who am I?" of *Ecce Homo*—the question "Who?" emerging where, in fact, very probably, metaphysics panics. For the enigma after all comes down to this: the *who*, in all sorts of ways, will have carried the metaphysics of the subject to its limit—and to the point of its "deadline" that is madness, where the deposing of the subject occurs. Or as Jacques Derrida makes me say, it shores up at the subject's *desistance* its resistant withdrawal.[1]

Who therefore cannot come after the subject. *Who*, enigmatically (and always according to the same enigma), is ceaselessly prior to what philosophical questioning installs as a presence under the name of subject.

A sign of this anteriority, but one that is more than a sign, is that if the question "Who?" has definitively arrived in philosophy (but a philosophy, it is true, that already no longer recognizes itself as philosophy, and certainly not as "philosophy of the subject"), it is in the wake opened by the guiding project of the *Kantbuch* of a "repetition of the establishment of the foundation of metaphysics" (in other words of a repetition of the Kantian "metaphysics of metaphysics," to the extent that the *Critique of Pure Reason* was interpreted as the "first explicit endeavor of a foundation of metaphysics"). We well recall that—I shall simply offer this brief reminder— because he takes his departure in the question of the possibility of the *metaphysica specialis* (rational theology, rational psychology, rational cosmology), Kant is ineluctably brought back to the question of the possibility of ontic knowledge and thereby to that of the possibility of ontological knowledge such that "the foundation of a *metaphysica specialis* is concentrated on the possibility of a *metaphysica generalis*," which, because it is given as "critique of pure reason," implies, as Heidegger said at Davos, that "it is pure *human* reason, that is, *finite* reason, which in advance and on its own strengths delimits the field of the problematic." The object of the critique is thus "to extract the essence of finite knowledge in general," that is to say, to delimit the metaphysical concept of sensibility as finite intuition (as originary reception). And this is what constrains Kant to introduce, with the received division between sensible knowledge (receptivity) and intelligible knowledge (knowledge by means of concepts), a third term that takes account of the finite originariness of knowledge, "a third source of the soul": the transcendental imagination, which is the "hidden root" of the division of reason. But in this, the unity of reason itself is affected: "reason," Heidegger continues, "as point of departure and reference, shatters . . . ; it flies in pieces." An abyss, in other words, opens in and as reason (*Vernunft*). What should have constituted the ground (*Grund*) shows itself as having no ground (*abgründlich*). And this is what is revealed to Kant as he goes in quest of the essence of *ratio*, which is to say, the essence of the subject.

It is before the abyss discovered in this way—and such is, as we know, Heidegger's thesis—that Kant had to recoil: he shrunk before the consequences of his own discovery, and that is why the repetition ought to radicalize (or better yet, aggravate) the Kantian questioning, with the result that in Kant's question (the transcendental question) that which did not come up to the question (but which, however, remained concealed within the question) can be repeated and liberated in its "inner force." Through the very fact of its consequence, Kant's question covered up the collapse of reason (of the subject)—and this is nothing else than the question of man. Since reason is that which metaphysically defines man (*zoon logon ekhon, animale rationale*) Kant's question required that the essence of man be rethought in an altogether different way. And that is moreover what Kant himself had already sensed under the heading of what Heidegger calls the "authentic result" of the Kantian ground, underlying the result he "explicitly" puts forth (the transcendental imagination as possibility of the ontological synthesis) in the form of the three principal questions of the *metaphysica specialis* (what can I know? What should I do? What am I allowed to hope?). Kant indeed sensed this, since these three questions find their unity in a fourth one: What is man? That Kant programmatically refers this question to a philosophical anthropology (which would thus provide the ground of the *metaphysica specialis*) only attests to his reticence. On the other hand it falls to the repetition of the Kantian question (and consequently of its "authentic result") to radicalize the question of the essence of man. This is why, if, by Kant's own admission, these questions derive from "the most profound interest of human reason," it is this interest itself that has to be put in question according to the principle itself of repetition, which is to question the question in its very possibility. And if reason in its essence is for Kant finite reason, if his interest—in terms also of his most intimate concerns—is consequently and can only be finitude (like the origin of human reason), this means that reason should render itself as finite. A difficult task, perhaps the most difficult of all tasks. (If an ethics can still exist, this is obviously where it will have its place: it consists in a duty and a respect— in a law.) What is required is that the question of the essence of man be understood as the question of the finitude of man.

This question orients what Heidegger still called, in 1929, a "metaphysics of *Dasein*," that is to say, fundamental ontology itself, since finitude is nothing other than the ability-to-question as such or, if one prefers, the finite transcendence from which point there arises, for "man" (in the caesura of the subject), the question of being. But in a certain way—and this is perhaps in spite of everything that held it to a certain extent still within the boundaries of a thinking organized around the subject—the "metaphysics of *Dasein*" proceeded from the question "What is?" that is to say, from a question of essence: *Das Wesen des Daseins liegt in seiner Existenz*. This is why if the question "Who?" should nevertheless arise within the horizon of such a "metaphysics of *Dasein*," it could only do so at the price of a second repetition—of an altogether different style and of an altogether different significance than the preceding one—and by abandoning fundamental ontology. And indeed, it is in 1935 in the *Introduction to Metaphysics*, but above all a year later, in the

204 / Philippe Lacoue-Labarthe

first part of the lecture on "Hölderlin and the Essence of Poetry," concerning one of Hölderlin's prose fragments in which it is stated that the task of language is to "say who man is," that the question "Who is man?" appears as the very question of *Dasein*. But *Dasein*, here, is— or is no longer—anything but the historial *Dasein*, which of course it had been since *Being and Time*, but in such a way, however, that Heidegger could still say at Davos that *Dasein* emerges par excellence in "the act of philosophizing," without, however, feeling the need to recall that "the act of philosophizing" is always historial.

But the question "Who?" as the first version of the lecture "The Origin of the Work of Art" (1935) demonstrates, is nothing other than the question "Who are we?" ("this knowledge or this nonknowledge—about that which the art and artwork can and must be in our historial *Dasein*—*jointly* determine the question of knowing *who we are*."). The "we," clearly, can refer to a "We Germans." Of course, "the Germans" or "Germany" (indeed, more largely, Europe or the Occident), inasmuch as their existence is precisely what is at the basis of the question, cannot be determined with any kind of positivity or as any kind of a *quid*. However, it is still the case that between 1929 and 1935 it is to a very real German *Volk* and to the regime that it had brought about that Heidegger had addressed the question of *Dasein*. I do not recall this in order to trounce Heidegger once more, as has become customary (the fact that he was constrained to pose the question "Who?" indicates quite sufficiently, moreover, the shock registered in his thinking by the "official" derailment of 1933–34). Nor am I raising the point in order to suggest that the question "Who?" is always necessarily a political one (we are well aware of this); I do so rather in order to accentuate an immense difficulty.

(Ten years later Heidegger himself recognized this difficulty: the "Letter on Humanism" explicitly challenges, in the same way it challenges the question "What?" the question "Who?" in that it presupposes, for every possible answer, a subject.)

This difficulty is none other than the difficulty of identification.

I do not use this term here in the sense that Freud introduced in the "Mass Psychology," i.e., in order to explain the formation of the social bond to the extent that it is not in essence libidinal. I use it therefore in the sense where it is at bottom the mimetic process whose task—probably untenable—is to account for the birth of the subject ("to identify *oneself* with" obviously presupposing a subject). I use the term in the much simpler sense of, for example, administrative language: in its transitive sense, as when one says that one identifies someone (or even something). The question of *who*—which only comes "after the subject" to precede the question itself—is, as the very question of existence, what I have called for want of anything better the question of identity. One can, and indeed one should, distinguish between a constituted identity and an identity that is not yet established or, in the experience of the *Werheit*, suddenly suspended, as though by a brusque and suffocating collapse of the subject into the "we." Even so, the question immediately turns around into this: As what do we exist if we do not (or no longer) exist as subjects?

We *live* as subjects, in the sense of daily living, that is to say, in the sense of being affected, but this is completely different. In daily life we never cease relating to ourselves: this relationship is what defines identity as subject. Such an identity, that is to say, the movement of relating to oneself, presupposes alienation in the dialectical sense: this, however, does not in any way affect the integrity of the subject's being. On the contrary. But the self forecloses existence, and this is why the question of alienation always arises, now in the pathological sense, now as what a certain Marxism was certainly not wrong in calling reification (if one at least endeavors to understand by that the coagulation of existing into a thing, Being-one's-Self as a thing, that is to say, the alienation of a native or originary alteration).

The alienation of a native alteration is propriation (identification). The perhaps inevitable slippage of the question "Who?" into the question "As what (do we exist)?" requires propriation. And, whatever one might say, this surely did not fail to keep Heidegger within the limits that he was the first to have drawn. One of these limits can be located in the motif of the people (of the *Volk*). This is not the least significant of limits, even if one objects that the people (the historial *Dasein*) cannot under any circumstances be confused with what constitutes a given nation. The slippage from the one to the other resulted in the confusion (and what a confusion!). Another of these limits is indicated under the motif of the sacred, and involves the entire thematic of poetry (*Dichtung*), language (*Sprache*), and myth (*Sage*). In each of the cases, it is a question of naming: Germany, the "sacred names." Propriation (identification) is carried out through naming—that designation that is fearful because it can be sacralizing.

The question is, therefore: how, if one has to ask "Who?," to avoid the fall of *who* into the sacralization of the name (in the alienation-reification of the "As what?"). It is a question that Nietzsche, in a sudden flash (the last one?), had perceived: "In the end, I am all the names of history."

Perhaps one should not begin by deploring "the lack of sacred names." But this is far from being an adequate response. Perhaps indeed we should be putting more in question—beyond the single question "What is?"—the philosophical mode of questioning, and the exorbitant privilege this mode of questioning grants the question. After all—here I repeat myself—the question "Who?" which is foiled by a simple "no one (No One)," a name without a name, is not a question for philosophy. It is not "worthy" of philosophy. Perhaps, then, one should leave to "literature" (I would willingly say: to writings, with no more identification than that) the effort of sounding that call: "Who?"—the effort of giving itself up to that call and of being summoned by it—so that the feeling "that there is someone" can tremble again, even if it were anonymous, and that from this *lethargy* there might arise the admiration for existence.

Notes

1. See J. Derrida, "Desistance," Introduction to Lacoue-Labarthe's *Typography: Mimesis, Philosophy, Politics,* ed. Christopher Fynsk (Cambridge, Mass.: Harvard University Press, 1989).

16

Philosophy and Awakening
Emmanuel Levinas

I

The independence or exteriority of being in relation to the knowledge that it commands in truth, and the possibility of this exteriority "interiorizing" itself in the knowledge that is also the *place* of truth, is the condition of the world in which an accord of thought and being is produced. This accord is not a mysterious adequation of the incomparable, an absurd equation between "psychic fact" and "physical (and spatial) fact"—which have, of course, no common measure—it is the fact of perception: the original union of the open and the graspable, of what is given and what is taken—or understood—in the world. And so the ideas of knowledge and being are correlative and refer us to the world. To think being and to think knowledge are to think in terms of the world. And so being and consciousness are attached to presence and representation, to the graspable solid that is the originary thing, to some*thing*, to the identical to be identified through its multiple aspects or, as we might say, to the Same. This is the ontic wisdom of perception— the wisdom of everyday life and of the nations that guarantee the universality of the science born of perception, the wisdom of truth and of the world.

In the way it is taught—but already in the forms of its direct discourse— philosophy has kept an ontic style. It seems to bear on *entities* (*étants*). Even when it wishes itself to be ontological. The being of the entity would, undoubtedly, no longer be a "something" since one cannot say that it *is*; the temptation nonetheless remains (and it is not the effect of a writer's clumsiness or carelessness) to speak of the truth of this being-verb and of the unveiling in which it manifests itself. Is it enough to reduce this ontic style to the logic of a certain language, one that is to be surpassed? Does it signify the truth of Kantism: the impossibility of any sensible thought that would not lead back, in one way or another, to a given, to the representation of being, to the presence of being, in the world? Does it signify, as

Translated by Mary Quaintance.

it does in another Kantian register, a new transcendental appearance? This language of representation has often been denounced in philosophy, where truths are stated as if they were the truths of some sublime perception, some sublimated sensibility, where they are understood like those of the science of Nature or of historical narrative and as if, in their scholarly and even sophisticated texture, they still referred to the functioning of a piece in some subtle clockwork of being. Jeanne Delhomme's effort, for example, from *Pensée Interrogative* through *La Pensée et le Réel* to *l'Impossible Interrogation*,[1] consists in finding in the language of philosophers a significance other than that of an ontic and even ontological speech, in separating philosophy and ontology and even, in a certain sense, philosophy and truth. Which is not to say—let us point it out in passing all the same—that philosophy would be the realm of the lie, which could not exactly be said of art.

But taken for an ontic knowledge, and considered alongside the coherent, communicable, universal results of scientific knowledge, philosophy has, in our time, lost all credibility. Disagreement among philosophers had already long since compromised its credibility. This disagreement is deplored in the *Discourse on Method*, and it is one of the motivations of the *Critique of Pure Reason* and of Husserl's phenomenological investigation, as Husserl demonstrates in 1910 in his famous article "Philosophy as Rigorous Science." But, behind the theme of the end of metaphysics, this depreciation of philosophy signifies in our time, perhaps most clearly, the awareness of a countermeaning perpetuated by a philosophy engulfed in its language, a philosophy that, in the guise of netherworlds, hypostasizes the meaning of its thoughts, in which it can find only ontic import. The work of the rearguard of this philosophy in retreat consists in deconstructing this so-called metaphysical language that, though ontic, is neither perception nor science, and in which one would like to find, through a psychoanalysis of the deconstructed materials, at least a signification of some ideological symptoms.

II

The philosophy of Hegel appears, even before today's crisis, to be informed by this *hubris* of a philosophy speaking the language of perception or expressing the arrangement of the cosmic order or the interdependence of historical events. Philosophic truth would not be an opening *onto* something, but the intrinsic rule of a discourse, the logic of its logos. Perception, science, narration, with their ontic structure of correlation between a subject and an object to which the subject conforms, no longer convey the model of truth; they constitute determined moments, peripeties of the dialectic. But discourse as logos is not, on its side, a discourse *on* being, but the very being of beings or, if you like, their being as being. It is a philosophy coherent to the point of having already broken with the realist prototype of truth in stating this rupture: Hegelian philosophy is already dialectical discourse when it is only at the point of rallying to the task. It never uses metalanguage, its exposition of itself is properly speaking without prefaces, whereas the philosophers who denounce a certain language system still speak the language they are in the process of condemning. It is a philosophy that recuperates the "truths" of the history of philosophy, despite their reciprocal contradictions and their apparent exclusions. The truths of *Representation* occupy, at determined moments of dialectical discourse, or of the movement of being as being, the place that logically comes back to them, but the process of thought and of being and its truth no longer pertain to Representation. Rationality consists in being able to pass from the *Representation* to the *Concept*, which is no longer a modality of *Representation*.

In so passing it preserves, however, an element that marks the rationality of our received philosophy and that still belongs to the wisdom of perception and of the narrative movement toward the graspable. To accede to the rational is to grasp. Knowledge is no longer *perception*, it is still *concept*. The rational is syn-thesis, syn-chronization of the historical, that is to say, presence; that is to say, being: world and presence. The thought of rational animality is realized in the *Idea* in which history presents itself. The dialectic, in which the moments that have been run through diachronically are recovered—that is, identified, sublated and preserved—tends toward this *Idea*. Philosophy of Presence, of Being, of the Same. A reconciliation of contradictories: from the identical and the non-identical, identity! It is still the philosophy of the intelligibility of the Same, beyond the tension of the Same and the Other.

In their Hegelian and neo-Hegelian form, the dialectical unfolding of rationality and the process of being in the guise of the logic of logos no doubt remain today as a possibility—perhaps the ultimate possibility—of a proud philosophy that, before the sciences, does not apologize for philosophizing: the possibility of a mature humanity, one that does not forget or no longer forgets its past. Neither the aftermath of the Hegelian system nor the crises that have marked the efforts, born of this system, to change the world can be absent from these memories; neither the paling of its rationality before the rationality that triumphs, communicating itself to all in the development of what we call the exact sciences and in the techniques they have inspired; nor the new disagreements between philosophers that the Hegelian message was unable to prevent; nor the discovery of the social and subconscious conditioning of human knowledge. The severe judgment that Husserl brings down upon the arbitrariness of speculative constructions, in his "Philosophy as Rigorous Science"—a critique disseminated more or less throughout his work— is aimed at Hegel. While remaining outside the Hegelian oeuvre in the details of its execution, this critique testifies to a profoundly felt disaffectedness, a disaffect- edness experienced by a whole epoch, and one that has not been dissipated during the sixty-six years—two-thirds of a century—that separate us from this Husserlian text. The influence of the phenomenology of the *Logical Investigations*, returning "to the things themselves," to the truth of the manifestness with which things "show themselves in their original character," attests not only to the difficulties of naturalistic positivism, but also to a suspicion with regard to dialectical discourse and even with regard to language itself.

But didn't the new promises of a scientific philosophy, Husserl's promises, prove to be just as fallacious? Untenable in the effort to return naively, in the integrity of spontaneous consciousness, to the truth—an opening onto the manifest-truth-of-the-given-being, to the being "in flesh and blood" down to its categorical forms—Husserlian phenomenology is itself caught up in a transcendental lesson in which the given-being-as-original constitutes itself in immanence. The beyond-of-language promised in the *Logical Investigations* does not exempt these very *Investigations* from relying upon the irreducible role played by linguistic signs in the constitution of meaning, and the *Ideas I* affirm the subjacence of doxic theses to all conscious life, which, from that moment, is apophantic in its most intimate structure, on the brink of making itself discourse in its spiritual articulation, even if this discourse must spurn dialectics. Furthermore, we cannot fail to recognize the relation, unceasing in Husserl, of consciousness to identified entities: consciousness as thought of the Same. The pre-predicative toward which—as if to put logical thought into question—the analysis returns, is developed from the outset around the *substrata*, the supports for all formal modifications of logic. And thus the substantive, the nameable, the entity and the Same—so essential to the structure of re-presentation and of truth as truth of presence—remain the privileged and originary terms of consciousness. But, above all, phenomenology itself disengages these structures by reflection, which is an internal perception in which the descriptive operation "synchronizes" the flux of consciousness, in knowledge. Phenomenology, in its philosophic act of the ultimate *Nachdenken*, thus remains faithful to the ontic model of truth. Perception, grasp, in its relation to the present, to the Same, to the entity, remains both the first movement of the naive soul in its pre-predicative experience (precisely insofar as it is experience) and the ultimate gesture of the reflective philosopher.

III

We nevertheless think that despite its gnoseological—ontic and ontological—expression, phenomenology calls attention to an aspect of philosophy in which it does not amount to a reflection on the relation of thought to the world, a relation that sustains the notions of being and the World. Husserlian philosophy would allow us to show thought as something more than explicitation of experience. The latter is always experience of being or presence in the world, thought that, even if it begins in astonishment, remains adequation of the given to the "signative," thought on the scale of the subject and that, precisely as such, is experience, the fact of a conscious subject, the fact of a unity held fast in its position, like the unity of *transcendental apperception* in which diverse elements come together under a stable rule. But this is not the only nor even the initial modality of the subjective in Husserlian analyses, which themselves are always more surprising than the "system" and programmatic discourse.

While appealing to intuition as if to the principle of principles where being presents itself in its original character and in its identity, and where indeed the origin of the notions of Being and the Same can be discovered, while referring itself to this presence in the manifest and to the horizons of the World in which it appears (or to the nostalgia for this presence) as if to the rationality of reason, Husserlian phenomenology *puts everything into question*, down to the formal logico-mathematic series whose objectivity, the *Prolegomenas* of the *Logical Investigations* assured against all psychologization. The appearance of presence not only deceives, but also functions as the obturation of living thought: useful for calculations, signs borrowed from language and from the opinions it conveys take the place of significations of living thought. In their objective essence, the latter are displaced, right before the eyes of the unwitting thinker. Knowledge as acquired knowledge, as a result deposited in a trust of various writings separated from living thought—and even knowledge given in the theme of a thought absorbed by what it thinks and that forgets itself in the object—does not subsist in the plenitude of its meaning. The slippages and displacements of meaning (*Sinnesverschiebungen*)—bewitching or bewitched games—play themselves out at the heart of objectivizing consciousness, of clear and distinct good conscience, without in any way disturbing its spontaneous and naive rational progress. But everything happens as if, in its lucidity, the reason that identifies being were sleepwalking or daydreaming, as if, despite its lucidity as regards objective order, it were sleeping off some mysterious wine in broad daylight. The full intelligence of the untroubled objective gaze remains defenseless against the deviations of meaning. This naiveté nonetheless still guides scientific research in its objectivizing integrity, in keeping with good sense, the most common thing in the world. As if the manifestness of the world as the condition of reason medused and petrified the rational life that *lived* this manifestness! As if the naive gaze, in its ontic intention as gaze, found itself obstructed by its very object and spontaneously underwent an inversion or in some way "imbourgeoised" its condition or, to put it another way, using an expression from Deuteronomy, *waxed fat*. As if, in consequence, the adventure of knowing— of knowing the world—were not simply the spirituality and rationality of the manifest, were not simply light, but instead a drowsiness of the spirit, and as if it required rationality in another sense. It is not a matter of overcoming any kind of limitation of *seeing*, of broadening the horizons belonging to the scheme in which seeing, thematized, appears and, thus, of being induced to recuperate totality from out of a part of totality by some sort of dialectic. To scan the objective horizon of the given in the theme where it appears would still be to take a naive course. There would be a radical heterogeneity—a difference threatening the dialectic—between the vision of the world and the life that underlies this vision. The scheme must be changed. But it is not a matter of adding an interior experience onto exterior experience. We must make our way back from the world to the life already betrayed by knowledge, knowledge that delights in its theme and is absorbed in the object to the point of losing its soul and its name there, of becoming mute and anonymous.

By a movement contrary to nature—because contrary to the world—we must make our way back to a psychism other than that of knowledge of the world. And this is the revolution of the phenomenological Reduction—a permanent revolution. Reduction will reanimate or reactivate the life that is forgotten or weakened in knowledge, called Life from that point on, absolute or apodeictically understood, as Husserl will put it when thinking in terms of knowledge. Beneath the tranquility in itself of the Real referred to itself in identification, beneath its presence, Reduction raises a life against which thematized being will already, in its smug sufficiency, protest and which it will have repressed in appearing. Dormant intentions brought back to life will open lost horizons, ever new, disturbing the theme in its identity as a result, reawakening the subjectivity of identity where it rests in its experience. The subject as intuitive reason in accord, in the World, with being, reason in the adequation of knowledge, thus finds itself brought into question. And doesn't the very style of Husserlian phenomenology, which multiplies gestures of reduction and untiringly effaces from consciousness any trace of subordination to the worldly in order to extract what we term pure consciousness, call attention to what betrays itself *behind* the consciousness submitted to its ontic fate in the thought of the Same?

Reduction signifies the passage from the natural attitude to the transcendental attitude. The *rapprochement* with the Kantian position that this language recalls is well known. And yet we also know that for Husserl it is less a matter of establishing the subjective conditions of the validity of the science of the world or of extracting its logical presuppositions than of giving full weight to the subjective life forgotten by thought directed toward the world. What is the proper interest of this transcendental life, and what rationality does it add to the rationality of natural consciousness aiming at the world? The passage to transcendental life, first accomplished on the Cartesian path, seems to seek certainty. From the inadequate evidence of the experience of the world, the path traces its way back to reflection on the cogitations of which experience is made, in order to measure the degree of certainty or uncertainty of this experience. We are still within a philosophy of knowledge—of being and the Same—within a theory of familiarity. But we could also say that, supported by the certainty of reflection, Reduction liberates sensible thought from the world itself, from norms of adequation, from obedience to the completed work of identification, from the being that is only possible as an assemblage complete within a theme, as the representation of presence. Transcendental reduction would thus not be just another fold in the certainty of the *cogito*, a standard of all meaning true in its manifestness and adequate to thought; it would be the teaching of a meaning *despite* the failure to achieve knowledge and identification, a failure affecting the norms that the identity of the Same commands. Nevertheless, if the reduction does not complete the incompletion of perception and of the science that bears upon the world, and where full coverage of what is targeted is impossible through seeing, it recognizes and measures this failure adequately, and is thus called apodeictic. In the adequation of reflection, a kind of knowledge thus fulfills itself and closes in upon itself, a knowledge that is at once knowledge of knowledge and of nonknowledge, but always sensible psychism.

IV

And so it is that in the *Cartesian Meditations* (§§6 and 9), this apodeictic rationality of a reflection upon reduced consciousness is no longer the condition of the adequation between intuition and the signative that it fulfills. Apodeicticity is lodged in an inadequate intuition. The indubitable character or principle of the apodeictic is not the result of any new piece of evidence, any new light. It is the result of a limited portion, a core of the field of consciousness considered "properly adequate." And it is there that, with emphasis on the word *living*, expressions like "this core is the living presence of the self to itself" (*die lebendige Selbstgegenwart*) and, further on, "the living manifestness of the *I am*" (*während der lebendigen Gegenwart des Ich bin*) appear. Can the living character of this manifestness or of this present be reduced to adequate recuperation? (We may ask ourselves, does the exception of the Cartesian *cogito* itself really, as Descartes says, result from the lucidity and distinction of its knowledge?) Must the liveliness of life be interpreted from the standpoint of consciousness: isn't it only, under the name of *erleben*, a confused or obscure consciousness, prior only to the distinction between subject and object, a prethematization, a foreknowledge? Don't we need another way to explain its psychism? Doesn't the adjective *living* accentuate the importance, from the beginning of Husserlian discourse, attributed to the word *Erlebnis* as an expression of the mode of the subject? Designated by the term *Erlebnis*—the lived— the prereflexive experience of the self is not just a moment of preobjectification, like a *hylé* before *Auffassen*. A living present—we know the importance that this term will assume in the Husserlian manuscripts on time, and the *Phenomenology of Internal Time-Consciousness* conveys, with the notion of *proto-impression*, its explosive and surprising character, similar to that of the present in Bergsonian duration. Unforeseeable, it is not in the least anticipated in any seed that might bear the past and the absolute traumatism that accompanies the spontaneity of its emergence, that is as important as the sensible quality it offers to the adequation of knowledge. The living present of the cogito-sum is not uniquely based on the model of self-consciousness, of absolute knowledge; it is the rupture of the equality of the "equal soul," the rupture of the Same of immanence: awakening and life.

In the *Phenomenological Psychology*, sensibility is experienced before *hylé* assumes the function of *Abschattung*. Its immanence is the gathering in passive synthesis of the time of self-presence. But this self-presence is produced according to a certain rupture, to the extent that the lived is lived for a self that within immanence distinguishes itself from it, that, beginning with the *Ideas I*, is recognized as "transcendence in immanence." In the identity of self-presence—in the silent tautology of the prereflexive—lies an avowal of difference between the same and the same, a disphasure, a difference at the heart of intimacy. This difference is not reducible to the adversity that remains open to conciliation and surmountable by assimilation. Here supposed self-consciousness is also rupture, the Other fissures the same of the consciousness that is thus lived: the other that claims it to be more profound than itself. *Waches Ich*—self in awakening. The sleeping "itself" is asleep to . . . without confusing itself with . . . Transcendent in immanence, the heart maintains its vigil without confusing itself with what solicits it. "The sleep to be looked at closely," writes Husserl, "has no meaning except in relation to the vigil and carries in itself the potential for awakening."[2]

V

But isn't the Self that emerges and in which the identification of the *hylé* with itself is broken in its turn an identification of the Same? We think that Reduction reveals its true meaning and the meaning of the subjective that it allows to be signified in its final phase of intersubjective reduction. The subjectivity of the subject shows up there in the traumatism of awakening, despite the gnoseological interpretation that, for Husserl, ultimately characterizes the element of spirit.

Intersubjective reduction is not simply directed against the "solipsism" of the "primordial sphere" and the relativism of truth that would result from it, wishing to assure the objectivity of knowledge that depends on an accord among multiple subjectivities. The explicitation of the meaning that a self other than myself has *for me*—for my primordial self—describes the way in which the Other tears me from my hypostasy, from the *here*, at the heart of being or at the center of the world where, privileged and in this sense primordial, I posit myself. But, in this tearing, the ultimate meaning of my "me-ness" is revealed. In the collation of meaning between "me" and the other and also in my alterity to myself, an alterity through which I can confer on the other the meaning of myself, the *here* and *there* come to invert their respective meanings. It is not the homogenization of space that thus constitutes itself; it is I—however manifestly primordial and hegemonic, however identical to myself, in what is "proper" to me, however comfortable in my own skin, in my *hic et nunc*—who pass to the second level: I see myself on the basis of the other, I expose myself to the other, I have accounts to render.

It is this relation with the other self, where the self is torn from its primordiality, that constitutes the nongnoseological event necessary to reflection itself, considered as understanding, and, consequently, to the egological Reduction itself. In the "secondarity" in which, before the face of the other (and all the expressivity of the other body spoken of by Husserl is the overture and ethical demand of the face), the primordial sphere loses its priority, subjectivity awakens from the egological: from egoism and egotism.

Contrary to the simple abstraction that moves from "individual consciousness" to "consciousness in general," through an ecstatic or angelic omission of its terrestrial weight and, in the intoxication or idealism of a quasi-magical sublimation—the Husserlian theory of intersubjective reduction describes the astonishing or the traumatising—trauma, not thauma—possibility of sobering up in which the self, faced with the other, is liberated from the self, is awakened from dogmatic slumber. Reduction, in reordering the discomposure of the Same by the Other that is not absorbed in the Same—and does not elude the other—describes the waking, beyond understanding, to insomnia or to the vigil (to the *Wachen*) of which understanding is only one modality. A fissure of the subject that does not protect the atomic consistency of the unity of transcendental apperception. An awakening that begins with the other—who is Other—who, incessantly, puts into question the priority of the Same. Awakening as a sobering up, beyond the sobriety of simple lucidity, which, despite the unsettling and the movements of an eventual dialectic, still remain conscious of the Same—identity of the identical and the non-identical—in its fulfillment and its repose. An awakening and sobering by the Other that does not let the Same alone and through which the Same from the outset resembles the living and, while it sleeps, is exceeded. It is not an *experience* of inequality posited in the theme of an understanding, it is the very event of *transcendence* as life. Psychism of the responsibility for the other that is the lineament of this transcendence and that is psychism in its essence. Transcendence in which, perhaps, the distinction between transcendence to the other man and transcendence to God should not be made too quickly.

VI

But this is no longer Husserl. To the end, with him, Reduction remains a passage from a less perfect understanding to a more perfect one, a reduction on which the philosopher decides almost miraculously, motivated only by the contradictions emerging in naive understanding. The psychism of the soul or the spirituality of the spirit remains knowledge; the crisis of the European spirit is a crisis of Western science. The philosophy that starts with the presence of being—equality of the soul to itself, resemblance of the diverse in the Same—will never explain its revolutions or its awakenings in terms other than those of knowledge. It nonetheless remains the case that, in Husserl, there is, beyond the critique of technique born of science, a critique of knowledge as knowledge, a critique of the civilization of science properly speaking. The intelligibility of knowledge finds itself alienated by its very identity. The necessity of a Reduction in Husserl's philosophy bears witness to a closure at the heart of the opening onto the given, to a drowsiness in spontaneous truth. It is what, protesting the unsettling of transcendence, we have called imbourgeoising, a self-complacency. In the identity of the Same, in its return to self where identifiable Reason pretends fulfillment, in the identity of the Same to which thought itself aspires as to repose, we would have to suspect a dazed stupidity, a petrification, or a laziness. Isn't the most reasonable reason the most awakened waking, the awakening at the heart of waking, at the heart of waking as a state? And isn't the ethical relation to the other the event in which this permanent revolution of sobering up is concrete life? Isn't the liveliness of life excessiveness, a rupture of the containing by the uncontainable, a form that ceases to be its proper content already offering itself in the guise of experience—an awakening to consciousness in which the consciousness of awakening is not the truth, an awakening that remains a first movement—a first movement toward the other of which the intersubjective reduction reveals the traumatism, secretly striking the very subjectivity of the subject? Transcendence. This term is used with no theological presuppositions. On the contrary, it is the excessiveness of life that all theology presupposes. Transcendence, as the amazement of which Descartes speaks at the end of the third meditation (in the French text): the sorrow of the eye exceeded by light, the Same disturbed and kept awake by the other that exalts it. If *from this transcendence of life* we think the idea of God, we can say that life is enthusiasm and that enthusiasm is not drunkenness but sobriety. Sobriety always to be sobered, a vigil on the eve of a new awakening. Ethics.

That this putting into question of the Same by the Other, and what we have called awakening or life, is, beyond knowledge, the condition of philosophy, is not only attested by the articulations of Husserlian thought that we have just shown, but also appears at the summits of philosophies: it is the beyond-being of Plato, it is the entry through the door of the agent intellect in Aristotle; it is the idea of God in us, surpassing our capacity as finite beings; it is the exaltation of theoretical reason in Kant's practical reason; it is the study of the recognition by the Other in Hegel himself; it is the renewal of duration in Bergson; it is the sobering of lucid reason in Heidegger—from whom the very notion of sobering used in this essay is borrowed.

It is not as understanding of the world—or of some sort of netherworld—nor as *Weltanschauung* that we have tried to explain the transcendence—the awakening and sobering up—from which point speak philosophies, permanent revolutions, as necessary to a knowledge that is anxious to reduce the naiveté of its consciousness as to one that prolongs itself in an epistemology that interrogates the meaning of its results. A transcendence that does not amount to an experience of transcendence, for palpably prior to any *position* of the subject and to any perceived or assimilated content. A transcendence or awakening that is the very life of the human, already unsettled by the Infinite. Whence philosophy: the language of transcendence and not the narrative of an experience: a language in which the speaker belongs to the narrative, thus a necessarily personal language to be understood beyond what it says, that is, to be interpreted. Philosophy is philosophers in an intersubjective "intrigue" that nobody resolves, while nobody is allowed a lapse of attention or a lack of rigor. We will not enter here into the perspectives thus opened by the ethical signification of waking and transcending and, notably, perspectives on time and diachrony as reference to the Uncontainable.

Notes

This text first appeared in *Les Etudes philosophiques* no. 3 (1977).

1. See *Pensée interrogative* (Paris: P.U.F., 1954), *La Pensée et le réel; Critique de l'ontologie* (Paris: P.U.F., 1967), and *L'Impossible interrogation* (Paris: Desclée, 1971).

2. *Phänomenologische Psychologie*, ed. Walter Biemel, *Husserliana IX* (The Hague: Martinus Nijhoff, 1962), p. 209.

17

Sensus communis:
The Subject in
statu nascendi

Jean-François Lyotard

These will be notes and remarks rather than an exposé: their community, in the sense of their reciprocal action that today we often call system, remains to be established. Although they are quite "common" in the sense of trivial, this time. My preference is no doubt imposed on me by my unpreparedness but equally by the subject. The unpreparedness proceeds from the subject. No one will ever be prepared for this *sensus*. Every community will forget and will have forgotten this *sensus*. Sensus communis is not *intellectio communis, der gesunde Verstand*, good sense, sound understanding, that of communication through the mediation of the concept. Even less is it *intellectio communitatis*, the intelligence of the community. It is a question of a community that is still—but that *still* presents a problem—unintelligent. Unintelligent, therefore, that is to say, proceeding without intellect. And unintellected, too, that is to say, one whose concept, *ex hypothesi*, will always be missed. And if we are condemned to think it, to think of it, by means of the concept (this is required by the exposé, the exposition, the Kantian *Exponieren*: "to reduce a representation of the imagination to concepts")[1], then the said "community" of sense, and through sense alone, can only be situated or put in place in the field of the *intellectio* negatively in my exposé in the mode of critical thought whenever it deals with taste: pleasure but without interest, universality but without concept, finality but without representation of an end, necessity but without argument. Unpreparedness is the very fact of my subject, *sensus communis*, which demands it. It demands that the intellect be at a loss. That it has got nothing ready. Without a show of readiness, something of which it is incapable, because it is spontaneous activity, *Selbsttätigkeit*. This *sensus* and this *communis* appear to be ungraspable in their exposition. The other of the concept. And so a good opportunity for metaphysics.

The understanding ought to stay disarmed, right up to where it touches this sense. Immunized against itself, letting itself touch, and be touched by, this

---

Translated by Marian Hobson.

common. But its "spontaneity," that activity whose principle is only in itself, its authoritarian munificence, the generosity of its office, of its *munus*—which is to synthesize by itself, off its own bat—cannot accept the sharing out of the munitions, the putting into common ownership of syntheses. The understanding will always find itself again in the community, it will refer the community back to its own power. It can only, at most, declare of its own accord that no, there *is* a synthesizing outside it, another way of synthesizing. But even in the apparent disavowal that the understanding makes of its activity, in the apparent modesty of this negative analytics (as one speaks of negative theology) its arrogance in distributing roles, in being master of communities can only continue to betray itself. Let us make no mistake about it: if thought, insofar as it is philosophical, consists in thinking by concepts, then with the *sensus communis* philosophy touches on that thought that is not philosophical, touches on it precisely because it cannot handle it. And it is this that should be understood in *sensus*. Is it by chance that the adverb *sensim*, which should mean "so that it can be sensed," mostly means "insensibly"? *A sensus* insensible to the *intellectus*. A community insensible to the community of argumentative syntheses. With the question of this sense we come, in particular, to the confines of literature and philosophy, of art and philosophy. These confines were called *Aesthetics* in eighteenth-century Europe. It is a matter of tact or tangent, at least for philosophy. Philosophy has difficulty in making contact with the *sensus*. It wants, by vocation, by hypothesis, to keep itself intact from the *sensus*, to prevent it from going off on a tangent. But also it wants to think everything, to think according to its rule, intellection, including therefore the unintelligent and the untouchable.

So all philosophy can do, just as all I can do only in expositing, is register that the concept, my concept, does not manage to touch the *sensus communis*. This sense is too near, or too far. More likely, this difficulty is not even a matter of distance, of interval. This *sensus* is indeed not situated in that space and time that the concept uses to know objects, neither in the space-time of knowledge, nor in the space-time that sensibility in the first *Critique* prepares precisely for knowledge by means of the schemata. For if there is a *sensus communis* it is made necessary by another necessity, another universality, and another finality than those that knowledge requires. So that even using these words gives rise to amphibology. For the cognitive community (the scientific one in its most determinate modality) these words "necessity," "universality," "finality," are names of categories that can be defined and exhibited, applicable in the space-time of experience. For the community that exists in and through sense they designate those movements of the imagination (called reflexion by Kant) that proceed obscurely (but this obscurity is qualified in this way by the understanding), Kant says, through comparison, through *Vergleichung*. It is this comparing that puts the intelligence in disarray, makes it unprepared in the face of the *sensus* which rounds it off: this is what cannot be avoided. It has to be said clearly: the *sensus* does not give rise to an experiencing, in the Kantian sense. The aesthetics of the beautiful is not the aesthetics of truth. Taste teaches nothing about the object, it has no object, no referent. If there are forms in play in these two aesthetics, those of the first *Critique* are oriented in their end toward knowledge, those of the third toward pure pleasure. And everything leads one to think that these last, more purely reflexive, more constitutive or productive, are diverted and tamed by the former. So, it is *not* really impossible to forestall the *sensus communis*. The mind will always have got itself pre-pared (after the fact, naturally), will always be able to comment on it, take it with itself into the mental community, into its authority, and begin it again. And yet it is indeed a question with this common sense of something "uncommon," out of the ordinary, of a singular according to intelligence:

> We often give to the judgement, if we are considering the result rather than the act of its reflection, the name of a sense, and we speak of a sense of truth, or of a sense of decorum, of justice, etc. And yet we know, or at least we ought to know, that these concepts cannot have their place in sense. (*KUK*, §40 *CJ*, p. 135)

Although in short we know that this sense is not a sense at all, nonetheless, Kant adds, even to that common understanding, to that minimal intelligence presupposed in every man, to the least privileged intelligence, the most vulgar but the most distinctive of the human mind, must be accorded this "mortifying [*krankende*] honour" of being called "common sense." Mortification: the understanding is demoted to a sense. Honour: this descent to the lowest is perhaps a new ascent to the well-springs of the capacity to judge, presupposed in every activity, intellectual even, and voluntary.

That may be what is at stake in the *Critique of Judgement* (aesthetic judgement). There would be judgment before the concept, and even before the schema, before the operation of synthesis, which is however very elementary, that brings together the pure diversity of sense-data (their matter) into unities that are apprehensible, reproducible and recognizable, and offers them as an experience to be grasped, to the *Ergneifen*, to the *Begreifen*, the categories of the understanding. Judgment, and so for Kant, synthesis, would not consist in determining regularities, as in the cognitive law, nor even in preparing them in sensible matter, by constructing spatio-temporal sequences that form objects in experience. A kind of nondenotative synthesis, not turned toward the object, and thus called strictly subjective, that is, exclusively felt (there's the *sensus*, which is feeling). This sentimental synthesis, this judgment that is feeling, deserves to be attributed to a *sensus*, unlike good sense. For with this *sensus* we are sent back to the most humble, the most "common" level of judgment, in a "state of mind" that as yet owes nothing (nothing as yet, or already nothing) to knowledge and its intrigues.

And in the same way (turning now toward the other elder sister, the other great faculty, not the theoretical this time but the practical), there would be judging and synthesizing independent of desire, whether it be empirical, as need or penchant, or transcendental, as pure will. That is to say, unlike every desire (I would add, although it is not Kantian: whether it is conscious or unconscious), a judgment not having "knowledge" of its end. One could say: a blind judgment, quite blind, without even the "clairvoyance" about what it has not got that is necessarily supposed by the psychoanalytical hypothesis of the "wish fulfilment" in the symptom, and by the accompanying hypothesis that this symptom can be deciphered thanks to this aim (even if it were to be illusory) for fulfilment. A judging blind to every end, but for this very reason, not a symptom. Or, as Kant says, "disinterested." Without interest in liberty nor in pleasure in the usual sense. A state of mind that owes nothing as yet (nothing as yet or already no more) to the intrigues of willing, whatever it may be. This feeling (since this *sensus* is sentimentality), when it is a question of tasting beauty, is precisely a feeling of pleasure, but a pleasure that does not come to fill up a lack nor to fulfill any desire at all. A pleasure before any desire. This aesthetic pleasure is not the purpose of a purposiveness experienced (or not experienced) beforehand as desire. It has nothing whatsoever to do with an end or purpose. It *is* finality, purposiveness itself, which has no end, no purpose in front of it and no lack behind it. So an instantaneous purposiveness, immediate, not even mediated by the diachronic form of the internal sense, nor by our way of remembering and anticipating. Certainly we (understanding, and reproductive imagination, memory), we remember this instant and we will try to reiterate it. We will try to integrate it, to give it a place in our intrigues, our narratives, our explanations, all our arrangements of every kind. But it will have been independent of them. On the occasion of a form, which itself is only an occasion for feeling, the soul is seized by a small happiness, unlooked-for, unprepared, slightly dynamizing. It is an animation or an *anima* there on the spot, which is not moving toward anything. It is as if the mind were discovering that it can do something other than will and understand. Be happy without ever having asked for it nor conceived it. An instant that will seem very long, measured by the clock of intrigue, but that is not in the purlieus of its timekeeping; a flash made of delayings (you tarry near beauty), a form, a little synthesis of matters in space-time, made sense, *sensus*. A sense that has to be thought of as absolutely singular. The occasion is the case. And it is this absolutely singular *sensus* that would be *communis*. So the finality, the purposiveness is end-less, purposeless, without a concept of its end. This is why the feeling of the beautiful has nothing to do with perfection, with this completion that *Vollkommenheit* connotes.

Here it is no longer the philosophy of intellect that cannot touch this *sense*, it is our occupational willing, our philosophy of will, of the infinite will established in the West at least since Descartes and Hobbes down to Nietzsche and Freud, to make no mention of the political all-comers bearing very diverse names. —What can a *communitas* be that is not bound to itself by a project?—this philosophy whispers to us. That has no Idea of what it wants to be and must be? Not having the Idea of its unity even as a horizon? These are false questions, directed by a line we have not questioned, by the prejudice according to which what comes first is the diverse, chaos (matter, according to Kant himself and many others) and that a principle is needed to unify it even if only into elementary forms. A gravitation, an interaction, I do not know, that can make a One out of this multiplex. Desire, the will, this is one of the names of this principle of interaction and integration. And pleasure or happiness, this will be when the desired, the will having been achieved, the synthesis is made between what one is and what one wants or desires to be. Even if it is explained to us that this does not exist, that it is always missed, that this happiness of fulfillment is a trap—this changes nothing about the principle that community is the desire experienced by diversity.

And as we know, this picture tells a story. With the willing of the will, there is displayed a time, memory and project, heritage and program. A narrative.

But if there really is a *sensus communis*, then it is a pleasure that has not been, will not have been, obtained by desire or willing, that has not come to a conclusion, or belted together the two ends of an Odyssey, not even for a moment. It will not have the character of a return, of a knot. And the *common* of this *sensus* will not have been a matter of project. This feeling creates no chronology, nor even a simple diachrony. It is not a question of an historical and social community that people of taste or artists, any more than people of science and will, form or want to form. It is not a question of "culture," or pleasure shared in, through, and for culture. And there is no progression promised to this pleasure of the beautiful, precisely because it is not desired.

As you see, that makes a lot of "no's" and "not's."

I quoted from Section 40 of the third *Critique*: "We often give to the judgment, if we are considering the result rather than the act of its reflection, the name of a sense." Sense as a result. *Sensus* is reflexion, the faculty of judging reflexively, but considered afterward, and not when it is operating, a little like an instance of sensibility. Now at the end of the same section:

> I say that . . . the aesthetical judgement rather than the intellectual may bear the name of a sense common to all [*eines gemeinschaftlichen Sinnes*], if we are willing to use the word "sense" of an effect of mere reflection upon the mind, for then we understand by sense the feeling of pleasure (*KUK* §40; *CJ*, p. 138).

The faculty of judgment, according to Kantian vocabulary, acts reflexively. The result of this operation (but probably it is not an "operation"), its effect on the mind, is the feeling of pleasure. The *sensus* is then like the seat of a capacity for pure reflexion. A seat established afterward. We know that Kant does not feel happy about assigning a place of residence to the intermediate faculty in the layered geography of the faculties—doubly layered (faculties of the soul, faculties of knowledge), each faculty being endowed with its a priori principle and with its domain or territory of reference—in this transcendental geography; the intermediate faculty, the "go-between" whose mission it is to make the link between intellection and desire, between theoretical understanding and practical reason. This capacity to negotiate is called, in the soul, the faculty of pleasure and pain, and in knowledge is called simply the faculty of judging.

Yet one judges everywhere, in every domain, and in all of them there is some *sensus* at work, a state of mind, even if it knows and wills. For the one that knows, Kant only explains things occasionally. There is, however (and this is transcendentally required), a feeling of pleasure, a euphoria associated with knowledge, that is, with the cooperation of sensibility and understanding required by knowledge, a subjective euphoria from the subsuming of an intuition under a concept, which guarantees objectivity. This is transcendentally required to such an extent that Kant has recourse to it in his deduction of the *sensus communis* in Section 21 of the third *Critique*. But this sentimental aspect of knowledge is kept rather clandestine. The transcendental *sensus* of ethical practice, on the contrary, has had considerable success, as we know, via the analysis of *Achtung*, of respect, in the second *Critique*. The fact remains that if we judge in ethics as we do in knowledge, the faculty of judging, the "go-between," must be in action here as well as in aesthetics. But it is hidden, and stays so. The intermediary erases itself, slides away, the faculty of judging leaves the office of synthesis to its elder sisters.

Bringing together is the mission of the concept and/or of the reproductive imagination (the schema) in knowledge as such, and the mission of reason in moral practice. The preliminary work of feeling is operating more openly in the latter case, in the name of respect (and in the name of its counterpart, humiliation of the empirical individual's presumption and self-love). But it is kept at the level of "motive," of *Triebfeder*, of the spring that projects an impure act of will, hung up in pathological motivations, toward the pure moral law. In this way, the faculty of judgment in its most humble form, feeling (here, pleasure and pain, for the feeling of obligation is mixed) is brought down, as in the case of the imaginative schema, to the rank of a mere sketch of a synthesis, is reduced by critical analysis to the role of mere precursor and sign of the veritable a priori ethical synthesis, of the true condition for morality that is not obligation but law, the free synthesis of "thy" action and of universal liberty, free, thanks to the free play of the "as if," of the *so daß* between the prescription to "act" and the universal principle of legislation valid for a community of reasonable and practical beings (also called "persons").

So the *sensus* and the *commune* are necessarily separated in the case of knowledge and in the case of ethics. The cognitive community or the community of people of learning is, as Habermas would say, "discursive," or as K. O. Apel would put it "one of argument." It is mediated by agreement, required pragmatically, over the rules for establishing a true judgment. And the ethical community, if there is one, can only indeed be an ideal of practical reason, a suprasensible society formed from beings with free will, but even so, it too is mediated by the recognition of the suprasensible character of freedom, by the Idea (which is an Idea of reason, and not a concept of understanding) of a moral law that contains tautologically, so to say, the principle of this community in its determinateness. In any case, it is neither feeling nor respect that makes up an ethical community, nor even that requires it.

Obligation only requires community because the law, whose feeling obligation is, contains this community in its definition.

I mean that there is no moral *sensus communis*, but only a reason that is common in its practical ethical use. Or again, the seat of the common, when it is a question of being just, is not in the feeling (even if the latter can forewarn us), but in an "unfathomable" concept, not found in experience, the Idea of freedom. Ethical community cannot be immediate, it must be mediate, mediated by an Idea of reason. So that it is subject a priori (but that must be argued for, proved) to a progression that is the progression of susceptibility (*Empfänglichkeit*) to the Ideas of reason. This is the question of culture, of the culture of the will, that is of reason in its practical use. In the end, there is only a possibility of progress and progression if there is a concept, if the *ambitus* (the register) of what is conceived (through the understanding and through reason) becomes wider, and richer. Now it is constitutive of the concept that it develops in its scope (its quantity) or its tenor (its quality): it is impelled by maximization, says Kant, haunted by the infinite. It is polarized by the principle of something suprasensible, whether cosmological or ethical. This is also why the feeling that can serve as a *signum* of the progress of humanity toward the best is not the immediate pleasure of the beautiful, and cannot be (even if the beautiful is a passable analogue for the good), but is the feeling of the sublime, which far from being immediate and simple is divided in itself and needs the representation of the Idea of freedom, and so the development of pure practical reason. History too has the infinite in it only through the concept.

But what might an aesthetical suprasensible be? The *sensus communis*, if we take *sensus* in the sense of feeling, cannot and must not be mediated by a concept. There, in aesthetics, the pure faculty of judgment, the capacity of bringing together the manifold without having the rule (concept) nor the law (Idea) of that bringing together—this is the definition of reflexivity—must operate without any additions, within the modesty of an immediate synthesis, the form, that makes the subjective synthesis, the feeling, immediately. In other words, reason in the broad sense, the theoretical faculty of *intellectio*, the practical faculty of *acta*, has no interest in it.

We are never done with the true and the just, but the beautiful does not develop. The feeling that it is does not belong to process.

The section in the first *Critique*, the Dialectic of Cosmological Ideas, that points out three interests of reason, theoretical, practical, and popular, needs analyzing in detail. These interests can be contradictory. What is meant by popular? What we call political, at least in part, in the part of it concerning the "public" or *Öffentlichkeit*. But aesthetics, which is certainly concerned in this latter, is not dependent on it, not at all, through its principle. For through its principle, on principle, aesthetics is not susceptible to any interest. Reason, be it popular, practical, or theoretical, can find no advantage in it. Of course this is because the aesthetic feeling is not mediated, whether by concepts or Ideas, and because it does not obey the impulse, which drives the concept, to extend the register of its domain of application. Because this feeling is not in the service of any concept, is not even subject to that kind of conceivable time that is the schema. In the pleasure of the beautiful, feeling is enough, absolutely enough. It announces nothing further. Is of no use to anything. A *go-between* in the process of coming and going, transmitting no message. *Being* the message. A pure movement that compares, that afterward we put under house-arrest in a seat called *sensus*. But this house-arrest is itself only analogical. One that we project on an object when we call it beautiful. But the object is merely an occasion. It is still impossible to capture in a name the capacity for reflection by and for itself, and the objectivity of beauty is still impossible to establish.

As for the *common* of this "sense," the "community" or communicability that qualifies it, that is certainly not to be observed in experience. It is certainly not what we call a "public." Not the society of art-lovers in museums, galleries, concerts, theaters, or who today look at reproductions of works (and, I may add, of landscapes) in their homes. The *sensus* must be protected from anthropologization. It is a capacity of mind. And yet . . . , only if the mind itself is not taken aback, interrupted by pure aesthetic pleasure. Only if the *anima* or the animation procured by the beautiful does not put the mind in a state of suspense. Only if, to sum up, the mind is not limited to the office and the exercise of intrigues.

So a secret *common*, that is, put aside, separated, secessioned, and as the expression goes in Latin *securus*, put out of reach of *cura*, of care, a common with no cares. *Sorgenfrei*, as Heidegger could never have written in 1927. Kant calls *anima*, soul, this mind free of care.

We know how Kant comes to detect this common in the analysis of taste. If pleasure is aesthetic, it is disinterested and without concept, but it also has to be universal in its quantity, unlike a particular preference, and it has to be necessary in its modality, unlike the pleasure that can be procured by an object in general (this pleasure is only possible, and the modality of its synthesis with the object will only be problematical), it has to be necessary also in opposition to the pleasure procured by an agreeable object (where the modality of the judgment made is assertoric: *de facto*, that pleases me).

If it were not to fulfil these conditions of necessity and universality, the first relative to the enunciation, the second to what is enunciated, a judgment of taste, the aesthetical feeling could never be isolated as such. And there would be no art because there would be no pure pleasure, independent of empirical or transcendental interests.

We are satisfied by an object that we find agreeable. But we do not require that this satisfaction be shared by every one, nor that it be posited as inescapable.

This said, neither the necessity of judging like this nor the universality of the attribution of the predicate "beautiful" to *this* rose can be deduced. Kant says, about universality, that the singular judgment of taste is *enjoined* (*ansinnen*) on everyone, and, about necessity, that it is not given apodictically, as the conclusion of a piece of reasoning, but as an *example*, always singular for a rule or norm of aesthetical feeling to which everyone should give their consent, but which always remains to be found, which is never found.

Before specifying, as far as an exposé can, the nature of this consent, enjoined and promised at the same time, just one observation: the analysis of quantity and that of modality, respectively, universality and necessity of the feeling of the beautiful, converge towards a strange pole, "surprising" says Kant, the *Einstimmung* or the *allgemeine Stimmung*: the beautiful must be declared in one single voice, in a chorus. This notion of *Stimme*, of voice, is introduced in Section 8, and is not developed. Should it be understood as what is voiced, or vocalized, what sounds "before" any consonant, before any conceptual synthesis? It can also be understood as a unity of votes in an election, here, that of a singular pleasure raised to the dignity of pure pleasure, of universal validity. What voice, what voices are concerned here? Whose are this or these voices? Those of empirical individuals? But what would these be doing in the transcendental determining of taste? I'm not saying that the Kantian text does not ask in passing for this anthropological reading. But the contrary recommendations—to stay inside strict critical analysis—are many, and seem to me to exclude understanding and hearing these voices as if they were phenomena. It is not a matter of social consensus, and even less of one obtained by ballot. The beautiful does not get elected like Miss World.

But the preliminary observation that I wanted to make is the following: the analysis of the quantity (universal) and the analysis of the modality (necessity) of the aesthetic judgment proceed by means of the same mainspring, I would say the mainspring of the *other*, or to use the word with which Kant designates the operator of reflexion, the mainspring of *comparison*, of *Vergleichung*. A sort of "pragmatics," excuse the word, for lack of something better, comes here to take over from the failing of the logical approach. For if the necessity is not apodictic, what can it be then? Exemplary, says Kant, and this makes us reflect on what an example is in transcendental logic. The state of the subject that is called taste, pleasure, or beauty, is a paradigm, a model for itself, at the same time that as a mere example it cannot turn itself into a model, fix itself as a thinkable Idea (to tell the truth, it can, there is an ideal of the beautiful, but the price paid is that an Idea of reason and an empirical concept are allowed to intervene in taste, and thus it loses its exemplary purity, its singularity).

And if universality is not in the attribution of a predicate to the subject of the statement, that is to say, to the object of knowledge, what can it be? Subjective, answers Kant. And that does not mean individual, that means: relative merely to the relationships of the faculties with each other in the subject. If there is a "pragmatics," that is, an examination of sense in terms of its destination (taste constitutes an example *for* the subject), then the senders and the receivers in action in this destination, in this *Bestimmung*, are the constitutive instances of the supposed "subject": imagination, understanding, at least. And the *Einstimmung*, that would be the chorus made up by these voices. A singular chorale, made piece by piece, one flower of vocal polyphony, another flower, then another, their suite not making a melodic intrigue, each one sufficing for itself in the internal comparison of voices, the suite only being constructed afterward, to make a whole. The comparison does not take place from one chord to the next, but on each occasion between the sounds.

Here is where the true difficulty of understanding (and hearing) the *sensus communis* begins, once the anthropological temptation has been chased away. That it really is a question of this harmonic agreement for Kant, when he does not let himself be carried away by the anthropological reading of what he is trying to think, can find a proof in Section 21 of the third *Critique*, where the authorization to presuppose the "sensus communis" is extorted, one might say, from reason, by means of a demonstration whose amplitude is surprising, in that it goes back to the communicability of every piece of knowledge of an object and of the *sensatio* (of the *Stimmung*) that accompanies it, and that even precedes it "in" the subject.

An argument directed against Hume and based on antiscepticism. If knowledge is not an empty subjective game, then it must be communicable. But besides, and first of all, knowledge would not be possible if the faculties in action to produce it did not come into harmony (here is the *Stimmung*) with one another, "on the inside" of the subject, so to speak. This harmony must not be less communicable than knowledge itself, since it produces knowledge.

What does this harmony, this agreement consist in? In a proportionality between the respective activity of the faculties that cooperate in knowledge. Now the proportion varies according to the objects of knowledge. (I imagine here a sort of transcendental chemistry of combinations of the faculties: the proportion of imagination, of sensibility, of understanding, of reason is not the same when that which is at stake is establishing a truth of experience, or a dialectical argument, or a pedagogical rule, or a moral principle. But we shall see that it is a question of music rather than one of chemistry. Of an interior music. Or better: of an intimacy of sounds.) The subject (but what subject—that is the point, as we shall see) is warned by its state about this variable proportion, or rather the feeling is at the same time this state and the signaling of this state. The *sensus* is *index sui*. This is the voice, the *Stimme*: the subject gives voice to itself "before" it sees itself or conceives of itself.

(I shall not develop this point here, though it seems to me highly important. It is always said that time, the internal sense, is the auto-affection of the subject. But the pure sentimental *sensus* is an auto-affection even more pure, a kind of transcendental coenesthesia, which "precedes" all diachronization. The agreements, the chords are only organized in a melodic line secondarily, through the organization of rhythm into diachronic time. And there is not even a harmonic rule or tempering to predetermine (inside themselves) their beauty or their singular exemplarity. The proportion Kant speaks of is not harmonic, architectural, because it is not the object of a concept. It is a "proportion" of timbres, of colorings, of vocal lights.)

So what is given voice in taste is the division of the subject as a division acc(h)orded for one moment, called together in convocation. The demonstration in Section 21 ends by saying "it is necessary"—it is quite necessary that, in the scale of all the possible proportions among the faculties in action for a piece of knowledge (always in the broader sense), there should be one that is "more appropriate." Appropriate to what? Kant says: to the knowledge that is in question. It seems that this is to give back an unexpected and unwelcome privilege to the cognitive function, the referential and determinant one (as if the concept came back into the description of the *sensus*). If, however, we give to the word "knowledge" the broad sense that it must have, and that it often has in Kant, especially in this text, the "appropriateness" of the said exemplary proportion can only be applied to this proportion itself, in the state in which the subject finds itself when such knowledge occurs, and of which, Kant reminds us straightaway, only feeling warns the supposed subject by "animating" it, by waking it up. This feeling is nothing other than this animation. Conclusion: it follows that this agreement, I dare not say and one must not say, perfect, but beautiful, or about beauty, or in beauty, ex-cellent like the knowledge that is its occasion, is a priori universally communicable. And as the *sensus communis* is necessarily presupposed in the communicability of this agreement, since this *sensus* is only the name given to the "seat" (invented afterwards) where these proportions, including the excellent one, are woven, it is indeed reasonable to accept the *sensus communis*.

I have said: the authorization to accredit a *sensus communis* is "torn" from reason by this demonstration. An uncertainty remains, or a confusion about the identity of the terms put into common ownership by the *sensus*: is it a question of faculties, as I am claiming, or of individuals? Written out in ordinary language, with all the risks that implies, the conclusion means that, seen transcendentally, every empirical individual is necessarily the possible seat of such a euphony (rather than euphoria). And, indeed, that is not too difficult. This is part and parcel of the general logic of the critique, in the very notion of an a priori condition of possibility. Kant does not say that the said euphony is necessary to every piece of knowledge. He says that a proportion among faculties is necessary for every piece of knowledge, and that it is necessary for one among all the possible proportions to be preeminently euphonious. It happens or does not happen empirically, and with anyone. But it must be able to happen.

We could stop there, have done here, on this strictly transcendental basis for the *sensus communis*. But the matter is a bit more complicated, or, what is the same thing, the demonstration in Section 21 is rather too a priori, I could even say: a bit too "first *Critique*." What makes matters more complicated, in the third *Critique*, is the way the appeal—let us call it the appeal—for euphony is described, the summons, the *Ansinnen* and the wait, the promise of euphony. More precisely, each individual internal (or subjective) agreement, each judgment of beauty, each state of taste, appeals to the agreement of others, in its individuality. And it seems here to be indeed a question of empirical individuals. Constitutively so, it seems. This appeal constitutes that which makes aesthetic pleasure into a pleasure distinct from every other pleasure. Every other pleasure, including the case where they are at first glance mixed in with the beautiful, is in the charge of an interest: an inclination, a theoretical or practical interest. The appeal to the other, contained in the beautiful, can itself give rise to a mistake about what is meant. And it did not fail to happen.

The appeal can be taken to be directed by an inclination to society. In Section 41, Kant protests against this confusion, which is almost the rule in English aesthetics until Burke, and which will be spread rapidly, after him, by Schiller, right up to the neo-Kantian and neo-neo-Kantian readings of the third *Critique*: it is said that taste prepares or helps on sociability. However, Kant writes, very clearly: "This interest that indirectly attaches to the beautiful through our inclination to society, and consequently is empirical, is of no importance for us now" (*KUK*, §41; *CJ*, p. 140). And he goes so far in disconnecting the "for the other" or the "to the other" that are contained in the empirical *sensus* from any empirical nature that in the following section he eliminates from pure taste everything connected with interest that could enter into it. Starting with the taste for human art, always suspected of "vanity," of "trickery," or procuring "social joys" (*CJ*, p. 142), and an impure content. A work is always the subject of a "mediate interest" (*CJ*, p. 142), turned toward its author's talent, an interest that has a priori nothing to do with the aesthetic feeling. On the contrary, the aesthetical pleasure that nature procures seems free from such mix-ups. but even there it will be necessary to purify the feeling that can be had from natural beauties, by extracting that element in pleasure that comes from what Kant calls the "charms" that these beauties offer.

I shall not say anything here about these "charms" except that what saves us from them, and sufficiently well, if Kant is to be believed, is the contemplation of "beautiful *forms*" (*CJ*, p. 141). Form is immediately felt, and is thus without any possible interest, since interest requires a finalized mediation. Form is without charm. What I will not say on this subject is that as a consequence, if disinterest is formal, then charm is material, that it is matter that exercises a charm on the mind, color, timbre. (This division is worked out in Section 14: line against color, harmony and composition against timbre. Kant resists with all his might an aesthetic of matter. At least when beauty is in question. For the sublime, it is another matter.) So again pleasure in landscape has to have expunged from it that which attracts us to it, empirical individuals that we are.

This lawsuit brought against matter, even natural matter, sheds light on the constitutive function that going via the other has in the judgment of taste. The attraction for a red or for the timbre of the breeze in a poplar tree is not communicable immediately a priori, it is not universalizable without a concept. No more than liking spinach. Each of us can only demand (enjoin, expect) unanimity about forms. Why? Because in sensation form is that by which the imagination can put itself in agreement with the understanding. The understanding has no materiological competence. It is only the principle of rules. Form is a rule sketched out in material presence. Relying on form, we rely on the universality of the potential rules of the understanding. But did I not say that the aesthetical forms of the third *Critique* are precisely not the schemas of the first, that they are freed from any cognitive destination?

Indeed, the freer form is from concept, and thus independent of schematic structures the purer the euphony of the two faculties will be. Because it is not right, either, that form should be subsumed directly under the concept, for that belongs to the constitution of objectivity; but it is necessary for taste that form, however dissonant it is in relation to the concept, however much a stranger, in its free production, from what the understanding can regulate, should indicate, however (even in its dissonance), a possible task for the faculty of rules. And this is how form animates that faculty, one would like to say: that form provokes, excites the understanding. The dissonant agreement, lack of harmony do not scare Kant—on the contrary.

Thus beautiful form does not need to emancipate itself just from matter, but also from the concept. The more distant (I would even say: improbable) the resemblance of the form to the schema and with it to the concept, the more free is beauty, the purer is taste. And thus: the more communicable, since it is guaranteed against any cognitive interest. The imagination producing forms freed from matter and concept, but forms that still invoke possible rules, this invocation or evocation being the secret of the true convocation of the faculties the one by the other, as faculties that make up the subjective euphony. Now to make certain of this formal purification is the mission of the comparison with the other person's judgment.

> But under the *sensus communis* we must include the idea of a sense *common to all* [*die Idee eines gemeinschaftlichen Sinnes*], i.e., of a faculty of judgment which, in its reflection, takes account (*a priori*) of the mode of representation of all other men in thought, in order, as it were, to compare its judgment with the collective reason of humanity, and thus to escape the illusion arising from the private conditions that could be so easily taken for objective, which would injuriously affect the judgment. (*KUK*, §40; *CJ*, p. 136)

And Kant adds, as if to aggravate the evidently anthropological character of this definition of the universalizing procedure, which to my great irritation seems completely to ruin the transcendental reading that I have just suggested: "This is done by comparing our judgment with the . . . judgments of others." After which, Kant continues on about the famous "maxims of common sense," to think on one's own, to think by putting oneself in an other's place, always to think in agreement with oneself. Maxims of which the second, called the maxim of "enlarged thought," is expressly assigned to the faculty of judgment.

The dossier seems heavy against my thesis or my hypothesis, according to which the common is transcendental, that it is an agreement, an uncertain polyphony, whose euphony is not measurable, preparable, but which most assuredly can "take place," as the phrase goes, on occasion, between faculties each endowed with their own timbre. The articles in this dossier suggest something quite different: the universality that is enjoined and promised in every judgment of taste is obtained by each human being when he compares his judgment with that of all the others. "This is done," writes Kant, "by comparing. . . ."

Let us look at it more closely. What is obtained, first of all? The Idea of a common sense, and you know what a Kantian Idea is, is a concept for which there is no corresponding intuition in experience. In Section 8, Kant writes: "The universal voice [*die allgemeine Stimme*] is, therefore, only an idea" (*KUK*, §8; *CJ*, p. 51). The "only" indeed says that there is no question of finding in experience a reality that corresponds to the Idea. Unless by succumbing to illusion, to transcendental appearance, against which all the Dialectic of the first *Critique* constructed the powerful defense mechanisms of the paralogisms, the antinomies, and the impossibilities of pure reason. But none of this will have stopped all well-meaning people, philosophers, politicians, theoreticians of art, from joyously going in between this impermeability of the Idea to experience.

In the third *Critique*, the antinomy of taste is organized in the same way around the status as Idea of the *sensus communis*. Thesis: there is no concept in the judgment of taste. If there were one, it would be possible to decide on the beautiful by means of a proof, by having recourse to the presentation of "realities" in experience. Antithesis: concepts are involved in the judgment of taste, otherwise we would not even "claim for our judgment the necessary assent of others" (*KUK*, §56; *CJ*, p. 184).

This seems to lead to the conclusion that the appeal to the *sensus communis* can be imputed to the part of the composition of taste that is the concern of the faculty of conception, that it draws its *communitas* from the necessity and the universality proper to the concept. And this also confirms the privilege accorded to form over matter in the purification of aesthetic pleasure. But the Antinomy also explains that this concept remains indeterminate and indeterminable, that is, without a possible intuitive proof in presentation, and that thus it is not a concept of understanding but a concept of reason, an Idea.

Is it a question of the Idea of *sensus communis* itself? No, the *sensus communis* as unanimity about the beautiful, unanimity required and promised in each singular aesthetic judgment, is the witness or the sign (and not the proof) "at the heart of" (but this must be investigated) subjectivity, the witness or sign of an Idea that relates itself to this subjectivity and that legitimates this requirement and this promise. This Idea is that of the suprasensible, explains Kant in the "Remarks" that follow Section 59. An Idea of a "suprasensible substrate of all his faculties" (*CJ*, p. 189), faculties of the subject, he writes. It is the Idea that it is in the nature of the subject (it is this "nature" that is the suprasensible in question in aesthetics) for all his faculties to agree to make possible knowledge in general. Understand by knowledge: thought, and thus judgment, and the most elementary, the most miserable, of the modes of thought, reflexion.

This principle of unification, or rather of unison, of the diverse voices of the faculties, a principle that on the mind's side makes certain the possibility of knowing, i.e., of thinking, that makes certain that even the most free form in the imagination keeps an affinity with the power to understand. And even more: this principle of subjective unison is even more enlivened, the "life" of the chorus of the faculties is even more intensified, when form seems to escape the intelligence. This suprasensible is brought into action in aesthetics as "the general ground of the subjective purposiveness of nature for the judgment" (*KUK*, §57; *CJ*, p. 185). The Idea is thus that of an "interior" purposiveness, which is not voluntary, nor conceived of, nor interested in any way, but which is natural to the mind, which is the nature of and in the mind. And this is why art at its basis belongs to nature, and why subjective nature is at bottom art.

I said music, because music is the art of time, and because time is internal sense and the unison in question is interior to the subject. But this time, once again, is not the schema. And the synthesis that it makes is not diachronic, melodic, according to a series that would announce or prepare the ordinal series of numbers. The synthesis is, let me repeat, synchronic, an unmeasurable and unforestallable harmony, a harmony of the timbres of the faculties, on the occasion of a form.

Let's take up the thread again. First, the *elaboration* of the problem: taste is a pleasure without mediation by intelligence or will; this pleasure is a judgment, one that is always singular; it requests, expects, demands, to be shared, it promises itself this; it has not conviction's means of argument, since it is itself unargued for; this is, however, why, although miserable and destitute, aesthetic pleasure distinguishes itself from the pleasures of interest; if we want to avoid making art sink into knowledge or ethics, then the spontaneous demand for unanimity implied in every judgment of taste must be founded, the appeal to an aesthetic sense common to all human beings must be founded.

So the *problem* is to be formulated thus: because aesthetic pleasure is stripped of all universality, of knowing as of willing, we must find the principle that legitimates the claim to universality, a claim that is included a priori in this judgment that is always singular.

Now, the *elaboration* of the *solution*: aesthetic pleasure is a feeling of pure internal euphony; this euphony can only be the "internal" agreement between the two faculties, the two modes of functioning of the mind—its capacity to make something present, to posit it there; its capacity to bring something under rules, to take it with, to con-ceive it; this agreement is an a priori condition of all "knowledge," not from the side of the "knowable," but from the side of the "knower"; if to present and to conceive were still absolutely heterogeneous operations, then not only would there not be any knowable experience, but there would not even be a subject; there would be an operator of presentations and elsewhere an operator of connections; since such is not the case (since knowledge is possible), there must therefore be an a priori principle of unison of the two faculties, which guarantees the possibility of a subject of knowledge in general; this principle cannot be itself knowable in the strict sense, since knowledge presupposes a unified or unifiable subject according to this principle; there is therefore only an Idea of it, or, which comes to the same thing, the principle is a "suprasensible substratum" and can be stated: there must be an affinity between the faculties for there to be knowledge in general.

At last, the *solution* of the problem is: if the euphony singularly felt in the pleasure of the beautiful or the judgment of taste brings with it right away the demand for universality, by appealing to a *sensus communis*, it is because this euphony is the immediate sign of the affinity of the faculties, which is universally required; taste is the feeling of the "natural" destination of the faculties to subjectivity; the principle of such a "nature" being universally valid, the feeling of this destination must also be so; this is why aesthetic pleasure can legitimately claim to be universalizable by demanding the consent of everyone.

This pattern of argument (I have given it the form, dear to Kant, of the logical or mathematical problem, of the *Aufgabe*), this pattern of argument that is also a "deduction" in the Kantian sense (to deduce is to establish the legitimacy of a "claim," to establish that a synthesis is well-founded when it claims truth or goodness or beauty), this pattern of argument calls for a large number of observations and questions. I shall formulate some of them. First, a correction.

I have said that the *sensus communis* called forth by taste is the sign "at the heart of" the subject of an Idea that relates to that subject. And that this "at the heart of" should be further investigated. The metaphor is not a good one. There is no heart, no interiority, in the judgment of taste. In so far as it calls for itself to be shared, pleasure in the beautiful is not experienced by an already constituted and unified subject. This *sensus* is not the internal sense, the aesthetic sentiment is not the auto-affection of the subject. The knowledge of experience, in the first *Critique*, demands a supreme principle of unification, the *I think*, as the originary synthetic unity of apperception. If this is accorded to Kant, it is quite easy to show that such a unity cannot grasp itself except in the form of the internal sense, which is time, for *I* is always behind on its knowledge; even when it tries to anticipate itself.

Compared to this deferred originarity of the *I*, the synthesis at work in aesthetical pleasure is at the same time more radical, less graspable, and wider in scope. For this synthesis is reflexive and not determining. In apperception, the *I* no doubt determines and redetermines itself ceaselessly from one moment to the other, but it remains haunted by determination. In the pleasure of the beautiful, heterogeneous powers find themselves in unison. Because the implied judgment is reflexive, and not determining, the unity is not presupposed, it is a state of "comparison," a sudden pairing up of the faculties. This pairing up does not establish a parity, the two parties are not a pair, they remain incomparable. There is no common measure for "presenting" something and for explaining it. The two parties defy each other. Between them there is defiance and mistrust, and, therefore, at the same time, confidence. I should like to say "fiance," "affiancing." There is too much for the understanding to think in the forms, especially the very free ones, that imagination delivers to it; and the imagination remains threatened by that regulation that the faculty of concepts could always impose on forms, by the intellectual "recuperation" of forms. It is according to this competition of the two powers that, on occasion, sometimes, their possible concert can be heard. Then the proportion will have been right. But that proportion remains indefinable, it cannot be prepared or forestalled. The sentimental congruence of the faculties is never brought to light in the determination. When the understanding tries to take over this affiancing, it can only determine the schematism, only the form that is aready determined and prepared for the concept. And it can only attribute this determinate synthesis to the determining faculty, that is, to itself. In this effort of determination, the deduction of the synthesis of forms leads necessarily to legitimating the synthesis, the synthetic apperception said to be originary, by the *I think*. For this is the origin of all the determining and determinable syntheses.

But it is not an origin for the reflexive syntheses. These happen without any *I think*. In a different light, in a different time. The critique of taste tries to make heard this bringing to light, this birth of a fiance between faculties. It finds its time and place in the light of reflexion, violent and gentle like a rivalry. It cannot be questioned. It is analysis, the Analytic that deduces its legitimacy from the principle of a substratum of affinity. This substratum is not a subject, not the subject, only an Idea that is not implied in the concert, but in the analysis of the concert. If we try to keep at the level of the pleasure in the beautiful, when describing it, then we must not say that it is experienced by the subject, it is an uncertain and unstable sketch of the subject. A subjectivity hears itself from far off and intimately at the same time, in this frail and singular unison, the subjectivity is being born, but it will never be born as such. Once born, the subject is only the *Ich denke*. And the aesthetical pleasure will always come along to disconcert it, to make it indeteminate, to make it be at a loss through its own concert, and its reflexive relation to itself.

And since the pleasure that is the affiancing cannot be inscribed in determination, even in the determination belonging to the temporal schema, this pleasure does not synthesize with itself in the course of time, and consequently it forgets itself. It is immemorial. This is also why each pleasure in beauty is a birth. Why the community of faculties remains discrete, secret, separated from itself, not inscribing itself in synthesizable time. But this is not at all the same reason why the cognitive *I* misses itself in its effort to determine itself. There simply is no aesthetic transcendental *I*. At the most a pre-*I*, a pre-cogito, a floating synthesis between the faculties, where the *I* of these faculties is not in charge, but, rather, nature is.

Consequently, it cannot be said that the Idea of a "natural" purposiveness of the subject for knowledge indicates itself by aesthetic pleasure "at the heart of" the subject, for this sign of pure pleasure cannot be inscribed "in" or "on" a subject since the subject is not present either as a temporal support or as a synthesizing power. The community has no interior that needs protecting.

And lastly it should not be said, either, that the community will have an interior once the subject is born, that we will move from sentiment to the concept, from art to philosophy, from *sensus communis* to *intellectus communis*, which is the *I think*. For this passage does not exist. There is no transition here between reflexion and determination, between the substratum of the faculties' affinity and the originary synthetic unity of apperception. Substance cannot make itself into subject. It is essential to the subject to misrecognize itself as substance. Sentiment is not transcribed in the concept, it is suppressed, without being "sublated." This sublation is the presumption of the concept. Knowledge demands that the imaginative syntheses should be subordinated to the understanding, subsumable under its rule. Knowledge puts an end to the rivalry. Forms are forced to keep step with the categories, in order to act as a test for them. Another proportion.

So much so that the community of faculties in the knowledge of the true is quite different from that which is in play in the sentiment of the beautiful. The first is a hierarchized, architectonic community, the second is free, and rather out of breath. I shall not develop this point. One of its implications is that we can wait without undue worry for this "death of art" prophesized by the philosophies of the concept. This does not mean that there is nothing to think about on this subject, especially when conceptual computable syntheses invade and occupy the field of art's materials and the domain of their forms. This I leave for discussion.

A second observation. The fact that the aesthetic community is transcendental does not absolve Kant from going back through anthropology in order to explain its nature. I return to the text of paragraph 40: "But under the *sensus communis* we must include the idea of a sense *common to all*, i.e., of a faculty of judgment which, in its reflection, takes account (a priori) of the mode of representation of all other men in thought"—to which Kant adds, as we have seen: "This is done by comparing our judgment with the possible rather than actual judgments of others" (*KUK*, §40; *CJ*, p. 136). This operation of comparison apparently occurs in a collectivity of individuals. Interpreted like this, this operation induces a realist empirical anthropological definition of the said *sensus*. How many illusions or political crimes have been able to nourish themselves with this pretended immediate sharing of sentiment?

However, looking more closely at the sentence, things are most hesitant. Kant writes "possible rather than actual judgments." And he reaffirms the condition for universalization already stated "by putting ourselves in the place of any other man. . . ." Now, in correct Kantian philosophy, the whole of all the others, as a totality, is not a category for which there can be a corresponding intuition in experience. It cannot be a question of an intuitable ensemble. This whole is the object of an Idea.

The required comparison is eidetic. The task is to form a pure aesthetic judgment by "imaginary variations," as Husserl would have said. The purposiveness of this mental "technique" is to remove from the pleasure in the beautiful any empirical individual charm or emotion. And thus to make certain that what is left after this "degreasing" is communicable. It will be communicable if it is well purified.

At the end of the same paragraph, Kant writes: "We could even define taste as the faculty of judging of that which makes *universally communicable* (without the mediation of a concept) our feeling in a given representation" (*KUK*, §40; *CJ*, p.

138). This definition is somewhat provoking ("We could *even* define"): the condition of the universal communicability of pleasure is enough to distinguish aesthetic pleasure from any other. It will be pure if it is really communicable. How to go on? The communicability is in proportion to the purity, transcendentally. Empirically, the purity can be gauged by the communicability. Let us say: the communicability is the *ratio cognoscendi* of purity, and the latter is the *ratio essendi* of the former. The formula of the eidetic comparison that makes certain communicability can seem "artificial," writes Kant, because it is "expressed in abstract formulas" (*KUK*, §40; *CJ*, p. 136). Nothing in itself is more "natural" than this abstraction. And, indeed, it is only a matter of letting oneself be guided by the principle of a substratum of affinity between the faculties, which is the suprasensible "nature" of the subject, or rather of the presubject—in order to eliminate the scoria of material interests and charms.

The *sensus communis* remains, therefore, a hypotyposis: it is a sensible analogue of the transcendental euphony of the faculties, which can only be the object of an Idea, and not of an intuition. This *sensus* is not a sense, and the sentiment that is supposed to affect it (as a sense can be affected) is not common, but only in principle communicable. There is no assignable community of sentiment, no affective consensus in fact. And if we claim to have recourse to one, or a fortiori to create one, we are victims of a transcendental illusion and we are encouraging impostures.

The essential is this: the sentiment of the beautiful is the subject just being born, the first pairing off of incomparable powers. This feeling escapes being mastered by concept and will. It extends itself underneath and beyond their intrigues and their closure. This is what Kant understands by the "natural substratum" that he takes, deductively, as his beginning. Thus it is a region of resistance to institutions and establishments where there is inscribed and hidden that which happens "before" we know what it is and before we want to make it into anything at all. This pleasure is an inscription without support, and without a code by which it can be read off. Miserable, if you like. It is the task of literatures and arts, the task of what is called writing, to reinscribe it according to its misery, without overwhelming it, and without getting rid of it.

Notes

1. *Kritik der Urteilskraft* (henceforth *KUK*) (Suhrkamp Verlag; 1974), vol. 10, § 57, note 1; in English see *Critique of Judgement*, Henceforth *CJ*, trans. J. H. Bernard (New York: Hafner, 1951), p. 180.

18

L'Interloqué

Jean-Luc Marion

I

Phenomenology has perhaps never had a more pressing task to confront than the determination of what—or possibly who—succeeds the subject. Nevertheless, it has never definitively decided between two kinds of succession, between either abolishing the subject forever, in order to replace it with the very absence of an heir (as Nietzsche claimed he had done) or hesitating to repeat, each time, the function of subjecti(vi)ty according to an always new mode. On the subject of the subject, phenomenology has never ceased oscillating between one and the other postulate, between the possibility of a heritage and that of a "new beginning." This hesitation allows us to inscribe phenomenology at times within the field of metaphysics, at times outside of its limits. The question of the subject's posterity will therefore not find even the outline of an answer as long as the way in which phenomenology claims to go beyond the subject, and hence beyond the metaphysical subject, has not itself been sketched out. Asked in another way: does phenomenology offer a path that leads to the overcoming of the subject? We shall examine this question through the obviously privileged case of *Dasein*, whose ambivalence Heidegger defined in *Being and Time*.

We ask then: to what extent does the analytic of *Dasein* accomplish the abolition of the metaphysical subject? *Dasein* reaches its specific and authentic truth in the figure of care (*Sorge*), which identifies it as anticipatory resoluteness: "*Dasein* becomes 'essentially' *Dasein* in that authentic existence which constitutes itself as anticipatory resoluteness [*vorlaufende Entschlossenheit*]."[1] We must therefore ask if this ultimate determination of the meaning of *Dasein*'s Being enables it to succeed the subject—or if we should still expect another.

Translated by Eduardo Cadava and Anne Tomiche

II

There wouldn't be any sense in denying that *Dasein* subverts the subject, even and especially when the subject is understood in terms of the Husserlian transcendental phenomenological subject. *Being and Time* not only calls into question the transcendental Kantian *I*; it calls into question the phenomenological *I* in general as well as the very core of this *I*, even when this *I* is understood in the sense given to it in the *Logical Investigations*. In what does this questioning consist? Subjecti(vi)ty no longer has as its objective the objectivization of the object, because the ultimate instrument of this objectivization—intentionality—no longer aims at the constitution of an object but at the opening of a world. The intentionality constitutive of an object remains, but it is limited to the status of a particular case of the fundamental determination of the Being-in-the-world of the one who, from then on, renounces the title of "subject," since he abandons the objective of the objectivization of the object, in favor of the title of *Dasein*. One must not be mistaken: the analysis of instrumentality occupies a central role in the analytic of *Dasein* because it establishes that what is in the world is not at first there in the form of objects constituted according to the objectivization exercised by a subject, but in the form of a specific manipulability that, in return, determines *Dasein* itself, handled, as it were, by that which it handles. *Dasein* is not in the world as a spectator, nor even in a constitutive way, but as a party possibly challenged by what it encounters. The world never amounts to the sum of constituted objects, since it in no way *consists* of objects, but is disclosed in the making of a (whole) world of objects. However, it can only be opened in this way inasmuch as, more essentially, *Dasein* produces the opening in general, by going into ecstasies. *Dasein*'s ecstasy lies in that, far from grounding itself in its being, or from grounding its being in itself, it is the entity for which what is at stake, each time, is nothing less than its Being—even better, the entity for which what is at stake, when what is at stake is *its* being, is also *the* Being of all other entities. Such an appropriation of Being to the *I*—"The Being of any such entity is *in each case mine* [*jemeines*]" (*Being and Time*, §9, p. 67)—must not be interpreted as a subjection of Being to the figure of the *ego*, indeed to that of egoism; if Being is each time mine, it is because *Dasein* is incapable of attaining Being in any other way than by staging itself in the first person, exposing itself to the possibility of death; Being is disclosed to *Dasein* only as a possibility reserved for the one who engages himself by naming himself as an irreplaceable first person. The "mineness" of Being no longer implies that the *I* would assume a substantially ineradicable subjectivity, but rather that Being remains inaccessible to *Dasein* as long as it does not risk exposing itself without reserve, without appeal, and without certainty, as if to the possibility of the impossible. From intentionality to "mineness," the subject, master of its being, and owner of its objects, disappears in order to give way to *Dasein*, which sets against the subject a double paradox: first, *Dasein* fails to constitute an object, but exposes itself to manipulation; second, *Dasein* has no substantiality, but arrives at its own Being only by taking the risk of exposure in person.

III

That *Dasein* realizes its own Being by risking itself in person is evidence that it sublates the subject. "Mineness," by which what is at stake is always only me in my being and even in Being, disqualifies all claims to the self-foundation of an unconditioned *I*. However, once understood, this still does not prevent us from asking another question: Under what condition does *Dasein* realize the "mineness" that characterizes its mode of being? The literal answer lies in a formula: "Resoluteness [*Entschlossenheit*] is a distinctive mode of *Dasein*'s disclosedness [*Enschlossenheit*]" (*Being and Time*, §60, p. 343). *Dasein*'s disclosedness displays itself, in a distinctive mode, at the moment of resoluteness. Resoluteness, understood as anticipatory resoluteness, brings out *Dasein*'s being as care (*Sorge*) and enables access to the meaning of being as temporality, thought in terms of the future. It is a question then of determining how the ecstatic structure of care (*Sorge*) is realized phenomenologically: What does resoluteness resolve, what decision does resoluteness lead *Dasein* to, in relation to what does it manifest *Dasein*? Resoluteness can be located in several phenomena that are organized around it: anxiety, the consciousness of guilt, Being-towards-death as anticipation. Each of these presents a common characteristic:

(a) Anxiety leads to the phenomenological experience of the nothingness of all entities, unchanging or else manipulable: "In that in the face of which one has anxiety, the 'It is nothing and nowhere' becomes manifest" (*Being and Time*, §40, p. 231). That this nothingness might, and even should be, interpreted as the world, does not in any way change the fact that anxiety opens upon nothingness, with nothing more than this very nothingness.

(b) The conscience that experiences its guilt (whatever this guilt might be) hears a call in this experience; however, this call neither evokes nor requires any compensation, any obligation, any ontically ascribable price. "What does the conscience call to him to whom it appeals? Taken strictly, nothing. The call asserts nothing, gives no information about world-events, has nothing to tell" (*Being and Time*, §56, p. 318). Conscience does not open *Dasein* onto the entity of the world but onto its own transcendence; strictly speaking it opens nothing to *Dasein*, except itself.

(c) Being-towards-death apparently marks an exception: so far as we know it is nowhere indicated that it might open upon the nothing to which the analysis nevertheless seems to appeal. It only opens *Dasein* onto the possibility of impossibility. But, more precisely, the anticipation of Being-towards-death (or rather *in* it) ultimately opens *Dasein* to absolute possibility—absolute since it even embraces the impossible—that privileges it as an ontological entity. If, "in Being-towards-death, *Dasein* comports itself *to-*

wards itself as a distinctive potentiality for Being" (*Being and Time*, §51, p. 296), one must conclude that it does not relate itself towards anything else. Thus the three phenomena that determine *Dasein*'s Being as care only define anticipatory resoluteness as an ecstasy opening upon—strictly—nothing.

Or, rather, anticipatory resoluteness leads to nothingness inasmuch as it is then a question of an entity's nothingness; but, by this very nothingness, it "isolates" (*vereinzelt*) *Dasein* by referring it to the ontico-ontological tránscendency that sets it apart from the intramundane entity. Such isolation does not by itself or first of all mean that *Dasein* should, following a traditional theme (Augustinian, for example), *in se redire*. *Dasein*'s isolation does not lead it back to itself, but realizes its essential determination: to be, without any possible substitution, itself. What was formulated at the beginning of the analytic of *Dasein* as "mineness" (*Jemeinigkeit*) is pronounced at the end as "Selfhood" (*Selbstheit*): "*Dasein*'s selfhood has been defined formally as a *way of existing* . . ." (*Being and Time*, §54, p. 312). *Dasein* exists as itself. Resoluteness does not resolve anything because what is at stake is the possibility of *Dasein* venturing towards its own destiny: to be the entity in whose being what is at stake is Being itself. *Selbstheit* must resolutely be understood as *constancy of the Self* (*Selbst-ständigkeit*), as Heidegger tells us directly:

> Selfhood [*Selbstheit*] is to be discerned existentially only in one's authentic potentiality-for-Being-one's-Self—that is to say, in the authenticity of *Dasein*'s Being *as care*. In terms of care the *constancy of the Self* [*Ständigkeit des Selbst*], as the supposed persistence of the *subjectum*, gets clarified. But the phenomenon of this authentic potentiality-for-Being also opens our eyes to the *constancy of the Self* [*Ständigkeit des Selbst*] in the sense of its having achieved some sort of position. . . . Existentially, '*Self-constancy*' [*Selbst-ständigkeit*] signifies nothing other than anticipatory resoluteness. The ontological structure of such resoluteness reveals the existentiality of the Self's Selfhood [*der Selbstheit des Selbst*]. (*Being and Time*, §64, p. 369).

Whether one understands the Self's *Selbst-ständigkeit* in the sense of an "autonomy," a "constancy of the self," or a "self-positing"[2] does not ultimately matter that much, provided these approximations really aim at thinking the prodigious paradox of the analytic of *Dasein*: for the ecstasy of care nevertheless leads to the radical autarky of *Dasein*, standing alone by itself, as the singular Self. Autarky: as paradoxical as it seems, the term is appropriate since all the extensions of intentionality (Being-in-the-world, anxiety, conscience, Being-towards-death) never have as their end the disclosure of an entity but rather—in order to lead *Dasein* back to its "mineness," then radicalized in a self-positing Selfhood—the disclosure of the nothingness of all entities. Resoluteness itself discloses the world through the ecstatic structure of care only by positing *Dasein*'s Self in itself and as

Self alone. Is it possible, then, that *Dasein* may only overcome the subject by once again miming it?

IV

Posited as such the Self's Selfhood—nonsubstitutable, by virtue of care and according to anticipatory resoluteness—defines *Dasein* in terms of a specific existential autarky. Assuming that it is actually achieved, this result gives rise to two interrogations directly linked to the question of a possible overcoming of the subject and of the seriousness of its succession.

(a) The first interrogation points to an aporia that is external to the project of *Being and Time*; if the Self's autarky still defines *Dasein*, to what extent does *Dasein* still "destroy" the metaphysical project of a transcendental *I* unconditioned because self-constituted? *Dasein* doubtless overcomes all subjecti(vi)ty by challenging the permanency of the *hypokeimenon* or of the subject of the *res cogitans*. However, the Self's autarky remains connected with the strange motto of a " . . . *ständig vorhandene Grund der Sorge*," i.e., constantly present-at-hand basis of care (*Being and Time*, §64, p. 322), in such a way that the reflexive characteristics of "to make up one's mind," "to exhibit *oneself*," "to precede *oneself*," "to anguish *oneself*," etc.—there each time for *nothing* else than the Self—might seem to mime the self-reflexivity that has been understood as self-constitutive of the transcendental subject, indeed of all subjectivity. *Dasein*'s confrontation with metaphysical egology (from Descartes to Hegel) may remain incomplete and even undecided, like a battle that is suspended before the winner is known.[3] Above all, *Dasein* may not completely overcome the thematics of the subject, as Heidegger's project for the "destruction of the history of ontology" nevertheless expressly implies in its second section. In short, we can risk the following hypothesis: the analytic of *Dasein* designates not so much that which succeeds the subject, but rather the last heir of the subject itself, to the extent that *Dasein* offers a path whereby it may tear itself away from subjectivity, without being successful. What—or who—must come after the subject will no doubt only be brought to the light of day through *Dasein*, but also after *Dasein*, indeed against it.

Hence the second interrogation,

(b) which designates an aporia that is internal to the project of *Being and Time*: If the Self's autarky defines *Dasein*'s specific transcendence, how might this autarky—which no entity can disrupt (precisely because it only manifests itself by transcending absolutely all entities)—care in any way for the question of Being in general? The distortion—very visible, even if not always discovered—between the question of Being in general and the analytic of *Dasein*, a distortion that traverses *Being and Time* and almost necessarily determines its incompleteness,[4] does not stem from a weakness in the presentation of *Dasein*; quite the contrary, it is precisely the exemplary success of this presentation that installs *Dasein* in the autarky of Self-positing, without any other determination than its own resolve toward its own opening; inasmuch as the analytic definitely leads, in the two sections of the published version of the text, to the identification of *Dasein* with the Self of autarkic resoluteness, it never confirms the project evoked by the "Introduction" to *Being and Time*—that of establishing phenomenologically a strict equivalence between the question of Being in general and *Dasein*'s Being in particular. Section 83 of *Being and Time* should perhaps be read as the *in fine* acknowledgment of the absolute impossibility of a regulated and phenomenologically guaranteed transition from *Dasein* as autarkic Self to the question of Being in general: "Can one provide *ontological* grounds for ontology, or does it also require an *ontical* foundation? and *which* entity must take over the function of providing this foundation?"—it is in terms such as these that the "problem of principle which still remains 'veiled' " is finally acknowledged (*Being and Time*, §83, p. 487). The aporia therefore lies in a contradiction that is all the more radical because it emerges from the exemplary success of the analytic of *Dasein*: the Self, positing itself as such through an anticipatory resoluteness towards possibility, does not accept any extrinsic determination: neither the world (which this resoluteness opens and therefore precedes), nor the entity (which it transcends), nor time (whose authentic temporality becomes phenomenologically accessible only through this resoluteness)—so that nothing, not even nothingness itself, can here evoke, say, or even sense Being. Here, Being does not yet exert any neutrality to the detriment, for example, of an other; on the contrary, neutrality goes against Being, according to the absolutely indeterminate autarky of the Self—absolutely indeterminate, except for its own resoluteness, the ultimate phenomenological face of *Dasein*. The Self's neutrality disqualifies Being itself.

Dasein may not accede to the question of Being in general as an autarkic Self; it may not appeal, at the moment of anticipatory resoluteness, to Being, since, in any case, it appeals only to itself: "*Dasein* is at the same time both the caller and the one to whom the appeal is made" (*Being and Time*, §57, p. 322). Heidegger found the solution to this paradoxical aporia only at the expense of the *Kehre*, which, in a sense, sacrifices everything that *Being and Time* had managed to thematize—the analytic of *Dasein*—in order to conform to what it had not achieved but only aimed at: the question of Being in general. This heroic reversal is marked, among other innovations, by the disqualification of *Dasein*'s autarky; since anticipatory resoluteness, as the self's appeal to itself, runs aground on ontological neutrality, it must submit to an appeal that it neither performs, nor controls, nor decides: this appeal—the appeal by which Being claims *Dasein* as the phenomenological agency of its manifestation[5]—is called, in the "Postface" to *What is Metaphysics?* as well as in the *Letter on Humanism*, the *Anspruch des Seins*. Contrary to *Being and Time*, where the appeal is always an appeal to itself (*Ansprechen seiner selbst*) (*Being and Time*, §25, p. 151), here Being's appeal claims *Dasein*, as it were, in advance and from the outside; a choice must be made between the Self's anticipatory resoluteness and the claim of that which is, from now on, called man (and not *Dasein*). Heidegger has chosen—the *Anspruch des Seins* comes before and therefore "destroys" *Dasein's* autarky. Man answers a call that claims him for Being, instead of *Dasein* deciding about and resolving itself to its own possibility as Self. By *man* one must understand, against all "humanisms," the one who comes after the subject, but also after the Self, because he lets himself be claimed by the *Anspruch des Seins*. He should be called *der Angesprochene*, the one upon whom a claim is made. After the subject, even beyond *Dasein*, emerges the one who knows how to hear Being's claim.

This thesis marks Heidegger's second advance beyond subjecti(vi)ty, a more radical move than the first, although more silent. This thesis, however, gives rise to a questioning that is even more redoubtable than the difficulties it had managed to overcome. For if *Dasein* indeed undergoes an analytic, which reveals it as resolute toward and in its autarkic Selfhood, the one who is interpellated, who is called upon by the claim of Being, does not, at least explicitly, benefit from such an analytic. But *if Dasein* answers the question of Being in general as interpellated much more than as resolute, the "new beginning" remains subject to an analytic of the claiming interpellation, which is precisely what is lacking. *Dasein* comes after the subject by renouncing the self-constitution of the transcendental *I*, but it still claims itself by the autarky of resoluteness; it remains for *Dasein* to let itself be claimed by an agency other than itself (here, Being), in order to finally succeed the subject without still inheriting subjecti(vi)ty. Only the one who is interpellated breaks with the subject, but *Dasein* does not yet abandon itself to interpellation.

V

The claim, then, calls me. I have not yet said *I*, since the claim has already hailed me, hence named and summoned me as *me*. Moreover, the only appropriate answer to the claim that names me is a "This is *me!*" without any *I*. Contrary to all appearances, it is not a question here of the classical critique of the objective *I/me* by the transcendental *I* (as it is in Kant, Husserl, and Sartre): for, to be precise, by denouncing the transcendent *I* as an empirical or constituted objective, the critique reestablishes an even more radical transcendental *I*, nonconstituted precisely because constitutive; here, in a metaphysical regime, the relativity of the empirical *I* stresses all the better the absolute primacy and, in this sense, autonomy of the constituting *I*. On the contrary, when the claim interpellates *me*, the *I/me* that it imparts to me thus designates not any autonomous and unconditioned transcendental *I*, but rather only the interpellation itself. The experience of the *me* whom I hear speak *myself* does not offer any proof of a transcendental *I*, but, as a pure and naked experience, it assigns me to the claim. The pole to which the *I/me* refers cannot be any hidden I—invisible because always already there, the singular pole of an already determined phenomenological horizon—but is rather an unconceivable, unnameable, unpredictable agency: the claim itself to be precise. No doubt, upon hearing myself interpellated, I experience an interpellated *me*, but, literally, *I* experiences a *me* orphaned of any transcendental and constitutive *I*; *I* experience *myself* means that the *I* (simple, without being double) experiences itself as a *myself/me*. I experience myself being claimed, that is, called upon in the accusative—interpellated as suspect and not as subject, named in the accusative and therefore dispossessed of any nominative function. The interpellated *me* marks the absence of any constituting *I*, under the—in this respect, totalitarian—authority of the claim. The *me* no longer testifies *a contrario* to the *I*, but acknowledges the nullity of the *I* under the authority of the claim which interpellates *me*.

The disaster of the *I*, that is, the sole overcoming of the subject, only occurs with the claim. However, does the extent of this disaster still allow the *me*, barely the phantom of a subject, to be named by a concept? We shall designate the *me* as the "interloqué" (*Angesprochene*):

(a) *Interloqué*, first, because it is summoned by the claim, with a radicality and a power that deny it not only the autonomy of a subject constituting itself in its atomic substantiality, but also the autarky of a resoluteness that is determined by nothing; the *interloqué* discovers itself always already compelled to a relation; in metaphysical terms, it would be necessary to say here that the derivative and secondary category of relation—which, in principle, must never apply to what is substantial, the primary category—not only applies to it, but also subjects it to the point of disqualifying it: the *interloqué* finds itself the derivative pole of a relation in which it no longer has any of the (autonomous, autarkic) substantiality implied by even the least subjecti(vi)ty.

(b) *Interloqué*, then, because the *me* experiences a surprise. The surprise here is strictly opposed to ecstasy (the ecstasy of intentionality as well as that of anticipatory resoluteness); ecstasy, indeed, institutes the subject outside of itself, but still in terms of itself as the originary pole of its own overcoming. On the contrary, the claim's surprise surprises the *interloqué* to the extent that it is deprived of any polarity of its own; surprise seizes the *interloqué* in the sense that it seizes all polarity of subjecti(vi)ty in the *me*: the *interloqué* is less torn away from the *me*—since it perceives itself precisely without even the least self—than constituted by an unassignable claim as a *me* without ground, without subject, without any place other than this very interpellation. Surprise, in the *interloqué*, is a reprisal against its very ecstasy: surprise dispossesses (*déprend*) the *interloqué* of its ecstasy.

(c) *Interloqué* finally, in the sense of an interlocutory judgment; *interloquer* means, according to ancient French judiciary language, "ordonner qu'une chose sera prouvée ou vérifiée, avant qu'on prononce sur le fond de l'affaire" (*Littré*), to establish the fact before speaking the law, and, in the meantime, to suspend the procedure. The *interloqué* is submitted, in a more essential sense, to an interlocutory judgment, since all *quid juris?* questions concerning its transcendental subjectivity, its powers, its limits, and its figures (including that of *Dasein*) must acknowledge that they are preceded by the question *quid facti?*

The irrevocable fact here consists in the claim itself, which, already and definitely, redefines all of the *interloqué*'s characteristics; nothing can be said of the *interloqué*—neither according to truth, nor according to evaluation, nor according to resoluteness—that would not at first be determined by the claim. The sole a priori, the claim still does not come from either conscience or the horizon, which it rather precludes. The sole fact, the claim, nonetheless comes before all limits and all rights, since this fact is not the fact of any subject and, perhaps, not even the fact of itself. Summons, surprise, precedent, the claim therefore institutes the *interloqué*, without defining it in any other way than by its status as *interloqué*. For before I am anything, before in me *I* exists or *I* invent, the possibility of being a subject or a *Dasein*, surprise must indeed summon me, *interloqué*. In the beginning, amazement; at first, admiration.

However, the thesis that only the *interloqué* comes after the subject is open to an objection: the claim can only install the *interloqué* as such if some agency performs it; it is necessary then that the claim ultimately be referred to a pole whose initial word tears subjecti(vi)ty. Who or what claims the *interloqué*? If we mention here God, the other, moral conscience, auto-affection, figures of difference, Being itself, etc., this only enables us to name the difficulty, not to solve it: as a matter of fact the *interloqué* would become in all cases a derivative and regional agency— a simple variation of the subject, situated or placed in relation to another agency; the *interloqué* would therefore regress to the level of a particularized subject. This objection relies, however, on an illusory assumption: that it is necessary to be able to name this agency that makes a claim on me, in order to know myself instituted as *interloqué*; on the contrary, according to the order of phenomenological description, I identify myself as *interloqué before* being aware not only of my subjectivity but also of what or who leaves me *interloqué*. The imprecision, indeed, the *confusion* of the claiming agency does not weaken the claim but rather testifies that the interpellation of the *interloqué* as such occurs from the very beginning; just as surprise surprises the subject, surprise surprises the surprisor himself; the *I* discovers itself *interloqué* precisely because it knows, at the moment of the claim, neither by whom nor by what it is claimed. Only the indeterminacy of the claiming agency enables the claim that, otherwise, would not *surprise* and hence would not institute any *interloqué*. What is at stake is an anonymous a priori, which functions perfectly, without identifying itself, since it consists only in the following: the *interloqué*'s recognition of a minimal a priori: the claim itself—the *I* recognizes itself as *interloqué* as a consequence of the claim itself. The *interloqué* provides the beginning— the most basic, hence the first, determination—that abolishes the subject: selfhood is initially wounded by the very fact that, before the self can constitute itself, the claim has already exiled it outside its "mineness." The wound that originally tears selfhood obscurely manifests the origin itself—the *interloqué*. Before ever knowing by what or by whom, the *I* surprises itself, as *interloqué*, and has always done so.

Notes

1. *Being and Time*, trans. John Macquarrie and Edward Robinson (New York: Harper and Row, 1962), §65, p. 370. All subsequent citations from this text are to this edition and will be cited parenthetically within my essay as *Being and Time*, section number, page number.

2. *Selbst-ständigkeit* is translated as "self-maintenance," "*maintien de Soi-même (autonomie)*" in *Etre et Temps*, translated by Martineau (Paris, 1985), pp. 227 and 316, and as "Self-constancy," "constance de soi-même" in *Etre et Temps*, translated by F. Vezin (Paris, 1986), p. 382. The ambiguity of the *Ständigkeit* attributed to *Dasein*, whose Self has just been emphasized (rather than opposed to) as "ständig *vorhandene* Grund" (my emphasis) seems to justify the use here of the Kantian term *positing*.

3. On this point, allow me to refer to my essay, "L'*ego* et le *Dasein*: Heidegger et la 'destruction' de Descartes dans *Sein und Zeit*," in *Revue de Métaphysique et de Morale* 1 (1987).

4. Similarly, on this point see "Différence ontologique et question de l'être—un indécidé de *Sein und Zeit*," in *Tijdschrift voor Filosofie* 3 (1987).

5. I draw here from my discussion of the emergence of the *Anspruch des Seins* in "L'angoisse et l'ennui: Pour interpréter *Was ist Metaphysik?*" in *Archives de Philosophie* 1 (1980).

19

After What

Jacques Rancière

"What comes after the subject?" this author is asked. How would he know? And how would he demonstrate it? Does his audience not remark, repeatedly, that they do not know *where* he is heading? He also knows, of course, that not knowing is too easy a way of creating his own image as a philosopher, all the easier in that philosophical questioning habitually knows more than its audience. Not knowing *who* to name, then, also means settling down in an *after* that, by designating the place or the home of the unknown one, perhaps says a lot in the end about his or her identity.

Questions about time are always advantageous. To talk about the end, the after, the *post-* lends a heroic tint to any idea concerning the end of a time when things were well-ordered and their meaning established. In the days of old, not so very long ago, there was—it is said—a time when all events took place in the light of grand narratives abut the self and the world, about God and people. Then would come the daring time of new days and adventurous paths. . . . But the very act with which this abandonment manifests itself as heroic effort or joyful drift restores a tranquil certainty concerning ties and places: we are now *in* the end or the after. All ruins hide a habitable temple, a temple already inhabited. The time defined as a time of loss, is still part of the continuum, of archaeology, and of our heritage. It makes sense and space. This means that it also gathers: to speak of epoch or *epochal* is to bring together, within the same destiny, the gathering of those who think in terms of an *after* and the indistinct masses who supposedly inhabit the ruins without knowing it. They are defined by that very supposition and thereby give to the corporation the mission of thinking for them that which is verified in their very muteness.

We know that the tranquility of this dual relation is not without its jolts. From time to time current events make it obvious that nine-tenths of humanity, or even a little more, suffer from that which the *epoch* has already passed beyond: the

---

Translated by Christina Davis

ancient stories of hunger, faith, and peoples. Gloomy sermonizers or pugnacious prosecutors then denounce the duplicity of the thinkers who think in terms of the *after*. Tragicomedy and vaudeville make game against a background of holocaust. Now the guardian of the temple announces betrayal by the corporation: we must return to the previous assurance of the subject who gathers up meanings and assigns values. Soon the keeper of the morgue comes to shame the guardian whose values— or whose forgotten values—have served the assassins. Yet again, the corporation, once proud of daring voyages far from the paternal lands of the subject, closes ranks in order to protect from any attempt at parricide the thinker of the end of metaphysics, the thinker who is also the only distinguished member of the corporation to have maintained some link, however tenuous, with the assassins.

These tribunals, periodically established where the affairs of the corporation encounter any affair or any sense supposed common, are perhaps the ransom for the commodity that it took over: that of the interminable capitalization of a misfortune whose resolution is indefinitely suspended. The temple and the charnel house, summoned up at its borders as concrete manifestations of its forgotten origins or its unacknowledged end, denounce at either limit the space/time where philosophical activity deliberately set up shop: that of the beginning of the end.

Indeed, whatever the philosophical good will put to radicalizing the question of the after, the terrain has been clearly marked by three *mise en scène* schemas that have become doxic configurations. Psychoanalytic theory first made the *time-after* into the time of the advent of the subject, perhaps thus dissimulating the enigmatic task of fidelity to the *time-to-come* hidden behind the visibility given to the parricidal event as origin of the meaningful sequence. Then comes the schema of extermination which represents the annihilation of the subject, not simply in the form of the mass liquidation of individuals, but also as a death without any remainder—no trace, monument, or immortality. Thus opens the horizon of a beginning of the end, projected into the two dimensions of past and future. On the one hand, the genealogies of horror trace, according to an origin that is always retreating, the beginning of an evil history, that of the subject bearing death; they follow its most minute advances. On the other hand, thoughts of tomorrow establish themselves in the twilight times that begin with the advent of the unthinkable. But behind the enigma and the horror comes a third schema, ever more triumphant, that of the particular redemption that is involved in the development of patrimonial policy. The latter brings into play a new immortality, henceforth attached to a monument and no longer to *that* which the monument represents: a colossal assurance against death, the holocaust and parricide, an ability to immortalize anything, to restore any temple, but also to monumentalize every object, to familiarize any strangeness in the filiation of a meaning that has escaped death.

The ordering of these three configurations gives us infinite resources as well as a plurality of times. To voice the beginning of the end, to speak in its name is to appropriate for oneself the powers of suspended death and the voyage through time. We speak in the present of raising the anchor, undoing the image, or erasing the name. But above all we settle into the singular schema of a retrospective apocalypse. We rewrite indefinitely, in the past tense, the prophecy of the wrong beginning (of forgetfulness, of disguise—or, just as well, of the lure of disguise or of forgetfulness) that makes us suffer endlessly the sequence of evils that result from the wrong schema, from the forgetful schema of subjectivity. An ethical fidelity to the recognized uncertainty of the subject and to the act of its *time-to-come* then reposes on the thought of extermination in order to install itself within the retrospective prophecies of the beginning of the end. But apocalypse in the past also continuously exchanges its performatory powers of threatening death with the resources in immortality of the patrimonial enterprise. Thus does philosophy succumb to the charms of rewriting, with the infinite possibilities of metonymy authorized by the richness of the text, the phrases of its history. Philosophy proposes itself as interminable future and offers, as the destiny of any given epoch, the rewriting that marks every phrase of the text with the threat of death and every utterance of a present event with the displaced repetition of a phrase of the text. These comings and goings between the text and an event, between the past and the future, between death and immortality, define the schema of an infinite resource that strangely resembles the *reserve* in which Heidegger's discourse on the apocalypse recognizes the essence of technological domination. Patrimony, the new technology of immortality, has perhaps become the vital element of that very philosophy that finds its force by denouncing this technological domination. By assuring philosophy a new time in which to make its statement, patrimony allows it to identify the inventory of its own heritage by deciphering the mortal enigma of the new times, and ensures its revenge on the social knowledge that had put it aside. From there, philosophy takes on a prominent role in all manifestations that conceive of and celebrate the monument, the archive, or the museum, the consequences of which seem positive.

This triumphant use of the *beginning of the end* should no doubt be considered within the continuity of the schema that I had earlier indicated: the determining function of *time*, of its availability or its absence, as the dividing line that stages philosophical activity by separating those who have the leisure to think from those whose business is not thinking.[1] I had indicated the continuity leading from the forthright affirmation by Plato of the privileges of the σχολή to the tortuous Sartrian analysis of the effects of a fatigue that takes away from the proletarian the time to think. The substitution of the time of urgency and the time of the beginning of the end for that of the leisure for philosophy should be thought about in terms of the schemas that today redefine the staging of philosophical activity and organize its δόξα under the new conditions of that activity in relation to its other: a mastery announced in the very name of time characterized by abandonment, a discourse whose gravity of utterance is due to its accounting for the common destiny of humanity, but which at the same time divides (as in the seventh book of the *Laws*) the watchmen of the beginning of the night from the sleep of the oblivious masses.

I am interested, however, in something else: the manner in which this plurality of times plays with horror and death, summons them up at the edge of discourse and then keeps them at arm's length indefinitely. There philosophy is playing with what was once its own: the assumption of death, the confrontation with fear and the passions that spring from fear—the frustration of "not yet having enough" and the fear of "no longer being" that accompany the destiny of the living possessed by word and representation. In the infinite reflection of apocalyptic prophecy and of redemption through patrimony, a certain *logos* unfolds whose paradoxical principle was once designated as the very principle of passion: the confusion of times, the perpetual enjambment of the present, this present that the Stoic master recommended circumscribing in order to keep at a distance the intermingling passions of expectation and regret. On the contrary, right before our very eyes that present continues to dilate, swelling with the comings and goings, the gains and losses included in the idea of the beginning of the end, in the exchange between holocaust and patrimony. Everything happens as if displaying the representation were a perfect replacement for the "use of representations," as if passion—that is, the confusion of times—had become the method.

Of course the anachronism is only valid here as displacement of perspective. We have at our disposal neither a "nature" nor a "hegemonic principle" that would guarantee this use. But this is precisely the problem: Do the themes of the end or the probably interminable death of the subject not live off the identification of any subjective schema with the archetypes of the *subjectum* or of the *substantia*? Is this identification of the "subject" with the wrong schema of presence (and thus with the presence of evil) not an only-too-convenient manner of getting rid of the question of the present, that is to say, eliminating the question of reason as well? If we had to play the familiar game of "forgetting" and "returning" I would willingly propose that what today is most forgotten or undermined is not Man, Thought, Rationality, Meaning, or any other of the victims over which the mourners hover, but simple reason in its nuclear definition: the art, for each one of us, of settling accounts with the confusion of times and the passions of expectation and regret that spring from it, an art of the present all the more necessary in that we have lost the assurance of the clearly delineated presence of a subject capable of preceding itself. Does not eliminating "the" subject with this schema, the present with the presence, mean abolishing the agency of that which—that who—is involved with the regulating of time and of fear?

What comes after the subject? We can say in a way that nothing comes after the subject, for it is precisely nothing that comes after, that risks continuing on its own account a text already started or a story already begun, that risks transforming, as Zarathustra said, the *es war* into a *so wollte ich es*, the very act in which the present is required to compensate for the lack of its *own* time. Identifying under every circumstance this will to risk with a "will to will" conceived of as the ultimate form of forgetting comes down to leaving in the background, behind or beyond the "subject" only the schema of a *some one* to whom nothing ever happens: a *nonsubject* unable to discern the specific schemas of forgetting, distress, or death, free from the necessity of verbalizing this discernment of those schemas and of doing something—

some deed—based on that declaration. Beyond the subject as thus defined, beyond his *ich wollte*, remains only consent to what *is happening*, in which *some* one can substitute for any other in the darkness of the indiscernible. Let us look, for example, to the commentary made in 1946 by Heidegger on a poem by Rilke giving voice in 1925 to the poetic schema of this "wish to risk": the very splendor of the commentary that reproaches the poet with having thus missed the bottom of the abyss is also that of the silence created around a hole, around the intervening twenty German years of which nothing clear is nameable in the discourse. After the subject, in the identification of the *after* with the *beginning of the end*, there is no longer any *use* for time.

Thus must we think of the *now*, as it were, in the form of the after, in the form of the dissociation of the *presence* and the *present*. But if we so posit the death of the subject or its exhaustion, we abandon the only thing that counts, that makes a difference: the interval between *es war* and *so wollte ich es*. On the contrary, we know only very little of this interval, of its use of time, in a word, of the effect of subject. And this very little that we know is, precisely, linked to the overly generous credit we give to the appearances of the subject's consistency, especially when this subject takes on the aspect of the other who supposedly is at repose in its blessed presence, becoming one with its representation.

This is at least what I attempted to demonstrate by confronting the schema of that privileged *other* of our political modernity, the subject called variously "proletariat," "working-class," or "labor movement," successively represented as the hero of a glorious epic, the instigator of the holocaust, or, finally, the subject of an archaic narrative, dead from obsolescence.[2] I tried to deconstruct the fiction of this *animal laborans* coming out of the caverns of the factory, the mine, or the slum, creating its image of self through contemplation of, and pride in, the tools of its trade, and gathering for the attack under the banners of its collective existence. As the basis for the forms of identification and the specific discourse creating the idea of a class and its combat, I suggested recognizing the singular phenomenon of a production of meaning that was neither the systematization of the ideas generated from the usages of the *animal laborans* itself nor the awareness of an avant-garde trained in the reasoning of objective science. I saw rather the product of the activity of a random network of individuals put, by way of different itineraries, in the position both central and out of bounds of spokesmen: not men and women bearing the word of the masses, but bearing simply the word; individuals separated from their supposed fellows because they had been led into the circuits of a word come from elsewhere and drawn into endorsing the discourse of the class and the movement, to give them an identity precisely because they could not create it on their own. Behind the supposition of an *animal laborans* waving the banner, heroic or deadly, of a new *homo politicus*, was necessarily to be seen the schema, both common and singular, of an *animal rationale*, believing in the words on its banners as does every being endowed with speech, every mortal in possession of language; as we believe, in general, *in what we say*—under the cover of duplicity. The *Hercule chrétien* celebrated in the 1840s by the editor of *Atelier* takes on the same appearance as the horseman—or centaur—in the starry sky of Rilke's sonnet: the union of two who go together without meaning or intending the same thing as their journey's aim; the always sufficient and forever disappointing schema of the bond: and in general any junction of words and every meeting of speaking beings rallying round certain words.[3] To think in terms of an *after* where we can exist in relation to the history of this connection requires at minimum that we take into account the *not yet*, the *just a minute*, and the *already no more* that mark it in each of its tenses and without which it would not be a story.

From this example, which is more than an example since it touches on the exemplary schemas of the other and the mourning which have structured our times, I shall offer this sole modest moral: he who wishes to say something about the time to come must also repudiate the schema of the beginning of the end and that of the supposed naïveté of the other. Discourse on time and discourse on the other constitute a common system and closure. He who wishes to extricate himself—and no one is required to do so—must confront the question of the subject, its reason and its passion, insofar as this question is not only the business of specialists but also of all those who live with the discrepancy of representation, the work of deciphering oneself in the *es war* and the essential fragility of the pact that makes of a singular reading the principle of a new community. He must face up to the necessary effort to deliver this roving search for meaning, this philosophy outside of itself, from all the cages—classes, cultures, mentalities, etc.—where it must unceasingly be locked by a learned reason both careful to guarantee its specificity through the naturalizing objectification of its other and desirous of disposing of this substantial world of meanings. This effort corresponds to what I analyzed in another study as the *verification of equality*: the exercise of a reason that can only be grasped through repudiation of any temporality proper to one who knows, of any presumed sharing between an elite of night watchmen and a mass of sleepers.[4] It can also be called an exploration of unknowing reason: that little bit of reason suspended from its singular decision to remain faithful, brought into play each time in the adventure that leads toward the end of the phrase, the exactitude of the word, the sign of understanding, the junction/disjunction begun over and over again.

Now, after . . .—the time is right for exploring the unknowing reason, that little bit of reason mixed in each *one* with the folly of the world, ever suspended from the act leading to its end, from the unexpected countenance of its decoding. A moral that is definitely temporary, accompaniment to an absent nature. Now, after . . .—therein is the place where this adventure comes to pass: the subject who speaks its truth in division and finds its peace in connection. Therein is the fragility of the reasonable community that holds together speaking beings without the guarantee of any law from before the law; a community that grants the leisure to search for the exact word while protecting itself from its wounds at any cost. Now, after . . .—it is time to return to sender not the all-knowing question but the brotherly solitude of the place from which it continues to reappear:

Sieh, nun heisst es zusammen ertragen
Stückwerk und Teile, als sei es das Ganze.
Dir helfen wird schwer sein.[5]

Notes

1. *Le Philosophe et ses pauvres* (Paris: Fayard, 1983).

2. *The Nights of Labor*, trans. John Drury (Philadelphia: Temple University Press, 1989).

3. *The Sonnets to Orpheus*, First Series, Sonnet 11.

4. *Le Maître ignorant* (Paris: Fayard, 1987). This text will soon appear in English as *The Ignorant Schoolmaster*, trans. Kriston Ross (Stanford: Stanford University Press).

5. "See, now we must bear the pieces and parts together, as if they were the whole. Helping you will be hard." *The Sonnets to Orpheus*, First Series, Sonnet 16. Translated by A. Poulin, Jr. (*Duino Elegies and The Sonnets to Orpheus*: Boston: Houghton Mifflin Company, 1977).

Name Index

About the Editors and Contributors

Sylviane Agacinski teaches at the Collège International de Philosophie. She is the author of *Aparté: Conceptions and Deaths of Søren Kierkegaard*, trans. Kevin Newmark (Tallahassee: Florida State UP, 1988). She has also written on Wittgenstein in *Mimésis des articulations* (Paris: Aubier-Flammaribn, 1975), and participated in the Groupe de recherches sur l'enseignement philosophique.

Alain Badiou teaches at the Université de Paris VIII. He is the author of *Peut-on penser la politique* (Paris: Seuil, 1985), *L'être et l'événement* (Paris: Seuil, 1988), and *Manifeste pour la philosphie* (Paris: Seuil, 1989).

Etienne Balibar teaches at the Université de Paris I. He has written, with Louis Althusser, *Reading Capital*, trans. B. Brewster (N.Y.: Pantheon, 1971), and is the author of *On the Dictatorship of the Proletariat*, trans. G. Lock (London: NLB, 1977) and *Spinoza et la politique* (Paris: PUF, 1985).

Maurice Blanchot has written numerous books and articles on philosophy and literature, including *Death Sentence*, trans. Lydia Davis (Barrytown, N.Y.: Station Hill Press, 1978), *The Space of Literature*, trans. Ann Smock (Lincoln: University of Nebraska Press, 1982), *The Writing of the Disaster*, trans. Ann Smock (Lincoln: University of Nebraska Press, 1986), and *The Unavowable Community*, trans. Pierre Joris (Barrytown, N.Y.: Station Hill Press, 1988).

Mikkel Borch-Jacobsen, Associate Professor of Romance Languages and Literature at the University of Washington, Seattle, is the author of *The Freudian Subject*, trans. Catherine Porter (Stanford: Stanford UP, 1988). He is currently working on a text to be entitled "L'inconscient revisité."

Jean-François Courtine teaches at the Université de Paris X and at the Ecole Normale Supérieure. He will publish three books this year: *Fondation et exstase de la raison: Etudes schellingiennes* (Paris: Galilée), *Heidegger et la phénoménologie* (Paris: Vrin), and *Suarez et le système de la métaphysique* (Paris: PUF).

Gilles Deleuze has recently retired from the Université de Paris VIII. His most recent publications in French include a book on Leibniz, *Le Pli* (Paris: PUF, 1990), and a collection of essays, *Pourparlers* (Paris: Minuit, 1990). Among his works in English translation are: *Kafka: toward a minor literature*, trans. Dana Polan (Minneapolis: Minnesota UP, 1986) and *A Thousand Plateaus*, trans. Brian Massumi (Minneapolis: Minnesota UP, 1987), both written with F. Guattari, and more recently *Logic of Sense*, trans. Mark Lester (Columbia: Columbia UP, 1990) and

Expressionism in Philosophy: Spinoza, trans. Martin Joughin (New York: Zone Books, 1990).

Jacques Derrida teaches at the Ecole des Hautes Etudes en Sciences Sociales and is Visiting Professor at both the University of California, Irvine and the City University of New York. Among his works available in English are *Glas*, trans. John P. Leavey, Jr. (Lincoln: Nebraska UP, 1986), *Truth in Painting*, trans. Geoffrey Bennington and Ian McLeod (Chicago: University of Chicago, 1987), *Limited Inc.*, trans. Samuel Webber (Evanston: Northwestern UP, 1988), and *Of Spirit: Heidegger and the Question*, trans. Geoffrey Bennington and Rachel Bowlby (Chicago: Chicago UP, 1989). His most recent publications include *Du droit à la philosophie* (Paris: Galilée, 1990) and *Le problème de la genèse dans la philosophie de Husserl* (Paris: PUF, 1990).

Vincent Descombes is Professor of French at Emory University. He is the author of *L'inconscient malgré lui* (Paris: Minuit, 1977), *Modern French Philosophy*, trans. Lorna Scott-Fox and Jeremy Harding (New York: Cambridge UP, 1980), *Objects of All Sorts: A Philosophical Grammar*, trans. Lorna Scott-Fox and Jeremy Harding (Baltimore: Johns Hopkins UP, 1986), and *Proust: la philosophie du roman* (Paris: Minuit, 1987). His most recent publication is *La Philosophie par gros temps* (Paris: Minuit, 1989).

Didier Franck teaches at the Ecole Normale Supérieure in Paris. His publications include *Chair et corps: sur la phénoménologie* (Paris: Minuit, 1986) and *Heidegger et le problème de l'espace* (Paris: Minuit, 1986).

Gérard Granel is Professor at the University of Toulouse–Le Mirail. He is the author of *L'équivoque ontologique de la pensée kantienne* (Paris: Gallimard, 1970), *Traditionis traditio* (Paris: Gallimard, 1972), and *De l'université* (Paris: Trans-Europ-Repress, 1982). His *Ecrits logiques et politiques* is due to appear this year.

Michel Henry has recently retired from the University of Montpellier. He has written *The Essence of Manifestation*, trans. Girard Etzkorn (The Hague: Hijoff, 1973), *Marx: A Philosophy of Human Reality*, trans. Kathleen McLaughlin (Bloomington: Indiana UP, 1983), and *Généalogie de la psychanalyse* (Paris: PUF, 1985).

Luce Irigaray teaches at the Université de Paris VIII. She is the author of *Speculum of the Other Woman*, trans. Gillian C. Gill (Ithaca: Cornell UP, 1985), *This Sex Which Is Not One*, trans. Catherine Porter, with Carolyn Burke (Ithaca: Cornell UP, 1985), and, recently, *Sexes et Parentes* (Paris: Les Editions de Minuit, 1987).

Sarah Kofman teaches at the Université de Paris I. She is the author of *Nietzsche et la métaphore* (Paris: Payot, 1972), *Le respect de femmes: Kant et Rousseau* (Paris: Gallilée, 1981), *The Enigma of Woman: Woman in Freud's Writings*, trans. Catherine Porter (Ithaca: Cornell UP, 1985), *The Childhood of Art: An Interpretation of Freud's Aesthetics*, trans. W. Woodhull (N.Y.: Columbia UP, 1988), *Socrate(s)* (Paris: Galilée, 1989) and, most recently, *Séductions* (Paris: Galilée, 1990).

Philippe Lacoue-Labarthe teaches at the University of Strasbourg and is Visiting Professor at the University of California, Berkeley. He is the author, with Jean-Luc

Nancy, of *The Literary Absolute*, trans. Philip Barnard and Cheryl Lester (N.Y.: SUNY Press, 1988), and author of *Typography: Mimesis, Philosophy, Politics*, ed. Christopher Fynsk (Cambridge: Harvard UP, 1989) and *Heidegger, Art and Politics*, trans. Chris Turner (Oxford: Blackwell, 1990). A collection of essays is forthcoming from the University of Minnesota Press.

Emmanuel Levinas is presently teaching at the Université de Paris X. He is the author of *Totality and Infinity*, trans. Alphonso Lingis (Pittsburgh: Duquesne UP, 1969), *Existence and Existents*, trans. Alphonso Lingis (The Hague: Nijoff, 1978), *Otherwise than Being, or Beyond Essence*, trans. Alphonso Lingis (Boston: Nijoff, 1981), and *Time and the Other, and additional essays*, trans. Alphonso Lingis (Pittsburgh: Duquesne UP, 1987). A recent collection of essays, *The Levinas Reader*, ed. Sean Hand, was published by Blackwell in 1989.

Jean-François Lyotard teaches at the Université de Paris VIII, and is Visiting Professor at the University of California, Irvine. He is the author of *The Postmodern Condition: A Report on Knowledge*, trans. Geoff Bennington and Brian Massumi (Minneapolis: Minnesota UP, 1984), *The Differend: Phrases in Dispute*, trans. George van Den Abbeele (Minneapolis: Minnesota UP, 1988), and, recently, *Heidegger and "the jews,"* trans. Andreas Michael and Mark S. Roberts (Minneapolis: University of Minnesota Press, 1990). A recent collection of essays, *The Lyotard Reader*, ed. Andrew Benjamin, was published by Blackwell in 1989.

Jean-Luc Marion teaches at the Université de Paris X. He is the author of *Sur la théologie blanche de Descartes* (Paris: PUF, 1981), *Dieu sans l'être* (Paris: Fayard, 1982), and *Sur le prisme métaphysique de Descartes* (Paris: PUF, 1989). His most recent publication is *Réduction et donation* (Paris: PUF, 1990).

Jacques Rancière teaches at the Université de Paris VIII. He is the author of *Le philosophie et ses pauvres* (Paris: Fayard, 1983), *The Nights of Labor*, trans. John Drury (Philadelphia: Temple University Press, 1989), and *Voyages au pays de peuple* (Paris: Seuil, 1990). *The Ignorant Schoolmaster*, translated by Kristin Ross, is forthcoming from Stanford University Press in 1991.

Eduardo Cadava teaches English at Princeton University. He has translated texts by Blanchot, Derrida, Lacoue-Labarthe, and Granel, and has co-edited, along with Avital Ronell, Derrida's *Mémoires for Paul de Man* (Columbia: Columbia University Press, 1986). He is currently working on a manuscript on Emerson's politics entitled *Nature's Politics: Emerson and the Institution of American Letters* and on the relation among technology, philosophy, and language.

Peter Connor is a doctoral candidate in the Department of French at the University of California, Berkeley.

Jean-Luc Nancy teaches at the University of Strasbourg and is Visiting Professor at the University of California, Berkeley. He has written *Le partage des voix* (Paris: Galilée, 1982), *L'impératif catégorique* (Paris: Flammarion, 1983), *L'oubli de la philosophie* (Paris: Galilée, 1986), and *L'expérience de la liberté* (Paris: Galilée, 1988). *The Inoperative Community* is forthcoming from the University of Minnesota Press, and a collection of essays, *The Birth to Presence*, is soon to appear from Stanford UP.